Selected Studies on Energy

Background
Papers for
Energy: The Next Twenty Years

Selected Studies on Energy

Background Papers for Energy: The Next Twenty Years

Hans H. Landsberg
editor

Sponsored by The Ford Foundation and
Administered by Resources for the Future

Ballinger Publishing Company ● Cambridge, Massachusetts
A Subsidiary of Harper & Row, Publishers, Inc.

International Standard Book Number: 0-88410-093-6

Library of Congress Catalog Card number: 79-24800

Printed in the United States of America

Library of Congress Cataloging in Publication Data
Main entry under title:

Selected studies on energy.

   Includes index.
   1. Energy policy—United States—Addresses, essays, lectures. 2. Power resources—United States—Addresses, essays, lectures. I. Landsberg, Hans H. II. Energy, the next twenty years.
HD9502.U52S45   333.7   79-24800
ISBN 0-88410-093-6

Contents

v

List of Tables

List of Figures

Energy: The Next Twenty Years
Study Group

LIST OF MEMBERS

Hans H. Landsberg (Chairman), Director, Center for Energy Policy Research, Resources for the Future

Kenneth J. Arrow, James Bryant Conant University Professor, Harvard University

Francis M. Bator, Professor of Political Economy, John F. Kennedy School of Government, Harvard University

Kenneth W. Dam, Harold J. and Marion F. Green Professor, University of Chicago Law School

Robert W. Fri, President, Energy Transition Corporation

Edward R. Fried, U.S. Executive Director, World Bank

Richard L. Garwin, IBM Fellow and Science Advisor to the Director of Research, Thomas J. Watson Research Center, IBM Corporation; and Professor of Public Policy, John F. Kennedy School of Government, Harvard University

S. William Gouse, Chief Scientist, The MITRE Corporation

William W. Hogan, Professor of Political Economy, John F. Kennedy School of Government, Harvard University

Harry Perry, Consultant, Resources for the Future

George W. Rathjens, Professor of Political Science, Massachusetts Institute of Technology*

*In January 1979, Professor Rathjens accepted a part-time appointment as Deputy U.S. Representative for Nonproliferation, with particular responsibility for U.S. participation in the International Nuclear Fuel Cycle Evaluation. His contribution to the study was substantially completed prior to that time.

Larry E. Ruff, W.R. Grace and Company

John C. Sawhill, President and Professor of Economics, New York University

Thomas C. Schelling, Lucius N. Littauer Professor of Political Economy, John F. Kennedy School of Government, Harvard University

Robert Stobaugh, Professor of Business Administration and Director of the Energy Project, Harvard University Graduate School of Business Administration

Theodore B. Taylor, Visiting Lecturer (Half-Time), Department of Mechanical and Aerospace Engineering, Princeton University

Grant P. Thompson, Senior Associate, The Conservation Foundation

James L. Whittenberger, James Stevens Simmons Professor of Public Health, Harvard University School of Public Health

M. Gordon Wolman, Chairman and Professor of Geography, Department of Geography and Environmental Engineering, Johns Hopkins University

Preface

This volume of papers supplements *Energy: The Next Twenty Years*, a report by a study group sponsored by the Ford Foundation and administered by Resources for the Future. Given the constraints imposed on the group by time and funding and the need to keep its size at a comfortable level, discussion of some relevant topics was based on commissioned background papers. A number of these have been selected for publication. They carry no endorsement by the study group, the Ford Foundation, or RFF, except the implied judgment that they merit being made available to a larger readership. The papers, for the most part, were completed in early 1979, before the later turbulent events that have affected energy supplies. Consequently, the analytical approach and methodology of some papers may be more significant than their precise quantitative aspects. In the interest of speedy release, they have undergone only light editing—done with customary competence by Ruth Haas, of RFF—and no attempt has been made to weld them into any kind of integrated presentation. They fall basically into two groups. One deals with largely domestic issues, the other with foreign experience and policies. The latter set of papers was especially useful in support of Chapter 8 of *Energy: The Next Twenty Years*. The study group gratefully acknowledges the contribution of the authors of these twelve papers.

Hans H. Landsberg
Editor
August 31, 1979

Selected Studies on Energy

Background
Papers for
Energy: The Next Twenty Years

Dimensions of Energy Demand

1

William W. Hogan

ENERGY DEMAND

Until recently, energy policy makers expected the aggregate demand for primary energy, measured in terms of the equivalent heat content of oil flowing from the well or coal extracted from the mine, to grow steadily. Prior to 1970, there were abundant supplies of cheap energy. Markets for new energy-using technologies, such as air conditioning, were expanding rapidly, and the growth in energy demand closely paralleled the growth in the gross national product. Between 1950 and 1970 the U.S. economy grew at 3.2 percent per year, the demand for energy grew at 3.4 percent per year, and the year-to-year changes in both were closely related (see Figure 1-1). This close linkage between energy and the economy led to a widespread presumption that growth in energy consumption was essential for the future growth and health of our economy.

Of course this period was also a time of great change in the energy system. The relative importance of coal decreased sharply, with petroleum and natural gas taking its place—the fraction of total energy consumption coming from coal dropped by half over this period,

Acknowledgments: Ben Ahn, Sergio Granville, Anthony Otten, Eugene Peters, and Stephan Regulinski assisted in collecting the data and preparing the calculations. The author benefited from comments by Joel Darmstadter, Martin Greenberger, Henry Lee, René Malès, Stephen Peck, Richard Richels, Henry Rowen, Walt Rostow, Milton Russell, John Weyant, and the members of Ford-RFF E:NTY Study Group. This paper is based on work done for the supporting analysis of the E:NTY Study Group. The author alone is responsible for any errors.

1

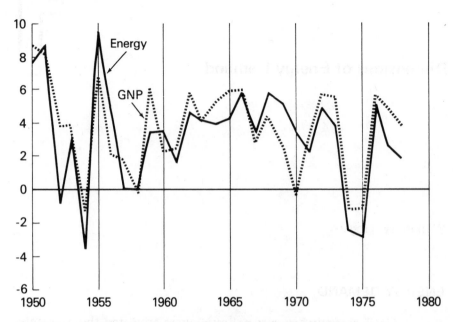

Figure 1-1. Changes in Primary Energy and GNP, 1950–1978.

Source: The data for GNP changes are from the *Economic Report of the President* (Washington, D.C.: Government Printing Office, January 1979). The energy data are from the Bureau of Mines for 1950–1974 and from the Department of Energy for 1974–1978.

while the proportion coming from natural gas increased by nearly the same amount. The form of energy used changed as well, with the energy going to electricity generation increasing from less than one-sixth to nearly one-fourth of all the primary energy used. These changes were of great importance to the energy industry, but passed unnoticed or were taken for granted by the average energy consumer.

By 1970, however, the energy system began to change its complexion in ways that affected our lives and our perceptions of the future. The regulation of natural gas prices became an increasingly controversial issue, and the first curtailments of natural gas consumption had begun in order to allocate limited supplies in the face of a growing demand. The domestic production of crude oil began to decline, with natural gas production soon to follow. The environmental problems associated with the burning of fossil fuels had moved to the forefront of national concern; for example, the regulation of power plant emissions had become a major element of national policy. Finally, the events of 1973, with the oil embargo and the abrupt increase in the price of oil, created a new concern with the energy economy and a fear that the future would be one of energy scarcity, unlike a past of energy abundance.

This new awareness of the importance of energy has led to a re-evaluation of both the role of energy in our economy and forecasts of the likely future demand for energy. At one extreme, there is the view that energy consumption is closely linked to the level of economic activity and that any expansion of the economy requires a proportional increase in energy supply. From this perspective, which seems supported by U.S. data from the years prior to 1970, economic growth determines energy demand, which must be treated as a requirement to be met through the sacrifice of great resources, the compromise of conflicting environmental goals, or both. At the opposite extreme, there is the view that the increased use of energy is only one of many ways to accomplish our real goals, and energy demand can be reduced without great sacrifices in welfare, preserving our limited energy supplies for the future and improving the environment today. The truth probably lies somewhere between these extreme views, but the evaluation of the potential flexibility of energy use will have a great influence on the types of policies recommended for our energy future. Those who see energy demand as inflexible will favor dramatic programs to expand energy supply, even to the point of subsidizing its production and use. Those who see more flexibility in the way energy is used will choose the energy conservation policies that could lead to sharp changes in our energy use patterns.

DIVERSITY OF ENERGY USES

Energy use is pervasive in our economy, and energy is used for many purposes. Ultimately, energy demand stems from consumer demand for all goods and services, either directly, as when we heat our homes or drive our cars, or indirectly, through the energy used to grow the food we eat or to make the clothes we wear. When we consider the indirect effects as well as the direct effects, we find that the total energy used by consumers in different income classes is roughly proportional to their total expenditures. As shown in Figure 1-2, an increase in income is associated with a decrease in the proportion of expenditures spent directly on energy, but with an increase in the proportion spent indirectly through the purchase of other goods and services. It is true that higher income groups spend a slightly smaller proportion on energy than lower income groups, but the drop is less than many might believe: rich and poor alike allocate nearly the same proportion of their expenditures to energy. Comprehensive

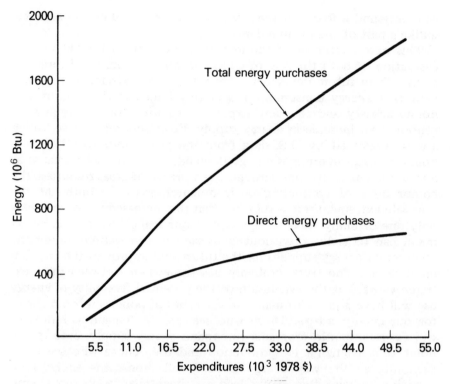

Figure 1-2. Energy Purchases versus Household Expenditures.

Source: The data are taken from R. Herendeen and J. Tanaka, "Energy Cost of Living," *Energy* 1, no. 2 (June 1976). The original data are in 1961 dollars and were converted here using the GNP deflator. Note that the Herendeen-Tanaka figures refer to household expenditure classes. We assume that, by and large, the findings are also applicable to income classes, although some groups (e.g., retirees) have spending characteristics not related to current income.

energy taxes, therefore, will affect the rich as well as the poor. Of course, as with any proportional tax, the burden will weigh less heavily on the higher income groups.

Energy consumption is more varied across regions than across income classes. Differences in weather patterns, travel distances, and industrial composition can produce dramatic differences in the level and type of energy used in different parts of the country. In 1971 the average dollar of output required 124,000 Btus per year in Louisiana but only 25,000 Btus per year in Connecticut.[1] And the

1. C. Starr and S. Field, "Energy Use Proficiency: The Validity of International Comparisons," *Energy Systems and Policy* 2, no. 2 (1978) 211-32. The figures are in terms of real 1978 dollars.

type of energy used exhibits a similar variability. Most of the imported residual fuel oil was consumed in New England, where it was attractive for environmental reasons but presented an especially acute problem after the price of imported oil increased in 1973.

The distribution of the fuel mix and the sectoral patterns of energy use are further evidence of the heterogeneous nature of energy consumption. For example, Table 1-1 shows the balance across fuel types and energy-consuming sectors in 1978. The industrial and electricity sectors used 98 percent of the total coal consumed, while the transportation sector alone accounted for 52 percent of the total petroleum consumption. Gasoline consumption amounts to over two-thirds of the petroleum used in transportation. More than half of the net energy demand is indirect; one-third is used by the industrial sector alone.

The diversity of energy consumption patterns is even more pronounced if we look within the industrial sector. The range of energy intensity—direct and indirect energy use per dollar of output—varies by a factor of ten across the industries in a ninety-sector industrial classification. Representative examples of industries with high and low energy intensities are indicated in Table 1-2. Clearly, a change in the composition of final demand for goods and services could have a

Table 1-1. Fuel Use by Sector for 1978 (quadrillion Btus).

	Residential/ Commercial	Indus- trial	Trans- portation	Total Net Energy Demand	Electric Utility	Total Primary Energy Demand
Coal	0.3	3.1	—	3.4	11.5	14.9
Petroleum	7.2	6.0	18.9	32.0	4.1	36.1
Natural Gas	8.4	8.4	—	16.8	3.2	20.0
Electricity	4.2	3.8	—	7.9	-7.9	—
Hydroelectric	—	—	—	—	3.0	3.0
Nuclear	—	—	—	—	3.0	3.0
Total	20.0	21.3	18.9	60.2	17.0	77.1

Source: The data for the energy balances are estimated from the Department of Energy *Monthly Energy Review* (MER) February 1979. The growth rates implicit in the MER data were applied to the accounting conventions used in the OECD *Energy Balances.* The OECD accounting conventions differ from those used in the Department of Energy or the Bureau of Mines, although the total primary energy figures are comparable. To maintain consistency in the comparison across countries, the OECD accounting conventions are used throughout. See Appendix B for further details. The residential and commercial sectors are combined in the OECD publication. In 1975, the commercial sector use was approximately 40 percent of the total residential and commercial consumption. Details may not add due to rounding.

Table 1-2. Energy Intensities of Selected Industries (1967 input-output table).

Industry	Primary Energy Intensity $(10^3 Btu/1978\$$ of output)
Water Transportation	117
Primary Iron and Steel	115
Chemical and Fertilizer Mining	103
Plastics	100
Air Transportation	99
Office and Computing Machines	19
Agricultural, Forestry, and Fishery Services	17
Radio and Television Broadcasting	14
Finance and Insurance	12
Communications	9
U.S. Average	38

Source: C. Bullard, B. Hannon, and R. Herendeen, "Energy Flow through the United States Economy," Center for Advanced Computation, University of Illinois at Urbana, 1975. (A 90 sector aggregation of the 1967 U.S. input/output table converted to the flow of embodied energy.) The data were updated from 1967$ to 1978$ using the GNP deflator. The U.S. average is from Bureau of Mines data on energy, which differ by 10 percent from the data of Bullard et al.

significant impact on the total demand for energy or the demand for any individual fuel.

Despite its statistical convenience, a concentration on equivalent heat content in measuring total energy demand disguises the diverse characteristics of the many forms of energy. Natural gas is a clean-burning fuel, but it is difficult to deliver except through a network of pipelines. Electricity is versatile and has a variety of specialized uses, but it is expensive for many purposes. Coal is an inexpensive fuel, but it is dirty when burned and there are handling problems that restrict its use to large-scale facilities. Oil is a good transportation fuel and can be used for many other needs, but at current prices, it is too expensive for use in large boilers. Each of these fuels has been used according to its specialized characteristics, and we have a complex balance of supply and demand as a result.

Except for the distribution across income classes, therefore, we see great variations in the nature and level of energy demand as we look at the types and locations of energy use. Variations over type and place suggest that the patterns of energy use may be varied over time as well. The flexibility of energy use, which we shall see is the key to understanding the impacts of future energy scarcity, may show a similar high degree of diversity. As we change the prices of different energy forms and change these prices in different ways, we may expect the mix of activities in the economy and the demand for energy in any one of these activities to change in a great variety of ways. Given the diversity of energy uses, and looking to a future of higher energy prices, the historical link between the growth of energy and the growth of the economy is not convincing evidence that no changes in energy use patterns are possible. We have observed changes in the composition of energy demand historically; perhaps with higher prices there will be changes in the level of energy demand.

FLEXIBILITY IN ENERGY DEMAND

Despite the strong link between energy and the economy suggested by Figure 1-1, there is evidence of a substantial potential flexibility in energy use per unit of output. This evidence is found through both the examination of the aggregate statistics of the past and the evaluation of the many energy-using technologies available now or likely to be in use in the future. Perhaps the most striking, and the most popular evidence of the inherent flexibility in energy demand, is found in the comparison of the energy utilization patterns of different countries. For example, the now familiar contrast between Sweden and the United States, countries with similar standards of living but very different levels of energy demand, is prima facie evidence that the level of economic activity does not by itself determine the level of energy demand. Consider Figure 1-3, which is typical of the comparisons that can be drawn with international data. The United States has a substantially higher energy use per dollar of output than other industrialized countries—more than one-third higher in the case of Sweden. Such simple statistics are found at the core of many of the charges that the United States is profligate in its energy uses; furthermore, these data are often used to call for great changes in the level and composition of energy use without sacrificing in any of the more fundamental dimensions of economic welfare.

These international comparisons can be misleading, of course, because the countries differ in several ways that might affect the level of energy demand and the experience in one country might not be transferable to another. This controversy, and the increased importance of energy, stimulated a careful examination of the international data, and the results indicate that the truth falls somewhere in between the possible extreme views.[2] On the average, approxi-

2. The data are from J. Darmstadter, J. Dunkerley, and J. Alterman, *How Industrial Societies Use Energy: A Comparative Analysis* (Baltimore: Johns Hopkins University Press for Resources for the Future, 1977).

Energy consumption (in quads)
per million dollars of GDP

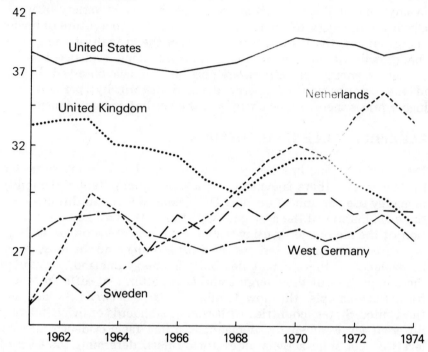

Figure 1-3. Energy-Output Ratios for Five Selected Countries, 1961-1974.

Source: From J. Darmstadter, J. Dunkerley, and J. Alterman, *How Industrial Societies Use Energy: A Comparative Analysis* (Baltimore: Johns Hopkins University Press for Resources for the Future, 1977). The data were converted to Btus per dollar of 1978 GDP by using 0.04 quadrillion (10^{15}) Btus per million tons of oil equivalent (see Darmstadter et al., p. 15) and the U.S. GNP deflator. See also L. Schipper and A. Lichtenberg, "Efficient Energy Use and Well Being: The Swedish Example," *Science* 194 (December 1976): 1001-13.

mately 40 percent of the difference in energy utilization between the United States and other countries can be attributed to the difference in the mix of activities in the different economies: compared with other countries, the United States has a larger proportion of expenditures for energy-intensive activities—chiefly energy purchases for household operations and gasoline for private automobile transportation. The balance of 60 percent is attributed to other factors— principally differences in the efficiency of energy use found in different countries. It is especially this latter component of lower energy utilization that might be transferable across countries. If we take Sweden, which uses 75 percent of the energy per dollar of gross domestic product as the United States, as the typical case, this would

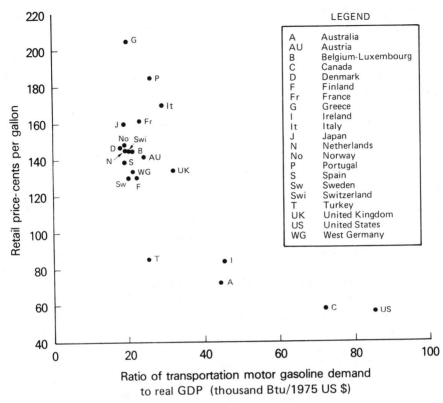

Figure 1-4. Cross-country Comparison of Motor Gasoline Demand in 1976.

Source: Data are from the *Economic Report of the President* (Washington, D.C.: Government Printing Office, 1978). The conversions to 1975 U.S. dollars are apparently based on the then prevailing exchange rates, not purchasing power priorities as used elsewhere in this chapter. Price is not the only explanation for the consumption differences; for example, the highest consumption is in countries with longest travel distances.

imply that the United States has the flexibility to improve its overall energy intensity by at least as much as 15 percent through efficiency improvements.

One explanation of the cause of these energy demand differences across countries is often found in the sharp differences in energy prices faced by consumers in the United States compared with consumers in other countries. The evidence is most striking in the prices paid for gasoline; Figure 1-4 displays the variation across many countries in the price paid for gasoline (with the variation in price due chiefly to differences in tax policies) and the quantity of gasoline used per dollar of economic output. The level of gasoline demand seems to be significantly affected by the price that the consumer must pay. When the price is low, there is little incentive to conserve on gasoline, and the consumption is high. But when the price is high, the consumer adjusts by using more efficient cars or switching to more efficient forms of transportation. A similar pattern exists in other sectors, although the more heterogeneous nature of the energy products makes the energy consumption profile more difficult to summarize in terms of a single index.

An examination of automobile efficiencies reinforces the evidence for the existence of a substantial potential flexibility in energy utilization patterns. It is a commonplace that the average car in the U.S. auto fleet consumes much more gasoline per passenger mile than its counterpart in other countries. This fact, and the central importance of automobile use in determining the demand for petroleum, prompted the U.S. Congress to legislate strict standards for automobile efficiency in an effort to reduce the dependence on imported petroleum. Starting at less than fifteen miles per gallon (mpg) in 1975, the average new car efficiency is required to improve to twenty-seven and a half mpg by 1985, and most analysts agree that this standard will be met. Of course, to the extent that higher gasoline prices would normally be accommodated by changing the efficiency of the fleet, as opposed to driving less or switching to other forms of transportation, the efficiency standards will reduce the incremental responsiveness of gasoline demand to gasoline price changes (by as much as two-thirds according to one estimate) because the mandatory standards preempt the consumer's option of selecting a more efficient car.[3] But other analyses indicate that the technological conservation potential for the automobile is not exhausted by the current standards; as much as a 40 percent further increase in automobile efficiency is feasible and might be economically attractive.[4]

To take another example, a careful analysis of household refrigerator-freezer combinations indicates the potential for as much as a 50 percent reduction in energy utilization, depending on the initial cost increase that the consumer is willing to absorb (see Figure 1–5).[5] Of course, it is difficult to tell what will be required to induce

3. J. Sweeney, "U.S. Gasoline Demand: An Economic Analysis of the EPCA New Car Efficiency Standard," in R.S. Pindyck, ed., *Advances in the Economics of Energy and Resources*, vol. 1, *The Structure of Energy Markets* (Greenwich, Conn.: JAI Press, 1979), pp. 105–33.

4. CONAES Demand and Conservation Panel, "U.S. Energy Demand: Some Low-Energy Futures," *Science* 200, no. 4338 (April 14, 1978): 142–52.

5. R. Hoskins and E. Hirst, "Energy and Cost Analysis of Residential Refrigerators" (Oak Ridge, Tenn.: Oak Ridge National Laboratory, January 1977). See also E. Hirst, "Effects of Energy Conservation Research, Development and Demonstration on Residential Energy Use," *Energy Systems and Policy* 3, no. 1(1979): 37–60. S. Peck observed that moving from the least to the most

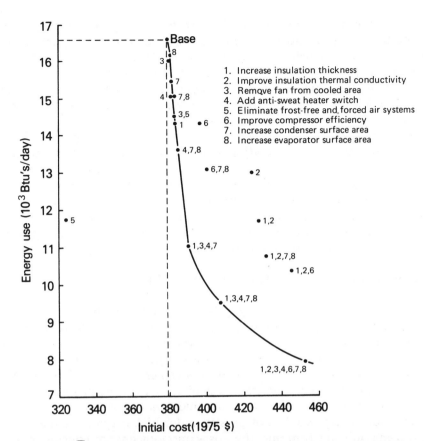

Figure 1-5. Energy Use versus Retail Price for Various Design Changes for a 16 cu. ft. Top Freezer Refrigerator.

Source: R. Hoskins and E. Hirst, *Energy and Cost Analysis of Residential Refrigerators* (Oak Ridge, Tenn.: Oak Ridge National Laboratory, January 1977).

consumers to adopt any particular technology, and there must be a gradual adjustment as old equipment is replaced, but evidence is accumulating that there is substantial potential flexibility in energy use. The most comprehensive and credible attempt at an analysis of individual technologies envisions the possibility of as much as a 40 percent improvement in the energy intensity for the entire economy, depending on the future increases in the price of energy to the consumers.[6]

energy-efficient combination saves 8,000 Btus per day. At $3 per million Btus, this is a savings of $10 per year achieved for an initial investment of $80, or a 12 percent rate of return on a ten year life cycle.

6. CONAES Demand and Conservation Panel. "U.S. Energy Demand."

This subject could be pursued further, examining individual energy-using technologies and the conservation problems and opportunities inherent in past legislation and existing institutions. But this selective inquiry into examples of the flexibility of energy use in a few specific applications suggests that the demand for energy can often be reduced without substantially impairing productivity in diverse processes that use energy as one among many inputs. In other work we have examined the economic role of energy in the aggregate and found that the ability to adjust energy use patterns will permit the growth in energy demand to be largely decoupled from the growth in the economy, albeit at the cost of rising energy prices and some slight reduction in economic output.[7] In the next section, we expand on these themes by further quantifying the flexibility in energy demand and examining the implications, in the large, for growth in energy demand over the next two decades.

ESTIMATING SUBSTITUTION POTENTIAL

The starting point of our aggregate analysis of energy demand is to treat energy as an economic good; in particular, energy is assumed to be only one input to production processes, only one item used to meet the needs of consumers. This assumption is motivated by the specific examples of the trade-offs between energy and other goods—for example, between energy and capital investment in refrigerators and from the basic common-sense judgment that our current demands for energy would not persist under higher price regimes. The profit-maximizing firm and the cost-conscious energy consumer will consider the prices of all inputs when making decisions about the mix of goods and services to be utilized. As the price of energy increases, we assume that energy users exploit the opportunities to substitute more energy-efficient machinery, to redesign production processes, to insulate homes, to install heat pumps, to switch to buses and subways—even to lower thermostat settings and observe speed limits. The energy user makes these and many other substitutions in order to reduce the cost of meeting the more fundamental objective of producing a product or achieving an acceptable standard of living.

The degree to which these adjustments will be made depends on

---

7. The reader may wish to pursue this examination of conservation options further, for example, in J. Sawhill, ed., *Energy Conservation and Public Policy* (Englewood Cliffs, N.J.: Prentice-Hall, 1979). Also see W. Hogan, "Energy and Economic Growth," in Sawhill, pp. 9–21, for a summary of recent work on the feedback between energy availability and economic growth.

many factors. The technical limits are constraints, but the actual substitutions may be motivated as much by convenience and personal taste as by the engineering characteristics of specific energy uses: the existence of hand-operated can openers does not imply that cooks will or should abandon the electric counterpart. The measurement of the energy substitution potential, therefore, must be based on the observed behavior of energy users confronted with different prices and the opportunity to make consumption choices. The result, if not the process, can be summarized by a proportional reduction in energy use, for a fixed level of activity, in response to a given percentage increase in the energy price. The ratio is the elasticity of energy demand (a convenient statistic that we will use extensively); hence, if the elasticity of demand is 0.5, a 10 percent increase in the price of energy produces a 5 percent decrease in energy demand, a decrease achieved by substituting a collection of other inputs and processes for the energy forgone.

The aggregate elasticity of energy demand will be useful in summarizing the substitution potential, but it is not useful for actually estimating the degree of potential substitution. As we have seen, energy is not a single commodity, and the full richness of the energy system must be considered when estimating the elasticity of energy demand. And only the most general linkage can be established between the disaggregated estimates of the many adjustments, made by different users, confronted with different prices, for different energy products, and the abstraction of the aggregate elasticity of total energy demand for all uses.

The links between the aggregate elasticity and the elasticities for individual sectors or fuels are obscured by the diversity of prices that must be considered. It is the price to the user that is the relevant price in determining the substitution among the many energy and nonenergy inputs for production or consumption. We often speak of the price of energy in terms of the price of primary energy or, more narrowly, in terms of the price of imported oil. But no consumer actually purchases energy at the price of production, and the prices to consumers do not vary in constant proportion with the price of primary energy. Hence, the same absolute price change and the same demand response will lead to different estimates of the price elasticity, depending on the point of measurement selected. For example, in 1972 the price of oil at the wellhead accounted for slightly over one-fifth of the cost of gasoline at the pump. Hence, assuming a straight pass-through of increased crude oil costs and no change in refinery operations, the elasticity of demand measured at the pump could be five times the elasticity measured at the wellhead.

Despite, or perhaps because of, these difficulties of measurement and interpretation, there have been many different attempts to examine the data and estimate the elasticities of energy demand. Many factors must be controlled (e.g., weather, population, economic activity) to isolate the effects of price alone, and the short-run effects must be separated from long-run adjustments that may take many years to complete. In addition, the data are not perfect, and there is no guarantee that the changes of the past, over one range of prices, will be indicative of the changes in the future, over a very different range of prices. The results are not without controversy, therefore, but some patterns do emerge. One survey of a number of different studies compared the long-run elasticities of demand for different consuming sectors, as shown in Table 1-3. These figures indicate a substantial elasticity of energy demand—that is, a significant flexibility in substituting for energy use. For example, the lowest estimate of the most likely range for the elasticity of demand for motor gasoline is consistent with the data in Figure 1-4 where consumption and prices were compared across countries.

These aggregate elasticities are roughly consistent with the potential reductions in energy utilization found in the detailed technological analyses cited above. The implication is that a doubling in the real cost of energy delivered to the consumer could produce up to a 50 percent reduction in the intensity of energy utilization. Of course, this would require more than a doubling of the cost of primary energy, but this represents a substantial flexibility in the long run for energy. And these aggregate figures disguise even greater adjustments in the demands for individual fuels: the increase in the price of any individual fuel will cause a shift away from that fuel, in addition to a reduction in the total energy demand. The evaluation of this more volatile shift in the mix of fuel demands requires a more complete

Table 1-3. Estimates of Long-run Elasticity of Energy Demand (delivered to the consumer).

Sector	Range of Studies	Most Likely Range
Residential	0.28 to 1.10	0.7 to 1.1
Industrial	0.49 to 0.90	0.8 to 0.9
Transportation (motor gasoline)	0.22 to 1.3	0.7 to 1.0

Source: R. Pindyck, "The Characteristics of Energy Demand," in J. Sawhill, ed., *Energy Conservation and Public Policy* (Englewood Cliffs, N.J.: Prentice-Hall, 1979), pp. 27–45. The survey by Pindyck covered several detailed econometric studies. The range of estimates was narrowed to the most likely range based on Pindyck's qualitative discussion of the results.

specification of the effects of the changes in energy prices; these fuel mix adjustments are discussed in more detail in a later section.

DEMAND FORECASTS

A forecast of energy consumption requires the simultaneous determination of the cost and availability of alternative forms of energy supply as well as the evaluation of a host of other factors that will determine the patterns of energy consumption. Our way of life, the design of our cities, the level and composition of economic activity, the stock of energy-using equipment, the changing nature of energy-using technologies—even the weather—will combine to determine the level of future energy demand. For many analytical purposes, the complete details are required—for example, evaluating the potential market for some new energy-using technologies—but most forecasts are based on one or another model that approximates the energy system by submerging many of the details in an aggregate analysis.

Many such forecasts of energy demand have been prepared, often through the use of simplifying assumptions that treat the major uncertainties by examining a number of possible energy futures. A sampling of these forecasts is collected in Table 1-4. Since 1973 there has been a steady decrease in forecast demand as well as a gradual convergence of the estimates. There is a similar convergence in the associated estimates of oil and gas imports. Important differences remain, however, and the differences become more pronounced when considering not only the level but the composition and rate of change of U.S. energy demand.

The broad purposes of the present study are not served by preparing yet another detailed assessment of the likely future composition and level of energy demand. As Table 1-4 testifies, this subject has been given extensive attention by others. The more pressing need is for the distillation of a qualitative understanding of the character of future energy demand and the sensitivity to variations in key uncertain parameters and assumptions.

The specification of the growth in the population, changes in the labor force, and the aggregate output of the economy must be the starting point of any projection of energy demand levels. The great potential flexibility of energy use is evidence that economic growth can be decoupled from the price and availability of energy in the long run; but the growth of the economy will be a key factor in determining the demand for energy at any given level of energy prices. This direction of effect, from the economy to the energy sector, is particularly important during the short run; witness the experience

Table 1-4.   Selected Forecasts: Total Primary Energy Demand and Imports (in quadrillion Btus)

Study	1985 Demand	1985 Imports	1990 Demand	1990 Imports	2000 Demand	2000 Imports
Project Independence,[a] 1974	102.9–109.1	6.6–24.8	—	—	—	—
FEA National Energy Outlook,[a] 1976	90.7–105.6	11.8–25.2	114.0–121.7	11.6–41.4	—	—
A Time to Choose:[a]						
Historical growth	116.1	—	—	—	186.7	—
Technical fix	91.3	—	—	—	124.0	—
Zero energy growth	88.1	—	—	—	100.0	—
USDI, Energy Through the Year 2000:[a]						
1972 Forecast	116.6	—	—	—	191.9	—
1975 Forecast	103.5	—	—	—	163.4	—
Shell:						
1976 Forecast[b]	96.2	24.0	110.0	22.0	—	—
1978 Forecast[c]	90.4	22.6	101.2	22.6	—	—
Exxon,[d] 1977	93.0	27.0	108.0	26.0	—	—
National Energy Plan,[e] 1977	97.0	23.0	—	—	—	—
CIA,[f] 1977	98.6	26.8	—	—	—	—
CONAES MGR,[g] 1977						
DESOM	—	—	112 –114	—	—	—
ETA	—	—	103.1–104.8	—	—	—
NORDHAUS	—	—	80.5–96.2	—	—	—
SRI	—	—	108.9	—	—	—
CRS,[a] 1977	91.2–98.4	19.7–38.9	104.5–113.4	20.5–45.2	94–136 (2010)	—
CONAES DEMAND, 1978[h]	—	—	—	—	—	—
MOPPS, 1978[i]	94.6	15.3	—	—	117.3	12.5
EIA, 1978[j]	91.2–96.9	21.4–22.9	100.7–109.4	24.1–29.7	—	—

Sources: These forecasts were collated with the assistance of Steven Regulinski. For those interested in a larger portfolio of forecasts, the International Energy Agency has compiled seventy-eight major forecasts prepared over the last ten years: J.R. Brodman and R.E. Hamilton, "A Comparison of Energy Projections to 1985" (Paris: IEA, January 1979).

[a]Extracted from *Project Interdependence: U.S. and World Energy Outlook through 1990*, Congressional Research Service, Committee Print 95–33, November 1977, p. 125.

[b]*National Energy Outlook*, Shell Oil Company, September 1976.

[c]*National Energy Outlook*, Shell Oil Company, February 1978.

[d]"Energy Outlook: 1977–1990," Exxon Corporation, August 1977.

[e]*National Energy Plan*, White House, April 1977, p. 96.

[f]"The International Energy Situation's Outlook to 1985," Central Intelligence Agency, ER77–102404, April 1977.

[g]Modeling Resources Group, Committee on Nuclear and Alternative Energy Systems (CONAES), "Energy Modeling for an Uncertain Future" (Washington, D.C.: National Research Council, 1978), for selected models.

[h]CONAES Demand and Conservation Panel, "U.S. Energy Demand: Some Low-Energy Futures", *Science* 200, No. 4338 (April 14, 1978): 142–52. The scenarios related here are scenarios III and IV, which range from no price increases to a doubling of prices by 2010. The panel also examined two cases where prices to consumers had quadrupled by 2010; in these cases, projected energy demand fell to a range of 60–75 quadrillion Btus.

[i]ERDA/DOE, "Market Oriented Program Planning Study," draft, 1978.

[j]Energy Information Administration, *Annual Report to Congress*, vol. II, 1977, released April 1978, DOE/EIA–0036/2.

since 1973. Energy demand grew only 0.5 percent per year between 1973 and 1977, compared with 3.1 percent per year for the four years preceding 1973. This deviation from the historical growth rate can be separated into equal parts of a reduction in the use of energy per unit of gross national product and a reduction in the growth rate of the economy. Without increases in energy prices, there would be no incentive to substitute other inputs to save energy, and the future growth of energy demand would be determined in large measure by the growth of the economy. The importance of the economic growth assumptions can be seen by examining the documentation for the forecasts collected in Table 1-4; a great part of the differences between the energy demand forecasts can be traced to different assumptions about the level of future economic growth.

The projection of aggregate economic activity is difficult enough; the translation of economic forecasts to energy demand forecasts is complicated further by the changes in the composition of output, as we have seen. This issue has been addressed, for example, by Hudson and Jorgenson through the application of their energy economic model considering the role of energy and the impacts of the changing composition of economic output. This analysis indicates that an increase in energy prices could change the intensity of aggregate energy utilization through a shift in the composition of output, away from the energy-intensive manufacturing and toward the less energy-intensive services and communications.[8]

The regulation of energy prices and energy-using technologies introduces additional uncertainties into any demand forecasts. The administrative control of prices prevents the consumer from recognizing the true scarcity of energy, which may distort, and increase, energy demand. Conversely, we have seen, in the case of the automobile, how the regulation of energy utilization can reduce both energy demand and future responsiveness to energy price changes. These countervailing effects of regulation must be recognized to avoid one type of double counting—forecasting a decrease of the same energy demand once because of higher prices and then again because of efficiency regulations. Of course, we can approximate the effects of price regulation by assuming a price of energy, in the near term, below the marginal cost of new supplies. Then, as this energy price increases, we can examine the response of the consumer in changing the level of energy demand.

The adjustments in energy demand, in response to increases in the

8. E. Hudson and D. Jorgenson, "The Economic Impact of Policies to Reduce U.S. Energy Growth," *Resources and Energy* 1, no. 3, (November 1978): 205-30.

price of energy, will not occur instantaneously. In the long run we may have a great deal of flexibility to substitute labor, materials, or new processes for energy, but in the short run the energy intensity of the economy is more narrowly restricted. The average consumer is not likely to replace or retrofit all energy-utilizing devices as soon as a higher energy price is encountered. The gradual turnover of the capital stock, with a slow adaptation to the optimum, long-run level of energy demand, is more likely to be the norm. In fact, the rate of adjustment to the long-run levels of energy utilization is probably slow enough for the price changes that have already occurred to have an impact on energy demand for the next twenty years: the energy system was not in long-run equilibrium in 1978. To the extent that improvements in energy efficiency occur primarily in conjunction with the purchase of new equipment, then the slowness of the turnover of the capital stock would guarantee that some residual part of the energy efficiency at the turn of the century will still be determined by the composition of the capital stock today.

These uncertainties, and the slow processes of adaptation in the energy system, imply that the next twenty years will be a period of change in energy demand. The next twenty years are not the long run, and the long-run analysis of the structure of energy demand provides only a rough outline of the destination of our journey. There is little in the long-run analysis to tell us of the route we might take; for this we need to consider the short-run adjustments in response to the recent and probable future increases in the price of energy.

ENERGY DEMAND ADJUSTMENTS

After many years of declining real prices and relatively stable demand growth in the energy system, in 1973 the sharp increase of oil prices marked the beginning of what may be a long period of change and adjustment in the level and composition of energy demand. Reinforced by the recognition of environmental problems and complicated by a high rate of general inflation, these adjustments were still very much underway more than five years later. Any investigation of future energy demand must consider both the continuing adaptation to past changes—for example, in the price of energy—and the effects of future rates of increase of energy prices and economic activity.

Our exploration of the possible energy demand adjustments will be improved by the refinement of our measure of aggregate energy consumption; we need a yardstick that can be related easily to the data and yet interpreted as an index of the final consumption level of the energy consumer. The difficulties inherent in the development of such an index are apparent: it must provide a consistent aggregation of diverse energy products, from the coal consumed in industry, at prices as low as $0.80 per million Btus, to the electricity consumed in the home, at prices as high as $10 per million Btus delivered. It is not possible to specify a perfect index, but it is possible to construct a good approximation through a careful accounting for the different prices paid for different energy products.

The aggregation employed here is essentially the one developed by Pindyck for an international comparison of energy demands.[9] The concept defined and the quantity measured for each year and each sector are the same as the net energy consumed—that is, the equivalent heat content delivered to the consumer, net of the energy losses in the generation, transmission, and distribution of electricity. (This follows the long practice of the Bureau of Mines as continued by the Department of Energy.[10]) The prices are those paid by consumers, as opposed to wellhead or primary energy prices, aggregated across sectors and weighted according to the value shares of expenditures. One advantage of measurement at this point is that it is the best approximation to the point where energy choices are actually made by the consumer. A disadvantage is that the resulting energy demand total is not the same as the total primary energy demand, which is the focal point of so many energy forecasts—for example, as in Table 1–4 —and the energy losses in electricity generation must be added to the net demand in order to obtain the equivalent primary energy demand.[11]

If the scale of economic activity is assumed not to affect the composition of energy demand, then the major uncertainty associated with economic forecasts can be avoided in the analysis by concentrating on the ratio between the delivered net energy demand and the

9. R. Pindyck, "The Structure of World Energy Demand" (Cambridge: Massachusetts Institute of Technology, September 1978). The data are taken primarily from the extensive data base assembled by Pindyck, and we used his translog aggregation equations to construct the energy price variable for each major sector. The aggregation across sectors was accomplished using a Cobb–Douglas price function with the 1972 value shares as weights. For further details, see Appendixes A and B of this chapter.

10. Energy Information Agency, *Annual Report to Congress*, vol II, 1977 (Washington, D.C.: DOE/EIA -0036/2, April 1978). Readers interested in a cogent discussion of alternative aggregation conventions will enjoy E.R. Berndt, "Aggregate Energy, Efficiency, and Productivity Measurement," in *Annual Review of Energy*, vol. 3 (Palo Alto, Calif.: Annual Reviews, 1978) pp. 225–74.

11. In 1978, electricity accounted for less than 15 percent of the distributed net energy. With a 30 percent efficiency of generation, 15 percent electricity would imply that primary energy demand was 1.35 times the net energy demand.

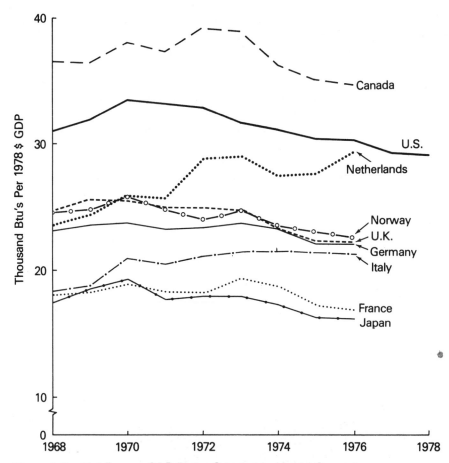

Figure 1-6. Net Energy-GDP Ratio: Selected Industrial Countries.

Source: Quantity data are from OECD *Energy Balances.* For further details, see Appendixes A and B of this chapter.

gross domestic product (GDP).[12] The data for the United States and selected industrialized nations are summarized in Figure 1-6, which can be compared with similar data for primary energy as shown in Figure 1-3; qualitatively, the two sets of data tell the same story. The net energy–GDP ratio for the United States is higher than that

12. The international comparisons are expressed in terms of the gross domestic product to remove the net factor income originating in overseas enterprises and investments, which is included in GNP. The difference between GNP and GDP is quantitatively small for the United States; in 1977 the difference amounted to less than 1 percent of GNP. For convenience, the U.S. figures for GNP are used as the estimate for U.S. GDP.

for most other countries, but has dropped steadily, from 33.4 thousand Btus per 1978 dollar of output in 1972 to 29.1 thousand Btus per 1978 dollar of output in 1978. The data from the other countries do not show quite so regular a pattern, but there is a general, if slight, reduction in the overall use of energy. Part of the explanation for this improvement in energy efficiency can be found in the trends in energy prices. The aggregate energy prices for the consumers in each of these countries are displayed in Figure 1-7. There has been a significant real increase, since 1972, in the price of energy, although the increase is much less than many would expect, given the dramatic changes that have been experienced for the prices of some important energy components—for example, for oil in the United States, which

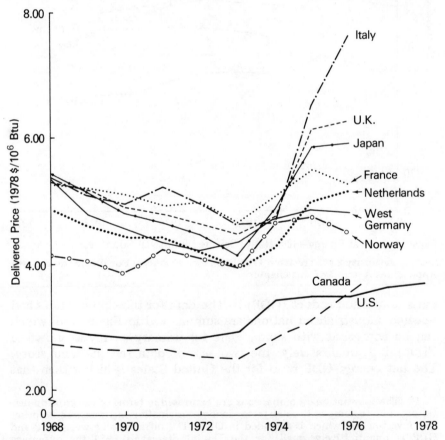

Figure 1-7. Price of Energy Delivered: Selected Industrial Countries.

Source: Price data are primarily from R. Pindyck, *The Structure of World Energy Demand* (Cambridge: Massachusetts Institute of Technology, September 1978).

increased by 120 percent between 1972 and 1978. The difference can be explained by noting that oil is only one component of aggregate energy input; many products are still sold under long-term contracts at low prices. And the costs of primary energy forms—for example, oil, coal, and gas—are only a part of the price of delivered net energy. Hence, the nearly threefold multiplication of imported oil prices since 1972 has led to only a 30 percent increase in the delivered price of all energy in the United States.

The uncertainties associated with future changes in energy prices can be addressed by projecting the net energy–GDP ratio using a number of different price assumptions. We examine primarily the data for the United States, from which we may draw analogies for the other industrialized nations. The construction of the aggregate price index involves several steps in order to integrate the prices of many fuels across many sectors, but the results can be summarized in terms of the relationship between the price of delivered energy and the price of primary energy. Assuming that (1) the average price of coal (in 1978$) gradually approaches $1.50 per million Btus, up from $0.95 in 1978, and is then unaffected by the price of oil; (2) the price of gas is equated to the price of oil, gradually approaching $4.50; and (3) the markups over the primary energy costs remain constant in real terms; then after all the long-run substitutions are made, the delivered price of net energy will be as in Figure 1–8.

If we assume that the change in energy efficiency takes place only with the introduction of new energy-using equipment (e.g., only by changing the efficiency of new cars, not by driving less), then the relationship over time between delivered net energy prices and the net energy–GDP ratio can be established once we specify the long-run price elasticity and the rate of introduction of new equipment. The result is a traditional demand curve, one for each year, with the price responsiveness increasing as we look further into the future. Consider the examples in Figure 1–9, based on data for the United States, for demand curves for the year 1978. Four curves are shown, one for each combination of two possible long-run elasticities (e) and two possible rates of introduction of new equipment (d). The price elasticities were selected to be compatible with the range of estimates from Table 1–3 and to include both high and low values ($e = 0.7$; $e = 1.0$); recall that these are the elasticities in terms of dilivered net, not primary, energy. The selection of the rate of introduction of new energy-using equipment is more problematical; two values are considered here ($d = 0.10$; $d = 0.20$). An introduction rate of 10 percent —that is, $d = 0.10$—implies that in any year, 10 percent of all energy-using equipment is newly installed and is assumed to be at the optimum energy efficiency at the price in that year. An economic growth

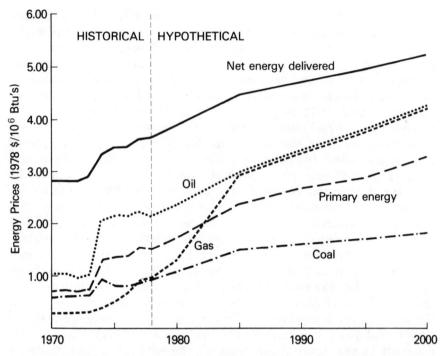

Figure 1-8. Illustration of Relation between Primary Energy Prices and the Energy Delivery Prices in the United States.

Source: The price data are from R. Pindyck, *The Structure of World Energy Demand* (Cambridge: Massachusetts Institute of Technology, September 1978), and his aggregation equations are used to construct the sector long-term price indexes, assuming that the commercial sector pays the same prices as a residential sector. The sectors are combined in a Cobb–Douglas aggregations produce the delivery price for all energy. See Appendixes A and B of this chapter for further details.

rate of 3 percent per year and an average life of equipment of fifteen years (six years) would be consistent with a rate of introduction of new equipment of 0.10 (0.20).

The demand curve in Figure 1-9 for each combination of demand elasticity and introduction rate is based on a forecast from 1969 through 1978 and can be compared with the actual outcomes for the intervening years. For example, in 1978 the net energy–GDP ratio was 29.1, down from the 1969–1970 average of 32.7, and the predicted value for the high elasticity, slow adjustment case ($e = 1.0$; $d = 0.10$) is 29.9; see Appendix A of this chapter for further details.

At least two lessons can be drawn from the data in Figure 1-9. First, there has been a notable reduction in the net energy–GDP ratio for the United States, consistent with our expectations given the rise

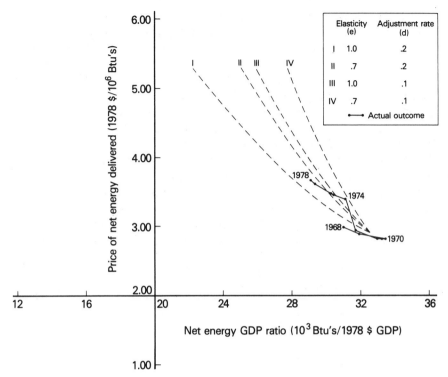

Figure 1-9. U.S. Net Energy Demand Curves for 1978: Selected Elasticities and Adjustment Rates.

Source: The data for 1968-1978 are from R. Pindyck, *The Structure of World Energy Demand* (Cambridge: Massachusetts Institute of Technology, September 1978), and the OECD. The demand curves are derived from a model with a Koyck lag adjustment process for the energy-GDP ratio. It is assumed that the prices change along the whole price path, between 1969 and 1978, by scaling the actual price path to match the proportioned change in 1978. For further details see this chapter's Appendix A.

in energy prices. But, second, it is too early to choose confidently, on the basis of these data alone, between the cases of low price elasticity, with a quick adjustment, and high price elasticity, with a slow adjustment. Of course, even the low price elasticity is higher than some of the estimates summarized in Table 1-3. This short-term evidence, despite its many limitations, supports the view gleaned from Table 1-3 and the studies of the long-run substitutability of energy: there is a substantial potential to change the intensity of energy utilization, and we are going through a period of adjustment to new patterns of energy consumption; further reductions in energy intensity can be expected, even if the final outcome in terms of the level of demand is in doubt.

If we focus on these two cases, high and low elasticity, we can exploit the same methodology to examine the likely range of energy demand over the next twenty years. By the year 2000, the adjustment to the recent price increases may be nearer completion, but further increases in prices are widely anticipated; hence, we may see an endless process of gradual change, with net energy–GDP ratios much different in the future than today. Figure 1-10 summarizes the two demand curves for the year 2000, based on the parameters for the two cases that best fit the data through 1978. Both curves imply that there could be a substantial further reduction in the demand for energy. For example, using our earlier assumptions, as in Figure 1-8, if the price of oil increases to $4.50 per million Btus, the price of delivered net energy would rise to approximately $5.50 per million Btus. According to Figure 1-9, the corresponding net energy–GDP ratio could be anywhere from 19 to 22; but in either case, more than

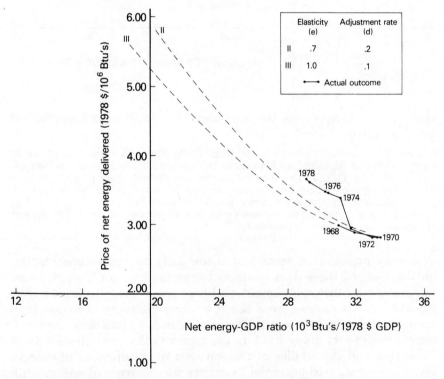

Figure 1-10. U.S. Net Energy Demand Curves for 2000: Selected Elasticities and Adjustment Rates.

Source: The method applied for Figure 1-8 was applied for a forecast through the year 2000, see note for Figure 1-9.

25 percent below the level of 1978. This would be a substantial reduction in the energy intensity of the economy, consistent with the lower forecasts in Table 1-4.

These figures can be converted to total primary energy demand, for comparison with other studies, by specifying (1) the degree of electrification (to account for the 70 percent of primary energy lost during conversion and distribution of electricity) and (2) the growth in the economy. In 1978, electricity accounted for less than 15 percent of the delivered net energy. If there is no major increase in the degree of electrification, then the ratio of primary energy to delivered net energy will be 1.35. With a 3 percent per year growth in the economy, total output will be four trillion (1978) dollars by the year 2000. Under these conditions, a net energy–GDP ratio of 22 implies a total primary energy demand in the year 2000 of 119 quadrillion Btus ($22 \times 1.35 \times 4 = 119$). If the growth in the economy is only 2 percent per year, or \$3.3 trillion by 2000, then the primary energy demand figure drops to 98 quadrillion Btus. These figures can be compared with the 1978 primary energy demand of nearly 77 quadrillion Btus. Other projections, consistent with the range of demand curves in Figure 1-10, can be prepared in the same manner.

The implications of a sensitivity analysis for the United States, based on Figure 1-10, are that some combination of high economic growth rates, low energy prices, or a major increase in the degree of electrification would be required to produce a primary energy demand in excess of 120 quadrillion Btus in the year 2000; conversely, low economic growth, high energy prices, or a decrease in electrification would tend to yield primary energy demands for the year 2000 less than 100 quadrillion Btus.

INTERNATIONAL ENERGY DEMAND

The extension of this sensitivity analysis to the examination of energy demand in other industrialized countries would produce similar results. Higher energy prices should reduce energy demand. The magnitude of the reduction may be less than for the United States, because the energy prices faced by consumers in most other countries are already higher than the prices in the United States. This will be especially true assuming that all the future increases in energy prices come only from increases in primary energy costs. Since primary energy costs are a smaller proportion of delivered net energy prices in other industrialized countries compared with the United States, the relative increase in delivered prices, when oil prices increase, will be correspondingly less. Reinforcing this lesser price effect, the economic growth rates in the other industrialized countries are likely to be higher than the U.S. growth rate. This has been true historically; between 1961 and 1970 the U.S. economy grew at 4 percent per year in real terms, and the remainder of the OECD countries grew at 5.5 percent per year.[13] Although output in these other economies should grow more slowly in the future than in the past, their share in world economic activity and world energy demand should be increasing. But with increasing energy prices, we would expect energy demand growth to be much slower in the future than in the past.

At the higher end of our range of sensitivity tests—that is, an elasticity of one—energy prices need only increase at the rate of economic growth in order for long-run energy demand to remain constant. Of course, we do not expect delivered net energy prices to increase this rapidly; there are abundant, but expensive, sources of energy supplies that should place a long-run ceiling on energy prices.

The ability to adjust to higher energy prices does not mean that higher prices are to be desired; there are real costs to be incurred when energy becomes more expensive. It only means that the flexibility in the energy system provides many means to accommodate the higher costs, minimizing the economic effects. But most of the evidence for this flexibility is drawn from analyses of data from the industrialized nations; we may be less sanguine about the outlook for the developing countries, at least for those developing countries that are not energy exporters. The structures of the economies in the developing countries are different from those of the industrialized nations. The acceptance of a single estimate for the elasticity of energy demand in all OECD countries is problematical; it would take a heroic leap to apply the same elasticity to the developing countries, and many observers argue that the elasticities are lower—for example, the limited investigation conducted by Pindyck, who provided our estimates of the elasticities for OECD countries, indicates that the price elasticity for gasoline demand is only 0.3 to 0.5 for selected developing countries.[14]

An even more serious problem that complicates the projection of energy demand for the developing countries relates to the effect of economic growth. For the United States, we assumed implicitly that a doubling of the level of economic activity would double the demand for energy, assuming that energy prices did not change. In fact, the increase in energy demand might be somewhat less—for example, because the increase in output might come from the service

13. Organisation for Economic Cooperation and Development, *National Accounts*, vol. 1 (Paris: OECD, 1976).
14. Pindyck. "Structure of World Energy Demand."

industries, which are less energy-intensive. We did not pursue this argument; it would only tend to reduce further our relatively low estimates for the likely range of energy demand. But for developing economies, the situation is likely to be reversed. Much of the current energy consumption in these countries is not part of the traditional energy trade, and this energy use does not appear in the statistics: wood and dung are not counted in our compendiums of quads. As the developing economies grow, and grow rapidly relative to the economies of the rest of the world, most of the demand for energy will be for the oil, gas, coal, and electricity of the industrialized world, especially for oil: our statistics will show the demand in developing countries growing at rates higher than their rate of economic growth.

When coupled with the recognition that developing economies should be growing rapidly over the next twenty years (this high rate of economic growth for LDCs is one of the major objectives of the community of nations), it is natural to conclude that the growing demand for energy in these countries will place a disproportionate demand on the world energy market as well as on their own balance of payments. The magnitude of this problem remains highly uncertain, however. Energy availability will continue to be a problem of the first importance to the LDCs, but estimates of the feedback effects on the world energy system, particularly in terms of oil supplies and prices, are presently the subject of much debate. Recent projections of the demand for commercial energy for the year 2000 in the LDCs range from as low as 50 quadrillion Btus to as high as 100 quadrillion Btus, compared with the 19 quadrillion Btus consumed in 1972.[15] By any account, this is a rapid rate of growth; at the upper range of the forecasts, the LDC demands could have a significant effect on the world energy market. Ensuring the production of this energy, and financing its purchase, remain major items on the agenda for energy policy in the international arena.

INTERFUEL SUBSTITUTION

The concentration on the analysis of aggregate energy demand is an important first step, particularly if the aggregate demand turns out to be lower than previously expected. In this event, the pressure to develop expensive, new supply technologies or stiff conservation measures may not be great, and there is time to test alternatives, conduct the basic research and development, and collect information as we go.

15. See Chapter 11, "Energy in Non-OPEC Developing Countries," by D. Baake.

The simple demand curve, relating net energy–GDP ratios to energy prices, is useful for sensitivity studies, to establish the likely range of energy demand, but it is not adequate for developing projections of the demand for individual fuels. From the perspective of U.S. national policy, the most pressing problems stem from the demand for oil and gas or, more directly, for imported oil and gas. A reduction in the aggregate demand for energy may be beneficial for many reasons—for example, improvement of the environment—but the extent to which it reduces the demand for imported oil depends in part on the degree to which it is possible to substitute abundant sources of supply, such as coal, for the imported oil. The opportunities for this interfuel substitution are not revealed through the use of the aggregate demand curve; a more disaggregated model is required for this purpose, and such models are available (with the cost of increased complexity) for studying alternative energy futures.

Most econometric demand models are constructed at a level of detail that captures the major fuel substitution possibilities; these interfuel substitution opportunities, such as substituting electricity for oil in heating, are even greater than those for saving all energy, as in the use of more efficient insulation to reduce heat loss. The potential sensitivity of demand composition to changes in the prices of individual fuels can be indicated by examining the estimates of own-price elasticities: the own-price elasticity is the percent reduction in the demand for any one fuel given a 1 percent increase in its price with the prices of all other fuels held constant, in contrast to the aggregate price elasticity, where the prices of all fuels may move together. Consider the case of electricity, for example, in Table 1-5. This is a metasurvey—namely, a survey of surveys of econometric estimates of the own-price elasticity of electricity, usually measured as delivered to the consumer. Although there is a substantial range of uncertainty in the estimates of this one parameter, the elasticity is

Table 1-5. Surveys of Own-Price Elasticity for Electricity (long run).

	Residential Sector	*Industrial Sector*
Taylor[a] (8 studies)	0.90 to 2.0	1.25 to 1.94
MRG[b] (3 studies)	0.78 to 1.66	0.69 to 1.03
Pindyck[c] (4 studies)	0.3 to 1.2	0.5 to 0.92

[a]L.D. Taylor, "The Demand for Electricity: A Survey," *Bell Journal of Economics* 6, no. 1 (Spring 1975): 74-110.

[b]MRG, "Energy Modeling for an Uncertain Future" CONAES (Washington, D.C.: Modeling Resources Group, 1978).

[c]R. Pindyck, "The Characteristics of Energy Demand," in J. Sawhill, ed., *Energy Conservation and Public Policy* (Englewood Cliffs, N.J.: Prentice-Hall, 1979), pp. 22-45.

large, and it will be important in determining the role that electricity might play in the nation's energy future.

The impacts of these large substitutions can cut both ways, increasing or decreasing the demand for electricity. With small increases in oil and gas prices and no change in electricity prices, there may be a continuing shift away from fossil fuels and toward electricity. But if electricity prices increase and oil and gas prices do not, the symmetric reduction in electricity demand would occur. The sensitivity of fuel mix and total demand is illustrated for example, in the more detailed studies conducted by the Demand Panel of the CONAES study;[16] this work employed both bottom-up engineering and top-down econometric analyses to explore the sensitivities of demand to dramatic changes in energy prices. The CONAES sensitivity tests were limited to one set of demand elasticities, which are consistent with the higher estimates considered here, and the results are similar —for example, the electricity demands for 2010 double if electricity prices are cut in half while other prices are held constant. This large potential for substitution was found in both the engineering and the econometric type analyses; there are even greater opportunities to change the mix of fuels used in producing electricity.

Two Disaggregated Models

Our simple demand curve could be extended, of course, to investigate the role of electricity, first by introducing two forms of energy —electric and nonelectric. But there are many other details that need to be included—for example, to adjust for the supply conditions and recognize the differential effects on the prices of electric and non-electric energy. To illustrate the range of variation that might exist for the composition of energy demands, two models have been compared. The first model was used by the Energy Information Administration (EIA) in preparing the *Annual Report to Congress.*[17] The second is the U.S. component of the OECD demand model developed by Griffin for the National Science Foundation.[18]

The EIA demand model is an econometric model estimated using a cross-section of data for regions in the United States. The aggregate elasticities of delivered net energy, in the model, are below the low end of the range of figures used in the previous sensitivity tests—for example, a long-run price elasticity of 0.5 for the residential sector and 0.3 for the industrial sector. Of course, the interfuel substitution elasticities are higher, often greater than 1. The Griffin model, in contrast, was estimated using a cross-section of data from different

16. CONAES Demand and Conservation Panel. "U.S. Energy Demand."
17. Energy Information Agency. *Annual Report to Congress.*
18. J. Griffin, "An International Analysis of Demand Elasticities Between Fuel Types," Report to the National Science Foundation, 1977.

countries, much like the Pindyck study mentioned above. The aggregate elasticities in this model are near the high end of the range of figures used in the previous sensitivity tests—that is, a price elasticity of 0.8 to 1.0. Again, the interfuel substitution elasticities are greater than the aggregate price elasticity.

These two models, therefore, have been selected to bracket the range of sensitivity tests that we have conducted; hence, we can obtain a consistent disaggregation of the sensitivity tests, to look once again at the aggregate demand and to examine the implications of changing prices for the changes in the demand for individual fuels. Two scenarios are reported here for each model by exploiting the extensive work done in the preparation of the EIA *Annual Report to Congress*. Two of the scenarios reported by the EIA correspond, roughly, to low and high price assumptions for the range of energy products. The EIA's scenario C is a medium GNP growth, medium oil price case. The EIA's scenario F is a medium GNP, high oil price case. The results of these two scenarios are taken from the EIA's report.[19]

19. EIA, *Annual Report to Congress*. The primary energy demand in quads per year for scenarios C and F in the two models are shown below. The data for the Griffin model were prepared by Sergio Granville and adjusted to match the actual outcome of 1975. Figures in parentheses are the adjusted values produced by scaling according to the ratio of the actual 1975 values to the estimated 1975 values.

	1975 (actual)	*1985* C	*1985* F	*1990* C	*1990* F
EIA					
Coal	12.82	21.2	21.7	25.4	27.3
Oil	32.74	43.9	42.4	48.5	43.6
Gas	19.95	19.1	19.4	19.3	19.9
Other	5.07	10.4	10.4	15.3	15.4
Total	70.58	94.6	93.9	108.5	106.2
Electricity Generation	6.56	10.4	12.6	10.5	12.9
Griffin					
Coal	14.9	13.2	14.2	14.2	16.4
	(12.8)	(11.4)	(12.2)	(12.2)	(14.1)
Oil	25.6	27.6	25.7	31.3	26.8
	(32.7)	(35.3)	(32.9)	(40.1)	(34.3)
Gas	21.8	21.1	20.0	20.2	19.4
	(19.9)	(19.3)	(18.3)	(18.5)	(17.8)
Other	5.1	12.4	12.4	15.9	15.9
	(5.1)	(12.4)	(12.4)	(15.9)	(15.9)
Total	67.4	74.3	72.2	81.6	78.5
		(78.4)	(75.8)	(86.7)	(82.1)
Electricity Generation	7.7	9.5	9.6	11.1	11.6
	(6.6)	(8.1)	(8.5)	(9.4)	(9.9)

Using the assumptions in the EIA report (in which the assumptions are spelled out with unusual care), Griffin's model was run for scenarios C and F, exclusive of the exogenous conservation savings assumed by the EIA.[20] The version of the Griffin model used has actual data only through 1973; hence, it is at a disadvantage relative to the EIA analysis, which begins in 1975. In an attempt to restore some consistency, the results from the Griffin model have been scaled so that the forecast from 1973 predicts 1975 demands exactly.[21]

The two scenarios involve very detailed price paths for a number of energy products. We use the price assumptions of the scenarios to exploit the richness of the models by permitting the prices of different fuels to change at different rates. The price assumptions for selected energy products are reported in Table 1-6, which is drawn from the EIA report. Both models were run with these prices as inputs. These varying rates of price change create the incentive for interfuel substitutions.

The results of the four model simulations, adjusted as described above, are shown in Figure 1-11. The differences here are substantial, reflecting the differences in the elasticities embedded in the two models: in comparing forecasts, it seems more important to agree on the model than on the price assumptions—for example, the delivered net energy-GNP ratios for 1985, scenarios C and F, are 27.1 and 24.5 for the EIA model and 20.3 and 19.5 for the Griffin model,[22] a greater variation across models than across scenarios. Most of the

20. S. Granville, "Runs of the Griffin Model under the DOE Price Assumptions," memo, Stanford University, July 28, 1978. This memo details the simulation of the Griffin model. The EIA conservation figures of 1.97 quads in 1985 and 3.2 quads in 1990 were not subtracted from the Griffin model.

21. We note in passing that the estimates from the Griffin model are below actual primary energy demand by 5 percent for 1975 and by 13 percent for 1977. This may be attributed to the lag parameters, which imply a very rapid adjustment to high energy prices. We are not aware of any similar test with the EIA forecast.

22. The assumed GNP level is $2,722 billion (1978 dollars) in 1985 and $3094 billion in 1990. The implied delivered net energy-GNP ratios in Figure 1-11 are:

	Scenario			
	1985		*1990*	
	C	F	C	F
EIA	27.1	24.5	28.3	26.0
Griffin	20.3	19.5	19.2	17.9

These values can be compared with the sensitivity tests with the simple demand curve. Note that most of the growth in primary energy demand projected with the EIA model comes from a rapid increase in electrification.

Table 1-6. EIA Energy Price Assumptions (1978$/10^6 Btus).

	Scenario C			Scenario F	
	1975	1985	1990	1985	1990
Industrial Coal	1.07	1.94	2.03	1.96	2.10
Industrial Gas	1.30	2.36	2.96	2.54	3.24
Residential and Commercial Gas	1.86	3.12	3.80	3.83	4.38
Residual Oil	2.30	3.06	3.23	3.66	4.58
Gasoline	5.52	6.09	6.28	6.68	7.74
Industrial Electricity	6.78	9.50	9.98	9.01	10.94
Residential Electricity	11.23	12.11	12.45	12.80	11.45

Source: Energy Information Agency, *Annual Report to Congress,* vol. II, 1977 (Washington, D.C.: DOE/EIA-0036/2, April 1978). Adjusted to 1978 dollars using the GNP deflator.

difference in the results of the two models is in the projections of oil and coal consumption. And the greatest difference in the detail is found in the forecasts of electricity generation, with the growth rate from Griffin's model one to two percentage points below the growth rate from the EIA model.

The detail of the two models tends to confirm the results of the sensitivity analysis with the simple demand curve. Prices and rates of price change will be important in determining energy demands during the next decade, but substantial uncertainty remains in the

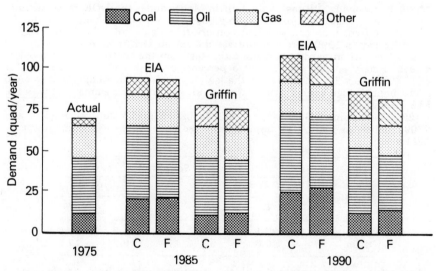

Figure 1-11. Composition of Primary Energy Demand (scenarios C and F).

measurement of the responses to higher prices. However, with all but the most pessimistic assumptions, the results suggest that energy demand may not grow as rapidly as indicated by the higher end of the range of forecasts in Table 1-4. The gradual response to higher energy prices and lowered expectations for economic growth may reduce some of the urgency for the development of new energy sources. Furthermore, if the price of oil increases more rapidly than the prices of other energy products, the substitution away from oil, in addition to the reduction of total energy demand, will reduce the demand for oil imports.

CONCLUSIONS

We should not rely on a single forecast of energy demand; concentrating on only one aggregate view of the future neglects unavoidable uncertainty. Energy markets are too complex, energy products are too diverse, and the unknowns are too many to be reduced confidently to one description of events far ahead in time. The growth of the economy, policies designed specifically to affect demand, the resolution of important environmental debates, and the evolution of energy prices will have dramatic effects on the level and composition of future energy demands. The uncertainties associated with these critical elements are great and can never be fully resolved until after the fact. But careful analysis can help us to understand the implications of the uncertainties and to delimit the range of future demand levels or the likely responses to changes in key conditions.

The shock of the events in 1973, with dramatic changes in world oil markets, stimulated many new studies of the options available for changing the growth in energy demand. Our examination of the results of these studies suggests that there are substantial opportunities to substitute insulation, new equipment, new production process, or changes in consumption patterns in order to reduce the consumption of energy. The evidence is found in both the examination of specific technologies—for example, the 45 percent improvement in efficiency now mandated for automobiles—and in the aggregate statistical data, where delivered net energy price elasticities as high as unity imply that a doubling of the delivered price of energy could improve energy efficiency by 50 percent.

In view of the evidence of many opportunities for reducing energy demand, it is not necessary to produce a precise forecast based on a single view of the future. The long-run economic impacts of higher energy prices may be much smaller than might be expected, at first glance, for a commodity as important as energy. If the effect of higher energy prices and reduced energy use is to substitute other materials, equipment, and process, in place of the forgone energy, rather than to curtail otherwise productive activities, then the economic cost of higher energy prices can be a relatively small proportion of the economy. And the best decisions today do not depend critically on the demand outcomes within the range that appears to be most probable. This is not to say that there is no cost to being wrong or that individual firms and consumers do not face many difficult energy choices. Rather, it means that the broad public policy recommendations for action today do not change if demand grows as suggested here, assuming that we exploit the opportunities to adapt as more information becomes available.

The adjustment process, en route to the exploitation of these long-run substitutions, may be another matter. The flexibility of the economy and our ability to change the mix of energy demands are substantially less in the short run. In the immediate future, the demands for energy will be determined largely by the composition and design of our stock of energy-consuming equipment, which can be modified only very slowly. All of the adjustments to the recent changes in prices may not be completed by the turn of the century. And the process of change, as we reshape the energy system, can have major impacts on large and important sectors of our economy and our society, albeit with the costs to the losers only slightly more than the gains of the winners, so that the aggregate change looks small.

The challenge, then, is to manage the adjustments. We have many opportunities to mismanage if we become blinded by extreme views that ignore the potential flexibility in the system or see a single panacea in energy conservation. We need to evaluate the costs and benefits of each energy use, and the best way to achieve this evaluation is to make sure that the energy consumer has the proper information, chiefly through the price system, to reflect the relative scarcity of the energy so that this scarcity may be compared with the benefits of the energy use.

If prices reflect the true scarcity of energy supply, including the many effects on resource exhaustion, the environment, national security, and so on, and the consumer pays these prices, then the level of energy demand must be, in a certain sense, correct. It is not so important to forecast the correct level of energy demand as it is to ensure that the system operates to give the correct signals to the consumer. The projections of very high energy demands are often the starting point for an analysis of impending crisis in the energy system. But if the difficulty of meeting the high demands is translated into higher energy prices, the flexibility to change the uses of energy will lead to a reduction in demand until the costs of further energy consumption just balance the benefits. This is the theory of the market system: where left alone, the market system for energy has worked reasonably well in the past, and it can be made to work well again in the future. The higher prices of energy are neither a crisis nor the essence of the energy problem. If we can manage the adjustment to a new era of energy scarcity, higher prices may be the solution to the energy problem. A sensible energy-pricing policy can help us manage the many adjustments that must be made by providing the incentives to make the substitutions that are possible. With these higher energy prices, future energy demand levels may be much lower than might be expected from the historical trend, a trend established during a period of decreasing energy prices. Conversely, if prices to consumers are held artificially low, we can make the problems of import dependence and supply allocation even more serious than the "crisis" situation we find ourselves in today.

APPENDIX A: ANALYTICAL FRAMEWORK

Aggregation

The analysis and discussion of energy prices and consumption quantities are simplified if we can speak in terms of a single measure applicable to all energy. Despite the common practice of adding together disparate Btus of oil, gas, or coal, however, it is clear that all forms of energy are not the same—for example, oil and electricity have different values and different uses, and they are certainly not the perfect substitutes that a simple addition would imply. To speak of a single form of energy, therefore, we must, at a minimum, account for the different values of the diverse energy products and the imperfect substitution possibilities among them. Even this may be a gross simplification.[23]

Prices. Although the complete set of conditions needed for consistent aggregation may not apply to the energy sector, we can develop price aggregation equations that serve as reasonable approximations that accommodate different values in use and different opportunities for substitution. It is fortunate for our study that

---

23. For further discussion of the heroic assumptions needed to create a consistent aggregate, see E.R. Berndt, and L.R. Christensen, "The Internal Structure of Functional Relationships: Separability, Substitution, and Aggregation," *Review of Economic Studies*, vol. 40, no. 123, pp. 403–417.

aggregation equations of this type are found in many econometric studies of energy demand, albeit usually restricted to some sectoral classification. In particular, we can benefit from the work of Pindyck in estimating aggregation equations applicable to a number of countries.

The approach used here is to adopt the price aggregation equations estimated by Pindyck in "The Structure of World Energy Demand." Pindyck assumes that, for each sector, the price of delivered energy is related to the delivered prices of the fuels according to the cost function:

$$P_E^j = C_j(P_1^j, P_2^j, P_3^j, P_4^j),$$

where P_E^j is the price of energy, P_i^j is the delivered price of fuel i (1 = solid fuels; 2 = oil; 3 = gas; 4 = electricity), and C_j is a positive function, homogeneous of degree zero, for the jth sector (1 = industrial; 2 = transportation; 3 = residential/commercial).

For purposes of estimation, a translog approximation for C_j was used—that is,

$$\ln P_E^j = \alpha_0^j + \sum_{i=1}^{4} \alpha_i^j \ln P_i^j + \sum_{i=1}^{4} \sum_{k=1}^{4} \beta_{ik}^j \ln P_i^j \ln P_k^j \qquad (1.1)$$

The parameters of this function describe the long-run substitution possibilities as the component energy prices change; hence, the estimates obtained from equation (1.1) will correspond to the long-run price of energy. This might by interpreted, for example, as the average price of delivered energy facing a consumer about to purchase new energy-using equipment when, because of the flexibility in choosing the new equipment, we may assume that the long-run substitutions apply.[24]

Pindyck provided estimates of the parameters of equation (1.1), except for α_0^j, for several OECD countries for the industrial and the residential and commercial sectors. For the transportation sector, we assume that $P_E^2 = P_2^2$—that is, that the price of energy for transportation is equal to the price of oil (gasoline) for transportation. We arbitrarily set α_0^j such that the index price, P_E^j, estimated from equation (1.1) for 1972 was equal to the quantity-weighted average of the prices of the four input fuels. The data sources for the prices are described in this chapter's Appendix B.

24. For further details on the derivation of equation (1.1), see Pindyck, "The Structure of World Energy Demand."

Sectors. Pindyck's price aggregation equations stop short of the aggregation across consuming sectors; yet this final, heroic step is needed if we are to obtain a single value for the price of energy. Over the range of the data considered here, the mix across sectors does not change enough to affect our qualitative conclusions, but there is some change in the total composition of energy consumption. To accommodate the implied substitutions, we have assumed that the aggregation across sectors was according to a Cobb–Douglas cost function with value shares estimated from the 1972 price and quantity data. In each case, this aggregation equation was benchmarked to yield a 1972 price equal to the quantity-weighted average of expenditures in that year:

$$P_E = c \prod_{j=1}^{3} (P_E^j)^{V_j} ,$$

where P_E = price of energy across all sectors, V_j = value share of expenditures in sector j, and c = a scaling constant.

Quantities. If the energy system is in long-run equilibrium, the data on total expenditures and the price of aggregate energy can be used to estimate the aggregate quantity of energy consumed. Unfortunately, the energy system was not in long-run equilibrium—at least not after 1973, the period of most interest to us. Presumably the full adjustments to the higher energy prices after 1973 had only just begun by 1978, and much of the energy intensity of the economy was still determined by decisions made at the lower, pre-1973 price level. The conceptually correct estimation of the aggregate quantities, therefore, depends upon the nature of the adjustment process, the very process we wish to examine.

If we assume the energy system was in long-run equilibrium in 1972, the benchmarking of our price index to the quantity-weighted average of the fuel price guarantees that the total quantity of delivered net energy was equal to the sum of the Btus of the individual fuels delivered to the consumer. But as the price of energy increased, the consumer is assumed to have changed both the aggregate level of energy consumption and the mix of fuels consumed. The sum of the Btus of the individual fuels was then no longer equal to the aggregate demand; however, the error of this estimate will be small if the long-run change in the fuel mix was small or if the adjustments completed were only a small part of the full, asymptotic adjustment.

Although the prices changed in different ways in different sectors and countries, the long-run, relative change in the mix of energy consumption should not be as large as the relative change in the total level of energy demand, and in the short run, the adjustment process is reasonably slow. We elected, therefore, to use the sum of the Btus of the delivered products as the best estimate of the aggregate delivered net energy consumed over the period 1968–1978. In the projections, of course, this assumption is no longer needed, and the estimates of future total energy requirements can be interpreted as the equivalent total Btus required at the 1972 equilibrium mix.

The construction of the aggregate energy quantity through the addition of the component quantities is at best an ad hoc procedure. The chief attractions are that the aggregation is exact in the base year of 1972 and the quantities relate to a familiar physical unit. But this approach is not consistent with the long-run equilibrium theory, and because of the relatively small changes in the aggregate, the choice among alternative aggregation schemes can have a significant effect on the results. For example, the use of price or value weights will greatly increase the importance of the residential and transportation sectors versus the industrial sector and of electricity versus the other fuels. This refinement in weights would be appealing for a long-run analysis, but it introduces the necessity of accounting for a greater short-run trend in the weighted energy-GNP ratio, a trend resulting from the increasing penetration of electricity. This extension would require an adjustment of our aggregate model (below) to introduce a trend in the energy intensity of the economy, stretching further the already strained assumptions needed to accept the aggregate analysis. It is not clear how this would change the resulting estimates of the long-run elasticities, but it is clear that (1) a deeper examination of the post-1973 data should be conducted with a disaggregated model that includes interfuel and interfactor substitution; and (2) the adjustment process must be specified more completely both to measure the dynamics of the system and to permit a better estimation of the proper aggregation of energy during the period of adjustment.

Data. The basic data sources are described in Appendix B to this chapter. The application of the several aggregation assumptions results in the aggregation parameters, aggregate prices, aggregate quantities, and aggregate energy–GNP/GDP ratios for the United States and eight selected OECD countries, for the industrial and residential and commercial sectors. The aggregation across sectors, combined with the transportation price data in Appendix B, was implemented with the Cobb–Douglas cost function and the relevant value shares. For purposes of comparison with the index prices from the aggregation equation (1.1), the quantity-weighted average prices were computed and presented. All these data were collected in Tables 1-7 through 1-9.

The hypothetical scenario for future delivered prices, as presented in Figure 1-8, was based upon an assumed trend in the primary energy prices. The five-step process for calculating the delivered energy prices was:

Step 1: Project primary fuel prices, $\overline{P}_{i,t}$ for $i = 1,2,3$. (1 = coal; 2 = oil; 3 = gas).

Step 2: Calculate $\overline{P}_{4,t}$, the primary fuel cost for electricity, from $\overline{P}_{i,t}$, as described in Appendix B—that is,

$$\overline{P}_{4,t} = \frac{3}{2.95} \left(\frac{\overline{P}_{1,t}}{0.49}\right)^{0.49} \left(\frac{\overline{P}_{2,t}}{0.34}\right)^{0.34} \left(\frac{\overline{P}_{3,t}}{0.18}\right)^{0.18} .$$

Step 3: Calculate delivered fuel prices from markups (assumed equal to real 1973 markups), for each fuel i and sector j—that is,

$$P_{i,t}^{j} = \overline{P}_{i,t} + M_{i}^{j} .$$

Step 4: Calculate aggregate energy price for each sector using the aggregation equations—that is,

$$\ell n P_{E,t}^{j} = \alpha_{o}^{j} + \sum_{i=1}^{4} \alpha_{i}^{j} \ell n P_{i,t}^{j} + \sum_{i=1}^{4} \sum_{k=1}^{4} \beta_{ik} \ell n P_{i,t}^{j} \ell n P_{k,t}^{j} .$$

Step 5: Calculate sectoral aggregation using 1972 value shares V_j, in a Cobb-Douglas price equation—that is,

$$P_{E,t} = c(P_{E,t}^{1})^{V_1} (P_{E,t}^{2})^{V_2} (P_{E,t}^{3})^{V_3} .$$

Modeling the Adjustments

The development of aggregate energy price, aggregate energy quantity, and energy-GNP estimates is useful for both the comparison across countries and for the examination of the early results of the energy system's response to the price shocks of 1973-1974. The comparisons of the international data are straightforward, once the aggregate statistics are available, and were discussed at greater length in the main body of this paper.

The examination of the energy system's adjustment process, however, depends upon the further elaboration of a dynamic model

Table 1-7.   Indexed Prices for the Industrial and Residential-Commercial Sectors, United States.

Year	Industrial		Residential-Commercial	
	Average Price	Indexed Price	Average Price	Indexed Price
1968	1.026	1.135	3.288	3.544
1969	1.001	1.091	3.176	3.380
1970	1.027	1.082	3.066	3.261
1971	1.129	1.147	3.171	3.292
1972	1.179	1.179	3.400	3.400
1973	1.275	1.211	3.903	3.590
1974	1.827	1.525	4.219	3.768
1975	2.095	1.659	4.384	3.862
1976	2.263	1.656	4.444	3.967
1977	2.532	1.753	4.905	4.219
1978	2.585	1.785	4.943	4.269

Coefficients (Industrial)

α_i	β_{i_1}
0.25550	-0.10170
0.05010	0.07390
0.47050	0.11950
0.22380	-0.09170

β_{i_2}	β_{i_3}	β_{i_4}
0.07390	0.11950	-0.09170
-0.01520	-0.07540	0.01670
-0.07540	0.05570	-0.09980
0.01670	-0.09980	0.17480

Coefficients (Residential-Commercial)

α_i	β_{i_1}
-0.01860	-0.25960
0.53360	0.00070
0.34920	0.15370
0.13520	0.10510

β_{i_2}	β_{i_3}	β_{i_4}
0.00070	0.15370	0.10510
-0.00320	0.10320	-0.10070
0.10320	-0.12410	-0.13280
-0.10070	-0.13280	0.12830

Summary Statistics

Year	Total Expenditure on Energy(T)	Demand(Q)	GNP	Q/GNP	Average Price	Indexed Price (C.D.FCN.)
1968	139.98	49.61	1601.27	30.98	2.8216	2.9891
1969	144.55	52.32	1642.32	31.86	2.7628	2.8989
1970	147.64	54.57	1634.00	33.40	2.7054	2.8182
1971	154.32	55.68	1682.64	33.09	2.7715	2.8270
1972	165.19	58.54	1779.92	32.89	2.8217	2.8217
1973	181.72	59.57	1877.20	31.73	3.0504	2.9153
1974	212.65	57.65	1851.36	31.14	3.6885	3.3905
1975	217.07	55.53	1827.04	30.40	3.9088	3.4529
1976	234.78	58.67	1938.00	30.27	4.0017	3.4731
1977	255.54	59.55	2033.76	29.28	4.2913	3.6117
1978	268.79	61.27	2105.35	29.10	4.3873	3.6598

Note: Indexed prices equal oil prices for transportation sector. Value shares are industry, 0.1725; transport, 0.4530, and residential-commercial, 0.3744. Prices are $1978 per million Btus and demand is in quads.

Table 1-8. Indexed Prices for the Industrial and Residential-Commercial Sectors, Canada.

	Industrial		Residential-Commercial	
Year	*Average Price*	*Indexed Price*	*Average Price*	*Indexed Price*
1968	1.410	1.442	2.593	2.698
1969	1.364	1.396	2.583	2.655
1970	1.363	1.399	2.603	2.632
1971	1.375	1.382	2.677	2.658
1972	1.261	1.261	2.589	2.589
1973	1.301	1.274	2.685	2.573
1974	1.936	1.591	3.391	3.061
1975	1.848	1.529	3.630	3.116
1976	1.938	1.519	4.319	3.853

Coefficients (Industrial)

α_i	β_{i_1}	β_{i_2}	β_{i_3}	β_{i_4}
0.23350	-0.10170	0.07390	0.11950	-0.09170
0.20990	0.07390	-0.01520	-0.07540	0.01670
0.29970	0.11950	-0.07540	0.05570	-0.09980
0.25690	-0.09170	0.01670	-0.09980	0.17480

Coefficients (Residential-Commercial)

α_i	β_{i_1}	β_{i_2}	β_{i_3}	β_{i_4}
-0.04540	-0.25960	0.00070	0.15370	0.10510
0.52360	0.00070	-0.00320	0.10320	-0.10070
0.28650	0.15370	0.10310	-0.12410	-0.13280
0.23530	0.10510	-0.10070	-0.13280	0.12830

Summary Statistics

Year	Total Expenditure on Energy(T)	Demand(Q)	GNP	Q/GNP	Average Price	Indexed Price (C.D.FCN.)
1968	12.02	4.46	122.28	36.50	2.6936	2.7267
1969	12.43	4.69	128.76	36.40	2.6516	2.6728
1970	13.17	5.01	132.06	37.97	2.6274	2.6372
1971	13.90	5.19	139.85	37.12	2.6769	2.6452
1972	14.61	5.78	148.05	39.06	2.5257	2.5257
1973	15.62	6.15	158.20	38.86	2.5411	2.5090
1974	18.57	5.89	162.70	36.21	3.1527	2.8287
1975	20.58	5.77	164.21	35.12	3.5691	3.0918
1976	24.32	5.99	172.71	34.69	4.0594	3.5432

Note: Indexed prices equal oil prices for transportation sector. Value shares are industry, 0.2175; transport, 0.4310, and residential-commercial, 0.3515. Prices are $1978 per million Btus and demand is in quads.

Table 1-9. Indexed Prices for the Industrial and Residential-Commercial Sectors, France.

Year	Industrial		Residential-Commercial	
	Average Price	Indexed Price	Average Price	Indexed Price
1968	2.004	2.251	5.746	5.915
1969	1.885	2.208	5.627	5.794
1970	1.864	2.190	5.431	5.790
1971	2.232	2.197	5.077	5.510
1972	2.272	2.272	5.592	5.592
1973	1.924	2.157	5.274	5.200
1974	2.124	2.157	5.710	4.834
1975	3.133	3.024	6.872	5.415
1976	2.862	2.696	6.665	5.511

Coefficients

Industrial

α_i	β_{i1}	β_{i3}	β_{i4}
0.24380	-0.10390	0.11840	-0.02370
0.38070	0.00930	-0.02400	-0.09160
0.19340	0.11840	-0.03400	0.06040
0.18210	-0.02370	-0.06040	0.17580

β_{i2}
0.00930
0.10630
-0.02400
-0.09160

Residential-Commercial

α_i	β_{i1}	β_{i3}	β_{i4}
-0.00510	-0.25960	0.15370	0.10510
0.26730	0.00070	0.10320	-0.10070
0.64160	0.15370	-0.12410	-0.13280
0.09630	0.10510	-0.13280	0.12830

β_{i2}
0.00070
-0.00320
0.10310
-0.10070

Summary Statistics

Year	Total Expenditure on Energy (T)	Demand (Q)	GNP	Q/GNP	Average Price	Indexed Price (C.D.FCN.)
1968	21.90	4.49	247.08	18.16	4.8809	5.2589
1969	23.09	4.85	264.31	18.35	4.7607	5.2149
1970	24.15	5.25	279.93	18.77	4.5974	5.1303
1971	25.72	5.43	295.11	18.41	4.7336	4.9573
1972	28.47	5.72	311.92	18.35	4.9729	4.9729
1973	29.01	6.38	329.22	19.39	4.5444	4.6368
1974	33.86	6.44	341.99	18.82	5.2617	5.0368
1975	37.11	5.99	344.21	17.41	6.1926	5.4980
1976	36.70	6.17	362.77	17.00	5.9499	5.2699

Note: Indexed prices equal oil prices for transportation sector. Value shares are 0.2241, industry; 0.4056, transport; and 0.3703, commercial. Prices are $1978 per million Btus and demand is in quads.

Table 1-10. Indexed Prices for the Industrial and Residential-Commercial Sectors, Italy.

Year	Industrial		Residential-Commercial	
	Average Price	*Indexed Price*	*Average Price*	*Indexed Price*
1968	2.750	2.907	5.177	4.488
1969	2.533	2.743	4.729	4.190
1970	2.269	2.519	4.345	3.979
1971	2.500	2.330	4.448	4.409
1972	2.251	2.251	4.242	4.242
1973	2.183	2.103	4.568	4.177
1974	2.424	1.964	4.413	3.948
1975	3.665	3.745	6.853	4.945
1976	4.269	4.211	8.638	6.289

Coefficients (Industrial)

α_i	β_{i_1}	β_{i_3}	β_{i_4}
0.23790	-0.10390	0.11840	-0.02370
0.40520	0.00930	-0.02400	-0.09160
0.14660	0.11840	-0.03400	0.06040
0.21040	-0.02370	-0.06040	0.17580

β_{i_2}			
0.00930			
0.10630			
-0.02400			
-0.09160			

Coefficients (Residential-Commercial)

α_i	β_{i_1}	β_{i_3}	β_{i_4}
-0.24450	-0.25960	0.15370	0.10510
0.24980	0.00070	0.10320	-0.10070
0.70650	0.15370	-0.12410	-0.13280
0.28810	0.10510	-0.13280	0.12830

β_{i_2}			
0.00070			
-0.00320			
0.10310			
-0.10070			

Summary Statistics

Year	Total Expenditure on Energy (T)	Demand (Q)	GNP	Q/GNP	Average Price	Indexed Price (C.D.FCN.)
1968	17.82	3.22	175.83	18.29	5.5417	5.3749
1969	18.14	3.49	185.66	18.79	5.2016	5.1013
1970	19.56	4.09	194.94	21.00	4.7778	4.9644
1971	21.53	4.05	197.92	20.48	5.3117	5.2124
1972	21.34	4.30	204.27	21.03	4.9681	4.9681
1973	21.91	4.64	217.02	21.39	4.7206	4.6337
1974	23.23	4.81	224.39	21.45	4.8273	4.6424
1975	32.58	4.63	216.51	21.39	7.0330	6.5574
1976	39.53	4.88	228.72	21.32	8.1086	7.6233

Note: Indexed prices equal oil prices for transportation sector. Value shares are industry, 0.2385; transport, 0.5109; and residential, 0.2506. Prices are $1978 per million Btus and demand is in quads.

Table 1-11.   Indexed Prices for the Industrial and Residential-Commercial Sectors, The Netherlands.

	Industrial		Residential-Commercial	
Year	*Average Price*	*Indexed Price*	*Average Price*	*Indexed Price*
1968	2.594	2.981	4.838	5.279
1969	2.367	2.559	4.763	4.874
1970	2.243	2.441	4.749	4.879
1971	2.544	2.272	4.826	4.842
1972	1.994	1.994	4.523	4.523
1973	1.923	1.847	4.550	4.467
1974	2.007	1.917	4.925	4.626
1975	2.927	2.421	5.146	4.923
1976	2.907	2.590	5.404	5.202

Coefficients (Industrial)

α_i	β_{i1}	β_{i2}	β_{i3}	β_{i3}
0.14860	-0.10390	0.00930	0.11840	-0.02370
0.41370	0.00930	0.10630	-0.02400	-0.09160
0.23110	0.11840	-0.02400	-0.03400	0.06040
0.20670	-0.02370	-0.09160	-0.06040	0.17580

Coefficients (Residential-Commercial)

α_i	β_{i1}	β_{i2}	β_{i3}	β_{i4}
-0.01910	-0.25960	0.00070	0.15370	0.10510
0.35460	0.00070	-0.00320	0.10320	-0.10070
0.63670	0.15370	0.10310	-0.12410	-0.13280
0.02790	0.10510	-0.10070	-0.13280	0.12830

Summary Statistics

Year	Total Expenditure on Energy (T)	Demand (Q)	GNP	Q/GNP	Average Price	Indexed Price (C.D.FCN.)
1968	6.65	1.43	60.49	23.58	4.6628	4.8993
1969	7.23	1.57	64.61	24.37	4.5903	4.6205
1970	7.78	1.80	69.07	26.03	4.3286	4.4400
1971	8.63	1.86	72.10	25.76	4.6462	4.4297
1972	9.02	2.15	74.90	28.69	4.1951	4.1951
1973	9.05	2.27	78.13	29.06	3.9844	3.9336
1974	9.57	2.24	80.73	27.72	4.2748	4.2495
1975	11.94	2.21	79.78	27.73	5.3970	4.9887
1976	13.30	2.44	83.47	29.29	5.4425	5.1679

Note: Indexed prices equal oil prices for transportation sector. Value shares are industry, 0.2284; transport, 0.3598; and residential-commercial, 0.4118. Prices are $1978 per million Btus and demand is in quads.

Table 1-12.   Indexed Prices for the Industrial and Residential-Commercial Sectors, Norway.

Year	Industrial		Commercial-Residential	
	Average Price	Indexed Price	Average Price	Indexed Price
1968	1.696	1.622	3.553	3.569
1969	1.688	1.682	3.441	3.504
1970	1.749	1.762	3.124	3.019
1971	1.860	1.814	3.629	3.626
1972	1.870	1.870	3.450	3.450
1973	1.758	1.700	3.602	3.441
1974	2.325	2.008	4.366	3.923
1975	2.284	2.180	4.543	4.115
1976	2.182	1.997	4.384	3.938

Coefficients

α_i	β_{i1}		α_i	β_{i1}
-0.06130	-0.10390		-0.08720	-0.25960
0.33170	0.00930		0.14690	0.00070
0.08880	0.11840		0.19470	0.15370
0.64080	-0.02370		0.74560	0.10510

β_{i2}	β_{i3}	β_{i4}	β_{i2}	β_{i3}	β_{i4}
0.00930	0.11840	-0.02370	0.00070	0.15370	0.10510
0.10630	-0.02400	-0.09160	-0.00320	0.10320	-0.10070
-0.02400	-0.03400	0.06040	0.10310	-0.12410	-0.13280
-0.09160	-0.06040	0.17580	-0.10070	-0.13280	0.12830

Summary Statistics

Year	Total Expenditure on Energy(T)	Demand(Q)	GNP	Q/GNP	Average Price	Indexed Price (C.D.FCN.)
1968	1.90	0.47	19.11	24.68	4.0200	4.1253
1969	1.97	0.50	20.07	24.80	3.9494	4.0464
1970	2.06	0.54	20.78	25.92	3.8301	3.8530
1971	2.28	0.54	21.72	24.79	4.2329	4.2315
1972	2.26	0.55	22.80	24.11	4.1166	4.1166
1973	2.25	0.58	23.75	24.58	3.8572	3.9368
1974	2.67	0.58	24.63	23.47	4.6188	4.6508
1975	2.84	0.59	25.49	23.06	4.8327	4.7325
1976	2.79	0.61	27.01	22.60	4.5666	4.4737

Note: Indexed prices equal oil prices for transportation sector. Value shares are industry, 0.2355; transport, 0.5329; and residential-commercial, 0.2316. Prices are $1978 per million Btus and demand is in quads.

Table 1-13.   Indexed Prices for the Industrial and Residential-Commercial Sectors, United Kingdom.

Year	Industrial		Commercial-Residential	
	Average Price	Indexed Price	Average Price	Indexed Price
1968	2.597	3.378	5.429	5.778
1969	2.451	3.019	5.186	5.406
1970	2.184	2.683	5.051	5.245
1971	2.447	2.550	5.221	5.337
1972	2.349	2.349	5.500	5.500
1973	2.238	2.312	5.624	5.323
1974	2.581	2.617	5.503	5.081
1975	4.158	3.445	5.913	4.902
1976	4.324	3.768	6.505	5.507

Coefficients

Industrial

α_i	β_{i_1}			β_{i_4}
0.17680	-0.10390			-0.02370
0.40370	0.00930			-0.09160
0.23620	0.11840			0.06040
0.18330	-0.02370			0.17580

β_{i_2}	β_{i_3}
0.00930	0.11840
0.10630	-0.02400
-0.02400	-0.03400
-0.09160	-0.06040

Commercial-Residential

α_i	β_{i_1}	β_{i_4}
-0.01040	-0.25960	0.10510
0.15470	0.00070	-0.10070
0.53800	0.15370	-0.13280
0.31770	0.10510	0.12830

β_{i_2}	β_{i_3}
0.00070	0.15370
-0.00320	0.10320
0.10310	-0.12410
-0.10070	-0.13280

Summary Statistics

Year	Total Expenditure on Energy (T)	Demand (Q)	GNP	Q/GNP	Average Price	Indexed Price (C.D.FCN.)
1968	31.13	6.40	258.60	24.76	4.8619	5.3559
1969	32.12	6.67	261.46	25.53	4.8128	5.2144
1970	31.26	6.83	267.17	25.56	4.5780	4.9257
1971	32.07	6.81	273.62	24.88	4.7110	4.8052
1972	32.44	6.99	280.67	24.89	4.6440	4.6440
1973	33.25	7.31	296.20	24.69	4.5473	4.4854
1974	33.78	6.96	298.65	23.32	4.8497	4.6684
1975	48.41	6.56	293.83	22.34	7.3752	6.1703
1976	48.66	6.71	301.49	22.26	7.2509	6.2761

Note: Indexed prices equal oil prices in transportation sector. Value shares are industry, 0.2632; transport, 0.3739; and commercial-residential 0.3628. Prices are $1978 per million Btus and demand is in quads.

Table 1-14.   Indexed Prices for the Industrial and Residential-Commercial Sectors, West Germany.

Year	Industrial		Residential-Commercial	
	Average Price	Indexed Price	Average Price	Indexed Price
1968	2.697	3.120	5.168	6.272
1969	2.506	2.773	4.726	5.817
1970	2.419	2.563	4.574	5.550
1971	2.562	2.381	4.899	5.448
1972	2.399	2.399	5.126	5.126
1973	2.300	2.285	6.045	5.781
1974	2.575	2.316	6.883	6.123
1975	3.000	2.385	7.116	6.213
1976	2.972	2.378	7.604	6.195

Coefficients

Industrial:

α_i	β_{i_1}
0.28640	-0.10390
0.35130	0.00930
0.13560	0.11840
0.22680	-0.02370

β_{i_2}	β_{i_3}	β_{i_4}
0.00930	0.11840	-0.02370
0.10630	-0.02400	-0.09160
-0.02400	-0.03400	0.06040
-0.09160	-0.06040	0.17580

Residential-Commercial:

α_i	β_{i_1}
-0.25160	-0.25960
0.29230	0.00070
0.57670	0.15370
0.38290	0.10510

β_{i_2}	β_{i_3}	β_{i_4}
0.00070	0.15370	0.10510
-0.00320	0.10320	-0.10070
0.10310	-0.12410	-0.13280
-0.10070	-0.13280	0.12830

Summary Statistics

Year	Total Expenditure on Energy (T)	Demand (Q)	GNP	Q/GNP	Average Price	Indexed Price (C.D.FCN.)
1968	31.96	6.95	299.43	23.22	4.5969	5.3354
1969	32.00	7.66	324.01	23.65	4.1755	4.8109
1970	33.16	8.14	343.24	23.71	4.0749	4.5608
1971	34.95	8.21	353.11	23.25	4.2573	4.3757
1972	36.08	8.54	365.17	23.39	4.2243	4.2243
1973	40.49	9.13	383.66	23.79	4.4367	4.3769
1974	44.91	9.02	386.03	23.37	4.9793	4.6874
1975	46.59	8.31	376.05	22.09	5.6097	4.8512
1976	50.69	8.77	396.99	22.09	5.7800	4.8226

Note: Indexed prices equal oil prices in transportation sector. Value shares are industry, 0.2862; transport, 0.3015; and residential-commercial 0.4123. Prices are $1978 per million Btus and demand is in quads.

Table 1-15.   Indexed Prices for the Industrial and Residential-Commercial Sectors, Japan.

	Industrial		Commercial-Residential	
Year	Average Price	Indexed Price	Average Price	Indexed Price
1968	2.846	3.365	6.876	6.777
1969	2.696	3.221	6.345	6.357
1970	2.518	2.949	5.781	5.917
1971	2.695	2.739	5.721	5.770
1972	2.653	2.653	5.435	5.435
1973	2.867	2.347	5.216	5.193
1974	3.134	2.360	7.126	6.174
1975	4.112	4.062	7.690	6.464
1976	4.238	4.264	7.677	6.414

Coefficients

α_i	β_{i1}	β_{i3}	β_{i4}
0.25710	-0.10390	0.11840	-0.02370
0.35730	0.00930	-0.02400	-0.09160
0.16380	0.11840	-0.03400	0.06040
0.22180	-0.02370	-0.06040	0.17580

β_{i2}	β_{i3}	β_{i4}
0.00930	0.11840	-0.02370
0.10630	-0.02400	-0.09160
-0.02400	-0.03400	0.06040
-0.09160	-0.06040	0.17580

Coefficients[a]

α_i	β_{i1}	β_{i3}	β_{i4}
0.04410	0.0	0.0	0.0
0.30430	0.0	0.0	0.0
0.11960	0.0	0.0	0.0
0.53190	0.0	0.0	0.0

β_{i2}	β_{i3}	β_{i4}
0.0	0.0	0.0
0.0	0.0	0.0
0.0	0.0	0.0
0.0	0.0	0.0

Summary Statistics

Year	Total Expenditure on Energy(T)	Demand(Q)	GNP	Q/GNP	Average Price	Indexed Price (C.D.FCN.)
1968	36.93	7.19	411.15	17.49	5.1375	5.4683
1969	40.18	8.41	455.29	18.48	4.7767	5.1630
1970	43.00	9.73	504.70	19.28	4.4183	4.8143
1971	44.49	9.52	541.25	17.59	4.6739	4.6679
1972	47.62	10.62	589.57	18.01	4.4833	4.4833
1973	51.90	11.57	647.40	17.88	4.4841	4.1206
1974	63.49	11.05	641.50	17.22	5.7464	4.8625
1975	69.15	10.71	656.95	16.30	6.4568	5.8932
1976	72.80	11.29	696.57	16.20	6.4497	5.9358

Note: Indexed prices equal oil prices in transportation sector. Value shares are industry, 0.3787; transport, 0.3558; and residential-commercial 0.2655. Prices are $1978 per million Btus and demand is in quads.

[a]Pindyck did not estimate an aggregation function for Japanese residential-commercial consumption. The Cobb–Douglas form is based on the 1972 value shares.

of energy demand. We have estimates from many sources of the long-run elasticity of energy demand (*e*), but it is assumed that this full adjustment is approached slowly. We are interested in comparing the post-1973 experience with the results of one model of this adjustment process. The model applied here was

$$\frac{E_t}{GNP_t^\gamma} = a(P_{E_t})^{-de} \left(\frac{E_{t-1}}{GNP_{t-1}^\gamma}\right)^{(1-d)} ,$$

where E_t = energy consumed in year t, GNP = GNP in year t, P_{E_t} = long-run price of (aggregate) energy in year t, e = long-run elasticity of energy demand, d = adjustment rate, γ = GNP-elasticity of energy demand, and a = a scaling parameter.

This simple equation is a common form found in econometric estimation of dynamic models. It would apply, for example, to a putty-clay situation wherein energy intensity was fixed at the time of installation of new equipment, and equipment was replaced at the rate of $100d$ percent per year. The short-run, one period price elasticity is de. The long-run, asymptotic price elasticity is e. The short- and long-run GNP elasticity is γ. The scaling parameter, a, can be fixed once an equilibrium price and E/GNP ratio are identified, in which case

$$a = \left(\frac{E}{GNP}\right)^d (P_E)^{de} .$$

In the main body of the chapter, we developed a range of estimates for the long-run price elasticity e. The aggregate GNP elasticity, γ, is probably less than unity. We tested values of 0.9 and 1.0, but all of the calculations presented in the chapter are based on γ = 1.0, which, ceteris paribus, will lead us to overestimate e during a period of rising energy prices. The adjustment rate, d, is more problematical; for the putty-clay model, an average life of new equipment of fifteen (six) years with a growth rate of 3 percent per year would be consistent with an adjustment rate of 0.10 (0.20); both values were tested. The scaling coefficient, a, was fixed by assuming that the average of 1968–1969 represented a long-run equilibrium.

With these assumptions, the dynamic model of U.S. energy demand can be simulated over the period 1969–1976 using the observed prices, and the predicted results for the energy-GNP ratio can be compared with the observed ratios. This naive test can provide an indication of the plausible range of values for the elasticities and adjustment rates that are consistent with the novel experience since the 1973–1974 price shock.

It should be emphasized that this is not a very powerful test, by itself. We have very few data points, and our theory suggests that the adjustment of the energy-GNP ratio, in response to higher energy prices, will be a slow process. Furthermore, despite the popular perception, the long-run aggregate delivered net energy prices have not changed more than 30 percent since 1972. This was an important change in prices, however, and the yearly accumulation of data should provide an ever-increasing precision in the range of estimates for d and e. But based on present data alone, it is not possible to rule out other explanations of the post-1973 reduction in the energy-GNP ratio; the trend through 1978, although persistent, was not outside the range of historical experience.

The most that can be said, at this step, is that the aggregate short-run adjustments were consistent with the independently derived long-run elasticity estimates. But this is an important increment to the weight of evidence supporting the estimate of a great degree of long-run flexibility in energy demand.

The results of these simulations were summarized in Figures 1-9 and 1-10. These represent the energy-GNP ratio that would have obtained under alternative price paths and parameter assumptions for the dynamic model; the demand curves can be compared with the actual experience with the changing energy-GNP ratio.

An alternative approach is to use the available data to estimate the elasticity in the dynamic model under different assumptions for the values of the income elasticity, γ, and the adjustment rate, d. The results of this estimation, with related statistics, are summarized in Table 1-16. This is not quite the same experiment as was done with the simulations because the econometric estimation always uses the observed value of the lagged energy-GNP ratio, not the forecast value; however, the general message to be gleaned from Table 1-16 is essentially the same: (1) there are few data points, and the test is not very robust; (2) but at slower assumed adjustment rates, the delivered net energy price elasticities implied by the data are at or above the high end of the range found in the examination of alternative estimates of long-run elasticities.

APPENDIX B: DATA SOURCES

Energy Consumption

Energy consumption figures for the three major energy-consuming sectors (industrial, transportation, and residential-commercial or "other") for the period 1969 through 1976 were taken from the OECD's *Energy Balances of OECD Countries: 1960-1974* and its

Table 1-16. Econometric Estimation (OLS) of Long-run Elasticity (e) in Dynamic Demand Model.[a]

Adjustment Rate (d)	GNP Elasticity (γ)											
	$\gamma = 0.8$				$\gamma = 0.9$				$\gamma = 1.0$			
	e	RSQ	t	D.W.	e	RSQ	t	D.W.	e	RSQ	t	D.W.
0.05	2.86	0.67	2.01	1.56	3.04	0.77	2.13	1.54	3.21	0.83	2.21	1.54
0.10	1.52	0.71	2.28	1.63	1.65	0.79	2.47	1.61	1.77	0.84	2.59	1.60
0.15	1.08	0.74	2.58	1.72	1.19	0.82	2.84	1.69	1.30	0.86	3.02	1.67
0.20	0.86	0.78	2.92	1.82	0.96	0.84	3.26	1.79	1.06	0.88	3.51	1.75
0.25	0.72	0.80	3.30	1.94	0.82	0.86	3.74	1.89	0.91	0.89	4.06	1.84

[a] $\ln(E_t/GNP_t^\gamma) = \ln a - e[d\ln P_{E,t}] + [(1 - d)\ln(E_{t-1}/GNP_{t-1}^\gamma)]$ for $t = 1969, \ldots, 1978$. See text for description of the data.

recent update, *Energy Balances of OECD Countries: 1974-1976.* In the case of the one year overlap between the two reports (1974), the more recent data of the 1974-1976 update were used. The OECD data were in millions of tons of oil equivalent (Mtoe) and were converted to British thermal units (Btu) at the rate of 0.0397 quadrillion Btu per Mtoe.

The OECD data are estimates of final sales. In particular, the figures given by the OECD represent consumption after end use conversions—that is, before electricity transmission losses, but after the conversion of fossil fuels to electricity and after on-site conversion of fuels to useful energy directly consumed. To distinguish from the more familiar primary energy, we refer to the OECD figures as "net energy." This definition of net energy does not coincide with the definition of net energy used by the Department of Energy (DOE).[25] Following the practice of the Bureau of Mines, DOE defines net energy consumption as the deliveries of electricity after conversion, transmission, and distribution losses plus the deliveries of primary energy for direct use but before on-site conversion losses.[26] We judged the MER convention to be the closest approximation to the measured quantities of energy actually purchased by final consumers; hence, it should yield the most compatible estimates of quantities purchased to be associated with the separate estimates of the retail prices. To maintain consistency across countries, therefore, we used the OECD estimates for the energy consumption data, but we adjusted the estimates to match the DOE-MER measurement conventions. As recommended in the preface to the OECD publication, the following conversions of the OECD figures were used: Solid fuel and oil consumption figures were divided by 0.95; natural gas figures were divided by 0.91; and electricity figures were divided by 1.00, but to account for electricity losses due to transmission and distribution, the electricity figures were multiplied by 0.91 (the average ratio of electricity sales to production for 1972-1976[27]). Before conversions from OECD net terms into DOE net terms, the OECD listed fuel consumption for nonenergy uses, by refineries and by the energy sector, and fuel losses were added to the industrial sector consumption totals.

These several adjustments were judged to make the measurement conventions as consistent as possible with the Department of Energy net energy consumption definition.

---

25. See DOE, *Monthly Energy Review,* February 1979, p. 22.

26. Note that DOE followed a different practice in the Energy Information Administration's *Annual Report to Congress,* p. 714, where "total net demand" included the energy lost in the transmission and distribution of electricity.

27. DOE, *Monthly Energy Review* (February 1979) pp. 59-61.

For 1977 and 1978, no OECD energy consumption figures were available; but for the United States, the *Monthly Energy Review* was used to estimate the percentage of increase or decrease over 1976 in each sector j (j = 1,2,3; 1 = industrial sector; 2 = transportation sector; 3 = residential-commercial sector) and for each fuel i (i = 1,2,3,4; 1 = solid fuels; 2 = oil; 3 = natural gas; 4 = electricity). The ratio obtained by dividing the MER estimate of average consumption for each year (1977, 1978) for fuel and sector (i,j) by the MER estimate of average consumption for 1976 for the same fuel and sector (i,j), was multiplied by OECD 1976 estimates of consumption for the same fuel and sector (i,j). The formula used in arriving at the updated figures was:

$\text{MER}_{(i,j)}^{77,78}$ = average consumption of fuel i in sector j, in 1977, 1978,

$\text{MER}_{(i,j)}^{76}$ = average consumption of fuel i in sector j for 1976,

$$\text{Estimated consumption}_{(i,j)}^{77,78} = \frac{\text{MER}_{(i,j)}^{77,78}}{\text{MER}_{(i,j)}^{76}} * \text{OECD consumption}_{(i,j)}^{76}.$$

In this way, a one year overlap of data was employed to incorporate the energy consumption growth implied by the MER into a consistent updating of the OECD yearly consumption figures.

This attempt at developing a data base that was consistent with both the OECD and U.S. Department of Energy data conventions was only partly successful. The aggregate consumption figures, for total primary energy, which includes all the losses in conversion, track fairly well once the OECD figures are converted to the DOE definitions. For example, Tables 1-17 through 1-27 display the

Table 1-17. U.S. Fuel Use by Sector, 1968 (10^{15} Btu).

Fuel	Residential-Commercial	Industrial	Transportation	Total Net Demand	Electric Utility	Gross Demand
Coal	0.50	3.92	0.02	4.44	7.88	12.32
Petroleum	5.57	5.16	13.51	24.24	1.18	25.42
Natural Gas	6.54	9.66	0	16.20	3.58	19.78
Electricity	2.13	2.58	0.02	4.73	-4.73	n.a.
Hydroelectric	0	0	0	0	2.37	2.37
Nuclear	0	0	0	0	0.14	0.14
Total	14.74	21.32	13.55	49.61	10.42	60.03

Source: OECD data.

n.a. = not applicable

Table 1–18.   U.S. Fuel Use by Sector, 1969 (10^{15} Btu).

Fuel	Residential-Commercial	Indus-trial	Trans-portation	Total Net Demand	Electric Utility	Gross Demand
Coal	0.42	3.91	0.02	4.35	8.21	12.56
Petroleum	6.23	5.24	14.05	25.52	1.65	27.17
Natural Gas	7.00	10.33	0	17.33	3.94	21.27
Electricity	2.35	2.76	0.02	5.13	-5.13	n.a.
Hydroelectric	0	0	0	0	2.71	2.71
Nuclear	0	0	0	0	0.16	0.16
Total	16.00	22.24	14.09	52.33	11.54	63.87

Source: OECD data.

n.a. = not applicable

Table 1–19.   U.S. Fuel Use by Sector, 1970 (10^{15} Btu).

Fuel	Residential-Commercial	Indus-trial	Trans-portation	Total Net Demand	Electric Utility	Gross Demand
Coal	0.40	3.78	0.02	4.20	8.42	12.62
Petroleum	6.54	5.59	14.53	26.66	2.08	28.74
Natural Gas	7.63	10.69	0	18.32	4.13	22.45
Electricity	2.48	2.90	0.02	5.40	-5.40	n.a.
Hydroelectric	0	0	0	0	2.67	2.67
Nuclear	0	0	0	0	0.25	0.25
Total	17.05	22.96	14.57	54.58	12.15	66.73

Source: OECD data.

n.a. = not applicable

Table 1–20.   U.S. Fuel Use by Sector, 1971 (10^{15} Btu).

Fuel	Residential-Commercial	Indus-trial	Trans-portation	Total Net Demand	Electric Utility	Gross Demand
Coal	0.38	3.45	0.01	3.84	8.37	12.21
Petroleum	6.55	5.69	15.20	27.44	2.42	29.86
Natural Gas	7.72	11.02	0	18.74	4.46	23.20
Electricity	2.65	3.00	0.02	5.67	-5.67	n.a.
Hydroelectric	0	0	0	0	2.90	2.90
Nuclear	0	0	0	0	0.43	0.43
Total	17.30	23.16	15.23	55.69	12.91	68.60

Source: OECD data.

n.a. = not applicable

Table 1–21.   U.S. Fuel Use by Sector, 1972 (10^{15} Btu).

Fuel	Residential-Commercial	Industrial	Transportation	Total Net Demand	Electric Utility	Gross Demand
Coal	0.34	3.83	0.01	4.18	8.65	12.83
Petroleum	6.97	6.00	16.16	29.13	2.88	32.01
Natural Gas	7.93	11.14	0	19.07	4.46	23.53
Electricity	2.95	3.19	0.02	6.16	−6.16	n.a.
Hydroelectric	0	0	0	0	2.88	2.88
Nuclear	0	0	0	0	0.59	0.59
Total	18.19	24.16	16.19	58.54	13.30	71.84

Source: OECD data.

n.a. = not applicable

Table 1–22.   U.S. Fuel Use by Sector, 1973 (10^{15} Btu).

Fuel	Residential-Commercial	Industrial	Transportation	Total Net Demand	Electric Utility	Gross Demand
Coal	0.31	4.14	0	4.45	9.67	14.12
Petroleum	6.42	6.21	16.87	29.50	3.62	33.12
Natural Gas	8.32	10.78	0	19.10	4.25	23.35
Electricity	3.16	3.36	0.01	6.53	−6.53	n.a.
Hydroelectric	0	0	0	0	3.02	3.02
Nuclear	0	0	0	0	0.96	0.96
Total	18.21	24.49	16.88	59.58	14.99	74.57

Source: OECD data.

n.a. = not applicable

Table 1–23.   U.S. Fuel Use by Sector, 1974 (10^{15} Btu).

Fuel	Residential-Commercial	Industrial	Transportation	Total Net Demand	Electric Utility	Gross Demand
Coal	0.28	3.82	0	4.10	9.47	13.57
Petroleum	5.99	5.66	16.70	28.35	3.80	32.15
Natural Gas	7.62	10.90	0	18.52	3.77	22.29
Electricity	3.38	3.30	0.01	6.69	−6.69	n.a.
Hydroelectric	0	0	0	0	3.14	3.14
Nuclear	0	0	0	0	1.23	1.23
Total	17.27	23.68	16.71	57.66	14.72	72.38

Source: OECD data.

n.a. = not applicable

Table 1-24. U.S. Fuel Use by Sector, 1975 (10^{15} Btu).

Fuel	Residential-Commercial	Indus-trial	Trans-portation	Total Net Demand	Electric Utility	Gross Demand
Coal	0.27	3.44	0	3.71	9.69	13.40
Petroleum	5.23	5.51	17.25	27.99	3.25	31.24
Natural Gas	7.72	9.34	0	17.06	3.42	20.48
Electricity	3.60	3.19	0.01	6.80	-6.80	n.a.
Hydroelectric	0	0	0	0	3.14	3.14
Nuclear	0	0	0	0	1.86	1.86
Total	16.82	21.48	17.26	55.56	14.56	70.12

Source: OECD data.

n.a. = not applicable

Table 1-25. U.S. Fuel Use by Sector, 1976 (10^{15} Btu).

Fuel	Residential-Commercial	Indus-trial	Trans-portation	Total Net Demand	Electric Utility	Gross Demand
Coal	0.27	3.49	0	3.76	10.87	14.63
Petroleum	6.75	5.66	17.78	30.19	3.58	33.77
Natural Gas	8.27	9.20	0	17.47	3.10	20.57
Electricity	3.77	3.47	0.01	7.25	-7.25	n.a.
Hydroelectric	0	0	0	0	2.98	2.98
Nuclear	0	0	0	0	2.06	2.06
Total	19.06	21.82	17.79	58.67	15.34	74.01

Source: OECD data.

n.a. = not applicable

Table 1-26. U.S. Fuel Use by Sector, 1977 (10^{15} Btu).

Fuel	Residential-Commercial	Indus-trial	Trans-portation	Total Net Demand	Electric Utility	Gross Demand
Coal	0.27	3.30	0	3.57	11.47	15.04
Petroleum	7.13	5.98	18.42	31.53	3.99	35.52
Natural Gas	8.01	8.93	0	16.94	3.22	20.16
Electricity	3.98	3.62	0	7.60	-7.60	n.a.
Hydrolelectric	0	0	0	0	2.44	2.44
Nuclear	0	0	0	0	2.71	2.71
Total	19.39	21.83	18.42	59.64	16.23	75.87

Source: OECD data.

n.a. = not applicable

Table 1-27.   U.S. Fuel Use by Sector, 1978 (10^{15} Btu).

Fuel	Residential-Commercial	Industrial	Transportation	Total Net Demand	Electric Utility	Gross Demand
Coal	0.29	3.14	0	3.43	11.49	14.92
Petroleum	7.16	6.02	18.85	32.03	4.10	36.13
Natural Gas	8.44	8.37	0	16.81	3.19	20.00
Electricity	4.14	3.75	0	7.89	-7.89	n.a.
Hydroelectric	0	0	0	0	3.04	3.04
Nuclear	0	0	0	0	3.03	3.03
Total	20.03	21.28	18.85	60.16	16.96	77.12

Source: OECD data.

n.a. = not applicable

Table 1-28.   U.S. Fuel Use by Sector, 1975 (10^{15} Btu).

Fuel	Residential-Commercial	Industrial	Transportation	Total Net Demand	Electric Utility	Gross Demand
Coal	0.2	3.8	0	4.0	8.8	12.8
Petroleum	5.7	5.5	17.9	29.2	3.2	32.7
Natural Gas	7.6	8.6	0.6	16.7	3.2	19.9
Electricity	4.0	2.6	0	6.6	-6.6	n.a.
Hydroelectric	0	0	0	0	3.2	3.2
Nuclear	0	0	0	0	1.8	1.8
Total	17.5	20.5	18.5	56.9	13.7	70.6

Source: DOE data.

n.a. = not applicable

aggregate energy balance tables extracted from the converted OECD data for 1968-1978. Table 1-28 displays the same energy balance data for 1975, the most recent comprehensive summary published by DOE, from the 1977 *Annual Report to Congress*, volume II.

Except for the different classification of the losses due to the transmission and distribution of electricity, which would make the DOE delivered electricity figure 9 percent smaller, Table 1-28 should agree with Table 1-24. The total consumption figure is approximately the same in both 1975 tables (74 quads). The sectoral totals, however, display larger, unexplained differences. This identifies a data problem that should receive attention in the DOE Energy Information Administration, which has responsibility for maintaining these data series for the United States. What are the explanations of the remaining differences in the figures from these two supposedly authoritative sources? Which figures are correct?

For the present study, with the emphasis on using consistent international comparisons, the OECD data, modified as described, are used throughout. The consumption figures for the selected countries are shown in Tables 1-29 through 1-37.

Delivered Energy Prices: United States

Retail prices for all fuels for all sectors, from 1968 through 1974, were obtained from Pindyck's World Oil Project Demand (WOPD) data base (the retail prices for oil in all three sectors were given through 1975). This data base was available on the MIT computer under the TROLL system; a description of the data base can be found in a paper by J. Carson[28] referred to below as the User's Guide. The prices were in constant 1975 dollars per trillion calories and were converted into constant 1978 dollars per million Btus, using the GNP deflator and the conversion of 252 calories per Btu as listed in the User's Guide.[29] These prices were updated from 1974 (or 1975, as appropriate) through 1976 or 1978 using several sources and methodologies, as detailed below.

During the updating of the price data from the WOPD data base, we compared the original data sources as identified in the footnotes in the User's Guide. These comparisons yielded a range of price differentials between the original sources and the WOPD data base. In some instances, particularly for the industrial prices for solid fuels, natural gas, and electricity, the price differentials between the original sources and the WOPD data were only a few cents per million Btus. This was judged as adequate to use the original sources directly. For other cases, where the cited data sources did not agree with the WOPD data base, we employed a more indirect updating scheme, as described below.

Direct Updates. Industrial prices for solid fuels, natural gas, and electricity were updated through 1977 by using the Edison Electric Institute (EEI) prices for solid fuels and natural gas found in the *Statistical Yearbook: 1977.*[30] It was assumed that the industrial sector as a whole paid prices for fuels that were equal to the prices paid by the electric utility industry. Coal prices, which were used as being representative of solid fuel prices, were given in current dollars per ton, and natural gas prices were given in current cents per million

---

28. J. Carson, "A User's Guide to the World Oil Project Demand Data Base" (Cambridge, Mass.: MIT Energy Laboratory, MITEL78-016NP, August 1978).

29. Ibid., Table 8.3.

30. Edison Electric Institute, *Statistical Yearbook: 1977* (Washington, D.C.: EEI, 1978) Table 45S.

Table 1-29.   Consumption by Sector and Fuel, United States.

Year	Solid Fuels	Oil	Gas	Electricity	Total
		Energy Demand (Delivered) in Quads			
Industry					
1968	3.92	5.16	9.66	2.58	21.32
1969	3.91	5.24	10.33	2.76	22.24
1970	3.78	5.59	10.69	2.90	22.96
1971	3.45	5.69	11.02	3.01	23.16
1972	3.83	6.00	11.14	3.19	24.17
1973	4.14	6.21	10.78	3.35	24.48
1974	3.82	5.67	10.90	3.31	23.69
1975	3.44	5.53	9.34	3.20	21.50
1976	3.49	5.68	9.20	3.47	21.83
1977	3.32	6.00	8.91	3.63	21.86
1978	3.14	6.26	8.37	3.74	21.51
Transportation					
1968	0.02	13.51	0.0	0.02	13.55
1969	0.02	14.06	0.0	0.02	14.09
1970	0.02	14.53	0.0	0.01	14.56
1971	0.01	15.20	0.0	0.01	15.23
1972	0.01	16.16	0.0	0.01	16.18
1973	0.00	16.87	0.0	0.01	16.88
1974	0.00	16.69	0.0	0.01	16.71
1975	0.00	17.21	0.0	0.01	17.22
1976	0.00	17.78	0.0	0.01	17.79
1977	0.0	18.29	0.0	0.0	18.29
1978	0.0	19.07	0.0	0.0	19.07
Residential/Commercial					
1968	0.50	5.56	6.54	2.13	14.74
1969	0.42	6.23	7.00	2.34	15.99
1970	0.40	6.54	7.63	2.48	17.05
1971	0.38	6.55	7.72	2.65	17.29
1972	0.34	6.98	7.93	2.94	18.19
1973	0.31	6.42	8.32	3.16	18.21
1974	0.28	5.99	7.62	3.37	17.26
1975	0.27	5.22	7.72	3.60	16.81
1976	0.27	6.75	8.27	3.76	19.05
1977	0.27	7.15	8.01	3.98	19.40
1978	0.30	7.43	8.77	4.19	20.69
Total Energy Demand					
1968	4.44	24.23	16.21	4.73	49.61
1969	4.35	25.53	17.32	5.12	52.32
1970	4.20	26.66	18.31	5.40	54.57
1971	3.84	27.44	18.73	5.67	55.68
1972	4.18	29.14	19.08	6.15	58.54
1973	4.45	29.50	19.10	6.53	59.57
1974	4.10	28.35	18.52	6.69	57.65
1975	3.71	27.96	17.05	6.81	55.53
1976	3.75	30.21	17.47	7.24	58.67
1977	3.59	31.43	16.92	7.61	59.55
1978	3.44	32.76	17.14	7.93	61.27

Source: OECD data.

Table 1-30. **Consumption by Sector and Fuel, Canada.**

Year	Solid Fuels	Oil	Gas	Electricity	Total
Industry					
1968	0.32	0.75	0.53	0.33	1.93
1969	0.28	0.76	0.63	0.35	2.02
1970	0.32	0.78	0.73	0.37	2.21
1971	0.26	0.84	0.76	0.38	2.25
1972	0.27	0.96	0.86	0.42	2.52
1973	0.25	1.11	0.98	0.45	2.79
1974	0.25	1.14	0.68	0.47	2.54
1975	0.24	0.97	0.69	0.45	2.35
1976	0.26	1.07	0.69	0.47	2.50
Transportation					
1968	0.0	1.01	0.0	0.0	1.01
1969	0.0	1.06	0.0	0.0	1.06
1970	0.0	1.15	0.0	0.0	1.15
1971	0.0	1.20	0.0	0.0	1.20
1972	0.0	1.28	0.0	0.0	1.28
1973	0.0	1.38	0.0	0.0	1.38
1974	0.0	1.47	0.0	0.0	1.47
1975	0.0	1.54	0.0	0.0	1.54
1976	0.0	1.58	0.0	0.0	1.58
Residential/Commercial					
1968	0.04	0.90	0.37	0.22	1.53
1969	0.04	0.92	0.41	0.25	1.61
1970	0.02	0.93	0.44	0.27	1.66
1971	0.02	0.96	0.47	0.29	1.74
1972	0.01	1.12	0.53	0.32	1.98
1973	0.01	1.10	0.53	0.34	1.97
1974	0.01	0.90	0.58	0.39	1.88
1975	0.01	0.87	0.60	0.40	1.88
1976	0.01	0.86	0.61	0.44	1.92
Total Energy Demand					
1968	0.36	2.65	0.90	0.56	4.46
1969	0.32	2.73	1.04	0.60	4.69
1970	0.34	2.86	1.17	0.64	5.01
1971	0.28	3.00	1.23	0.68	5.19
1972	0.29	3.37	1.40	0.73	5.78
1973	0.26	3.59	1.51	0.79	6.15
1974	0.26	3.51	1.26	0.86	5.89
1975	0.25	3.38	1.29	0.85	5.77
1976	0.26	3.51	1.31	0.91	5.99

Energy Demand (Delivered) in Quads

Source: OECD data.

Table 1-31. Consumption by Sector and Fuel, France.

Year	Solid Fuels	Oil	Gas	Electricity	Total
Energy Demand (Delivered) in Quads					
Industry					
1968	0.74	1.21	0.15	0.26	2.37
1969	0.75	1.41	0.17	0.28	2.61
1970	0.74	1.62	0.19	0.30	2.85
1971	0.62	1.61	0.23	0.31	2.78
1972	0.58	1.65	0.25	0.32	2.81
1973	0.60	1.91	0.29	0.35	3.14
1974	0.63	1.99	0.29	0.36	3.27
1975	0.54	1.67	0.32	0.34	2.87
1976	0.53	1.62	0.36	0.36	2.88
Transportation					
1968	0.0	0.76	0.0	0.0	0.76
1969	0.0	0.83	0.0	0.0	0.83
1970	0.0	0.89	0.0	0.0	0.89
1971	0.0	0.94	0.0	0.0	0.94
1972	0.0	1.03	0.0	0.0	1.03
1973	0.0	1.13	0.0	0.0	1.13
1974	0.0	1.13	0.0	0.0	1.13
1975	0.0	1.16	0.0	0.0	1.16
1976	0.0	1.25	0.0	0.0	1.25
Residential/Commercial					
1968	0.42	0.71	0.11	0.11	1.35
1969	0.38	0.78	0.12	0.12	1.41
1970	0.35	0.88	0.14	0.14	1.51
1971	0.29	1.10	0.17	0.15	1.71
1972	0.25	1.26	0.20	0.17	1.89
1973	0.25	1.43	0.24	0.19	2.11
1974	0.24	1.34	0.25	0.21	2.03
1975	0.19	1.27	0.27	0.23	1.96
1976	0.18	1.30	0.31	0.26	2.05
Total Energy Demand					
1968	1.16	2.69	0.27	0.37	4.49
1969	1.13	3.02	0.29	0.41	4.85
1970	1.09	3.39	0.33	0.44	5.25
1971	0.91	3.66	0.40	0.46	5.43
1972	0.83	3.95	0.46	0.49	5.72
1973	0.85	4.47	0.53	0.54	6.38
1974	0.87	4.46	0.55	0.56	6.44
1975	0.73	4.10	0.59	0.57	5.99
1976	0.72	4.17	0.67	0.62	6.17

Source: OECD data.

Table 1-32. Consumption by Sector and Fuel, Italy.

Year	Solid Fuels	Oil	Gas	Electricity	Total
	Energy Demand (Delivered) in Quads				
Industry					
1968	0.25	1.05	0.26	0.24	1.80
1969	0.24	1.12	0.31	0.25	1.92
1970	0.28	1.46	0.33	0.26	2.34
1971	0.26	1.29	0.34	0.27	2.16
1972	0.28	1.30	0.39	0.29	2.26
1973	0.29	1.50	0.42	0.31	2.52
1974	0.32	1.61	0.45	0.32	2.70
1975	0.29	1.41	0.46	0.31	2.47
1976	0.28	1.45	0.52	0.35	2.59
Transportation					
1968	0.0	0.61	0.0	0.0	0.61
1969	0.0	0.66	0.0	0.0	0.66
1970	0.0	0.70	0.0	0.0	0.70
1971	0.0	0.73	0.0	0.0	0.73
1972	0.0	0.77	0.0	0.0	0.77
1973	0.0	0.82	0.0	0.0	0.82
1974	0.0	0.80	0.0	0.0	0.80
1975	0.0	0.80	0.0	0.0	0.80
1976	0.0	0.77	0.0	0.0	0.77
Residential/Commercial					
1968	0.11	0.52	0.08	0.08	0.80
1969	0.11	0.62	0.09	0.09	0.91
1970	0.09	0.76	0.10	0.10	1.05
1971	0.07	0.85	0.13	0.11	1.16
1972	0.07	0.93	0.15	0.12	1.26
1973	0.07	0.93	0.18	0.13	1.31
1974	0.05	0.92	0.22	0.14	1.32
1975	0.04	0.91	0.27	0.14	1.36
1976	0.04	1.01	0.31	0.15	1.51
Total Energy Demand					
1968	0.37	2.19	0.34	0.32	3.22
1969	0.36	2.40	0.39	0.34	3.49
1970	0.37	2.92	0.43	0.37	4.09
1971	0.33	2.87	0.47	0.38	4.05
1972	0.35	3.00	0.53	0.41	4.30
1973	0.36	3.25	0.60	0.44	4.64
1974	0.37	3.33	0.66	0.46	4.81
1975	0.33	3.12	0.73	0.45	4.63
1976	0.32	3.22	0.83	0.50	4.88

Source: OECD data.

Table 1–33.   Consumption by Sector and Fuel, the Netherlands.

		Energy Demand (Delivered) in Quads			
Year	*Solid Fuels*	*Oil*	*Gas*	*Electricity*	*Total*
Industry					
1968	0.08	0.42	0.15	0.06	0.71
1969	0.09	0.42	0.18	0.07	0.75
1970	0.09	0.49	0.24	0.07	0.89
1971	0.07	0.45	0.27	0.08	0.88
1972	0.07	0.52	0.35	0.09	1.03
1973	0.07	0.55	0.40	0.09	1.11
1974	0.09	0.56	0.41	0.09	1.14
1975	0.08	0.46	0.39	0.09	1.03
1976	0.08	0.57	0.41	0.10	1.17
Transportation					
1968	0.0	0.22	0.0	0.0	0.22
1969	0.0	0.24	0.0	0.0	0.24
1970	0.0	0.26	0.0	0.0	0.26
1971	0.0	0.28	0.0	0.0	0.28
1972	0.0	0.30	0.0	0.0	0.30
1973	0.0	0.31	0.0	0.0	0.31
1974	0.0	0.29	0.0	0.0	0.29
1975	0.0	0.31	0.0	0.0	0.31
1976	0.0	0.34	0.0	0.0	0.34
Residential/Commercial					
1968	0.07	0.25	0.14	0.04	0.50
1969	0.07	0.26	0.22	0.04	0.59
1970	0.04	0.29	0.27	0.05	0.65
1971	0.03	0.27	0.35	0.05	0.70
1972	0.02	0.28	0.46	0.06	0.82
1973	0.02	0.28	0.49	0.06	0.85
1974	0.01	0.21	0.52	0.07	0.80
1975	0.01	0.20	0.60	0.07	0.88
1976	0.00	0.23	0.62	0.08	0.93
Total Energy Demand					
1968	0.15	0.89	0.29	0.10	1.43
1969	0.15	0.92	0.39	0.11	1.57
1970	0.13	1.04	0.50	0.12	1.80
1971	0.10	1.00	0.63	0.13	1.86
1972	0.09	1.10	0.81	0.15	2.15
1973	0.08	1.14	0.89	0.16	2.27
1974	0.09	1.06	0.92	0.16	2.24
1975	0.09	0.97	0.99	0.16	2.21
1976	0.08	1.15	1.04	0.18	2.44

Source: OECD data.

Table 1-34. Consumption by Sector and Fuel, Norway.

Year	Solid Fuels	Oil	Gas	Electricity	Total
		Energy Demand (Delivered) in Quads			
Industry					
1968	0.03	0.11	0.0	0.12	0.26
1969	0.03	0.11	0.0	0.12	0.26
1970	0.03	0.13	0.0	0.12	0.28
1971	0.03	0.12	0.0	0.13	0.28
1972	0.03	0.12	0.0	0.13	0.28
1973	0.03	0.15	0.0	0.14	0.31
1974	0.04	0.14	0.0	0.15	0.33
1975	0.03	0.13	0.01	0.15	0.32
1976	0.03	0.13	0.01	0.15	0.33
Transportation					
1968	0.0	0.09	0.0	0.0	0.09
1969	0.0	0.10	0.0	0.0	0.10
1970	0.0	0.11	0.0	0.0	0.11
1971	0.0	0.11	0.0	0.0	0.11
1972	0.0	0.11	0.0	0.0	0.11
1973	0.0	0.11	0.0	0.0	0.11
1974	0.0	0.10	0.0	0.0	0.10
1975	0.0	0.12	0.0	0.0	0.12
1976	0.0	0.12	0.0	0.0	0.12
Residential/Commercial					
1968	0.01	0.06	0.00	0.05	0.12
1969	0.01	0.07	0.00	0.05	0.14
1970	0.01	0.08	0.00	0.06	0.15
1971	0.01	0.08	0.00	0.06	0.15
1972	0.01	0.08	0.00	0.06	0.15
1973	0.00	0.09	0.00	0.07	0.16
1974	0.00	0.08	0.00	0.07	0.15
1975	0.00	0.07	0.00	0.07	0.15
1976	0.00	0.08	0.00	0.08	0.17
Total Energy Demand					
1968	0.04	0.26	0.00	0.18	0.47
1969	0.04	0.28	0.00	0.17	0.50
1970	0.04	0.32	0.00	0.18	0.54
1971	0.04	0.31	0.00	0.19	0.54
1972	0.04	0.32	0.00	0.19	0.55
1973	0.03	0.34	0.00	0.21	0.58
1974	0.04	0.32	0.00	0.22	0.58
1975	0.04	0.32	0.01	0.22	0.59
1976	0.04	0.33	0.01	0.23	0.61

Source: OECD data.

Table 1-35.   Consumption by Sector and Fuel, United Kingdom.

	Energy Demand (Delivered) in Quads				
Year	Solid Fuels	Oil	Gas	Electricity	Total
Industry					
1968	1.16	1.57	0.16	0.36	3.26
1969	1.15	1.71	0.20	0.39	3.43
1970	1.08	1.80	0.26	0.40	3.53
1971	0.94	1.84	0.36	0.40	3.54
1972	0.80	1.92	0.51	0.40	3.64
1973	0.79	2.00	0.59	0.44	3.82
1974	0.71	1.80	0.61	0.41	3.54
1975	0.66	1.52	0.60	0.41	3.20
1976	0.65	1.57	0.64	0.43	3.29
Transportation					
1968	0.0	1.03	0.0	0.0	1.03
1969	0.0	1.07	0.0	0.0	1.07
1970	0.0	1.12	0.0	0.0	1.12
1971	0.0	1.16	0.0	0.0	1.16
1972	0.0	1.21	0.0	0.0	1.21
1973	0.0	1.29	0.0	0.0	1.29
1974	0.0	1.24	0.0	0.0	1.24
1975	0.0	1.23	0.0	0.0	1.23
1976	0.0	1.27	0.0	0.0	1.27
Residential/Commercial					
1968	1.03	0.41	0.35	0.32	2.11
1969	0.97	0.46	0.39	0.35	2.17
1970	0.89	0.49	0.43	0.37	2.18
1971	0.74	0.50	0.48	0.38	2.10
1972	0.65	0.53	0.55	0.41	2.14
1973	0.63	0.55	0.59	0.43	2.21
1974	0.60	0.48	0.67	0.43	2.18
1975	0.51	0.48	0.73	0.42	2.14
1976	0.47	0.49	0.78	0.42	2.15
Total Energy Demand					
1968	2.19	3.02	0.51	0.69	6.40
1969	2.12	3.23	0.59	0.73	6.67
1970	1.96	3.41	0.69	0.76	6.83
1971	1.68	3.50	0.84	0.79	6.81
1972	1.45	3.66	1.06	0.81	6.99
1973	1.43	3.84	1.18	0.87	7.31
1974	1.31	3.53	1.28	0.84	6.96
1975	1.17	3.23	1.33	0.84	6.56
1976	1.12	3.33	1.41	0.85	6.71

Source: OECD data.

Table 1-36. Consumption by Sector and Fuel, West Germany.

		Energy Demand (Delivered) in Quads			
Year	*Solid Fuels*	*Oil*	*Gas*	*Electricity*	*Total*
Industry					
1968	1.26	1.82	0.19	0.43	3.70
1969	1.32	2.01	0.23	0.47	4.02
1970	1.18	2.20	0.32	0.49	4.20
1971	1.07	2.19	0.42	0.51	4.20
1972	0.95	2.33	0.49	0.53	4.30
1973	0.99	2.52	0.60	0.57	4.69
1974	1.08	2.26	0.80	0.59	4.73
1975	0.81	1.87	0.76	0.54	3.99
1976	0.82	2.04	0.70	0.59	4.15
Transportation					
1968	0.0	0.98	0.0	0.0	0.98
1969	0.0	1.05	0.0	0.0	1.05
1970	0.0	1.17	0.0	0.0	1.17
1971	0.0	1.27	0.0	0.0	1.27
1972	0.0	1.33	0.0	0.0	1.33
1973	0.0	1.37	0.0	0.0	1.37
1974	0.0	1.30	0.0	0.0	1.30
1975	0.0	1.38	0.0	0.0	1.38
1976	0.0	1.44	0.0	0.0	1.44
Residential/Commercial					
1968	0.74	1.19	0.13	0.21	2.27
1969	0.73	1.46	0.17	0.23	2.59
1970	0.66	1.66	0.19	0.26	2.77
1971	0.50	1.74	0.22	0.29	2.75
1972	0.44	1.84	0.29	0.33	2.90
1973	0.40	1.96	0.34	0.36	3.06
1974	0.39	1.88	0.36	0.37	2.99
1975	0.30	1.86	0.38	0.39	2.93
1976	0.26	2.04	0.46	0.42	3.18
Total Energy Demand					
1968	2.01	3.99	0.32	0.63	6.95
1969	2.05	4.52	0.39	0.70	7.66
1970	1.85	5.03	0.51	0.75	8.14
1971	1.57	5.19	0.64	0.80	8.21
1972	1.39	5.51	0.78	0.86	8.54
1973	1.39	5.86	0.94	0.93	9.13
1974	1.46	5.44	1.16	0.96	9.02
1975	1.11	5.11	1.15	0.93	8.31
1976	1.08	5.51	1.16	1.01	8.77

Source: OECD data.

Table 1-37.   Consumption by Sector and Fuel, Japan.

Year	Solid Fuels	Oil	Gas	Electricity	Total
Energy Demand (Delivered) in Quads					
Industry					
1968	1.32	2.60	0.12	0.66	4.70
1969	1.55	3.09	0.12	0.75	5.51
1970	1.65	3.82	0.13	0.86	6.45
1971	1.64	3.37	0.13	0.91	6.04
1972	1.66	4.00	0.14	0.99	6.80
1973	1.70	4.37	0.19	1.08	7.35
1974	1.92	3.87	0.13	1.02	6.95
1975	1.85	3.54	0.14	1.04	6.56
1976	1.82	3.89	0.14	1.12	6.97
Transportation					
1968	0.0	1.05	0.0	0.0	1.05
1969	0.0	1.18	0.0	0.0	1.18
1970	0.0	1.34	0.0	0.0	1.34
1971	0.0	1.39	0.0	0.0	1.39
1972	0.0	1.50	0.0	0.0	1.50
1973	0.0	1.66	0.0	0.0	1.66
1974	0.0	1.66	0.0	0.0	1.66
1975	0.0	1.73	0.0	0.0	1.73
1976	0.0	1.81	0.0	0.0	1.81
Residential/Commercial					
1968	0.17	0.98	0.12	0.16	1.44
1969	0.15	1.23	0.15	0.20	1.72
1970	0.13	1.42	0.16	0.22	1.94
1971	0.10	1.55	0.18	0.26	2.09
1972	0.08	1.75	0.20	0.30	2.33
1973	0.08	1.94	0.22	0.33	2.57
1974	0.20	1.66	0.22	0.36	2.43
1975	0.17	1.62	0.23	0.40	2.42
1976	0.16	1.68	0.25	0.42	2.51
Total Energy Demand					
1968	1.49	4.64	0.24	0.82	7.19
1969	1.69	5.50	0.26	0.95	8.41
1970	1.78	6.58	0.29	1.08	9.73
1971	1.75	6.31	0.31	1.16	9.52
1972	1.74	7.25	0.34	1.29	10.62
1973	1.78	7.97	0.41	1.42	11.57
1974	2.12	7.19	0.35	1.38	11.05
1975	2.02	6.88	0.36	1.44	10.71
1976	1.97	7.38	0.39	1.54	11.29

Source: OECD data.

cubic feet. Both prices were put into constant 1978 dollars per million Btus by using the GNP deflators given in the *Economic Report to the President*, 1979, and the fuel conversion factors given in the User's Guide.[31] Industrial electricity prices were derived from EEI figures.[32]

Indirect Updates. For oil prices in all three sectors and natural gas prices in the residential and commercial sectors, the price comparisons between the WOPD and the cited sources yielded differences as large as 20 cents per million Btus. This large deviation would dominate our results if we mixed the price series directly; hence, we elected to adopt a more indirect updating procedure. For the sake of consistency, the WOPD data base was accepted as definitive, and the updating from 1974 to 1976 or 1978 was accomplished through the use of overlapping data series: the data for the final year overlap between the WOPD numbers and the alternative data source for updating were employed along with a ratio method to estimate the implied price changes over time. In this way, intertemporal consistency was maintained with the WOPD numbers while capturing the more recent information in the several data sources. (We did not attempt to pursue this issue further, but the problems encountered in comparing alternative data bases represent an opportunity for further research and data base development. The WOPD data base may well be the most comprehensive international energy data base in existence; it has been an invaluable resource in this study, but more work needs to be done if future researchers are to build upon the substantial efforts of Pindyck and his colleagues.)

The ratio method takes advantage of a year of price data overlap between the WOPD prices and those from the selected updating source: for each fuel i in the sector j, with 1974 as the base year, the general formula is:

$$P^{75,76,77}_{(i,j)\,WOPD} = \frac{P^{75,76,77}_{(i,j)}}{P^{74}_{(i,j)}} * P^{74}_{(i,j)\,WOPD},$$

where $P^{75,76,77}_{(i,j)}$ and $P^{74}_{(i,j)}$ are constant dollar prices from the updating sources.

To update the industrial prices for solid fuels, natural gas, and electricity from 1977 to 1978, a constant price markup from the

31. Carson, "User's Guide," Table 8.3.
32. EEI, Table 45S. The prices given under the heading "Commercial and Industrial/Large Light and Power" were used to arrive at the current dollar prices through the use of GNP deflators and Table 8.3 of Carson's User's Guide.

primary fuel price to the retail fuel price was assumed. Thus, the difference between the 1978 and 1977 primary fuel prices for fuel (i,j) was added to the updated WOPD 1977 retail price for the same fuel (i,j). Primary fuel prices are described below.

Residential-commercial electric prices were updated from 1974 through 1978 in the same manner as industrial electric prices.[33] For prices from 1974 through 1977, a ratio update was used. Each constant dollar price for residential electricity from 1975 through 1977 from the EEI was divided by the constant dollar price for 1974, again from EEI. This ratio was then multiplied by the WOPD 1974 residential-commercial price for electricity. The update of the residential-commercial price from 1977 to 1978 was again done with a constant markup over primary fuel costs: the difference in primary energy costs per unit of electric output between 1978 and 1977 was added to the WOPD price for residential-commercial electricity in 1977.

The oil prices for the industrial, transportation, and residential-commercial sectors, as well as the prices for residential-commercial natural gas, were updated through the use of the DOE *Monthly Energy Review*. Oil prices were updated for 1976 through 1978, and the natural gas prices were updated for 1975 through 1978, using a ratio update. For industrial oil prices, the average annual retail prices for low-sulfur residual number six oil were used. For motor gasoline, we calculated an average of the prices for leaded regular and leaded premium at a full service pump. Finally, residential-commercial oil prices were taken from the average annual retail price of heating oil. For natural gas in the residential-commercial sector, the average annual retail price of natural gas sold to residential customers was used. For all oil and natural gas prices, only the data from the first six months of 1978 were used, and the data from the base year of 1975 were adjusted to an average of the prices over the first six months.

To update the prices for residential-commercial solid fuels, we assumed a constant markup over primary fuel costs. The difference in the primary fuel price of coal from 1974 to each more recent year was added to the 1974 WOPD residential-commercial retail price for solid fuels. The final retail prices, as adjusted and updated, are reported below after a description of the data sources for price from the eight related OECD countries.

---

33. EEI, Tables 33S and 45S. Table 33S, entitled "Revenues—Total Electric Utility Industry," provided weights to obtain the average price for residential-commercial electricity according to the relative value of consumption in the two subsectors.

Table 1-38. Price Accounting Conventions.[a]

	Solid fuels	*Oil*	*Gas*	*Electricity*
Residential/ Commercial	Domestic anthracite	Domestic kerosene	Domestic natural gas	Domestic electricity
Transportation	n.a.[b]	Inland transport gasoline (premium)	n.a.	n.a.
Industrial	Industrial steam coal	Industrial heavy fuel oil	Industrial natural gas $(500 \times 10^{16}$ kcal)	Industrial electricity

[a]To relate accounting conventions in R. Pindyck, "The Structure of World Energy Demand" (Cambridge: Massachusetts Institute of Technology, September 1978), to the classification scheme in OECD, "Energy Statistics: 1974/1976" (Paris, 1978).
[b]n.a. = not available.

Delivered Energy Prices: OECD

The retail prices for fuels in Canada, France, Italy, the Netherlands, Norway, United Kingdom, West Germany, and Japan were estimated from two sources. Prices for 1968 through 1974 were taken from the WOPD data base, adjusted from 1975 dollars per trillion calories to 1978 dollars per million Btus. The only other similarly comprehensive data base for prices is the OECD publication, "Energy Statistics: 1974/1976,"[34] which reports prices for 1968 through 1976. This latter source was used, with the ratio method and the 1974 data overlap, to update the WOPD data base to 1976.

The OECD publication uses a different set of accounting conventions to record their price data. For the purposes of the updating of the WOPD data base, we used the mapping summarized in Table 1-38.

The use of the ratio method, after adjusting for price inflation in each country, implies that the currency conversions embedded in the WOPD data base are also applicable to the prices reported here in 1978 dollars per million Btus. The conversion factors used by Pindyck were estimates of purchasing power parities, not the volatile currency exchange rates (see the User's Guide).

The prices for the United States and the eight related OECD countries are shown in Tables 1-39 through 1-47.

34. (Paris: OECD, 1978).

Table 1-39. Prices by Fuel and Sector, United States.

Year	Solid fuels	Oil	Gas	Electricity
Industry				
1968	0.399	0.619	0.478	4.840
1969	0.394	0.585	0.462	4.671
1970	0.423	0.644	0.464	4.623
1971	0.467	0.858	0.475	4.797
1972	0.481	0.920	0.490	4.911
1973	0.488	1.099	0.523	4.990
1974	0.705	2.351	0.677	6.015
1975	0.814	2.136	0.930	6.805
1976	0.795	2.025	1.199	6.954
1977	0.821	2.129	1.441	7.438
1978	0.881	1.945	1.489	7.541
Transportation				
1968	0.0	5.155	0.0	0.0
1969	0.0	5.087	0.0	0.0
1970	0.0	4.940	0.0	0.0
1971	0.0	4.825	0.0	0.0
1972	0.0	4.630	0.0	0.0
1973	0.0	4.709	0.0	0.0
1974	0.0	5.785	0.0	0.0
1975	0.0	5.714	0.0	0.0
1976	0.0	5.665	0.0	0.0
1977	0.0	5.744	0.0	0.0
1978	0.0	5.817	0.0	0.0
Residential/Commercial				
1968	3.302	2.284	1.528	11.312
1969	3.240	2.239	1.486	10.694
1970	3.079	2.206	1.480	10.208
1971	2.999	2.256	1.528	10.246
1972	2.967	2.541	1.572	10.413
1973	2.880	3.811	1.560	10.361
1974	3.276	3.723	1.633	11.018
1975	3.108	3.358	1.844	11.408
1976	3.096	3.389	2.097	11.586
1977	3.156	3.696	2.440	12.160
1978	3.216	3.686	2.572	12.263

Note: All prices are in $1978 per million Btus.

Table 1-40. Prices by Fuel and Sector, Canada.

Year	Solid fuels	Oil	Gas	Electricity
Industry				
1968	0.704	1.308	0.650	3.531
1969	0.706	1.254	0.640	3.433
1970	0.802	1.332	0.626	3.369
1971	0.905	1.269	0.637	3.398
1972	0.926	1.063	0.636	3.241
1973	0.977	1.272	0.613	3.066
1974	1.156	2.337	0.653	3.232
1975	1.156	2.121	0.795	3.232
1976	1.156	2.121	1.068	3.232
Transportation				
1968	0.0	5.304	0.0	0.0
1969	0.0	5.216	0.0	0.0
1970	0.0	5.088	0.0	0.0
1971	0.0	5.113	0.0	0.0
1972	0.0	4.915	0.0	0.0
1973	0.0	4.838	0.0	0.0
1974	0.0	4.958	0.0	0.0
1975	0.0	6.130	0.0	0.0
1976	0.0	7.096	0.0	0.0
Residential/Commercial				
1968	2.308	1.816	1.636	7.330
1969	2.354	1.814	1.588	7.150
1970	2.437	1.798	1.541	7.073
1971	2.673	1.905	1.520	7.047
1972	2.591	1.947	1.443	6.792
1973	2.433	2.094	1.383	6.626
1974	2.768	2.717	1.489	7.846
1975	3.261	3.161	1.567	7.697
1976	3.190	3.161	1.793	10.178

Note: All prices are in $1978 per million Btus.

Table 1-41. Prices by Fuel and Sector, France.

Year	Solid fuels	Oil	Gas	Electricity
Industry				
1968	1.428	0.916	1.774	8.899
1969	1.386	0.790	1.716	8.749
1970	1.653	0.767	1.665	8.452
1971	1.848	1.245	1.576	8.621
1972	1.782	1.275	1.855	8.543
1973	1.678	0.909	1.766	8.076
1974	1.770	1.193	1.755	8.210
1975	2.007	2.198	2.842	9.833
1976	1.979	1.838	2.577	9.001
Transportation				
1968	0.0	12.260	0.0	0.0
1969	0.0	12.370	0.0	0.0
1970	0.0	11.943	0.0	0.0
1971	0.0	11.464	0.0	0.0
1972	0.0	11.185	0.0	0.0
1973	0.0	10.458	0.0	0.0
1974	0.0	13.571	0.0	0.0
1975	0.0	12.597	0.0	0.0
1976	0.0	11.899	0.0	0.0
Residential/Commercial				
1968	5.171	1.982	10.839	26.325
1969	5.109	2.006	10.393	25.213
1970	5.060	1.921	9.364	24.890
1971	4.876	1.737	9.976	24.374
1972	4.921	2.532	10.610	23.268
1973	4.721	2.101	11.157	22.252
1974	4.109	2.648	11.045	21.000
1975	4.737	2.832	13.354	23.492
1976	5.123	2.706	12.140	21.336

Note: All prices are in $1978 per million Btus.

Table 1-42. Prices by Fuel and Sector, Italy.

Year	Solid fuels	Oil	Gas	Electricity
Industry				
1968	2.192	1.429	1.348	10.797
1969	2.103	1.236	1.293	10.359
1970	2.444	1.133	1.212	9.676
1971	3.122	1.335	1.130	9.146
1972	2.944	0.997	1.227	8.597
1973	2.789	1.139	1.190	8.007
1974	3.712	1.517	1.103	7.544
1975	3.266	2.628	2.452	10.521
1976	2.936	3.405	2.414	11.758
Transportation				
1968	0.0	14.200	0.0	0.0
1969	0.0	13.624	0.0	0.0
1970	0.0	13.787	0.0	0.0
1971	0.0	14.958	0.0	0.0
1972	0.0	14.103	0.0	0.0
1973	0.0	12.797	0.0	0.0
1974	0.0	13.633	0.0	0.0
1975	0.0	17.754	0.0	0.0
1976	0.0	20.061	0.0	0.0
Residential/Commercial				
1968	3.401	1.740	10.058	24.551
1969	3.306	1.661	9.778	22.450
1970	3.154	1.605	9.327	21.218
1971	3.922	1.676	8.816	21.136
1972	4.090	1.631	8.276	19.465
1973	4.081	2.092	7.414	18.395
1974	6.690	2.078	6.193	16.552
1975	8.814	4.465	5.264	24.579
1976	9.156	5.898	8.490	26.849

Note: All prices are in $1978 per million Btus.

Table 1-43.   Prices by Fuel and Sector, the Netherlands.

Year	Solid fuels	Oil	Gas	Electricity
Industry				
1968	1.241	1.042	1.134	18.558
1969	1.143	0.919	0.997	16.624
1970	1.415	0.917	1.076	15.758
1971	1.602	1.371	1.078	15.175
1972	1.411	0.834	0.934	13.643
1973	1.392	0.864	1.094	12.211
1974	1.473	1.018	1.023	13.017
1975	1.519	2.246	1.265	15.125
1976	1.465	1.954	1.386	15.916
Transportation				
1968	0.0	10.969	0.0	0.0
1969	0.0	11.251	0.0	0.0
1970	0.0	10.366	0.0	0.0
1971	0.0	10.872	0.0	0.0
1972	0.0	10.979	0.0	0.0
1973	0.0	9.773	0.0	0.0
1974	0.0	11.371	0.0	0.0
1975	0.0	14.255	0.0	0.0
1976	0.0	14.143	0.0	0.0
Residential/Commercial				
1968	4.521	2.033	6.242	18.240
1969	4.508	1.722	6.102	16.288
1970	4.601	1.862	5.890	15.703
1971	4.527	2.140	5.345	15.164
1972	4.527	2.140	5.345	13.713
1973	4.474	2.820	4.546	12.213
1974	4.147	4.138	4.204	12.919
1975	5.277	4.083	4.568	12.645
1976	4.838	4.736	4.468	14.961

Note: All prices are in $1978 per million Btus.

Table 1–44. Prices by Fuel and Sector, Norway.

Year	Solid fuels	Oil	Gas	Electricity
Industry				
1968	1.071	1.175	4.078	2.300
1969	1.145	1.134	5.026	2.363
1970	1.455	1.382	7.030	2.223
1971	1.534	1.558	6.576	2.209
1972	1.772	1.481	5.728	2.251
1973	1.658	1.487	4.785	2.070
1974	1.563	2.818	5.592	2.042
1975	1.818	1.932	5.592	2.524
1976	1.805	1.759	5.592	2.330
Transportation				
1968	0.0	11.258	0.0	0.0
1969	0.0	10.771	0.0	0.0
1970	0.0	10.269	0.0	0.0
1971	0.0	11.162	0.0	0.0
1972	0.0	10.686	0.0	0.0
1973	0.0	10.261	0.0	0.0
1974	0.0	12.312	0.0	0.0
1975	0.0	12.014	0.0	0.0
1976	0.0	11.455	0.0	0.0
Residential/Commercial				
1968	2.882	2.095	5.328	5.238
1969	3.099	2.025	6.549	5.319
1970	3.447	1.825	9.100	4.821
1971	3.568	2.288	8.537	5.541
1972	3.554	2.016	8.355	5.367
1973	3.351	2.265	8.068	5.196
1974	3.793	3.836	7.689	4.963
1975	3.793	3.616	7.689	5.461
1976	3.793	3.711	7.689	5.056

Note: All prices are in $1978 per million Btus.

Table 1–45. Prices by Fuel and Sector, United Kingdom.

Year	Solid fuels	Oil	Gas	Electricity
Industry				
1968	1.211	1.461	3.999	11.314
1969	1.106	1.385	3.323	10.719
1970	1.050	1.079	2.393	10.145
1971	1.152	1.567	1.588	10.261
1972	1.273	1.528	1.330	9.692
1973	1.268	1.313	1.652	9.049
1974	1.178	1.633	1.289	11.042
1975	1.846	4.053	1.368	12.353
1976	2.148	3.870	1.539	13.315
Transportation				
1968	0.0	10.837	0.0	0.0
1969	0.0	11.647	0.0	0.0
1970	0.0	11.193	0.0	0.0
1971	0.0	10.674	0.0	0.0
1972	0.0	10.027	0.0	0.0
1973	0.0	9.539	0.0	0.0
1974	0.0	10.178	0.0	0.0
1975	0.0	18.307	0.0	0.0
1976	0.0	16.068	0.0	0.0
Residential/Commercial				
1968	2.918	3.073	6.471	15.370
1969	2.778	2.866	5.992	14.080
1970	2.813	2.657	5.601	12.999
1971	2.944	2.949	4.927	12.891
1972	3.180	3.131	5.106	12.815
1973	3.193	3.624	5.458	11.947
1974	2.796	3.384	5.089	12.377
1975	2.706	5.424	4.596	12.536
1976	3.015	5.916	4.599	14.687

Note: All prices are in $1978 per million Btus.

Table 1-46. Prices by Fuel and Sector, West Germany.

Year	Solid fuels	Oil	Gas	Electricity
Industry				
1968	1.675	1.106	1.601	12.998
1969	1.633	1.028	1.445	11.861
1970	1.694	1.010	1.338	11.122
1971	1.759	1.333	1.260	10.607
1972	1.818	1.031	1.276	10.485
1973	1.791	0.986	1.226	10.083
1974	1.865	1.392	1.283	10.193
1975	2.292	1.916	1.283	10.193
1976	2.458	1.671	1.283	10.193
Transportation				
1968	0.0	10.458	0.0	0.0
1969	0.0	9.197	0.0	0.0
1970	0.0	8.854	0.0	0.0
1971	0.0	8.487	0.0	0.0
1972	0.0	8.152	0.0	0.0
1973	0.0	8.145	0.0	0.0
1974	0.0	9.334	0.0	0.0
1975	0.0	9.970	0.0	0.0
1976	0.0	9.842	0.0	0.0
Residential/Commercial				
1968	4.348	1.854	11.647	23.024
1969	4.207	1.504	11.284	21.906
1970	4.338	1.552	11.028	19.912
1971	4.594	1.759	12.105	18.822
1972	4.647	1.531	13.264	18.548
1973	4.961	2.657	14.353	17.916
1974	4.933	3.424	15.487	18.040
1975	6.168	2.906	17.220	18.040
1976	6.906	2.749	19.849	18.040

Note: All prices are in $1978 per million Btus.

Table 1-47.   Prices by Fuel and Sector, Japan.

Year	Solid fuels	Oil	Gas	Electricity
Industry				
1968	1.380	1.212	8.510	11.262
1969	1.330	1.161	8.031	11.004
1970	1.282	1.127	7.661	10.300
1971	1.227	1.273	7.338	9.986
1972	1.222	1.327	7.003	9.759
1973	1.122	1.817	6.495	9.207
1974	1.122	2.411	6.495	9.207
1975	1.426	2.389	6.495	14.460
1976	1.762	2.604	6.495	13.652
Transportation				
1968	0.0	13.021	0.0	0.0
1969	0.0	12.177	0.0	0.0
1970	0.0	11.594	0.0	0.0
1971	0.0	11.714	0.0	0.0
1972	0.0	11.317	0.0	0.0
1973	0.0	10.523	0.0	0.0
1974	0.0	14.640	0.0	0.0
1975	0.0	13.623	0.0	0.0
1976	0.0	13.281	0.0	0.0
Residential/Commercial				
1968	8.510	2.728	9.491	28.248
1969	8.031	2.525	8.971	26.638
1970	7.661	2.345	8.307	24.808
1971	7.338	2.399	7.957	23.662
1972	7.003	2.207	7.593	22.504
1973	6.495	2.309	7.582	20.266
1974	10.109	3.824	6.248	21.162
1975	10.109	3.753	6.248	23.319
1976	10.109	4.045	6.248	22.013

Note: All prices are in $1978 per million Btus.

U.S. Primary Fuel Prices; GDP Statistics

The price of primary fuels is defined here as the cost of extraction from the ground of each fuel (solid fuel, oil, natural gas) plus the cost of transportation from the mine or wellhead to the fuel's user. Thus, the primary fuel price is the price that the oil refiner must pay for oil or the price that the utility must pay for solid fuel.

All the yearly primary prices were obtained in current dollars per a nonuniform unit—per ton for coal, per barrel for oil, and per million cubic feet for gas. The prices were put into constant 1978 dollars through the use of the GNP deflators given in the *Economic Report of the President*, 1979. The conversion to million Btus from ton, barrel, or million cubic feet was according to the conversion Table 8.2 in the User's Guide.

The prices for solid fuels were obtained from *Coal Data: 1975*, for 1968 through 1974, as the average f.o.b. price plus the average railroad freight cost. For 1975 through 1978, price figures were obtained from the *Monthly Energy Review*, as the average price for coal delivered to utilities.

For oil, price data for 1968 through 1973 were taken from the *Basic Petroleum Data Book*, published by the American Petroleum Institute. The price for each year was arrived at by taking the domestic wellhead price and adding $0.30 per barrel to cover shipment to the refineries. For 1974 through 1978, the "Refineries Acquisition Cost" table from the *Monthly Energy Review* was used. The average price for each year was taken, and since the price included shipment to the refineries, no additional charge was added (for 1978, the price for the month of June was used, instead of a six-month average). It was assumed that the average domestic wellhead price for 1968 through 1973 was representative of all oil prices in those years, because it was not until 1974 that the large price differential between domestic and imported oil, plus taxes and tariffs, occurred.

Natural gas prices for 1968 through 1973 were obtained from the *Basic Petroleum Data Book*. No additional charges were added on to the price as given. To update the prices through 1978, the table of "Total Purchases of Interstate Pipeline Companies" in the *Monthly Energy Review* was used, again taking the average price for the year (the month of May only was used for 1978).

There is a simple, one-to-one link between the primary fuel costs and the delivered products, except for electricity. Since the forecast assumptions about primary fuel costs are used to estimate the delivered energy price, using a constant real markup over primary energy costs, the fuel cost for electricity must be estimated to accommodate for fuel substitution as prices change in the future. The approach adopted here was to assume: (1) a Cobb–Douglas cost function for primary fuel use in electric power generation; and (2) a 33.3 percent energy efficiency in the generation of electricity.

Using the consumption figures from EIA's *Annual Report to Congress*, 1977,[35] and the estimates of primary cost for the individual fuels, we derived the following formula for the primary energy cost in electric power generation:

$$\overline{P}_4 = \frac{3}{2.95} \left(\frac{\overline{P}_1}{0.49} \right)^{0.49} \left(\frac{\overline{P}_2}{0.34} \right)^{0.34} \left(\frac{\overline{P}_3}{0.18} \right)^{0.18},$$

35. EIA, *Annual Report to Congress* (Washington, D.C.: Department of Energy, 1978), Table 5.29.

Table 1-48. Estimated Primary Energy Costs, United States (1978 dollars per million Btus).

Year	Solid Fuels	Oil	Gas	Electric-Power Generation
1968	0.503	1.02	0.30	1.67
1969	0.515	1.02	0.29	1.68
1970	0.586	1.00	0.29	1.77
1971	0.610	1.00	0.29	1.81
1972	0.622	0.97	0.29	1.80
1973	0.634	1.03	0.31	1.88
1974	0.969	2.05	0.39	3.05
1975	0.802	2.14	0.49	2.95
1976	0.790	2.13	0.67	3.09
1977	0.850	2.21	1.87	3.41
1978	0.910	2.14	0.92	3.51

where $\overline{P}_i$ is the primary energy cost for $i = 1$ (solid fuel), 2 (oil), 3 (natural gas), 4 (electricity). The resulting primary energy cost estimates for the United States are summarized in Table 1-48.

The constant dollar GNP figures for the United States were taken from the *Economic Report of the President*, 1979. The constant dollar GDP figures for the eight selected OECD countries were taken from the International Monetary Fund publication, *International Financial Statistics*, May 1978.

Energy Policies and Automobile Use of Gasoline

James L. Sweeney

The OPEC oil price increase and embargo of 1973 fueled a desire to curb reliance on foreign petroleum and to reduce domestic consumption. One result was a significant increase in policy attention given to automotive use of gasoline. The annual growth of gasoline consumption now is below the preembargo rate,[1] although the actual use of gasoline continues to rise. In 1978 Americans consumed 7.4 million barrels of gasoline daily, 39 percent of the country's total petroleum use. Passenger cars accounted for 74 percent of gasoline consumed, nearly 30 percent of the entire petroleum consumption. Continued concern over gasoline use has led to proposals for new federal programs to reduce consumption.

This paper offers several approaches toward examining the influence of federal programs on automotive gasoline consumption and uses these methods to estimate the impacts of past, present, and proposed future federal policies. No estimations are provided for other than automobile uses of gasoline. The analysis strongly suggests that under current law, sufficient incentives will exist to motivate auto-

The author would like to thank, without implicating, John Weyant and Zakia Rahman for computer assistance, Emmett Eggleston for editorial assistance, and Hans H. Landsberg for suggestions on content and style.

1. According to Federal Highway Administration data, until the embargo, gasoline consumption for passenger cars increased 5.2 percent a year for more than two decades, while the total consumption of gasoline for all uses increased at 4.4 percent per year (3.6 percent yearly, according to the Bureau of Mines). Between 1973 and 1978, however, total consumption of gasoline has increased only 11 percent, an average increase of 2.1 percent a year. From 1977 to 1978, the increase was 3.3 percent.

93

mobile manufacturers to meet the average efficiency standards mandated through the year 1985. And it will be argued that in the presence of the efficiency standards, only programs that work by changing driving patterns—such as the now discarded gasoline standby tax—will significantly influence gasoline consumption by automobiles. Moderate programs that are intended to work through increasing new car efficiency will have no effect.

PERSPECTIVE: POLICIES AND PROGRAMS

Prior to the 1973 oil embargo, four federal policies or programs probably affected gasoline consumption: the federal gasoline tax, the oil import quota, the construction of the interstate highway system, and the imposition of noxious emissions standards on new cars. Gasoline is taxed by both the states and the federal government, with the largest tax imposed by states. State taxes vary from a minimum of 5 cents per gallon in Texas, to a maximum of 11 cents per gallon in Connecticut. The federal gasoline tax has remained at 4 cents per gallon since 1959.

The second preembargo program that tended to increase the price of gasoline was the Mandatory Oil Import Program, established in 1959. By restricting oil imports, this program increased domestic crude oil prices and increased the consumer price of refined petroleum products. It is estimated that until quotas were abandoned in 1973, this program added about three-quarters of a cent per gallon to the price of gasoline.

In 1956, the revenues from the federal gasoline tax were earmarked for the Federal Highway Trust Fund. The fund's primary activity has been to develop an interstate highway system, which has reduced the time cost of driving by increasing the average speeds for long trips. By decreasing travel time, the program probably has increased miles traveled and therefore increased gasoline consumption.

The final preembargo policy, the noxious emissions standards for new cars, was implemented by the Environmental Protection Agency in 1968, and the standards have subsequently become tighter. These standards, which specify maximum quantities of noxious emissions per mile for new cars, led manufacturers to modify engines and carburation. The result has been less engine efficiency and increased gasoline consumption, but the magnitude of the impact has been smaller than commonly believed.

The period since the 1973 oil embargo has been marked by the abandonment of import quotas, adoption of a petroleum price control system, and implementation of a national speed limit and new car efficiency standards. The federal gasoline tax has remained unchanged. However, other federal programs now decrease the price of crude oil below the world level, rather than increase it above the world level.

Price controls on domestically produced oil, coupled with the entitlements program, have decreased the average price of oil relative to the imported price by about $2 per barrel,[2] which in turn may reduce gasoline price by 4.8 cents per gallon.[3] Thus, the net effect of the federal gasoline tax and the crude oil price controls has been to reduce the price of gasoline by about 0.8 cents per gallon below what it would have been in the absence of these programs. The 55 miles per hour national speed limit was adopted in order to reduce the consumption of gasoline per mile driven. The noxious emissions standards remained.

Because future congressional action is uncertain, and for analytical purposes, it will be assumed that these programs and policies continue throughout the period of analysis.

The Energy Policy and Conservation Act (EPCA), passed into law in 1975, marked a major change for gasoline consumption trends. The Act includes mandatory efficiency standards for newly purchased cars, with the standards first becoming effective in the 1978 model year. The standards mandate a mean efficiency[4] for all cars sold by each manufacturer. Large civil penalties are imposed for noncompliance.

In the National Energy Plan (NEP) several policies were proposed. The first, aimed at new cars, combined a "gas guzzler" tax on new automobiles that fail to meet federal mileage standards with a rebate on new autos that exceed the standards. The second was a standby tax on gasoline. The gasoline tax has been quickly disapproved by Congress, while the "gas guzzler" tax, in a weakened form, was ultimately signed into law.

President Carter announced that he would issue an executive order requiring that the federal fleet of new cars meet an average mileage standard that is 2 miles per gallon higher than the EPCA average fuel

2. James L. Sweeny, "Energy Regulation—Solution or Problem" in *Options for U.S. Energy Policy* (San Francisco: Institute for Contemporary Studies, 1977).

3. This paper implicitly rejects the Phelps–Smith argument that petroleum product prices are set on world markets and that therefore domestic controls do not influence product prices; see Charles E. Phelps and Rodney T. Smith, "Petroleum Regulation: the False Dilemma of Decontrol," Report R-1951-RC (Santa Monica: The Rand Corporation, 1977).

4. More precisely, a minimum harmonic mean of miles per gallon is mandated. This is equivalent to a maximum arithmetic mean of gallons per mile for new cars.

Table 2-1.   Estimated Impacts of Federal Policies on Passenger Car Gasoline Consumption.

Federal Policies and Programs	Components of Consumption		Equilibrium[b] Vehicle Miles (percent)	Long-run[c] Equilibrium Gasoline Consumption (percent)
	New Car Efficiency (percent)	Operating[a] Efficiency		
Preembargo Conditions				
Gasoline tax	+9.3	+	-0.8	-9.2
Oil import quota	+1.7	+	-0.2	-1.9
Highway construction			+	+
Emissions standards	-2.2		-0.5	+1.7
Postembargo Conditions				
Before efficiency standard				
Gasoline tax	+4.3	+	-0.4	-4.5
Crude oil price controls	-4.7	-	+0.4	+5.3
55 mph limit		+	-	-
Emissions standards	-2.2		-0.5	+1.7
After efficiency standards[d]				
Efficiency standard	+46[e]		+8.8[f]	-25[g]
Gasoline tax		+	-1.3	-1.3
Crude oil price controls[h]		-	+1.5	+1.5
55 mph limit		+	-	-
Emissions standards				0
Federal purchases				0
Proposed policies[i]				
NEP gas guzzler tax[j]				0
NEP gasoline tax[k]		+	-6.8	-6.8
Minimum efficiency standard[l]				0

Notes:

[a]Changes in operating efficiency due to maintenance, speeds driven, and so forth for new car efficiency held constant.

[b]Vehicle miles driven by automobiles in long-run equilibrium after fleet of autos fully adjusts. The effect before full adjustment of the fleet will be greater.

[c]Measured after fleet of autos fully adjusts. The effects over a few years, before fleet fully adjusts, will be significantly smaller. The column excludes the effects on operating efficiency, effects which I believe to be relatively small. Estimates of long-run equilibrium gasoline consumption have been derived using equation (2.1), with the percentage change of miles per gallon equal to the percentage change of miles per gallon for new cars.

[d]All impacts of policies assume the efficiency standard to be fixed and other programs to be added or deleted.

[e]These are based on 1985 estimates. For 1980 and 1990 the figures would be +8 percent and +46 percent, respectively, for new car efficiency, assuming a 27.5 mpg standard in 1990.

[f]The 1980, 1985, and 1990 changes would be +0.4, +3.9, and +6.9, respectively, based upon the model in James L. Sweeney, "The Demand for Gasoline: A Vintage Capital Model," in *Select Papers from Workshops on World Energy Supply and Demand* (Paris: International Energy Agency, 1978).

[g]The actual 1980, 1985, and 1990 changes would be -1.3, -12, and -20 percent, respectively, based upon the model in James L. Sweeney, "The Demand for

Table 2-1. continued

Gasoline: A Vintage Capital Model," in *Select Papers from Workshops on World Energy Supply and Demand* (Paris: International Energy Agency, 1978).

[h] Assumes the controls continue to decrease domestic price by about $2 per barrel and that this reduces gasoline price by about 4.8 cents per gallon.

[i] Effects in addition to existing programs, including the efficiency standards.

[j] For 1980, 1985, and 1990, new car efficiency increases would be +8.5, 0, and 0 percent respectively; vehicle miles would increase by 0.6, 0.4, and 0 percent; gasoline consumption would change by -2.2, -1.3, and -0.7 percent, all based upon the model in James L. Sweeney, "The Demand for Gasoline: A Vintage Capital Model," in *Select Papers from Workshops on World Energy Supply and Demand* (Paris: International Energy Agency, 1978).

[k] 1985 estimates. The tax would have begun at 5 cents per gallon in 1979 and would increase by 5 cents per year to a maximum of 50 cents per gallon.

[l] This would impose a minimum 18 mpg standard on all cars.

economy standard in 1978 and 4 miles per gallon higher in 1980 and afterward. However, to the author's knowledge, this order has never been issued.

There have been a number of proposals, notably from the U.S. Senate, to impose minimum efficiency standards on each automobile sold, as opposed to the mean efficiency of all cars built by a manufacturer. And, finally, there are several proposals to help fund the development of alternative technologies to increase the efficiency of new cars.

Estimated Impacts: A Preview

The theory and the econometric relationships described at a later point in this chapter will be used to develop rough quantitative estimates of the impacts of federal policies on gasoline consumption by automobiles. Table 2-1 provides a summary of these results. It is based on evaluations of federal influences on automotive gasoline use in three specific areas—new car efficiency, operating efficiency, and vehicle miles traveled. These components ultimately dictate gasoline consumption.

The first column lists the various federal policies and programs whose effects are estimated. Columns 2 through 4 provide an analysis of the impacts on gasoline consumption of the various policies and programs, listing percentage changes in the relevant variables. Blanks appear whenever the program is judged to have no impact on a particular variable. Column 2 estimates the percentage changes in new car efficiency associated with the various policies. Column 3 indicates the directions of operating efficiency changes, changes in the fuel efficiency of a given auto as a result of driving habits, maintenance patterns, and so on. No quantitative estimates are provided.

Column 4 estimates the percentage impacts on long-run equilibrium vehicle miles, i.e., impact on vehicle miles after the fleet of automobiles fully adjusts to any change in new car efficiency. This column includes the direct effect on vehicle miles associated with each program and the indirect effect through changes in the fleet efficiency.

The last column provides summary estimates of the long-run impacts of the various policies on gasoline consumption. The numbers in this column represent the percentage changes in gasoline consumption (from the base case) caused by the specific policies or programs. This column includes the effects of policies on new car fuel efficiency and on fleetwide vehicle miles, but excludes the impacts of the policies on operating efficiency.

For example, the effects of the efficiency standard are estimated in Table 2-1. This standard will reduce long-run gasoline consumption by 25 percent from what it would be otherwise. New car efficiency will be increased by 46 percent, while vehicle miles will increase by 8.8 percent. Operating efficiency will be unchanged. The net effect will be a consumption reduction of 25 percent. Discussion of the estimated impacts of federal policies on gasoline consumption by automobiles appears in the last section of this chapter.

DETERMINING GASOLINE USE BY AUTOMOBILES

Gasoline consumption by automobiles depends critically upon three factors: (1) the technical characteristics of the fleet of automobiles, (2) the manner in which autos are maintained and driven, (3) and the number of vehicle miles obtained by the fleet. The first two factors combine to determine the mean fuel efficiency of the fleet at any time. This will be measured by $\overline{mpgF}$, the fleetwide mean miles driven per gallon of gasoline consumed. The last factor, the utilization of the fleet, is represented by VM, the total vehicle miles obtained by the fleet.

Vehicle miles and mean fuel efficiency combine very simply to determine gasoline consumption by autos (GAS):

$$GAS = VM/\overline{mpgF}. \qquad (2.1)$$

This tautology is useful because it allows an analysis of gasoline consumption whenever one can evaluate policy impacts on vehicle miles and mean fuel efficiency. The remainder of this section describes the determinants of VM and $\overline{mpgF}$, including the influence of gasoline price and the feedback effects between the two variables.

Vehicle Miles

Fleet vehicle miles are determined primarily by human mobility decisions—how far away to live from work; how far to drive on a vacation; what mode of transport to use for vacation, commuting, business, or social trips; how frequently to make such trips; whether to carpool or otherwise modify load factors. These decisions are quite complex and difficult to model explicitly, since they are determined primarily by behavioral rather than technological relations.

While a comprehensive analysis of the determinants of vehicle miles is generally not possible, both economic theory and econometric testing provide some results. Perhaps the two most important driving forces behind vehicle miles are population and income. As population increases, vehicle miles tend to increase proportionately. And as income increases, so do vehicle miles. People tend to engage in more activities requiring mobility (e.g., vacation trips) as their incomes go up. And higher incomes imply a higher valuation of time and hence a decreased willingness to sacrifice time to reduce travel costs. Finally, as incomes increase, the number of cars per family increases, thereby increasing total vehicle miles while reducing vehicle miles per car. The empirical literature suggests a near unity (per capita) income elasticity of vehicle miles. However, as incomes continue to increase, this may show some significant saturation effects. The elasticity of vehicle miles with respect to population is also about unity.

In general, decisions determining vehicle miles can also be expected to depend upon time cost and fuel cost of travel, with increasing cost reducing vehicle miles. However, the elasticities seem to be quite small. An elasticity of vehicle miles with respect to gasoline price of between -0.1 and -0.25 is consistent with the available empirical evidence. No reliable elasticities of vehicle miles with respect to time cost are available.

Fuel cost per mile of driving depends not only upon gasoline price but also the efficiency of the fleet of autos. In particular, fuel cost per mile is simply the ratio of gasoline price to the average efficiency of the fleet of automobiles. Thus policies that increase fleet efficiency reduce fuel cost per mile and lead to increases in vehicle miles. The elasticity of vehicle miles with respect to fleet efficiency is equal to the negative of the elasticity of vehicle miles with respect to gasoline price. Therefore a 10 percent increase in fleet efficiency would tend to increase vehicle miles between 1 and 2.5 percent, using the elasticity estimates of the preceding paragraph. This feedback effect from mean efficiency to vehicle miles offsets 10 to 25 percent of the consumption reduction obtained as the efficiency of the fleet increases.

New Car Efficiency

All cars, both old and new, have relatively fixed characteristics determining gasoline use. Although patterns of operation and maintenance play a part, the mean fuel efficiency of autos from a given model year, or vintage, depends principally on two factors—the miles per gallon obtained by the specific models and the market shares captured by each model. Average fuel efficiency of a given vintage will increase as a result of either an increase in the fuel efficiency of each car or a shift in market shares from less efficient to more efficient automobiles. This is illustrated in Figure 2-1.

The graph on the bottom left of Figure 2-1 shows two distributions of market shares by weight of automobiles. The first distribution (MSW_A) has a greater proportion of low weight cars than does the second distribution (MSW_B). The graph on the upper left-hand side shows the relationship between weight of an automobile and the miles per gallon obtained by that auto, for two different measures of technical efficiency. This expresses the empirically observed relationship that the miles per gallon obtained by an individual automobile are roughly inversely proportional to its weight for any given model year. The constant of proportionality is a measure of technical efficiency and will be denoted by EFF.[5] In the graph, the first level of technical efficiency (EFF_1) is lower than the second (EFF_2): for a given automobile weight, the miles per gallon obtained under the second are higher than under the first level of technical efficiency. The graph on the upper right-hand side shows three alternative distributions of market shares by miles per gallon. Distribution MSM_{A1} will have the lowest mean miles per gallon for the vintage, while MSM_{A2} will have the greatest fuel efficiency for the vintage.

Figure 2-1 illustrates that a given technical efficiency and a given distribution of market share by weight translates into a given distribution of market share by miles per gallon and, hence, a given mean fuel efficiency of the vintage. Note that a shift in the distribution of market share by weight toward heavier cars results in a lower mean fuel efficiency of the new cars. Similarly, an increase in the technical efficiency, ceteris paribus, will increase the mean miles per gallon of all automobiles sold.

The two factors—the market share distribution by weight and the technical efficiencies—are not independent. An increase in technical

---

5. More precisely, EFF will be a normalized constant of proportionality.

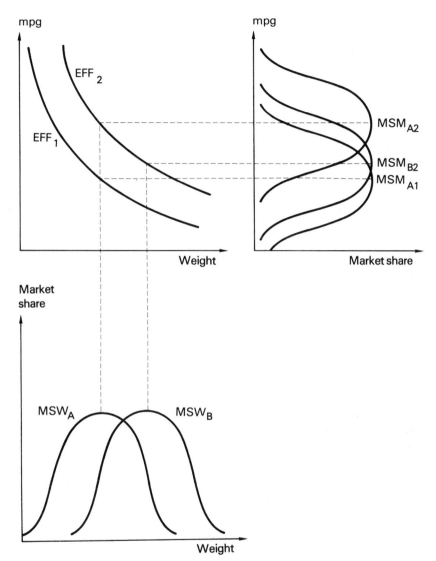

Figure 2-1. Technical Efficiency, Market Shares by Weight, and Market Shares by Miles per Gallon.

efficiency, say from EFF_1 to EFF_2, will shift the weight distribution of automobiles toward heavier cars, since an increase in technical efficiency reduces the relative cost of driving large cars and leads consumers to purchase heavier cars than they would otherwise. Thus, an increase in efficiency may cause the weight distribution to change from MSW_A to MSW_B, with a net effect of changing the miles per gallon market distribution from MSM_{A1} to MSM_{B2}. This shift in market shares may offset a significant component of the apparent increase in technical efficiency.

The induced shift in market shares occurs because individuals purchasing new cars consider capital costs and projected operating costs (as well as other characteristics) of the available array of automobiles. Assuming that the consumer uses current gasoline prices as a forecast of future prices, the estimated operating cost and hence the market share of each model will depend upon the ratio of gasoline price to miles per gallon of that model. A simultaneous doubling of gasoline price and of fuel efficiency for each car will leave all operating costs, and therefore all market shares, unchanged. But since the efficiency of each car sold would double in this case, the mean fuel efficiency would also double.

In general, if there are proportional shifts in the fuel efficiencies of the various models, represented by a shift in EFF, then the mean efficiency of newly purchased cars ($\overline{mpg}$) can be expressed as follows:

$$\overline{mpg} = EFF \cdot f(P_{gas}/EFF), \tag{2.2}$$

where $f(\cdot)$ is some increasing function of the ratio P_{gas}/EFF and where P_{gas} is the real gasoline price. This is demonstrated in the mathematical appendix.

Equation (2.2) shows a striking relationship between the elasticity of mean miles per gallon with respect to EFF and the elasticity of mean miles per gallon with respect to gasoline price:

$$\eta_{EFF} + \eta_{P_{gas}} = 1, \tag{2.3}$$

where
$$\eta_{EFF} = \frac{\partial \ell\eta \ (\overline{mpg})}{\partial \ell\eta(EFF)} \text{ and}$$

$$\eta_{P_{gas}} = \frac{\partial \ell\eta \ (\overline{mpg})}{\partial \ell\eta \ (P_{gas})}$$

are the two elasticities of $\overline{mpg}$.

Equation (2.3) implies that the larger the elasticity of mean miles per gallon with respect to gasoline price, the lower will be the elasticity with respect to technical efficiency. Note that if an increase in technical efficiency did *not* induce a shift in market shares toward larger cars, the elasticity of average miles per gallon with respect to technical efficiency would equal unity. For example, if the empirically estimated elasticity of $\overline{mpg}$ with respect to gasoline price were 0.7, then the elasticity with respect to technical efficiency would be only 0.3. The induced shift in market shares would offset 70 percent of the gain in mean efficiency resulting from a technological change which increased EFF.

The theory discussed above has been tested econometrically and shown to explain the historically observed pattern of mean efficiencies. Some empirically estimated equations developed by the author are presented in this chapter's appendix. This empirical research supports an elasticity of $\overline{mpg}$ with respect to a gasoline price of about 0.7 and an elasticity of $\overline{mpg}$ with respect to a technical efficiency of 0.3.

The elasticity of $\overline{mpg}$ with respect to price of 0.7 is not accepted by all researchers. Models based upon explicit estimation of the market shares captured by various size classes tend to provide lower elasticities. The DOE/JFA model, developed by Difiglio and Kulash[6] (three size classes), has an implicit elasticity of less than 0.07; the WEFA model, developed by Schink and Loxley[7] (five size classes), has an implicit elasticity of less than 0.05; the C-R-S model, developed by Cato, Rodekohr, and Sweeney[8] (three size classes), has an implicit elasticity of 0.3. Sweeney[9] compares the four models, but the sources of the differences are not fully understood. One speculation, however, is that the market shares approach rules out, by assumption, intraclass shifts in automobile purchases motivated by price changes. This omission tends to bias downward elasticities derived from models that estimate market shares of a limited number of size classes and assumes that consumers do not shift choices within a size class.

A number of federal policies described earlier also can be expected to influence mean efficiency of newly purchased cars in the absence

6. Carmen Difiglio and Damian Kulash, "Methodology and Analysis of Ways of Increasing the Effectiveness of the Use of Fuel Energy Resources: Increasing Automobile Fuel Economy via Government Policy," presented to the U.S.–USSR Joint Energy Commission: Information and Forecasting, October 1977.

7. George R. Schink and Colin J. Loxley, "An Analysis of the Automobile Market: Modeling the Long-Run Determinants of the Demand for Automobiles," (Philadelphia, Pa: Wharton EFA, Inc., 1977).

8. Derriel Cato, Mark Rodekohr, and James L. Sweeney, "The Capital Stock Adjustment Process and the Demand for Gasoline: A Market-Share Approach," in *Econometric Dimensions of Energy Demand and Supply*, A. Bradley Askin and John Kraft, eds. (Lexington, Mass: D. C. Heath, 1976).

9. James L. Sweeney, "Structural/Econometric Modeling of Gasoline Consumption," in *Proceedings: Second Lawrence Symposium on Systems and Decision Sciences* (North Hollywood: Western Periodicals, 1978).

of an efficiency standard. The gasoline tax, the oil import quota, and the crude oil price controls all have an effect on the price of gasoline and thus can be expected to influence the efficiency of new cars, as indicated by equation (2.2). The noxious emissions standards decrease technical efficiency and therefore induce a shift toward smaller cars. The effect of these standards on mean efficiency of new cars will be less than proportional to the changes in technical efficiency of the various models.

Another factor influencing the market shares is the array of new car prices. Increases in the prices of large cars relative to those of small cars will induce shifts in market shares toward smaller cars and will increase the mean efficiency of cars purchased. The gas guzzler tax and the average efficiency standard could be expected to increase the efficiency of new cars through changing the prices of new cars of different efficiencies. This effect will be discussed further in a subsequent section.

New Car Efficiency Under the EPCA Efficiency Standards. New car minimum mean efficiency standards were mandated as part of the Energy Policy and Conservation Act (EPCA) of 1975. Under the provisions of the EPCA, each manufacturer must meet or surpass the new car standard of 20 miles per gallon[10] in 1980 and 27.5 miles per gallon in 1985. EPCA also specified a non–tax deductible civil penalty to be imposed upon each manufacturer failing to meet the minimum standards. For such manufacturers, the penalty per automobile increases linearly with the difference between the mandated standard and the mean efficiency obtained. For manufacturers above the standard, no tax is levied.

This standard is applied not to individual automobiles, but rather to the mean of all automobiles sold by the manufacturer. Thus, the manufacturer can sell cars less efficient than the standard, avoiding all penalties if enough cars more efficient than the standard are also sold.

The fine under the EPCA is described by:

$$F = \begin{array}{l} t(mst - \overline{mpg})N, \text{ for } mst \geqslant \overline{mpg} \\ 0 \qquad\qquad , \text{ for } mst \leqslant \overline{mpg} \end{array} \tag{2.4}$$

where F is the equivalent before tax penalty cost of the fine, mst is the standard, N is the number of cars sold, and t is the penalty rate.

10. As measured by EPA. The procedures used significantly overstate on the road performance.

Under the EPCA, *mst* equals 20 mpg in 1980 and 27.5 in 1985; *t* equals $100/mpg-car, under the assumption of a 50 percent marginal corporate tax rate.

In the presence of the EPCA standard, there is a strong incentive to meet the mandated mean efficiency but no incentive to exceed the standard. The incentive stems primarily from the financial penalty but may also be strengthened by the fear of adverse publicity should the standard not be met. This section ignores the adverse publicity incentive and focuses entirely upon the financial incentives.

Figure 2-2 presents the major conclusion based upon analysis of the financial incentives embedded in the EPCA. Without the standard, the mean fuel efficiency of newly purchased cars ($\overline{mpg}$) would be an increasing function of gasoline price. In the presence of the EPCA standard, the mean fuel efficiency of new cars will not be smoothly

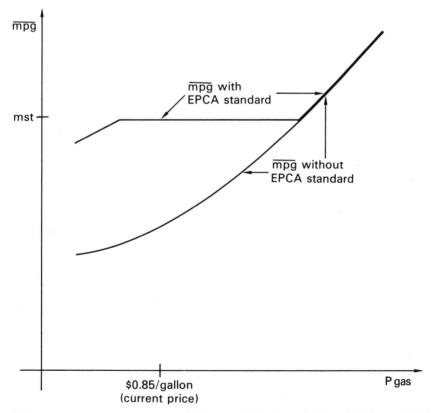

Figure 2-2. Mean Efficiency in 1985, with EPCA Standards and Without EPCA Standards.

increasing. Rather, there will be a broad range of gasoline prices, including the current price and extending to at least twice the current price, over which the average efficiency will just equal the standard. For even higher gasoline prices, the new car mean fuel efficiency will not be influenced by the existence of the standards.

If a much smaller elasticity of $\overline{mpg}$ with respect to gasoline price were chosen, then Figure 2-2 would remain qualitatively the same. However, the flat region of the curve ($\overline{mpg}$ with EPCA standard) would begin above the current price.

A similar diagram having the same form could be drawn for other policy instruments. For example, under current gasoline prices, the imposition of a gas guzzler tax would leave fuel efficiency precisely at the standard unless that tax were large enough to cause the standards to be surpassed. In such a case the existence of the standard would be irrelevant in determining mean efficiency. Similarly, changes in fuel efficiency standards for government vehicles would lead to movements along a flat region in which mean fuel efficiency remains at the standard. Decreases in fuel efficiency of privately purchased cars would just balance increases in fuel efficiency of governmental automobiles.

In the broad intermediate range, changes in gasoline price, or moderate changes in most other policy instruments, will have no effect on new car mean fuel efficiency. Automobile manufacturers will simply change pricing and marketing strategies to compensate for any policy shift so as to continue to just meet the standards. While such moderate policy changes can be expected to alter the relative prices of new cars of different fuel efficiencies, they will be totally ineffective in modifying new car mean efficiencies.

The remainder of this subsection, except for the last three paragraphs, presents an analysis supporting the conclusions presented above and can be skipped with no loss of continuity. A more mathematical treatment appears in another work by this author.[11]

For a firm faced with the efficiency standard, two types of economically motivated response may occur. The first may be an improvement in the efficiency of automobiles with given characteristics (an increase in EFF). The manufacturer would adopt those technology changes that would pay for themselves by reducing penalty costs. The second response would involve the pricing of automobiles. Increasing the price of low mpg cars and/or decreasing the

11. James L. Sweeney, "U.S. Gasoline Demand: An Economic Analysis of the EPCA New Car Efficiency Standard," in *Advances in the Economics of Energy and Resources*, vol. 1. *The Structure of Energy Markets*, Robert Pindyck, ed. (Greenwich, Conn: JAI Press, 1979).

price of high mpg cars would shift consumers toward more efficient autos, reducing the penalty. Thus the rational manufacturer is induced to account for penalty costs in setting pricing and marketing strategies.

The manufacturer's decisions on which technologies to adopt and on what prices to charge depend critically upon the magnitudes of the financial incentives incorporated in the penalty structure. These incentives will be examined more carefully.

The EPCA penalty structure imposes a set of marginal penalty costs for selling one more car of a given fuel efficiency. The marginal penalty costs can be calculated explicitly using equation (2.4). The calculation is presented in the mathematical appendix. These marginal penalty costs are plotted as a function of the manufacturer's mean efficiency in Figure 2–3 for two auto models, one more fuel-efficient than the standard and one less fuel-efficient. These marginal costs are highly nonlinear functions of mean efficiency of autos sold by the manufacturers. Most important, however, for mean efficiency below the standard, the marginal penalties are generally nonzero, while for mean efficiency equal to the standard, the marginal penalty costs are reduced discontinuously to zero. For $\overline{mpg}$ above the standard, the marginal penalty costs remain at zero.

Table 2–2 presents the marginal penalty costs in 1980 and 1985

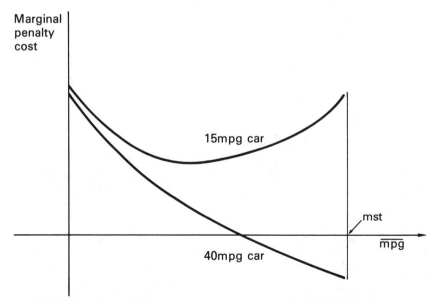

Figure 2-3. Marginal Penalty Costs Under EPCA for Two Automobiles.

Table 2-2. Manufacturer Pricing Response to Current Legislation and NEP Proposed Gas-Guzzler Tax

New Car mpg	Current Law: Manufacturer Incremental Costs		NEP Proposed Taxes	
	1980	*1985*	*1980*	*1985*
5	$6,000	$12,375	$666	$2,488
10	2,000	4,183	666	2,488
15	667	2,292	333	1,603
20	0	1,030	0	733
25	-400	275	-199	219
30	-667	-229	-333	-121
35	-857	-598	-428	-362
40	-1,000	-859	-473	-493

for selling one more car of various fuel efficiencies (mpg) for fuel efficiencies ranging from five to forty. These are applicable for a manufacturer just failing to meet the standard. For example, if the manufacturer sold one additional car with a mpg rating of 15, its pretax equivalent penalty would increase by $667 for 1980 sales and by $2,292 for 1985 sales. Selling one more car with a mpg rating of 40 would reduce the penalty by $1,000 in 1980.

For comparison, the NEP–proposed "gas guzzler" tax and subsidy is also presented in Table 2-2. The incentives existing in the current law are larger than those that were proposed in the NEP to assure compliance with the standards!

How do the EPCA marginal penalty costs modify profit-maximizing decisions of manufacturers? The rational manufacturer will treat these penalty costs in the same manner as any new marginal costs.[12] However, the discontinuity of the penalty cost at the standard must be explicitly recognized.

The simplest situation occurs in an industry that is competitive. In this case the equilibrium price charged by a manufacturer will equal his marginal cost of selling an additional car, including the marginal penalty cost.[13] Technologies would be adopted if their adop-

---

12. When these subsidies and penalties are passed through to the consumer, the net amount collected will precisely equal the total penalty cost. That is, the marginal penalty cost for a given model type multiplied by the number of sales of that model, summed over all models, will equal the fine given in equation (2.4) This follows mathematically from the linear homogeneity of the fine as a function of auto sales.

13. This marginal cost is not dependent upon the number of cars the manufacturer sells. This result follows because the penalty cost is a linear homogeneous function of the number of sales.

tion would reduce the penalty cost by more than the cost of the technology.

If the standard is not met, the marginal penalty cost increases the price of cars with low fuel efficiency and may either increase or decrease the price of cars that are highly fuel-efficient. If the standard is surpassed, this marginal penalty cost, equaling zero, does not influence prices.

If the equilibrium mean efficiency equals the standard, then the profit-maximizing strategy would be to impose a fraction of each (positive or negative) marginal cost on the sales price. This fraction would be the same for each efficiency of car, and it would be chosen so that the standard would be precisely met. In making technology adoption decisions, the same fractional marginal penalty costs would be utilized to compare against the costs of the technical improvements.

The discontinuity of marginal penalty costs at the standard leads to a situation in which changes in market conditions simply cause manufacturers to change the fraction of the marginal penalty cost passed on to consumers. This fraction is changed so as to maintain the equilibrium at the standard (at the discontinuity). This is the primary reason for the results illustrated by Figure 2-2. For low gasoline price, the full marginal penalty costs are imposed, but the mean efficiency of autos purchased remains below the standard. For a wide range of higher gasoline prices, imposition of the full marginal penalty costs would lead to a mean efficiency above the standard, while imposition of no marginal penalty costs would lead to a mean efficiency below the standard. Therefore, a fraction of the marginal penalty costs are imposed, with that fraction calculated to just reach the standard. For high enough gasoline prices the standard will be surpassed, and therefore no marginal penalty costs will be imposed.

If the industry is not competitive, then the price changes are not so simply calculated. However, the basic logic will continue to apply.

The preceding paragraphs have described the response of auto manufacturers to the standard and in so doing have established that the general form of the Figure 2-2 curve is correct. However, they have not established that with the current gasoline price the standards will be met. To do so requires further quantitative analyses.

The preceding section described the relationship between mean efficiency of new cars and gasoline price in the absence of the EPCA standards. In order to relate that analysis to the questions of this section, the device of an equivalent gasoline tax will be utilized.

The marginal penalty cost derived from equation (2.4), if fully passed on to the consumer, would have the same present value of cost for each automobile as would a combination of a lump sum subsidy and a gasoline tax. The gasoline tax, which is financially equivalent to the marginal penalty cost structure, will be called the equivalent gasoline tax.

The marginal penalty costs are imposed on a manufacturer, whereas a gasoline tax would be imposed directly on the consumer. However, which agent initially bears the given cost increase will not influence the market equilibrium. This corresponds to the normal results from economic theory and holds independently of market structure. Thus, the equivalent gasoline tax can be calculated from marginal penalty costs without examining which agents ultimately bear the cost changes. The equivalent tax will be independent of whether the automobile industry is competitive or monopolistic.

The concept of an equivalent gasoline tax allows the analysis to be reduced to two dimensions. The equivalent gasoline tax, ET, depends upon $\overline{mpg}$. For a given ET, the resulting consumer response determines $\overline{mpg}$. The market equilibrium is obtained when the two relationships are satisfied simultaneously.

Figure 2–4 illustrates the market equilibrium. An "optimal pricing" curve is illustrated, based on the marginal penalty costs and their equivalent gasoline tax. The figure also gives two possible demand response curves, illustrating two possible degrees of consumer responsiveness to price changes. In both cases $\overline{mpg}$ is an increasing function of ET.

The equilibrium of the system will be one of two types. Point A illustrates the equilibrium obtained with very low demand elasticities. In this case, the full marginal penalty costs (or the full equivalent tax) are imposed, but consumers do not respond sufficiently for the standard to be met. Point B illustrates the equilibrium obtained with a higher elasticity. The standard is met with a fraction of the full equivalent tax imposed. Which type of equilibrium obtains will depend upon the level of the standard and the responsiveness of consumers to higher prices.

The equivalent gasoline tax can be calculated. For a manufacturer just below the standard in 1985, the equivalent gasoline tax is 88 cents per gallon of gasoline[14] for a consumer with a 10 percent

---

14. The following formula was used to calculate ET: $ET = (1/1.14)(\$100)$ $(\overline{mpg}^2/TVM)$. TVM (total discounted vehicle miles) equals 84,000 for $r = 6$ percent, 76,000 for $r = 10$ percent, and 68,000 for $r = 15$ percent. The factor $(1/1.14)$ was obtained because the law is based upon the EPA-measured efficiency, which overstates lifetime average on the road performance by about 14 percent. See the appendix to this chapter for a derivation.

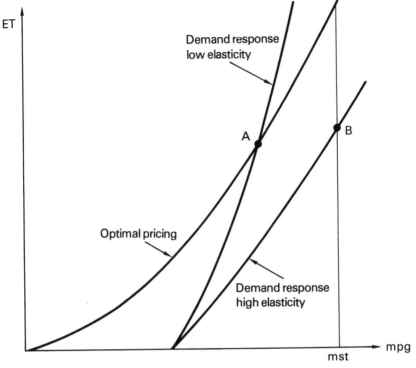

Figure 2–4. EPCA-guided Market Equilibrium.

real discount rate (70 cents for 6 percent and 97 cents for 15 percent discount rates).

In order to evaluate whether the standard will be met, the question becomes: Would a gasoline price increase of 88 cents per gallon (or possibly 79 or 97 cents) be sufficient in the absence of the standards to motivate a 1985 mean new car fuel efficiency above 27.5 miles per gallon? If the answer is yes, then the standards will probably be met.

A simple analysis can be conducted to answer this question. A constant elasticity specification of equation (2.2) can be assumed:

$$\overline{mpg} = B \left\{ \frac{P_{gas}}{EFF} \right\}^{\alpha} \times EFF, \qquad (2.5)$$

where α is the elasticity of $\overline{mpg}$ with respect to gasoline price and B is a constant. α and EFF will be treated as parameters in order to determine whether the standard would be met for various combinations. The constant, B, can be calibrated by using 1976 data and normalizing EFF to unity in that year. To obtain the demand response curve, the gasoline price, P_{gas}, can be replaced in equation (2.5) by the gasoline price plus the equivalent gasoline tax.

The 1976 value of $\overline{mpg}$ used is 16.8 mpg, the mean efficiency of domestically produced cars. The value of ET of 88 cents per gallon is used. Assuming a constant real price of crude oil from 1979 through 1985 (a conservative assumption), decontrol of crude oil prices adding 6 cents per gallon to gasoline prices, a 1979 gasoline price of 85 cents per gallon, and a 6 percent annual inflation rate from 1979 through 1985 gives a 1985 Consumer Price Index (CPI) of 3.09 and gasoline price of $1.29 per gallon (compared to 1.95 and 67 cents respectively in 1978).

The results are presented in Figure 2-5, which shows the 1985 values of $\overline{mpg}$ obtained for various assumed increases in EFF ($\Delta EFF/EFF$) and values of α. A line has been drawn through the table to separate combinations of EFF and α for which the financial incentives are sufficient for compliance from combinations for which they are not. For low values of α and EFF the incentives are not sufficient, while for higher values they are. Note that for large enough values of α or of ($\Delta EFF/EFF$), the other parameter can be zero and yet the standard would still be met. If the demand elasticity exceeds 0.7, then the standards could be met even with no improvements in technology. Similarly, if technical efficiency increases by 70 percent or more from its 1976 level, then the standards would be met even if demand were perfectly inelastic. The greater the technology improvement, the less important will be the demand response, and conversely, the greater the demand elasticity, the less will be the required technology improvement.

$\Delta EFF/EFF$					
α	0	20 Percent	40 Percent	60 Percent	80 Percent
0	16.8	20.2	23.5	26.9	30.2
0.2	19.4	22.4	25.4	28.2	31.0
0.4	22.4	24.9	27.4	29.6	31.8
0.6	25.8	27.7	29.5	31.1	32.6
0.8	29.8	30.9	31.8	32.7	33.5
1.0	34.3	34.3	34.3	34.3	34.3

Figure 2-5. Maximum Values of $\overline{mpg}$—1985 Demand Response Curve.

The econometric estimates in the chapter appendix suggest a demand elasticity of 0.72, so that under currently legislated incentives, the efficiency standard will be met even if there is no improvement in technology and no increases in the real price of gasoline. If a technical efficiency improvement of as little as 30 percent were to occur between 1976 and 1985, then any elasticity above 0.50 and 0.40 would imply that the incentives are sufficient for compliance with the standard. However, if an elasticity as low as 0.2 were correct, then a 60 percent increase in technical efficiency would be required to meet the standard.

The quantitative evidence cited here supports the conclusion that the new car efficiency standard will be met in 1985. A similar analysis supports the conclusion that the newly promulgated intermediate year standards (20, 22, 24, 26, and 27 mpg for 1980, 1981, 1982, 1983, and 1984, respectively) will also be met. Thus it can be concluded that if the elasticities estimated here are correct, then independent of most possible policy or program changes, the EPCA new car efficiency standard will be just met in each year through 1985. Modest policy changes will neither increase the average efficiency nor decrease it below the standards.

If consumers are much less responsive to prices than is assumed here, the EPCA standards may not be met. However, in that case, policies that impose price or cost changes on consumers could be expected to have little impact on gasoline consumption in relationship to the magnitude of the price changes.

If the standards are not met, then the cost changes passed on to consumers are equivalent in present value terms to a gasoline price increase of over 80 cents per gallon. Thus, one might question whether any market failures associated with gasoline use justify a tax incentive equivalent to over $33 per barrel of gasoline. The author is aware of no analysis that justifies so large an incentive. A complete analysis is beyond the scope of this chapter. But casual considerations suggest that if elasticities are small enough that the EPCA standards are not met, then the goal of economic efficiency dictates policy changes toward allowing less efficient autos than mandated and thus motivating more gasoline consumption than would occur under the current policy.

Other Factors Determining Gasoline Use

The efficiency of newly purchased cars ultimately is the primary determinant of fleet efficiency. However, fleet efficiency ($\overline{mpgF}$) adjusts only slowly to changes in new car efficiencies. The rate of adjustment of fleet efficiency depends upon the number of new cars purchased each year as a fraction of the total stock of automobiles and upon the relative intensity of utilization of cars of different vintages. These factors have been discussed elsewhere[15] and will not be described here.

Average fleet efficiency also depends upon the way that automobiles are operated. This operating efficiency depends on the frequency of tuneups, carburetor adjustments, the average speed of highway travel, the rural-urban mileage split, rates of acceleration, and other factors. While no attempt is made here to quantify the various policy impacts on operating efficiency, qualitative judgments are presented. In general, the higher the price of gasoline, the greater the incentive to take those actions that reduce gasoline consumption, including those actions that increase operating efficiency. Thus a gasoline tax could be expected to increase operating efficiency. The 55 mile per hour speed limit can be expected to increase operating efficiency since gasoline consumption is an increasing function of speed above a certain point. Noxious emissions standards, new car average efficiency standards, gas guzzler taxes, minimum efficiency standards, and federal fleet efficiency standards have their sole impact at the point of new purchase and cannot be expected to influence operating efficiency.

Automobiles comprise 74 percent of total gasoline consumption. This chapter does not examine the impacts of federal programs on the other uses of gasoline. This may be a serious limitation if policies directed at passenger cars inadvertently influence consumption by trucks, boats, and so forth. A particular case in point may be the impact of the EPCA mean efficiency standards on the sales of vans and light duty trucks. Consumers with a preference for vehicles having a fairly large carrying capacity may find that the EPCA standards reduce the availability of satisfactory automobiles. They may be motivated to purchase a light duty truck or van instead, since these vehicles are not governed by the same EPCA standards. Thus the total gasoline consumption reduction may be less than that predicted from an analysis of passenger cars only. Similarly, increasing gasoline prices will lead to a lessening of the incentives discouraging the purchase of automobiles and may thereby reduce the market shares of vans and light duty trucks. This would increase the sales of automobiles, keeping their mean efficiency constant, and decrease the sales of vans and trucks, thereby reducing gasoline consumption. Such phenomena have not been adequately assessed.

15. Sweeney, "The Demand for Gasoline."

Price Elasticities Over Time

A previous paper documents a simulation model that incorporates the relationships described above. In developing the model, the theoretical relationships described in the previous section have been empirically estimated using national data. The underlying data sources, the econometric estimates, and a model following the diagram of Figure 2-6 are described elsewhere and will not be discussed here in any detail.[16]

Two relationships in the model are most critical for describing the price elasticities over time—the vehicle mile elasticities and the new car efficiency elasticities. Vehicle miles depends upon the gasoline cost per mile—the ratio of gasoline price to fleet efficiency. This elasticity is −0.225. New car mean efficiency is specified as in equation (2.5). The elasticity of $\overline{mpg}$ with respect to gasoline price is 0.72.

The model was simulated both with and without the EPCA standards by increasing the price of gasoline by 10 percent in each year (beginning in 1979) and observing the percentage changes in gasoline consumption, vehicle miles, fleet efficiency, and new car efficiency over time. The results are presented in Table 2–3. The first column labels the number of years during which the price change has been effective. Year 1 therefore corresponds to 1980. The second column presents the price elasticity of gasoline consumption.[17] Columns 3–5 provide an analysis of the changes in gasoline consumption. Column 3 describes the elasticity of vehicle miles with respect to gasoline price, including the feedback through fleet efficiency. Column 4 presents the elasticity of fleet efficiency and column 5 presents the elasticity of new car efficiency, both with respect to gasoline price.

For example, without the EPCA standards, a 1 percent increase in gasoline price maintained over time would reduce gasoline consumption by 0.5 percent in the fifth year. This reduction would be the result of a 0.16 percent reduction in vehicle miles and a 0.34 percent increase in fleetwide fuel efficiency. New car efficiency would increase by 0.72 percent.

Without the EPCA standard, the one year price elasticity of gasoline demand is accounted for virtually entirely by changes in vehicle miles, while the long-run elasticity is accounted for virtually entirely by changes in fleet efficiency. The long-run elasticity of demand is

16. Sweeney, "The Demand for Gasoline."
17. This elasticity is calculated as $\ell n(GAS'/GAS)/\ell n(1.1/1)$, where GAS' is gasoline consumption with the 10 percent price change and GAS is consumption without the price change. All the other elasticities are calculated analogously.

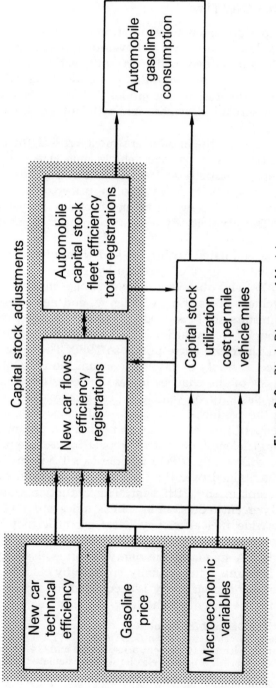

Figure 2-6.   Block Diagram of Model.

Table 2-3. Price Elasticities of Gasoline Demand.

Year	Gasoline Consumption	Vehicle Miles	Fleet Efficiency	New Car Efficiency
		With Efficiency Standards		
1	-0.22	-0.22	0	0
2	-0.22	-0.22		
3	-0.23	-0.23		
5	-0.23	-0.23	↓	↓
10	-0.24	-0.24		
∞	-0.24	-0.24	↓	↓
		Without Efficiency Standards		
1	-0.22	-0.22	0	0
2	-0.32	-0.20	0.12	0.72
3	-0.39	-0.19	0.20	
5	-0.50	-0.16	0.34	↓
10	-0.66	-0.11	0.55	
∞	-0.78	-0.06	0.72	↓

roughly four times the short-run elasticity, with a 50 percent adjustment occurring in three years.

The fleet efficiency adjusts gradually over time following the (assumed) instant response of new car fuel efficiency to the price rise. A 50 percent adjustment of fleet efficiency occurs in five years.

The vehicle mile elasticities decline over time. This occurs because there is a feedback from fleet efficiency to vehicle miles, with increasing fleetwide fuel efficiency leading to increasing vehicle miles. The elasticities of vehicle miles reported here are the net results of two opposing terms: an instantaneous gasoline price increase and a gradual fleet efficiency increase.

In the presence of the EPCA standards, the pattern of elasticities over time is quite different. Virtually the entire elasticity of gasoline demand is associated with changes in vehicle miles. Thus the long-run elasticity of demand is much smaller in the presence of the EPCA standards than in their absence, while the short-run elasticity is the same. The small, virtually unnoticeable, change in fleet efficiency occurs because higher gasoline prices reduce driving—and hence, the demand for new cars—and finally the rate at which the new, more fuel-efficient cars are absorbed into the fleet.

SUMMARY AND CONCLUSIONS

In the preembargo period, the gasoline tax and the oil import quota increased the price of gasoline, increasing new car efficiency and operating efficiency and decreasing equilibrium vehicle miles. The long-run equilibrium gasoline consumption by automobiles was decreased by a total of 11 percent. On the other hand, highway construction led to an uncertain increase in long-run equilibrium gasoline consumption.

The noxious emissions standards on automobiles may have reduced technical efficiency on the order of 7.5 percent for a number of years,[18] although it is not clear that there was any significant reduction in technical efficiency after the introduction of the catalytic converter. However, a 7.5 percent reduction in technical efficiency would lead to only a 2.2 percent reduction in new car efficiency, since most of the effects of changing technical efficiency would be offset by the induced shift of demand toward smaller cars. The reduction in auto efficiency would make it more costly to drive, reducing long-run equilibrium vehicle miles by 0.7 percent. Thus, the overall long-run equilibrium gasoline consumption perhaps would have increased by only 1.7 percent in the preembargo period as a result of a long-run 7.5 percent reduction in technical efficiency.

In the postembargo period, before the efficiency standards became effective, the gasoline tax and the crude oil price controls worked in almost equal, but opposite, directions, canceling each others' effects. The noxious emissions standards remained during that period.

The impact of programs after the efficiency standard becomes effective depends very critically upon whether the efficiency standard will be met. The previous sections show that the current law incorporates financial incentives equivalent (in present value terms) to a gasoline tax of over 80 cents per gallon ($33 per barrel). It is concluded that these incentives are sufficient so that the EPCA standards will be met.

Since the efficiency standard will be precisely met, no other program designed to influence the mean efficiency of newly purchased cars will succeed, unless the program alone is sufficient to increase the average efficiency above the EPCA mandated levels. Thus, neither gasoline tax, crude oil price controls, noxious emissions standards, the federal fleet efficiency standards, the NEP "gas guzzler" tax, nor the proposed minimum efficiency standard on individual cars would influence the mean efficiency of newly purchased cars. To the extent that any such program tends to influence mean efficiency, manufacturers can be expected to compensate by changing their pricing

18. U.S. Environmental Protection Agency, "Fuel Economy and Emission Control" (Washington, D.C.: Office of Air and Water Programs, Mobile Source Pollution Control Program, November 1972).

policies so as to always precisely meet the standard. Thus, programs could influence the mix of motivating factors that cause the standards to be met (e.g., the gasoline price increases versus automobile price differentials), but would not increase the resultant fuel efficiency above the standard.

The efficiency standard alone significantly increases the new car fuel efficiency from what it would have been otherwise. The 46 percent increase indicated in Table 2-1 measures the increase in new car efficiency from what could be expected to obtain given the existing programs—the 4 cent gasoline tax, the crude oil price controls, and the noxious emissions standards. The effects of these programs have not been eliminated before estimating the change in new car efficiency. The effects on operating efficiency of the various programs are probably not changed by the efficiency standard.

These various postembargo, postefficiency standard programs could influence long-run equilibrium vehicle miles. In particular, the efficiency standard, by increasing the average miles per gallon of the automobile fleet, will at the same time increase equilibrium vehicle miles by about 9 percent. The net long-run equilibrium adjustment in gasoline consumption will be a net reduction of about 25 percent, with about 12 percent occurring by 1985. Again, the gasoline tax and the crude oil price controls roughly offset one another.

Of the proposed policies, the "gas guzzler" tax would have very little additional effect on gasoline consumption. Its only effect would be directly through new car efficiency. In early years of the program, the "gas guzzler" tax would have been large enough to increase the efficiency of newly purchased cars above the mandated standard. By 1985 the NEP "gas guzzler" tax alone would not be sufficient to bring average new car efficiency above the standard. Thus, manufacturers would continue to set prices so as to precisely meet the efficiency standard. However, in 1985 the fleet of automobiles would be more efficient because in early years more efficient automobiles would have been purchased and would remain in the fleet. In 1985 the NEP "gas guzzler" tax would have reduced gasoline consumption by 1.3 percent.

The very large standby gasoline tax proposed in the NEP would have no effect on new car efficiency, since it would not be sufficient alone to cause the average efficiency of cars to exceed the standard. Thus, any reduction in gasoline consumption caused by this tax would be through a reduction in the vehicle miles obtained. Finally, the minimum efficiency standard on individual cars would not move the average of all cars purchased above the EPCA efficiency standard, and therefore this proposal would have no effect on gasoline consumption, although by reducing consumer flexibility, it could be expected to reduce economic efficiency.

The logic of the efficiency standard is all-encompassing. The law provides strong incentives to meet the average standard but no incentive to surpass it. Thus, if the standards are met initially, no policy option will increase average efficiency unless that option is strong enough to increase average efficiency above the standard even in its absence, and if the elasticities of new car efficiency with respect to gasoline price are as high as estimated here, then the standards will be initially met. Only under much lower elasticities will manufacturers fail to meet these standards.

Dynamic price elasticities of demand with and without the EPCA efficiency standard are quite different from one another. Based upon the model diagrammed here, without the standard, gasoline demand elasticity may be about -0.2 in the short run and -0.8 in the long run, reflecting changing vehicle miles in the short run and changing fleetwide fuel efficiencies in the long run. However, in the presence of the EPCA standards, both the short-run and the long-run elasticities can be expected to be about -0.2, reflecting only changes in vehicle miles, not changes in fleetwide fuel efficiency.

MATHEMATICAL APPENDIX: DERIVATION OF EQUATION (2.1)

Let S be a vector whose elements, S_i, indicate the market shares captured by the various automobile models; let G be a vector whose components, G_i, indicate the gallons of gasoline consumed per mile driven for the ith car, (G_i is the inverse of mpg_i); and let $\overline{mpg}$ represent the mean efficiency of all newly purchased cars. Then the following identity relates G, S, and $\overline{mpg}$:[19]

$$\overline{mpg} = l/[G \cdot S] . \tag{2.6}$$

The vector S is assumed to depend upon operating costs of the various autos. The operating costs of a given model depend upon maintenance costs, physical characteristics of the model, and fuel costs. Gasoline price enters only through the last factor and then only insofar as it influences the fuel cost per mile driven. Hence, operating costs of the ith model are influenced by the product of gasoline price and G_i.

19. Two vectors separated by a dot will indicate the inner product of the two vectors. For example $G \cdot S$ represents $\sum_i G_i S_i$.

Holding all factors constant but gasoline cost and the model efficiencies, the above discussion leads to the mathematical relationships:

$$\overline{mpg} = l/[G \cdot S(P_{gas} \ G)], \tag{2.7}$$

where P_{gas} is the (scalar) gasoline price.

By equation (2.7), the average new car efficiency can be influenced by the gasoline price or by the efficiencies of the various models. A gasoline price change can be expected to alter the market shares of the various models and thus to change the weights used for averaging efficiencies.

The properties of equation (2.7) generally depend upon the matrix of own- and cross-elasticities of demand for the various models. Thus little can be said about the response to arbitrary changes in model efficiencies. However, it can be expected that in any year, the miles per gallon obtained by a car are roughly inversely proportional to its weight and directly proportional to EFF, the measure of technical efficiency. Therefore, it is useful to examine the case in which the efficiency of each model changes by the same percentage. Thus, let efficiencies of each vintage vary so that

$$G = G^{o}/EFF, \tag{2.8}$$

where G^{o} is a fixed vector of efficiencies. Then equation (2.2) becomes:

$$\overline{mpg} = l/\left[\frac{G^{o}}{EFF} \cdot S\left(\frac{P_{gas}}{EFF}\right)G^{o} \right] \tag{2.9}$$

This equation can be rewritten very simply into the form of equation (2.1) in the body of the paper:

$$\overline{mpg} = EFF \cdot f(P_{gas}/EFF). \tag{2.1}$$

Optimal Pricing Under EPCA

The EPCA penalty from equation (2.3) is:

$$F = \begin{cases} t(mst - \overline{mpg})N, & \text{for } mst \geqslant \overline{mpg} \\ 0 & , \text{for } mst \leqslant \overline{mpg} \end{cases}. \tag{2.3}$$

Let $x \, x_1, x_2, \ldots, x_n$ be the vector describing the numbers of cars sold of model $1, 2, \ldots, n$. Then:

$$N = \sum_{i=1}^{n} x_i. \qquad (2.10)$$

The mean efficiency, $\overline{mpg}$, is defined by equation (2.6). Therefore, the fine equals the following, for $mst \geqslant \overline{mpg}$:

$$F = t \left[mst \cdot N - \frac{N^2}{G \cdot x} \right]. \qquad (2.11)$$

The total nonpenalty cost of manufacturing and marketing cars is represented as $C(x)$, assumed to be a concave function. Revenue is $P(x) \cdot x$, where $P(x)$ is a vector of prices. Then profit becomes:

$$\pi = P(x) \cdot x - C(x) - F. \qquad (2.12)$$

Differentiating equation (2.12) provides necessary conditions for profit maximization for the individual firm:

$$MR_i = P_i + \sum_j x_j \frac{\partial P_j}{\partial x_i} = \frac{\partial C}{\partial x_i} + T_i, \text{ for each } i, \qquad (2.13)$$

where

$$T_i = \lambda (\overline{mpg})^2 / mpg_i + \lambda (mst - 2\overline{mpg}) \qquad (2.14)$$

and where

$$0 \leqslant \lambda \begin{cases} = t \text{ , for } \overline{mpg} < mst \\ \leqslant t \text{ , for } \overline{mpg} = mst \\ = 0, \text{ for } \overline{mpg} > mst \end{cases} \qquad (2.15)$$

The T_is are the marginal penalty costs used within the body of the paper. To derive the equivalent gasoline tax, note that equation (2.14) has two terms on the right-hand side. The second term— $\lambda (mst - 2\overline{mpg})$—corresponds to a lump sum subsidy (or penalty) on all autos purchased from a given manufacturer. This term does not depend upon the fuel efficiency of the individual car, but only upon mean efficiency. The first term—$\lambda (\overline{mpg})^2/mpg_i$—can be related to the equivalent gasoline tax.

Consider an increase in gasoline price of ET for each year. If a car obtains a fuel efficiency of mpg_i and is driven $m_1, m_2, \ldots m_q$ miles per year for its life of q years, then the discounted cost increase facing the owner of the car would be:

$$\frac{ET \cdot TVM}{mpg_i}, \tag{2.16}$$

where

$$TVM = \sum_{j=1}^{q} m_j \left(\frac{1}{l+r}\right)^j . \tag{2.17}$$

TVM is simply the discounted miles driven over the life of the car. Equating expression (2.16) to the first term of equation (2.14) gives:

$$ET = \lambda \frac{(\overline{mpg})^2}{TVM}. \tag{2.18}$$

This equivalent gasoline tax is that used in the body of the paper.

It should be noted that the magnitudes of the lump sum subsidy and of the equivalent gasoline tax are independent of the auto industry structure. Thus the interpretation does not depend upon a competitive industry assumption.

Econometric Equations for $\overline{mpg}$ and VM

In order to estimate efficiency of newly purchased cars, equation (2.1) was fitted in a log-linear form using data from 1957 through 1974. Complete documentation appears elsewhere.[20] Equations were fitted by constraining the sum of elasticities (with respect to EFF and with respect to P_{gas}) to unity and then were reestimated without constraining the sum. Equation (2.19) presents the constrained estimation results, while equation (2.20) presents the unconstrained estimates.[21]

20. Sweeney, "U.S. Gasoline Demand."
21. t-Statistics are in parentheses. Lagged gasoline price was used rather than contemporaneous price to compensate for data timing mismatch: The variables mpg and EFF are for model year, while P_{gas} is for calendar year.

$$\ell n \ \overline{mpg} = \quad 3.344 + \quad 0.721 \ \ell n \ P_{gas} \ (-1) + 0.279 \ \ell n \ EFF$$
$$(32.0) \qquad (7.9)$$

$$R^2 = 0.86 \qquad\qquad D.W. = 2.1 \qquad\qquad\qquad (2.19)$$

$$\ell n \ \overline{mpg} = \quad 3.325 + \quad 0.703 \ \ell n \ P_{gas} \ (-1) + 0.249 \ \ell n \ EFF$$
$$(28.9) \qquad (6.9) \qquad\qquad\qquad (2.2)$$

$$R^2 = 0.86 \qquad\qquad D.W = 2.0 \qquad\qquad\qquad (2.20)$$

where $P_{gas}(-1)$ is the lagged gasoline price.

Equations (2.19) and (2.20) fit the theory well, implying that the elasticity of average miles per gallon with respect to gasoline price and the elasticity with respect to technical efficiency sum approximately to unity, even when no constraint is imposed. The preferred equation (2.19) implies that the elasticity of vintage efficiency with respect to gasoline price is about 0.72. Thus, in response to increases in technical efficiency, the induced shift in market shares offsets over 70 percent of the apparent efficiency gain.

In estimating vehicle miles, variables were fitted in per capita form. Per capita vehicle miles were estimated as a function of the cost per mile of driving, the per capita disposable income, and other variables describing the state of the economy. The equations are tabulated in Table 2-4. Here, C is the constant, $GCPM$ is gasoline cost per mile of driving, YD/N is per capita disposable income, Ru is

Table 2-4.   Vehicle Miles per Capita (VM/N) Equation.[a]

C	$GCPM$	YD/N	Ru	$HPEA$	$PCR(-1)$ / $N(-1)$	R^2	$D.W.$
-0.389 (-1/0)	-0.139 (-1.3)	1.040 (28.0)				0.99	0.5
-0.433 (-1.7)	-0.119 (-1.6)	1.076 (39.8)	0.015 (4.2)			0.99	1.7
5.60 (3.8)	-0.219 (-2.9)	0.821 (13.7)		-1.657 (-4.1)		0.99	1.4
3.106 (1.7)	-0.17 (2.5)	0.933 (12.3)	-0.0095 (2.1)	-0.975 (-2.0)		0.995	2.2
1.372 (0.6)	-0.225 (-2.7)	0.632 (2.3)	0.0059 (1.1)	-0.952 (-2.0)	0.306 (1.1)	0.996	2.2

[a]Sample period 1957–1974.

All variables expressed in logarithmic form except Ru, which is not transformed.

the unemployment rate, *HPEA* is the weekly hours of production workers (a measure of free time), and $PCR(-1)/N(-1)$ is the per capita stock of passenger cars in the previous time period. This last variable is included to allow the possibility that the stock of cars helps determine the vehicle miles demanded.[22] Other equations documented elsewhere include a measure of time cost plus gasoline cost, but this theoretically superior measure proved to be empirically inferior to *GCPM*.[23]

22. The variable is lagged to eliminate the simultaneous equation bias.
23. Sweeney, "U.S. Gasoline Demand."

The Electric Utilities Face the Next Twenty Years

Irwin M. Stelzer

This paper will discuss two broad types of problems that the electric utility industry faces in the next twenty years: those particular to the industry and those arising for the industry from general issues society is having difficulty resolving.[1]

PARTICULAR PROBLEMS

The three most important particular problems facing the electric utilities are earnings, rates, and the need to recuperate from self-inflicted wounds. Let me consider these in turn.

Earnings

State commissions limit the regulated gas and electric monopolies under their jurisdictions to a fair return on invested capital. This return, generally set as a range in recognition of the difficulty of quantifying such concepts as risk, investors' requirements, and the like, is arrived at by a variety of methods. It would be a needless digression to examine the claims made for each of these methods or to ask the reader to come down on one side or another of the arguments concerning the adequacy of the resultant earnings levels. .

---

1. These broad categories are not clearly separated by some fine line, but have been chosen to simplify exposition.

Instead, I shall attempt three simple demonstrations and offer some solutions:

1. An empirical demonstration showing that most utility stocks are selling at prices below their book values;
2. A demonstration that this limits their ability to engage in economically appropriate expansion; and
3. An argument that this is contrary to the administration's perception of the national interest.

Data.   An examination of the market price–book value ratios of the ninety-six electric utilities traded on the New York Stock Exchange,[2] using averages for the first six months of 1978, shows that sixty-seven companies found the price of their stock below book value; only twenty-nine achieved at least book value; and only three had stocks selling at or above 1.2 times book value, a level generally felt to be sufficient to permit the issuance of new equity without major problems.

Limitation on Ability to Expand.   This means that, to sell common stock, most utilities must dilute the values held by existing shareholders by selling stock below book value. In essence, they transfer to the new stockholder a portion of the claim on earnings held until then by the old stockholder. This is fine—until the next round, when the new stockholder is now the old stockholder and must die by the very sword by which he had lived. Sooner or later, holders of capital will see what is in store for them if they make it available to companies with stocks selling below book value and with a perceived obligation to expand. And they will demand premiums for their capital—or refuse to make it available.[3]

Nor will utilities be in a very good position to raise debt capital. With embedded interest costs rising steadily as old, low cost debt is rolled over, utilities' ability to sell new debt without running into coverage problems is limited. Our studies suggest that this problem will force utilities to reduce their debt-equity ratios by the mid-1980s—that is, to rely even more heavily on the equity

2. These companies account for over 90 percent of all revenues of privately owned electric utilities. A later tabulation (July 31, 1979) of seventy-five utilities found only nine with stocks at or above book value. See First Boston Corp., "Progress Report," August 6, 1979.
3. For a fuller—and clearer—exposition of this problem, see Herman G. Roseman, "The Impact of the Energy Bill on Utility Financing," Testimony before the Ad Hoc Committee on Energy, U.S. House of Representatives, Thomas J. Ashley, Chairman, June 16, 1977.

capital that we have just shown will be so difficult for them to raise.

Keep in mind the fact that, even with the new lowered expectations concerning growth rates, utilities are voracious consumers of capital. In 1976, capital expenditures of investor-owned utilities came to almost $20 billion ($19.76 billion), equal to over 12 percent of net plant.[4] And over 70 percent of these funds was raised in the capital markets.[5] Since new plants cost about twice as much as existing plants,[6] even modest growth rates in required capacity will result in proportionately much higher capital requirements. For example, if capacity is growing 5 percent per year, the high cost of new plant will mean that total book capital must grow 10 percent per year. Unless one believes that growth rates will be so close to zero as to make these capital-raising difficulties of no consequence,[7] this issue must rate as one of the most important facing the industry.

Contravening the National Interest. There are several ways in which a utility capital crunch creates problems of a national character. If we assume that one goal of any energy policy that may eventually evolve is to reduce dependence on imported oil,[8] then it is important that utilities not have a societally uneconomic incentive to avoid relatively capital-intensive technologies, such as nuclear and coal, in favor of the fuel-intensive technology, oil. If utilities are not able to raise the funds to construct the more highly capital-intensive, but less fuel-intensive, coal and nuclear power-generating facilities, then they will be forced to meet future energy demands with the less capital-intensive, but more fuel-intensive, oil-burning power plants designed to meet peak requirements. The consequence would be needlessly higher future energy costs and an increased dependence upon imported oil. For example, if owing to a lack of funds,[9] a utility decides to cancel a more capital-intensive power-

4. Edison Electric Institute, *Statistical Year Book of the Electric Utility Industry for 1977* (New York, 1978), pp. 59–60.

5. Ibid, pp. 59 and 64.

6. "Cost" is used here in its accounting sense.

7. Recent forecasts include the 5.4 percent figure used by the National Electric Reliability Council, 4.1 percent by the Department of Energy, and 4.7 percent by Electric Power Research Institute, for varying future periods.

8. Executive Office of the President, Energy Policy and Planning, *The National Energy Plan* (April 29, 1977), p. 93 (hereinafter, NEP) (Washington, D.C.: Dept. of Energy).

9. Even if a utility is able to raise the money, if it is earning less than its cost of capital, it will not have the financial incentive to do so. When a utility's stock is selling at less than book value, it is very probably earning less than its cost of capital.

generating facility (nuclear) that is less fuel-intensive in the long run, in favor of a less capital-intensive facility (oil) that is more fuel-intensive in the long run, then all of society is forced to pay a higher price (pecuniary as well as nonpecuniary) for energy.[10] Such a decision would, of course, also increase U.S. dependence on foreign oil. Indeed, decisions of that type have already had a devastating effect on our national goal of reducing oil imports. Responding to declining demand projections and inadequate earnings,[11] utilities have slashed construction budgets. In 1974, U.S. electric utilities planned to have 178,000 megawatts (MW) of nuclear capacity in operation in 1984; they now plan 121,000 MW for that year. So, too, with coal: plans made in 1974 called for 324,000 MW of coal-fired generation by 1984; current plans call for only 290,000 MW of such capacity. To the extent that these curtailments reflect the inability of utilities to raise adequate funds, they will result in higher oil (and gas) consumption by the electric utility industry.[12] This is a giant step backward on the road to "independence" and an enormous retreat in the "war" on the energy problem.[13]

Clearly, if the NEP's goals are to be even approximated, the state regulatory authorities will have to permit some improvement in the industry's ability to finance coal and nuclear facilities. This can be accomplished in one of several ways or by some combination of these methods.

Possible Solutions.

Increase Earnings. This is the most direct method. Its consequences would be at least twofold. First, with higher earnings on

10. This is especially the case since the canceled units are likely to be baseload generators and the substituted oil-fired equipment is likely to be peaking capacity not economically appropriate for the uses to which it would be put.

11. It is impossible to tell the relative importance of these two factors, but it is important to note the different implications of these two causes for construction cancellations. If planned power-generating facilities are canceled because revisions in energy demand forecasts indicate that they are no longer needed, then society is not wasting scarce resources by creating excess energy capacity. However, if these reductions in construction programs are due to the inability of utilities to generate the necessary funds, then the impact of these reductions will be to produce a suboptimal generating mix.

12. A useful rule of thumb: A single 1,000 MW steam generating plant fired with fossil fuels will consume approximately 11 million barrels of oil (or its equivalent) per year. Over its life, it will consume something like 300 million barrels of oil. If all this oil were to be imported, the annual increase in the nation's imports of oil due to the installation of a single 1,000 MW fossil fuel generating plant would come to about $130 million.

13. The NEP called for oil imports of 7 million barrels of oil per day by 1985. The change in utility plans would increase imports by 2 million barrels per day.

equity, coverage ratios will be higher, permitting utilities to sell more debt at lower interest rates. Moreover, if utilities can maintain or raise their debt ratios, the amount of common stock that they will have to sell will be that much smaller and their ability to sell stock will be that much less in doubt.

Second, if the return on equity is high enough, the danger of a cumulative downward spiral in the price of the stock is averted, and the company will be able to sell stock as required. This is true even if the higher return does not increase the price-book ratio, which, of course, it can generally be expected to do.

How much does this mean in rate increases? To raise price-book ratios to levels that would permit utilities to finance without dilution would require an average rate increase of about 4 percent. For the industry as a whole, this means an increase of about $2 billion in annual revenues. When compared with the private industry's capital expenditures of $17 billion per year, this increase does not seem all that large.

Change Accounting Practices. It is impossible to describe the intricacies of regulatory accounting here, but it can be noted that a variety of devices are available to enable utilities to increase cash flow. One would be to include in the rate base the money invested in facilities under construction—a device that would raise rates now but keep them lower in the future. This, of course, is the CWIP (construction work in progress) controversy—one I will not discuss here.

Eliminate Regulatory Lag. In rate case after case throughout the country, commissions make determinations of the fair return an electric utility should be permitted to earn under the new rates that the commissions authorize. And in case after case, the utility does not in fact achieve the return the commission intended. The actual earnings on equity of many companies have been running about two or three percentage points below the levels that their commissions have most recently allowed. The shortfall tends to be larger for those electric utilities that are experiencing above-average growth in capital requirements—the very companies for which it is not in the national interest to have an uneconomic incentive to use oil-intensive technologies. Working with stale data and often inadequate staffs, regulators do not permit utilities to earn the amounts that the regulators themselves have found to be required. Given this environment, some form of automatic adjustment clause, designed to raise or lower rates to produce a range of earnings on equity and/or coverage of interest payments, may now well be in the consumers' interest. Automatic adjustment clauses that permit companies to earn at the levels that their commissions have themselves found appropriate would provide greater assurance that utilities would be able to carry out their plans for the optimum mix of facilities, even though such plans involved large investments in high capital cost facilities with long lead times.

Managements today are faced with a continuing problem of trying to match their plans for (1) the best way of achieving the appropriate quality of service at the lowest total cost with (2) the limitations on their ability to carry out such plans because of a potential lack of financing capability as their companies repeatedly fail to realize the return that commissions find to be just and reasonable. If, and to the extent that, an automatic adjustment clause removes that uncertainty, companies would be able to make longer term commitments, such as those involved in high capital cost–low fuel cost generating facilities.

The adoption of an automatic adjustment clause would also reduce the current very significant disincentive to undertake fuel economies. For example, a coal plant will cost more to build than an oil plant, but will have lower fuel costs. Similarly, a nuclear plant will cost more to build than a coal plant, but will have lower fuel costs. At present, most utilities can recover their fuel costs through an adjustment clause, but cannot so recover their capital costs. Thus, the present system of regulatory lag gives utilities an incentive to build plants that use less capital and more fuel.[14] Many companies, for example, could under the present circumstances improve earnings at the expense of their customers and the national interest by substituting oil-fired for planned coal and nuclear facilities since oil-fired facilities require less capital per unit but have much higher fuel costs. Under an inclusive automatic adjustment clause, this incentive to inefficiency would be removed.

In the one instance (New Mexico) in which this approach has been adopted, the results have been salutary: the cost of both equity and debt capital was sharply lowered—by one percentage point in the case of equity and by one-half a percentage point in the case of debt. These are substantial savings; equally significant is the fact that elimination of regulatory lag permitted the construction of facilities using a more optimum mix of fuel and capital than would otherwise have been possible.

Whatever the device used, state regulators can conform with

14. Harvey Averch and Leland L. Johnson, "Behavior of the Firm Under Regulatory Constraint," *American Economic Review* (December 1962): 1052-69.

national policy objectives by adopting less restrictive attitudes toward utility earnings. But I am pessimistic that they will.

Rates

Even if utilities are given a reasonable opportunity to earn a return that will permit them to raise capital efficiently, they will still face a second problem—rate structures. The National Energy Plan calls for rates equal to "true" or "marginal" replacement costs[15] —an economically unexceptionable goal. And assume further that marginal cost is the proper basis for rates.[16] Assume, finally, that environmentalists, conservationists, academics, and thoughtful members of the Department of Energy staff will press for rates based on marginal costs. Then utilities will find themselves with several problems.

1. They will at the same time be raising rates (in response to inflation, environmental pressures, and investor demands) and restructuring those rates. Thus, if a utility needs a 15 percent rate increase and seeks at the same time to revise the structure of its rates, it will have to raise some rates by more than 15 percent, increasing consumer dissatisfaction. This adds to the realistic pressures against rate reform: across-the-board increases evoke less consumer opposition in the short run. In the long run, of course, failure to conform rates with marginal cost leads to excessive increases in consumption and investment and, hence, to higher rates than would otherwise be necessary. But consumers tend to think in short-run terms.

2. Utilities will be required to make management changes, such as elevating ratemakers to higher policy levels. The company's revenue requirements cannot be determined without reference to rate structure. We know too much about demand elasticity to believe it to be zero or equal for all customer classes or at all times of the day and year. Accumulation of data on the demand side, combined with marginal cost information, permits much more intelligent analysis of the relationship between the required level of

15. NEP, pp. 29 and 49. See also p. 46, calling for peak load pricing.
16. The literature on this point, both pro and con, is voluminous. See, for example, Alfred E. Kahn, *The Economics of Regulation: Principles and Institutions* (New York: Wiley, 1970), especially vol. 1, pp. 63–99; Electric Power Research Institute, Electric Utility Rate Design Study, "Rate Design and Load Control: Issues and Directions," A Report to the National Association of Regulatory Utility Commissioners, November 1977; and Sam Schurr, Joel Darmstoadter, Harry Perry, William Ramsay, and Milton Russell, *Energy in America's Future: The Choices Before Us* (Baltimore: Johns Hopkins University Press for Resources for the Future, 1979). A contrary view can be found in James Ranniger, "Electric Rates—Where We Have Been, Where We Are Going," *Public Utilities Fortnightly*, May 12, 1977.

rates and the rate structure. Whether utilities will view this as an opportunity or a burden remains to be seen.

3. No matter how utilities view the rate structure question, they will find themselves in a crossfire. Industrial customers in most instances continue to resist anything resembling comprehensive rate reform.[17] Other groups attempt to use utility rate structures as a device to redistribute incomes, even though electric rates are a demonstrably inefficient device for such redistribution and un- economically high rates to industry reduce economic growth rates and available employment. All fight against rate increases. The utility industry will find itself hard pressed to withstand these conflicting pressures.

Self-inflicted Wounds

That the electric utility industry is a handy, visible target for those who oppose it on particular issues, no one can question. And the fact that several broad, societal issues affect electric companies with particular force will be demonstrated below. But the industry makes the problems it faces even more difficult by defending itself in ways that add to, rather than reduce, the damage of the attacks made upon it.

The industry has an extraordinary record of performance. For decades it rendered reliable service, at steadily declining real prices, to millions of satisfied customers. Given the many service territories, the varying conditions of terrain and weather, the extraordinary range of customer requirements and other such problems, the indus- try's engineer-planners had reason to be proud of what they had created—and of the rules of thumb they had developed: one genera- tion outage every ten years, reserves equal to the largest unit, and so on.

But two things happened in the 1960s. First, costs began to rise sharply. Second, and not unrelated, "outsiders"—academicians, politicians, better informed regulators—became interested in the industry and began to ask questions. They wanted to know how much reliability was costing: Would it be possible to save money by lowering reliability standards? They wanted to know what out- ages cost. Was it possible that shortage costs were not as great as everyone had believed? They wanted to know whether the industry was optimally configured, both between its vertical levels and in terms of its ownership structure. Was a more economic mix of

17. They do, of course, support selected reforms such as wider availability of interruptible rates.

generation and transmission attainable? Should separate systems be merged into large, regional units?

The people who had engineered the beautifully functioning industry had two choices. They could respond to these questions by attempting to dismiss them—by arguing that the rules of thumb that made the industry great are engineering concepts and should not be subjected to cost-benefit analysis. Or they could attempt to demonstrate that the savings from reduced reliability would be more than offset by the costs of the resultant outages and shortages—that the externalities associated with less adequate power supply exceeded the dollar savings from lowered capacity requirements.

Unfortunately, the industry exhibited the tendency I have described as self-inflicted wounding: it dug its heels in and defended, but refused to quantify, its rules of thumb. And not without reason. I share the suspicion that the public places a low value on reliability—until a lower reliability is manifested. Then public outcry and political pressures mount, forcing uneconomic investments.

But it would have been far better if the industry had addressed its critics, using cost-benefit analysis as a tool to bring some sense to the debates. Instead, time was lost, and only now is the industry developing a methodology to enable it to present its critics with hard choices. For example, we recently completed a study of the cost, employment, and other effects of varying degrees of shortage created by a continuation of California's restraints on construction of new generating capacity.[18] A few of our more interesting findings are:

1. The consumption-weighted average cost of outages for all California manufacturing is 27.8 cents/kWh.[19]
2. If California bans new construction but permits already begun plants to be completed, and if demand grows at the 3.8 percent annual rate projected by the conservationist-inclined California Energy Commission, the 1995 loss of load probability will be so high that some load will have to be curtailed for twelve out of every twenty-four hours or rationing imposed requiring usage reductions of 14 to 17 percent (and even then loads will have to be curtailed from two to five and a half out of every twenty-four hours). The annual shortage cost would be between $1.4 and $3.2 billion.

18. National Economic Research Associates, Inc., *California's Electric Power Future: Electricity Supply Alternatives for California* (San Francisco: California Council for Environmental and Economic Balance, August 19, 1978).
19. Based on 1975 values.

3. Given the assumptions stated above, electric rates will be 11 percent higher in 1995 than they would otherwise be, and employment would be reduced by some 170,000 to 320,000 jobs.

These empirical findings suggest that when the electric utility industry finally gets around to examining its own position in a calm and systematic way, it will find that many of its intuitive preconceptions are correct. Better to measure the cost of a shortage and find it large, even though finite, than to refuse to measure it in the hope that everyone will believe it to be infinite. But the industry is often reluctant to quantify, to treat questions reasonably, to abandon the notion that outsiders are incapable of raising interesting questions and of rationally appraising quantified responses. Just as its critics tend to judge the entire utility industry by the most reactionary of its executives, so the industry often tends to judge all its critics by the silliest and most irresponsible ones. And this often leads the industry to avoid genuine issues.

GENERAL PROBLEMS

The electric utility industry is not immune to the general problems facing our society. Indeed, those problems often hit the industry with special force; witness the devastating effect on utilities of the oil embargo, inflation, increased environmental awareness, concern over nuclear proliferation, and a host of other societal concerns. Three of these general concerns create such difficult problems that they are worth addressing here: the no growth controversy, nuclear policy, and federal-state relationships.

No Growth

Ever since the Club of Rome study appeared, the growth versus no growth argument has raged. Those who fear the consequences of continued growth on what they see as our finite resources have arrayed themselves against those who see continued growth in output of material goods as an important societal goal, particularly for the poor.

Those who oppose economic growth know that such growth is at minimum more difficult and perhaps even impossible without new generating capacity. They also know that the procedures established for certifying such capacity are ideally suited to delay. It is not unfair to cite the reaction of the opponents of the Seabrook nuclear plant to their defeat in the endless EPA and other proceedings as support for the proposition that it is not due process they pursue, but an end to new construction. This does not mean that intervenors have not made valuable contributions by raising variants of the no growth argument: they did cause increased internalization of external costs; they did push the cause of economic pricing; they did urge a reconsideration of demand forecasting techniques to reflect elasticity responses. But these successes will not diminish this group's desire to resist economic growth: unhappy with such growth and unpersuaded of its importance in the fight to retain an upwardly mobile society, it will remain influential in national policymaking. And the general background color this issue provides to specific arguments will make it extraordinarily difficult to obtain licenses for new mines and plants.

Nuclear Policy[20]

Uncertainty about the future of nuclear power in the United States has risen in the wake of the accident at Three Mile Island. Using our electricity supply model,[21] we have made a preliminary assessment of the impacts, through the year 2000, of three alternative policies regarding the growth of nuclear power on utility costs, consumption of oil, emissions of sulfur dioxide, and the number of fatalities associated with the production and movement of fuel and generation of electricity. Each of the policies was evaluated under alternative assumptions about electricity growth, oil prices, nuclear costs, and limits on coal capacity additions. While it is not possible, or appropriate, to discuss all of the results here, I will summarize briefly some of our findings (see Table 3-1).[22]

By comparison with a policy in which nuclear power continues to grow, one that prohibits any new nuclear capacity beyond that currently on line would, in 2000:

1. Raise annual utility costs by $11.16 billion (expressed in 1977 dollars);

20. Because of the heightened interest in nuclear policy in light of Three Mile Island, I have included here our most recent assessment of the impacts of alternative nuclear policies.

21. The NERA electricity supply optimization model is designed to determine the effects of a wide variety of energy and environmental policies on the electric utility industry. For each of twenty-one demand regions, the demands for electricity and fuels are specified; supply schedules are determined for nineteen coal supply regions and for four oil and gas supply regions; in the case of uranium, a single national supply schedule is specified. Fuel and capital costs are determined and given various assumptions about environmental and other policies; optimal generating mixes are determined by regions. Fuller descriptions are available upon request.

22. The complete national and regional results are available upon request.

Table 3-1.   Assumptions Contained in NERA Energy Model.

Growth in Demand
  1977-1987: at 5 percent per year to 3,428 million megawatt hours
    in 1987
  1988-1997: at 3.9 percent per year to 5,026 million megawatt
    hours in 1997
Prices
  Low-sulfur oil and gas (1977 dollars)
  1977-1987: Increase 1.5 percent per year to $17.41 per barrel and
    $2.90 per Mcf
  1988-1997: Increase 1.5 percent per year until 1990 and then 4.0
    percent per year to $23.96 per barrel and $3.99 per
    Mcf by 1997
Costs
  Capital: Increase 1.5 percent per year in real terms, 1977-1997
  Coal:[a] Increase 1 percent per year in real terms, 1977-1997

---

[a]Coal prices may increase at a different rate from costs, the difference representing rents.

2. Increase utility oil consumption by 2.17 million barrels per day;
3. Increase sulfur dioxide emissions by 2.11 million tons annually and, consequently, offset a major part of the reduction in emissions expected to be achieved under the 1977 amendments to the Clean Air Act;
4. Raise by 22,000 the expected number of fatalities related to electricity generation over the 1979-2000 period.

The effects by 2000 under a more severe policy of nuclear curtailment that requires all existing nuclear capacity to be decommissioned by 1985 would:

1. Increase annual costs by $17.54 billion (over the shorter term such a policy could impose energy shortage costs as high as $25.87 billion a year);
2. Increase oil consumption by 2.75 million barrels per day;
3. Increase sulfur dioxide emissions by 2.56 million tons per annum;
4. Raise the expected number of fatalities associated with electricity generation by 30,100.

These results are based on the following key assumptions (summarized in Table 3-2): (1) Electricity demand will grow at an average annual rate of 3.6 percent between 1978 and 2000; (2) oil prices will remain at $15 per barrel (expressed in 1977 dollars) through 2000; and (3) nuclear costs will not rise significantly as a result of

Table 3-2. Projected Capacity Additions and Fuel Use.

	Coal	*Nuclear*	*Other*
		(Megawatts)	
Capacity			
1984–1987	99,800	54,100	8,000
1988–1997			
No new nuclear	301,000	0	102,300
Optimal mix	19,700	302,700	80,400

	Oil[a]	*Coal*[b]
	(Million barrels)	*(Million tons)*
Fuel		
1976	1,102	679
1987	223.4	1,184
1997		
No new nuclear	275.6	2,114
Optimal mix	201.5	1,298

Source: NERA electricity supply optimization model (see footnote 21).
[a]Consumption by utilities, including gas.
[b]Includes industrial steam coal.

Three Mile Island. Changes in these assumptions will alter the results discussed above. For example:

1. If growth should proceed at 4.5 rather than 3.6 percent annually, by 2000 the effect on annual costs, oil consumption, and emissions will be greater.
2. Should oil prices rise to $25 per barrel (in 1977 dollars) rather than remain at $15 per barrel, the impacts on annual costs, emissions, and the number of deaths will be greater, but the effects on oil consumption will drop sharply if coal can be substituted for oil.
3. If nuclear costs increase significantly as a result of Three Mile Island (but oil prices remain at $15 per barrel), the impacts on annual costs, oil consumption, emissions, and the number of fatalities will be reduced.

A recitation of the cost consequences of various policies does not, of course, resolve the issue. Society may decide that the costs of a no nuclear policy are more tolerable than the risks of having nuclear plants in optimal numbers. But it seems unlikely, at this

writing, that reasoned comparision of costs and benefits will ultimately decide the question.

Federal-State Relationships

There seems little question that electric utilities are caught up
in the competing jurisdictional claims of the state and federal governments. The conflict affects the energy industry with particular
force for three reasons peculiar to the production of energy.

First, the external costs associated with producing energy are
local; the benefits are regional and national. The external costs of
strip mining are borne by the local residents, to whom elected
state officials feel themselves responsible. The electrical energy
generated from that coal benefits residents of a much wider area.

Second, the costs of expanding our capacity to produce electrical
energy *are imposed now*; the benefits come *later*. This is perhaps
best exemplified by the "boom town" phenomenon—the social
costs of rapid growth are felt now; the revenues from taxes on
mining do not begin until extraction begins. Local governments
are more concerned with the "here and now" costs, federal officials
are a bit more inclined to give more weight to the longer run.

Third, national policies are geared[23] to making energy more
expensive, in order to encourage conservation and to discourage
imports of oil. But it is one thing to favor such a policy in a general
way; it is quite another to approve the specific, higher utility rates
that implement that policy. The federal government may support
the concept of replacement cost pricing of energy, but may find its
implementation on the national level politically difficult and its
reflection in state regulatory policies blurred by a host of local
considerations.

And always, the utilities are caught in the middle. National policy
calls for the pricing of energy at replacement cost; the state agencies
tell utilities to exclude CWIP from rate base—a position in which
still other federal agencies join. The states want coal transported to
utility boilers as cheaply as possible to keep electricity rates down;
the Department of Transportation wants coal-shipping rates set
high enough to subsidize other losing rail traffic. The EPA wants
clean air; local officials want nuclear plants located somewhere
else.[24]

Little wonder that utilities are confused and schizophrenic on

23. Not consistently.
24. The attitude of antinuclear groups in sparsely populated affluent suburbs
is very much like the attitude of those residents toward low income housing—
a wonderful idea, but somewhere else, please!

the subject of state versus federal control. On the one hand, they recognize that state commissions are inclined to a narrower view of the need for a long-term adequate supply of power, to a more niggardly attitude toward rate relief requests. They recognize that states like California can shortchange utilities, discourage expansion, and rely on beggar thy neighbor policies—relying on federal allocation of power from neighboring states in an emergency. On the other hand, utilities fear the remoteness of federal bureaucrats; the horrendous inefficiency of DOE (described by John Gardner as the product of the combined sciences of pediatrics and geriatrics—an agency senile at birth); the penchant of federal officials for social tinkering with, and eventual nationalization of, the industry.

The solution, partial at best, seems to be continuation of pressure by the federal government on state agencies to move in a direction indicated by national policy needs. Experience with the so-called rate structure reform issue is a case in point. Taking as an indication of federal policy needs the provisions of the utility section of the energy bill, we conducted a survey of state commissions to see if there was a tendency by the agencies to move in federally indicated directions before the passage of PURPA (Public Utilities Regulatory Policy Act) made it a bit less voluntary to do so.[25]

Of greatest interest is that part of the survey that dealt with state activity in the area of rate structures. Our survey offers no support for the extremist view that state regulation is characterized by pervasive inactivity in key areas. Take the question of declining block rates, covered in both the House- and Senate-passed bills. Thirty-one states have considered the cost justification of declining block rates; of those that have not, fourteen nevertheless have a policy of discouraging declining block rates; two others have officially approved flat rates; and two others are flattening rates, even if not as part of an explicit policy. Only Rhode Island is without a policy or direction in this area. Should the entire weight of the federal government be brought to bear in this area to whip Rhode Island into line? After all, our survey shows that Rhode Island is experimenting with time of day rates and had scheduled a generic hearing, so even there things are moving forward.

There has also been progress in other aspects of the cost-rate area. The House-passed bill provided that rates for each class shall

25. Every state commission was interviewed in depth; written summaries were sent to the respondents for verification or amendment; follow-up telephone calls cleared up remaining ambiguities. The response was complete—we have 100 percent coverage. Fifty states, Puerto Rico, and the District of Columbia were surveyed. Puerto Rico and Nebraska do not regulate electric utilities. The term "states," as used herein, means all entities except the latter two.

reflect "the costs of providing electric service" to that class. To do this, utilities must, of course, measure the costs of providing electric service to each class, which the bill also requires; utilities in some forty states were reported by their regulators to be doing that. The bill also stated as minimum standards the availability of rates based on time of day and seasonal cost differentials—points on which the Senate bill was in general agreement. In twenty-three states, utilities already measured time of day and/or seasonal cost differentials. In even more states—twenty-six in the case of time of day and forty-one in the case of seasonal rates—time differentiated rates were in effect, in some instances on an experimental basis.

So, too, with interruptible rates: thirty-one states had approved rates for interruptible service. Finally, let us look at master metering. The House bill would restrict its use; the practice was already being discouraged or reviewed in twenty-six states.

The question of efficiency is equally interesting. My own conversations with congressional staffers led me to feel that they view utilities as inefficient, in some undefined way, and see their regulators as willing to allow such inefficiency to be reflected in rates by following cost-plus policy. In this view, little regulatory attention is paid to the question of efficiency. The facts are at variance with this prejudice: forty-three states monitor their fuel and other adjustment clauses; twenty-five state commissions have initiated management audits, while in eight other states, companies have done the same; in only seventeen states have no such efficiency audits been undertaken.

These results, and other parts of our survey, support the view that state regulation is moving forward. But that does not dispose of the question of the appropriate role of the federal and state governments. For just as clear as the progress was its lack of universality: some states did not move forward. And much of the state-by-state progress was a response to the threat of federal action. Finally, the reaction of industry members to the EPRI report on rate structures leaves little doubt that a significant segment of the industry will continue to use pleas for "additional research" to avoid long overdue reforms. Hence, we did eventually see the passage of PURPA, relying on continued state regulation with a bit of a federal nudge.

So, where do we stand? Clearly, the federal government, responsible for defense and foreign policy, has an interest in utility rates. Certainly, the states have made substantial progress, without intervention. What is needed now is a subtle blending of government and private resources, each section performing the functions best suited to it. How can this be achieved?

First, further work will be needed to refine our body of knowledge and to fill in some of the details on the already legible map of rate reform. This the federal government is best able to finance and administer. Also, the Federal Energy Regulatory Commission can help by providing leadership by example. Where has it been in the fight for marginal cost pricing? The Department of Energy can help by making its expertise available to state commissions in rate and generic proceedings.

Second, some initiatives are needed from the utilities themselves. Perhaps an incentive to the innovators, provided by treating as "excess" only that revenue from marginal cost-based rates that exceeds allowed rates of return, would be helpful. Were this offered, the recalcitrants would at least be put on the defensive within their own companies.

Finally, and most crucially, an agency somewhere between the federal government and state regulators is needed. Perhaps the National Association of Regulatory Utility Commissioners (NARUC) can play this role. It is in a position to promulgate guidelines. If it is reluctant to do so, or if individual commissions choose to defy it, the case for federally imposed standards would be considerably strengthened.

How could NARUC, or some new agency, do this? It could adopt that part of the EPRI report that constitutes the "clear message screaming to be released," to use the words of one commentator. The economics of the industry combine with the need to adopt a rational approach to the use of our energy resources to dictate that time-related rates, based on marginal costs to the greatest extent feasible, be adopted. Consumers will then receive proper price signals and be able to make economic choices between use and conservation. That so many states are already moving forward without federal compulsion shows that the task is necessary and feasible.

If an absence of federal intervention is deemed so desirable, NARUC should see that the job is completed.[26] It should get guidelines requiring each commission to adopt marginal cost-based, time-differentiated rates or to prove them either administratively infeasible or cost-ineffective. Proof, of course, differs from assertion. It could perhaps be submitted to a NARUC blue ribbon panel drawn from people favorable to rate innovation but willing to entertain the possibility that specific exceptions might exist. This panel might include a regulator, a utility rate person, an EPRI representative, and some federal official.

Clearly, this is a middle ground. It does not leave the states free

26. There is some precedent for this sort of thing: separations in the telephone industry.

to ignore national policy, but it assigns a lesser role to the federal government than some seek for it. I reach the conclusion that some intermediate intervention is required with reluctance, and only because I am not certain that state commissions alone can handle the added responsibility. Their approach to rate relief requests has certainly left much to be desired. All too often, commissions have shied away from approving rate levels that would permit companies to finance adequate construction budgets without stockholder subsidization of ratepayers—known to some as selling stock below book and, to others, as confiscation. The subterfuge used is to approve rates of return on equity that seem adequate but will never actually be earned, to hope that managements will sell stock below book value if necessary, and to pray that all those demand projections being presented are wrong!

But I am not certain that the federal government would do any better. Its own proposals recklessly increase utility capital requirements, without addressing the industry's ability to finance those requirements; it contemplates huge increases in the use of coal that its own policies may make unavailable and increases in the use of nuclear power by plants that it will not license. Most important, the proponents of a large federal presence in rate structure revision are often completely insensitive to the danger of rate relief delay. So we are left with an imperfect situation—a need to make progress using a federal apparatus that threatens delay, a state apparatus reluctant to grant needed relief, and an industry not famous for rushing forward to embrace new ideas. But perhaps all is not lost: rate structures can be revised to comport with sound economic principles by continuing a federal role in research and rate case intervention, offering an incentive for utilities to move forward and developing a role for some agency between the federal and state levels as a promulgator of guidelines for the individual commissions.

CONCLUSION

Can utilities overcome the particular and general problems they face? If by "overcome" we mean "survive in the face of," the answer is "yes." If we mean provide economically optimal energy in amounts adequate by past standards, I doubt it. The best we can hope for is to approach some optimal level.

Price Regulation and Energy Policy

4

Philip Mause

Virtually all energy consumed in the U.S. economy, except for coal used directly by industry (roughly 4 quadrillion Btus [quads]), is either subject to price regulation itself or is converted into price-regulated electricity. Although the direct price regulation of petroleum is a relatively recent phenomenon, natural gas and electricity have long been (and promise long to be) subject to price regulation. At present, roughly 50 percent of the energy consumed in the United States is sold through price-regulated natural gas and electric utilities.[1] Most of this 50 percent is subject to price regulation by state utility commissions whose policies are affected by the uneven quality of their members, a lack of adequate funding, and a constant concern that certain policies may cause industrial users of energy to relocate. The *distribution* of natural gas and the *distribution* of electricity appear to be natural monopolies, and even if price regulation of natural gas at the wellhead is discontinued, gas pipeline and distribution utilities will continue to be regulated. An understanding of utility regulation and its peculiar impact upon energy supply and demand is therefore vital to any analysis of energy policy in the United States.

UTILITY REGULATION

Prices for regulated utilities are generally set in lengthy and complex proceedings designed to establish a price level that will provide the

1. Natural gas and electricity each account for roughly 20 quads of domestic energy consumption. Some 3 quads of natural gas are used to generate electricity.

utility a fair rate of return upon its rate base. The rate base is calculated with reference to the original cost of the utility's existing plant.[2]

A utility's decision to add capacity is generally based upon its projection of the demand for service at regulated prices. Unlike many other companies, utilities generally do not compare the profitability of an investment in increased capacity with other possible investments. Only when new capacity is completed and added to the rate base does its cost become relevant to prices charged the consumers of a utility's service.[3]

The requirement that utilities serve whatever demand materializes under rates set to provide a fair rate of return on their original investment in their existing plant has necessarily, since the early 1970s, been relaxed with respect to gas pipeline and distribution utilities. Price regulation of the production of natural gas has made it impossible to satisfy demand. However, as a practical matter, gas utilities generally behave, to the extent that they are able, as described above. That is, they tend to add new supply, regardless of its cost, as long as unsatisfied demand—at prices currently being charged—exists. The costs of adding the new supply are averaged in with other supply sources to determine the rates that will prevail once the new supply is brought on line.

In a period in which the costs of new supply greatly exceed the original costs used to establish the rate base, this system of regulation has some very important effects upon the demand for energy and upon the choice among energy supply sources. In general, it tends to produce energy consumption in excess of that which would exist were utility prices set with reference to marginal costs. It also biases energy supply investment in favor of investments that can be made by utilities and against those that can be substituted by consumers for utility service. It frequently will result in an investment

2. Original cost has not always enjoyed such overwhelming popularity as the benchmark for determining rate base (and therefore prices). Under Smythe v. Ames, 169 U.S. 466 (1898), rate base was determined with reference to "fair value" or "present cost of construction." This practice—which in an era of declining costs led to lower rates than would have existed under an "original cost" approach—proved to be difficult to administer because of the controversy connected with establishing the reproduction cost of existing facilities. See Alfred Kahn, *The Economics of Regulation* (New York: Wiley, 1970) vol. I, p. 39; and the Southwestern Bell Telephone case, 262 U.S. 276, 289–312 (Brandeis, J., dissenting). In Federal Power Commission v. Hope Natural Gas Co., 320 U.S. 591 (1944), the Supreme Court held that use of the "fair value" or reproduction cost standard was no longer required.

3. In some cases, a utility is allowed to include the costs of construction work in progress in its rate base. This reduces, but does not close, the gap between prices and replacement costs.

in the expansion of utility capacity, even when the same amount of energy could have been produced less expensively through conservation or energy supply alternatives produced through investments made by the consumers of a utility's service. This paper will examine how utility regulation has these effects, provide some examples of these effects, and review some policy measures that would alleviate such inefficiencies.

PRICE REGULATION IN AN ERA OF RISING COSTS

The system of utility price regulation and capacity expansion described above has generated increasing controversy in recent years. As capacity expansion has necessitated large rate increases, the rate-setting process has attracted more participants. Much of the controversy has been in connection with utility rate structure—reflecting a common-sense concern that declining block rates and volume discounts should be reexamined in an era of rising costs, as well as insights drawn from economics that indicate the desirability of basing prices upon marginal costs.

The issue has become more and more critical because of the relatively recent phenomenon of an enormous gap between utility rates and the marginal costs confronted by utilities.[4] This phenomenon has been dramatic in the past five years for three basic reasons:

1. For a variety of reasons, real construction costs have escalated so that the replacement cost of a utility's plant far exceeds its original cost. Because rates are based upon a fair rate of return on original cost, rates do not accurately reflect the costs of expanding capacity.
2. While the OPEC price action increased the market-clearing price for oil and gas, price regulation and the operation of long-term contracts have held oil and gas prices considerably below the cost of an extra barrel of oil to the U.S. economy.
3. Inflation itself can widen the gap between original cost-based rates and replacement costs by driving up the nominal cost of new capacity. In essence, utilities are not allowed to account for

4. One indication of the rapid change in the relationship between prices and marginal costs is the fact that Alfred Kahn's excellent work, *The Economics of Regulation*, treats the rate structure issue in a chapter entitled "Decreasing Costs and Price Discrimination" and focuses almost entirely upon the problem of setting rates for utilities whose marginal costs are below the level of rates necessary to ensure an adequate return on investment.

inflation by writing up their assets to the level of replacement costs.

As a result, gas utilities that charge industrial users $1.75 per million cubic feet (Mcf) are simultaneously adding new supply at costs of between $3.50 and $5.50 per Mcf, and electric utilities that charge industrial users 10 mills or less per kilowatt hour are busily adding capacity at costs of between 30 and 40 mills per kilowatt hour. Although it may mitigate the disruption associated with higher energy prices in the short term, this practice tends to produce a number of inefficient distortions in the economy:

1. The low rates encourage consumption, which can be supplied only at a higher replacement cost. Investments in energy conservation or substitute fuels, which may be cheaper than the costs of the new supplies a utility is adding, will not be undertaken if they are not also cheaper than the utility's rates.
2. Very expensive new sources of energy can be added without any real market test. Because their costs are "rolled in" with cheaper, older sources of energy, no consumer is confronted with a price that accurately reflects these costs.
3. Customer's choices among utilities—both regionally and by fuel type—are distorted. The utilities with the lowest rates have an advantage in competing for new hookups, while rational policy would dictate encouraging new hookups to utility systems with the lowest marginal costs.

AN EXAMPLE FROM THE NATURAL GAS INDUSTRY

To present these problems more clearly, a hypothetical example from the natural gas industry will be used. Pipeline A currently sells natural gas at a price of $1.60 per Mcf to four industrial users—B, C, D, and E. B would switch to number 6 oil if the price of gas reached $2.40 per Mcf. C is considering on-site intermediate Btu coal gasification and would install such a system if the price of natural gas reached $2.75. D has an aggressive energy manager and has been told that there are a whole series of energy conservation investments it can make; of course, the higher the price of gas, the more of these investments are economically justified. E wants to expand its operations and to increase its use of gas. E's processes are such that there is no real substitute for natural gas.[5]

5. Let us assume that the value of additional gas to E is $8 per Mcf.

Pipeline A is experiencing gradually decreasing deliveries of natural gas and proposes to build:

1. An SNG (petroleum gasification) plant that will produce gas at a cost of $4.25 per Mcf.
2. An LNG facility that will supply gas at a cost of $3.50 per Mcf (of which, roughly $1.50 per Mcf is paid to Algeria).
3. A coal gasification plant that will produce gas at a cost of $5.50 per Mcf.

Because A continues to have a considerable supply of cheap, regulated gas, the new sources can be added and averaged in with the existing supply without driving the price to B, C, D, and E above $2 Mcf.

Under current pricing policy, A will go forward and make the investments, even though gas could have been obtained much more cheaply through substitution or conservation than through the supply side investments. The cost of this distortion may be as high as $2-3 per Mcf. That is, without incremental pricing, there are likely to be ways of saving or substituting for gas at costs of $2 to $3 per Mcf below the costs of the new supply that is added instead.

On the other hand, if A is not allowed to make these investments in new supply sources, there will be insufficient gas to serve all of the demand that exists at a price of $1.60 per Mcf. A curtailment plan must then be administered. In all likelihood, customer E will not be allowed to increase its consumption of gas. B, C, D, and E may be ordered to cut back consumption in the same percentage of the amount they each used during a base period. Or possibly, B may be ordered off the system entirely because it has the cheapest alternative to gas. Of course, if E could somehow buy gas directly from A, B, C, or D at the marginal cost, he would be more than willing to do so. Unfortunately, the regulatory system generally does not allow this outcome to occur.

With respect to balance of payments and national security, the following patterns emerge:

1. Rolled-in pricing may keep a number of industrial users on gas, rather than oil. To the extent that the gas comes from domestic sources (i.e., coal gasification), rolled-in pricing may help reduce net imports. Unfortunately, it also keeps industrial users on high Btu gas rather than conserving or switching to intermediate Btu coal gasification. To the extent that the gas is derived from foreign sources (e.g., LNG), negative balance of payments and national security consequences may follow.

In general, holding down the price of oil and simultaneously exhorting regulators to reduce its consumption leads to the replacement of oil, not by its least expensive alternatives, but by those that have the greatest regulatory convenience. Rolling in LNG or SNG is convenient under the current regulatory system[6] and therefore becomes a key strategy for reducing oil imports.

2. The price we pay for LNG probably reflects the fact that LNG is rolled in. That is, if LNG were incrementally priced, it would not be able to compete with oil at current prices. This competitive pressure might well force the Algerians (and other suppliers) to take a smaller royalty.

3. Energy conservation—and substitute energy supply investments—are given inadequate incentives by the current pricing system.[7] All of the gas that could be saved by energy conservation investments could, of course, directly or indirectly replace oil in the energy market.

4. What gas is available is not rationally allocated among consumers. The curtailment process only crudely approximates economic efficiency in allocating an important resource.

5. Some serious long-term dangers to the utilities are created by rolled-in pricing.

The long-term dangers are best understood by following the example above into the future. Imagine that pipeline A continues to add expensive new supply projects. Meanwhile, its cheap, old gas is either no longer available or is provided only at a higher price. Not very gradually, pipeline A's price rises from $2 to $2.25, $2.50, and finally $3 per Mcf. Customers begin deserting the pipeline in favor of cheaper substitutes. An upward price spiral commences because reductions in sales force A to raise its prices in order to recover its fixed costs (the costs of the pipeline itself and the costs associated with LNG and coal gasification facilities) over lower sales volumes. Each price increase drives more customers off the pipeline and thereby necessitates further price increases. The rolled-in price reaches $3.25 per Mcf.

6. Perhaps too convenient. If gas from LNG and coal can be rolled in and sold below cost, so too can gas from naphtha and propane conversion plants.

7. For example, low and intermediate Btu coal gasification is generally suitable for direct, on-site industrial use but cannot produce pipeline quality gas that can be rolled in as high Btu gas can. It is placed at a competitive disadvantage by current pricing policies because the incentive for its development is the price that industrial users actually pay for natural gas—a price well below the costs of high Btu coal gasification. Thus, current pricing policy tends to distort the choice among coal gasification technologies and to create situations in which high Btu coal gasification facilities will be constructed even if the same amount of energy could have been produced much less expensively through low or intermediate Btu coal gasification.

Suddenly, substantial quantities of pipeline quality gas become available (from Mexico, geopressurized brine, tight sands, deep drilling in the Anadarko basin, Devonian shale, biomass, and so on) at a cost of $2.10 per Mcf. Pipeline A would like to buy some of this gas, but at a price of $3.25 per Mcf, the market for gas in its service territory is glutted. Customer B would switch from oil to gas, if he could buy the gas for less than $2.40 per Mcf, but in order to sell it to him, pipeline A would have to depart from rolled-in pricing and price the new gas incrementally. Such a result hardly seems "fair" to pipeline A's other customers, who are now paying $3.25 per Mcf.

ELECTRIC UTILITY RATES AND MARGINAL COSTS

Although it has attracted somewhat less attention, a similar set of problems occurs in connection with electricity. The problem is more confusing because of the greater complexity associated with allocating marginal costs correctly between peak and off-peak periods. In addition, some electric utilities have substantial excess capacity that tends to drive rates up, but may actually reduce marginal costs (by diminishing the need for new capacity). Still, there is general agreement that marginal costs are considerably in excess of rates currently being charged,[8] although the size of the gap varies markedly from system to system. Generally, four factors are at work:

1. *Fuel Costs*—The fuel costs experienced by electric utilities (and passed on to consumers) often are below the replacement cost of the fuel utilized. A number of electric utilities still burn low-cost (in the 70-90 cents per Mcf price range)[9] natural gas under long-term contracts. Oil is still price regulated, and thus the price a utility pays is below replacement cost.

---

8. National Economic Research Associates has studied the marginal costs of a number of electric utilities. These studies have generally resulted in findings that marginal costs substantially exceed current rates. There is, however, a great deal of variation in the pattern. In the Pacific Northwest, where prices are very low, reflecting the high percentage of hydroelectrical capacity, marginal costs may be 100 percent or more in excess of current prices. In other parts of the country, there is a smaller gap, and in some areas, prices may even exceed marginal costs. It is difficult—and probably not very useful—to estimate a weighted national average gap, but it is probably substantial.

9. As of February 1978, the national average cost of gas consumed by electric utilities was $1.35 per Mcf. In the South Atlantic region, the average price was 98.4 cents per Mcf—reflecting considerable gas consumption by Florida utilities under low cost, long-term contracts.

2. *Plant Construction Costs*—The rate base (and, thus, the rate level) of an electric utility is based on the original cost of its existing plant. New plant (especially new generating plant) costs considerably more than existing plant. Nuclear plants have experienced the most dramatic cost escalations, but there have been major increases in the cost of fossil fuel plants as well.[10]

3. *Changing Fuel Mix*—Certain utilities are in a transition with respect to their fuel mix. The most dramatic example of this is in the Pacific Northwest, where cheap hydroelectric power provides a large share of current consumption, and this guarantees that prices remain low. Expansion of capacity, however, will be in the form of fossil fuel or nuclear facilities—at a cost of roughly ten times the cost of electricity generated by hydroelectrical sources.[11]

4. *The Cost of Money*—The utilities borrowed heavily in the late forties and early fifties—usually with long-term (thirty year) bonds at low (2 to 4 percent) interest rates. This low-cost money helps hold down prices to consumers, while new facilities have to be financed at interest levels of between 8 and 10 percent.

The result is a considerable gap between current prices and replacement costs. There is enormous regional variation in prices,[12] some regional variation in replacement costs, and thus considerable variation in the size of the gap.

The incremental versus rolled-in pricing dilemma may be even more serious in the case of electricity than it is for gas. This is due to the enormous number of new hookups and appliance acquisitions and the growth in industrial and commerical use. This is probably most striking with respect to electric heating. While only 14 percent of the homes in the country had electric heat as of 1976, *half* of the new homes completed in 1977 had electric heat.[13] Consumer decisions to increase electricity consumption are likely to be prem-

10. The average cost (in mixed current dollars) per kW of nuclear generating capacity rose from $243 in 1972 to $527 in 1977. Coal-fired capacity costs rose from $170 to $308 in the same period.

11. Although hydroelectric energy accounted for 11 percent of the electricity generated in 1976, it is expected to decline to roughly 7 percent by 1986. Theodore J. Nagel, "Operating a Major Electric Utility Today," *Science* 201 (September 15, 1978): 985-92.

12. An industrial customer using 200,000 kWh with a maximum (peak) consumption of 500 kW paid (as of July 1978) a monthly bill of $14,634 in New York City, $7,039 in Detroit, $4,657 in Forth Worth, and $1,540 in Seattle.

13. See *Energy Daily*, September 14, 1978, p. 2. A number of these hookups are in the service territories of utilities that burn oil and/or gas. Many hookups of electric heating occur because of a ban on new hookups of gas. Our regulatory system is such that the alternative of allowing gas-burning electric utilities to sell the gas directly to new residential users in their own or other service territories is not systematically evaluated.

ised on current prices, which have little relationship to the costs of expanding the electrical system to serve such consumption. An example that may best illustrate the problem is the hypothetical city of Pompeii:

Electricity is supplied to residential users by a largely hydro-electrical system at a price of 15 mills per kWh, but expansion of the system will require the construction of nuclear reactors. The cost of the electricity generated in nuclear reactors and delivered to residential consumers will be 40 mills per kWh in current dollars.

A prospective homeowner, given current prices, will elect to install an electric resistance heating system. If the price of electricity were 2 cents per kWh, he would insulate his attic. If the price of electricity were 3 cents per kWh, he would install a heat pump.[14]

Obviously, there is a strong argument for some public policy measure that would correct the distortion and lead the prospective homeowner to behave as if he were confronting the marginal costs the system is experiencing. The policy choices appear to be:

1. Charge all electric users 4 cents per kWh.
2. Revise the rate structure and charge only new users 4 cents per kWh.
3. Mandate insulation and prohibit electric resistance heat through a regulatory program.
4. Allow the electric utility to help pay the costs of attic insulation and the heat pump system—perhaps by providing interest-free loans.[15]

The same pattern occurs with respect to the industrial use of electricity. One of the major impediments to the increased use of cogeneration is the fact that electricity is available at prices substantially below marginal cost, while the cogeneration facilities themselves must be constructed at marginal costs.

OIL PRICE REGULATION

The same pattern discussed above prevails with respect to petroleum. The distortions exist to the extent that entitlements have value—that is, to the extent that there is a gap between the average refiner

---

14. The heat pump has a higher first cost that is not justified at lower prices of electricity.

15. One utility in the Pacific Northwest is actually doing this, premised on the common-sense argument that insulation is cheaper than new generating capacity. See "Oregon Electric Consumers Flock to Utilities' Free Lunch," *Energy Daily*, September 1, 1978, p. 3.

acquisition cost and the cost of imports. The incentive to conserve or to develop alternatives at the point of end use is the price under regulation, a price below the marginal cost of additional consumption.

The Department of Energy has recently proposed to extend entitlement benefits to various synthetic substitutes for petroleum (oil shale, oil from biomass, coal liquefaction, for example).[16] This would provide incentives for the development of these petroleum substitutes equal to the benefits obtained by refiners who utilize OPEC oil.

SOLUTIONS

All of the solutions to the above dilemma that have been proposed fall into essentially four categories:

1. Raise the price of energy to all users to the marginal cost level;
2. Resolve the problem by revising rate structure to raise the price selectively to (a) the most price elastic users, (b) new users, (c) growing users, or (d) all users for use over a certain level;
3. Equalize the economic incentives for new supply and for conservation by allowing utilities to make investments in energy conservation; and
4. Require a variety of decisions to be made by regulatory action (after cost-benefit analysis based upon consideration of the marginal costs of energy) rather than by the marketplace.

Each proposed solution has its own combination of political, administrative, and legal pitfalls.

Raising the Price Level

If the first approach is to be adopted, then utilities will collect much more revenue. This revenue must be either kept by the utilities themselves or taxed away.[17]

One of the most intractable issues connected with raising prices to the level of marginal costs through energy taxes is the distribution of the revenue that would be raised under such a tax. Because the gap between marginal costs and prices varies in different regions of the country, the revenue produced by a tax designed to raise energy prices to the level of marginal costs would not be generated evenly throughout the country, but would tend to be produced dispropor-

16. See 43 F.R. 38844 (August 31, 1978).
17. For example, electric utilities could simply be allowed to use replacement cost accounting.

tionately from certain parts of the country. Unless the funds produced by the tax could be returned in a regional pattern similar to the pattern in which they were raised, a substantial interregional transfer of wealth could result.

Reforming Rate Structure

The second solution has a great deal of appeal. Total utility revenue would remain the same, but rate structure would be manipulated to produce correct price signals. In practice, however, revising rate structure to reflect marginal costs while the total revenue a utility is allowed to earn is based on original costs presents various problems. A variety of approaches have been proposed.

One frequent proposal is to reserve the cheap, "old" energy for certain customers (either all "old" customers or all residential customers) and to charge other customers the costs of new supply.[18] This, of course, fails to provide the favored customers with a marginal cost price signal—and actually holds their rates below the level they would have reached had rolled-in pricing been used. If a distinction is drawn between "old" and "new" customers, then a kind of "vintaging" of customers must take place, with each customer's bill becoming dependent upon the year in which he was hooked up. With respect to natural gas, the argument has been made that the customers who would otherwise have been curtailed should pay for expensive natural gas supplements, since they are the ones who benefit from them. This can become complicated, as curtailment varies from year to year because of the temperature-sensitive nature of the demand for gas, while most supplements involve capital-intensive projects requiring a long-term commitment rather than an annual search for purchasers. It has the advantage of subjecting expensive natural gas supplements to a market test.

Another approach is to tilt the rate structure so that all customers receive some small amount of service at a low price, but pay a price reflecting marginal costs in their "tail" block of consumption. For example, each customer could be provided with, say, 75 percent of his historic use (determined in some base period) at a low rate and charged a price reflecting marginal costs for use in excess of this amount. This would correctly signal customers concerning the cost—to the utility—of added consumption and the benefits of conservation. It would have to be implemented quickly or an incentive would be created to use more during the transitional years

18. This is required, by statute, with respect to sales made by the Bonneville Power Administration. The favored customers are municipalities and, indirectly, the largely residential and commerical load they serve.

so as to establish a higher historic use level.[19] The revenue stability of the utility would be threatened, since a warm winter or cool summer would drastically reduce most customers' tail block consumption and thereby reduce a utility's gross revenues.[20] An automatic adjustment clause could be designed to resolve this problem —for example, the size of each customer's block of cheap energy could be made subject to temperature adjustment (and, therefore, be smaller in a warm winter)—but this added complexity would, at least initially, provide a challenge both to the competence of many utility commissions and to the understanding of a utility's customers.

Another alternative would be to try to determine which customers' demand was least price-elastic and reduce their bills—the "inverse elasticity rule."[21] While theoretically attractive, this would add a new—and unwieldy—issue, price elasticity, to rate proceedings.

The entire issue is complicated, of course, by the potential for fuel switching and the concern that charging customers of one utility the marginal costs of service may cause an undesirable switch to another fuel—unless we are confident that all fuels are priced at marginal cost. This lends a "Catch-22" quality to efforts aimed at causing gas, for example, to be incrementally priced. Unless electricity and oil are also priced at marginal cost levels, such pricing may lead to undesirable fuel switching. This, of course, leads back to the old debate concerning the price of oil. If, given national security, balance of payments, and other considerations, oil is underpriced, then it is difficult—and maybe even dangerous—to price gas and electricity correctly.

This problem is most acute with respect to the industrial user of gas. Industrial gas users may have enormous coefficients of elasticity as the price of gas nears the price of oil. Of course, as noted above, rolled-in pricing does not really offer long-term protection from massive fuel switching either. The conclusion that, under either rolled-in or incremental pricing, massive fuel switching and the specter of a natural gas surplus side by side with increasing oil imports may be an inescapable danger has led to the convoluted formulations of the natural gas compromise. The solution adopted—to raise gas prices to levels just below those high enough to cause

19. If a period of time from the too remote past is selected for determining "base use," problems of fairness and efficiency could arise.

20. Because a utility's books are based on accountants' cost analysis, there would not be a corresponding reduction in the utility's costs—as reflected on its books—and the utility's net revenue could be impaired.

21. More accurately, the respective ratios of price to marginal cost (P-MC) /P for different customers—or groups of customers—would be inversely proportional to their respective elasticities of demand. See Kahn, *Economy of Regulation*, p. 144.

fuel switching—is probably a sensible one, if such levels can be correctly identified. Of course, this solution fails to subject expensive gas supplements to a market test. Even this defect could be cured by an ironclad decision rule not to add such supplements if their cost exceeded the cost of oil, but of course, the advocates of such supplements generally argue that one of their selling points is that the additional gas will reduce oil consumption—an implicit argument that oil is underpriced.

Utility commissions have attempted to attack these problems, and progress is likely to occur over time. Certainly, rate structure can be reformed to provide consumers with more rational price signals. On the other hand, the gap between marginal costs and current prices is in some cases so great, and the institutional problems so formidable, that a reliance upon rate reform alone to provide adequate incentives for conservation and alternative sources is probably misplaced.

Utility Investments

The lengthy debates over the role of utilities in solar energy, insulation, and other conservation or alternative sources have been clouded by rhetoric concerning "metering sunlight" and by a general suspicion of utilities. The reason for a governmental policy supporting such a role is relatively straightforward. Given the insufficient incentive provided by utility prices for such alternatives, some added incentive—either in the form of direct utility investment or a utility subsidy—is desirable to ensure that these alternatives are actually implemented when they are, in fact, less expensive than the expansion of a utility's conventional plant.[22]

Unfortunately, a number of problems arise:

1. Allowing a utility to subsidize some of its customers appears unfair to the others. Those who insulated last year at their own expense may not be impressed by arguments that the provision of free insulation to their neighbors is cheaper than the next nuclear power plant.
2. A utility arguably is unfairly advantaged in competing with a private contractor. This could be mitigated by requiring utilities to subcontract all work—but placing the power to select subcontractors in the hands of an already disliked utility may be difficult.

22. In terms of our example above, if an investment in insulation saves electricity at a lower cost than a nuclear power plant produces it, and yet current pricing policy blocks the investment in insulation, one would simply allow the utility to make an investment in insulation by subsidizing, in whole or in part, its installation.

3. Although this solution ensures that some measures will be taken when they are less expensive then expanding a utility's plant, others (e.g., turning down thermostats) will not be.

Regulation and Government Subsidy Aimed at Inducing Energy Conservation and Investments in Alternative Supply

Economic regulation tends to spread; there is no reason for this to be less true when regulation holds prices below marginal costs than when it artificially increases prices.[23] Appliance efficiency standards, building design standards, tax credits for solar installation, and even enforcement of thermostat turn-down rules all take on a different light in a world in which the price of energy is held below its marginal cost. Such measures are inexact, often perverse, usually incompetently and occasionally corruptly administered, frequently regressive with respect to income distribution, and costly to implement. In almost every respect, they are hopelessly inferior to the use of accurate prices as a means for inducing efficiency in the use of energy. The enthusiasm with which they have nevertheless been embraced by politicians of all ideologies may be an accurate index of our society's extreme reluctance to resolve the energy problem through the price mechanism.

CONCLUSION

The regulatory, rolled-in pricing phenomenon produces the distortions discussed above. It also has some other implications:

1. It probably adds stability to energy forecasting. The faster we grow into high-priced new sources of energy, the higher prices will rise due to the averaging in of more expensive new supplies. This price rise should, in turn, dampen demand. Forecasts based on pre-1970 data are likely to be useless because, before 1970, exactly the opposite relationship existed. That is, growth in consumption and the consequent capacity expansion generally lowered utility costs[24] and therefore resulted in price decreases. Growth in consumption and price reductions were mutually reinforcing.

23. See Kahn, *Economics of Regulation* vol. II, pp. 28–32, for a discussion of the tendency of regulation to spread when prices are held above marginal costs.

24. Between 1948 and 1968, the "heat rate" of electric utility plants (the fuel consumption per kWh) declined by 33 percent, and the real cost of plant per kilowatt of capacity declined. See M.J. Young, "Rate Reform: Outcome of New Economic Setting," *Energy User News*, September 25, 1978, p. 22.

2. When marginal costs go up suddenly (as they did in 1973), prices to ultimate consumers go up more slowly. Even after marginal costs stabilize (as they have in the oil market), consumer prices will continue a gradual increase if more and more " new supply" is averaged in. In a sense, consumer prices reverberate after marginal costs have stabilized.
3. The share of investment claimed by regulated utilities is larger than it would otherwise be because these utilities expand even when the markets they serve could be served more cheaply by substitutes. Thus, the "regulated" sector of our economy grows.
4. As long as there is a large gap between marginal costs and current prices, expansion in energy consumption is highly inflationary even if marginal costs remain stable. Expansion drives prices up by forcing the addition of new, expensive supply sources.

As long as roughly 50 percent of the energy utilized in our economy is sold through regulated utilities, any hope that a laissez-faire approach will produce economically optimal results is simply unrealistic. The distribution of electricity and the distribution of gas are natural monopolies[25] and will, in the foreseeable future, be regulated. The inexorable conclusion is that our society has to face an economically complex and politically distasteful set of choices.

In general, the gap between marginal costs and current prices may be politically impossible to close. Instead, a combination of efforts to revise rate structure to provide more accurate price signals to consumers and various regulatory measures will probably have to be undertaken. Active utility involvement in energy conservation and alternative energy supply investments, appliance efficiency standards, building standards, and mandatory industrial efficiency standards may all be necessary to ensure that those conservation investments which are less costly than new supply will actually be made.

APPENDIX

After this paper had been made available to the members of the study group and discussed, Kenneth Arrow raised a number of questions in a letter to Philip Mause and elicited a detailed response that adds to the original paper. Both the letter and the reply are hereafter reproduced, with permission of both writers.

---

25. The deregulation of natural gas production will ameliorate, but not resolve, the dilemma. Long-term contracts at low prices will still ensure that consumers do not confront the cost of new gas.

Letter from Kenneth J. Arrow[26]

I have read Philip Mause's first draft. While it is very well written and certainly lays out important issues, there are additional points on which I would welcome exposition.

The most important is a full discussion of what natural gas pricing is. I may be wrong, but it seems to be at three distinct levels: the wellhead price, the price of delivery by the pipeline to the local distributor and the price to the consumer. I badly need some full explanation of who determines which of these prices and what the criteria are. Does the regulation of price charged by the pipeline to the local distributor influence greatly the pattern of pricing by the local distributor to individual consumers?

Also, while there is some discussion of charging different prices to new customers as opposed to old (which I guess is called "incremental" pricing, though Mause does not use that term) and also of lifeline rates and other variations in price structure, I would welcome a little more discussion of the economic effects of these. For example, it is true that if we *assume* historical cost pricing, then anything which slows down the rate of expansion keeps prices down. Hence, the rates should be highest for those with the most elastic demand, which resembles the Ramsey rule.

There are a few specific points that should be conveyed to him. There is repeated emphasis on the "second-best" problem, that the discrepancy between the marginal cost and price of oil affects other margins. But this can be overdone. The discrepancy between the roll-in price of oil and the world price is after all only about ten percent. This is probably much less than the discrepancy between marginal cost and the price in electricity and perhaps also in gas, though I know less about the latter. I think the oil problem has been overweighted in this discussion.

The examples on pages 148–51 leave me somewhat uneasy. When the cheaper gas (at $2.10 for Mcf) becomes available, why can't the pipeline go back to lower pricing. Is the problem that they have long term contracts with the more expensive gas? In any case to the extent that the price is higher because the throughput is below capacity, they certainly could lower prices to fill it up. "Promotional" pricing is after all very well known.

On page 152, in referring to the cost of money, I may be mistaken but I thought that the total return allowed was the current market rate of return multiplied by the rate base or is that true only of the

26. At the time of writing, Kenneth J. Arrow was James Bryant Conant University Professor at Harvard University.

equity component? The point has to do with whether low interest rates in the past keep prices down now; of course low structure of costs certainly do that.

On pages 154-55 Mause refers to the fact that marginal cost pricing will cause windfall profits to electric generating plants. He notes that the tax scheme will not be equally fair in all parts of the country but after all electricity regulation is a local matter and why not simply let the localities do their own taxing?

I hope you can pass these comments on to Mause.

Author's Reply (November 12, 1978)

1. In general, there are three levels of natural gas price regulation. The first is wellhead price regulation—the price producers charge to interstate pipelines. This is controlled by the Federal Energy Regulatory Commission and has been the primary issue of interest with respect to natural gas regulation over the years. The second level is the rates charged by pipelines to local distribution utilities. These rates are also controlled by the Federal Energy Regulatory Commission. Finally, the rates charged by distribution utilities to individual customers are generally regulated at the state level. There are some important exceptions to this pattern. For example, many large industrial users buy directly from interstate pipelines and, therefore, are not subject to any form of state price regulation.

At each step of the process, the costs of the recipient of the gas are the prices set by the regulatory agency that controls the sales. Thus, a distribution utility's cost structure is largely controlled by the rate structure set by the Federal Energy Regulatory Commission with respect to sales by pipelines to that distribution utility. As a general rule, gas is rolled in—that is, a distribution utility is charged a commodity price that reflects the average cost of all of its pipeline's gas supplies. The costs of the transmission and distribution systems are also allocated—again, usually on the basis of embedded rather than marginal costs.[27] There are some exceptions, but as a general result, distribution utilities confront a set of costs from pipeline utilities that do not accurately reflect the marginal costs experienced by the pipelines themselves. This is one of the serious impediments to achieving reform in rate structure.

2. There are a number of approaches to "incremental" or "marginal cost" pricing. Unfortunately, each of them involves various administrative—and in some cases, legal—difficulties. One

27. Of course, in a transmission system with chronic excess capacity, this results in charges in excess of the marginal cost of increased use of the system—which may be close to zero.

approach is to differentiate old and new customers. In many states this might be illegal. Another approach would be to give each customer a percentage of historic use at a low price and to charge a higher price for use in excess of that percentage. This presents certain administrative problems. It was the approach adopted by the Wisconsin Public Service Commission in the recent Wisconsin Power and Light order—with respect to large customers. Yet another approach would be to invert the rate structure. This presents difficulties because of varying amounts of use by different customers. Some customers would find that their marginal consumption fell within the low cost initial blocks of an inverted rate structure and would, therefore, have a reduced incentive to conserve gas under an inverted rate structure.

It is probably impossible to identify elasticity of demand on a customer-by-customer basis. There have been some studies that have attempted to do it with respect to different classes of customers (industrial, commercial, and residential), but even in this area, the quality of the data is very bad because they were generated in periods of stable or declining energy price levels. I think the recent Wisconsin order illustrates the opportunities—and the pitfalls—in the way of actual implementation of incremental cost pricing at the state level. Of course, these difficulties are more extreme when the divergence between marginal costs and embedded costs is larger.

3. Although at the current time the gap between the world oil price and the crude oil acquisition cost to American refineries is not great, the important point to recognize is that our regulatory structure is such that, if there is a rapid increase in the world oil price, the gap will become greater. This prospect, I would think, should be considered in any intermediate term view of the energy problem. For example, if there is a rapid increase in the world's oil price in the mid-1980s, what kind of regulatory system do we want to have in place, in advance, to allow us to respond to that world oil price increase? Is the current regulatory structure adequate for anticipated future supply and price patterns, or should it be replaced? Would a modest tax on oil imposed now allow us to cushion the economy against a future increase in the world oil price? It has taken natural gas prices five years to come even close to catching up to the oil price increase that occurred in 1973–1974; if there is another dramatic price increase, do we want to build in a mechanism that would allow natural gas prices to catch up more quickly—or is the pattern we have just lived through satisfactory?

Another way to look at this is to try to determine what policy would be desirable in the event of a rapid increase in the world oil price and then to analyze current policies to determine whether, as a matter of practical politics, they are likely to result in the adoption of sound policy in the event of a rapid price increase.

4. A separate problem is created by our national schizophrenia with respect to oil imports. If the reduction of imports is popularly perceived as desirable, but we are unwilling to raise the price of oil to encourage alternatives, then a whole series of political pressures build up to either compel or subsidize the use of alternatives. Because no one has decided what it is worth to reduce oil imports, interest groups can have a field day advocating subsidies and regulations, using the politically incontrovertible argument that it is in the national interest to reduce oil imports. A veritable cornucopia of subsidies for Amtrak, home insulation, coal gasification, sociological studies of the effects of lifestyle on energy consumption, and endlessly supported research and development opens up as soon as it is generally agreed that there is a national interest in reducing oil imports that is not reflected in the price charged to users in the United States. On the other side, all sorts of mandatory regulatory schemes—which would normally be viewed as unacceptable government interference—suddenly become palatable when they can be justified as reducing oil imports. For example, ten years ago, a very low probability would have been assigned to the enactment of legislation mandating the end of traditional full size automobiles, much less its being signed into law by a Republican president from Michigan.

Some of these regulatory measures and subsidies please some of us for other reasons; we may perceive certain types of consumption as garish or "wasteful" or may feel that the environmental externalities connected with energy consumption justify regulations to reduce its level. Americans have never been shy about trying to legislate their moral principles for the edification of those in the population who are not sufficiently enlightened to adopt them voluntarily.

Much as the Cold War was used to justify student loans, highway construction, foreign aid, physical fitness, fallout shelters, and also some nasty regulatory measures, the "energy crisis" can be used to justify government measures that would normally be completely unacceptable. There is no lack of pressure groups able to devise and forcefully advocate such measures; resistance is much more difficult when the need for government action can be justified under the rubric of a generalized need to reduce oil imports at any cost.

The policies that are developed in response to these pressures will not be the result of any intelligent overview of our energy situation nor will they reflect the efficiencies of a free marketplace. Instead, they will be the result of political pulling and hauling by various pressure groups. If the forces behind high Btu coal gasification are strong enough, one form or another of subsidy will be arranged "in the national interest," even if the energy output costs the equivalent of $35 per barrel of oil. Utilities will be ordered to stop burning oil, not because that is necessarily a sensible policy, but because they are large and unpopular and can easily pass on the costs of conversion. A possible result may be an unmanageable glut in the world residual oil market. Our refusal to ship Alaskan oil to Japan is probably another example of various pressure groups banding together, wrapping themselves in the American flag, and successfully lobbying for an uneconomic policy that is implemented because of a general perception that "it is in the national interest to reduce oil imports." A network of subsidies and regulations will be created—and they will all develop constituencies that will make policy change very difficult.

My modest suggestion is that America would be a better place in which to live if oil were taxed and it was agreed that the tax was the only government policy to reduce oil imports. This would reduce government interference in the marketplace and tend to assure that those alternatives to oil that are least expensive would be developed first.

5. Of course, in the hypothetical example, the rational solution in a system with excess transmission capacity and the prospect of $2.10 per mcf gas would be to charge the most elastic users a price, probably slightly above $2.10. The difficulty is that the regulatory system does not always allow this to occur—for a variety of reasons. One of them is that the more expensive supplies may be under "take or pay" long-term contracts. Another institutional problem is that liquefied natural gas, synthetic natural gas, and coal gasification facilities are usually owned by the pipeline companies themselves, whereas the $2.10 gas might be purchased from an independent producer. The pipelines have a strong incentive to use the facilities that they actually own and to allow those facilities to be depreciated. There was a recent investigation of the Columbia Gas Transmission Company in which it was alleged that part of the reason for the shortage of gas in the winter of 1976 was that Columbia refused to take gas from producers in Texas, so that it could operate its own SNG plant in Green Springs, Ohio. The gas from the SNG plant cost roughly three times what the Texas production would have cost, but from the accounting perspective of the transmission company may have been an advantageous choice. Another problem is illustrated by the recent difficulties of the Pacific Gas and Electric Company in California. Pacific Gas and Electric can receive some domestic gas at roughly $1.80, but is also locked into long-term LNG and Canadian

gas contracts. The California commission has not allowed Pacific Gas and Electric to sell the $1.80 gas to customers capable of fuel switching. The Wisconsin order embodies what I think is an intelligent solution to this problem by allowing the gas company to conduct an auction. My confidence that other state commissions will show similar enlightenment is not high.

6. A utility's rate of return is based upon the weighted average of the costs of its various sources of financing. It is true that the rate of return on common equity reflects current money market conditions; but the overall rate of return permitted is a weighted average of the return on equity and the actual cost of debt. The debt portion of the rate of return is generally determined by calculating the weighted average interest rate for all outstanding bonds that the utility has issued. If the utility has issued long-term low interest bonds in the past, this tends to hold down the cost of debt and to reduce the overall rate of return that the utility is permitted to earn on its rate base. An admittedly oversimplified example will illustrate this.

Assume that a utility has issued long-term bonds, some at 5 percent and some at 7 percent; in recent years, interest rates have increased to 10 percent. The utility commission has allowed the utility a 14 percent rate of return on common equity to reflect current market conditions. As illustrated in Table 4-1, the overall rate of return that the utility will be allowed to earn will be 9.2 percent—assuming the capital structure set forth in Table 4-1. On the other hand, the cost of new capital, even assuming the same relative mix of funding sources, may be considerably higher—as illustrated by Table 4-2. It is this cost of new capital that must be incurred by any consumer of electricity who considers making a new investment in equipment that may reduce his consumption of electricity (e.g., cogeneration, heat recuperators, more efficient motors).

Table 4-1. Capital Structure and Rate of Return.

	Capital Ratio	Annual Cost Rate (percent)	Weighted Cost (percent)
Long-term Debt at 5 percent	25	5	1.25
Long-term Debt at 7 percent	25	7	1.75
Preferred Equity at 8 percent	10	8	0.80
Short-term Debt at 10 percent	5	10	0.50
Common Equity at 14 percent	35	14	4.9
	100		9.2

Table 4-2. Cost of New Capital.

	Capital Ratio	Annual Cost Rate (percent)	Weighted Cost (percent)
Long-term Debt at 10 percent	50	10	5.0
Preferred Equity at 11 percent	10	11	1.1
Short-term Debt at 10 percent	5	10	0.5
Common Equity at 14 percent	35	14	4.9
			11.4

7. Allowing localities to manage the gap between marginal cost prices and current revenue requirements probably could work in those areas in which state regulatory authorities set utility rates. However, with respect to both the Bonneville Power System and the Tennessee Valley Authority, the federal government's role looms large, and it is unlikely that the state of Tennessee, for example, could tax TVA electricity and retain the revenue itself without some changes in federal legislation. Perversely enough, these are the very two systems in which the gap between marginal costs and current prices is probably the greatest, largely because they are both hydro-electrical systems in the process of a transition to a greater percentage of coal and nuclear generating capacity. Another argument for federal involvement is the concern about "industrial blackmail" often presented in state commission proceedings. That is, industries threaten to leave states that raise industrial rates. Of course, a state could rebate the taxes it earned on electricity through a reduction in corporate income or property taxes and thereby attract some corporations that would not have entered the state had it simply refrained from taxing electricity. It is likely that the state would attract a less energy-intensive mix of industry, and if marginal costs are higher than embedded costs, this might be desirable. Very few state regulators or politicians see the logic of this argument, however, and plant closings tend to be more newsworthy than plant openings. Whether the political impact of "industrial blackmail" is sufficient to justify some larger federal role in this area is very questionable. On the other hand, it is part of the dynamic of the rate-setting process that has to be borne in mind in analyzing the likelihood that rates will actually be set at marginal cost through local taxation.

Institutional Obstacles to Industrial Cogeneration

Norman L. Dean

    With all the effort being devoted to increasing the efficiency of electric power production through development of fuel cells, magnetohydrodynamic generators, and solar collectors, it comes as a surprise to most people to hear that the nation already possesses a method for generating electricity that can produce a kilowatt hour (kWh) of electricity using one-half to two-thirds the fuel required by the most efficient utility power stations now in operation. Even more surprising is the fact that this method uses proven technologies, is economic, and is in widespread use in other industrialized nations, but provides less than 5 percent of U.S. electricity consumption. This method is known as cogeneration, and it involves simply the sequential generation of industrial process steam or heat and electricity from the same primary fuel source.

    The development of cogeneration has been hindered in the United States by numerous institutional barriers. This paper outlines those barriers and examines what can be and is being done to overcome them. The first sections of the chapter describe the cogeneration concept, its technologies, and its fuel-saving and other advantages. The relatively long center section of the chapter outlines the many institutional barriers to cogeneration and suggests several approaches for lowering them. The final sections review the ongoing federal and state policy initiatives for encouraging the concept and suggest the need to shift the focus of the present policy debate.

THE COGENERATION CONCEPT

Cogeneration saves fuel by integrating two inherently wasteful processes—industrial process steam generation and central station utility electric power production. Industry uses roughly one-seventh of the nation's energy consumption to generate steam for process use. Most of that steam is required at temperatures of less than 400°F, in a process that has been aptly described as the thermodynamic equivalent of "cutting butter with a chain saw." At the same time, electric utility plants are discharging about one-fifth of the nation's energy consumption into the environment in the form of "waste heat."[1] It makes considerably more sense to generate both of these together—using the high thermodynamic potential of fossil fuel combustion to first generate electricity and then employing the remaining heat as industrial process steam.

Cogeneration can take one of two forms: electricity can be generated as a by-product of industrial processes, or industrial process steam (or heat) can be generated as a by-product of electricity production. This latter approach, which typically involves the siting of industrial plants adjacent to central station utility plants, is less appealing for both physical and practical reasons. Utility power plants now discharge their waste heat at about 100°F. To be most useful in industrial processes, utility operations would have to be modified to produce heat at 200–400°F. This would reduce the electrical output and could lead to an overall loss in efficiency unless essentially all of the utility's waste heat were used by industry.[2] Only in rare cases is this likely to be feasible in view of the many practical difficulties associated with co-siting industries and utilities. The two would have to be located very close together since it is costly and inefficient to ship steam over long distances. Space limitations and environmental concerns make it increasingly impossible or inadvisable to clump several large facilities together on a single site. Moreover, utilities and industries have considerably different planning horizons and construction lead times, which makes cooperation extremely difficult. In view of these many difficulties, this chapter focuses on the generation of power as a by-product of industrial operations. This approach will be referred

1. Robert H. Williams, *Industrial Cogeneration* (Princeton, N.J.: Center for Environmental Studies of Princeton University, 1978), p. 2.
2. Marc Ross and Robert Williams, *Assessing the Potential for Fuel Conservation* (Albany, N.Y.: Institute of Policy Alternatives, 1975), p. 15.

to as industrial cogeneration. The use of the term industrial cogeneration is not intended to suggest that utilities will have no role in the process. Indeed, utilities are likely to be heavily involved—as potential owners of the equipment, as suppliers of backup electricity, or as purchasers or at least distributors of much of the power produced.

THE TECHNOLOGY OF
INDUSTRIAL COGENERATION

Industrial cogeneration can take place using either "topping" or "bottoming" cycles. These terms are used to describe the point in the process at which electricity is generated. In the topping cycles electricity is generated first, with the remaining heat used in an industrial process. In the bottoming cycles the fuel is first used in an industrial process, with the remaining heat being then used to generate electricity. With the bottoming cycles an industry typically has no additional fuel costs. It recovers the "free" waste heat from a process unit (such as a cement kiln) and uses that to generate power. In the case of the topping cycles, an industry burns a sufficient additional amount of fuel to generate power and to leave enough leftover waste heat for its process needs. Over 90 percent of the fuel-saving potential of cogeneration is associated with the topping cycles.

Cogeneration topping cycles can use steam turbines, gas turbines, or diesel engines to generate electricity. The gas turbine and diesel engine cycles produce considerably more electricity per unit of industrial process steam and thus offer the greatest fuel-saving potential. They are incapable, however, of burning coal. This suggests that one obvious strategy for increasing the fuel-saving potential is the development of coal-burning engines with a high ratio of electric to steam (or heat) output. Possible candidates include pressurized fluidized bed combustors or coal-fired gas turbines.

In view of the fact that the only coal-burning cogeneration system presently available has a relatively low energy-saving potential, it may be advisable either to pace coal conversion to take advantage of the development of new technology or to exempt from coal conversion requirements those industries that are willing to cogenerate using either oil- or gas-fired diesel or gas turbine cogeneration systems.

FUEL-SAVING POTENTIAL OF
INDUSTRIAL COGENERATION

A vigorous debate now rages as to the overall short-term potential for industrial cogeneration. The various studies of the "economic" potential for cogeneration in 1985 have produced estimates that range from 20 to 260 gigawatt electric (GWe) of central station generating capacity that could be displaced by cogeneration capacity.[3] This means that by 1985 anywhere from 20 to over 250 central station power plants could be replaced by cogeneration, with a resultant fuel savings of between 200,000 and 2.5 million barrels of oil equivalent per day. These widely varying estimates are the result of different assumptions as to technologies, costs, the relationship of industrial facilities to the existing utility grids, taxes, and laws and regulations. All of the studies are conservative in the sense that they employ estimates of average rather than long-run incremental electric power costs.

What is the long-run potential for cogeneration? Few thoughtful estimates have been made. Robert Williams of Princeton University estimates the overall "technical" potential for cogeneration in the year 2000 at 1,000 GWe with a practical potential of 208 GWe of equivalent central station generating capacity. If this practical potential were achieved, the nation would save over 2 million barrels of oil equivalent per day.[4]

ADVANTAGES OF COGENERATION

Aside from its enormous fuel-saving potential, industrial cogeneration has several other notable advantages:

- *Capital Savings*—Since industry already needs much of the steam boilers, piping, and other equipment that is required to generate power, cogeneration can substantially reduce the amount of capital required to generate electricity.
- *Reduced Electricity Rates*—The reduced fuel and capital requirements of cogeneration can reduce the cost of power to consumers.

3. Williams, p. 35.
4. Ibid. pp. 70–75. The estimate of the maximum technical potential assumes that all industrial process steam would be associated with diesel cogeneration units. The estimate of practical potential assumes, among other things, that 45 percent of all process steam capacity in the United States will be associated with cogeneration capacity using the following mix of technologies—20 percent coal-fired steam turbines, 15 percent coal-fired fluidized bed combustors used with gas turbines and gas-steam turbine cycles, 5 percent oil-fired gas turbines and gas-steam turbine cycles, and 5 percent oil-fired diesels.

- *Reduced Environmental Damage*—Cogeneration can reduce the discharge of waste heat by power plants and can reduce the discharge of air pollutants in proportion to the reduction in fuel consumption.
- *Increased System Reliability*—Cogeneration's reliance on a large number of relatively small generators could reduce the probability that large portions of the power system will fail simultaneously. Consequently, it could reduce the amount of "spinning reserves" and reserve margins needed by the utility system.
- *Improved Ability to Adjust to Changes in Demand*—Since a cogeneration facility can be brought on line in less than four years compared with a typical lead time of from eight to ten years for central station generating plants, reliance on cogeneration can increase the nation's flexibility to respond to unexpected changes in demand and can reduce reliance on historically unreliable long-range demand forecasts.

INSTITUTIONAL BARRIERS TO IMPLEMENTATION

Despite these many advantages, cogeneration continues to provide only a small fraction of the nation's electric power. This is due mainly to a large number of institutional barriers that are arrayed against the concept. These can be roughly divided into three types—attitudinal barriers, economic barriers, and regulatory barriers. Naturally, these barriers are interrelated—attitudes affect the exercise of regulatory authority, many of the relevant costs are controlled by regulatory policies, and economics clearly affects attitudes. However, this chapter will treat each separately.

As can be seen, many of these barriers arise out of the need of a cogeneration facility to be connected to existing power grids. Interconnection is required to enable the cogenerator to obtain power when its facility is out of service for repair or routine maintenance or to enable a cogenerator to sell any power it generates in excess of its own needs.[5]

Attitudinal Barriers

The most nebulous but in many ways the most important barriers to cogeneration involve people's attitudes toward the concept and

5. It is estimated that it is technically possible for the petroleum refining, pulp and paper, and chemical industries to generate over eleven, four, and three times their on-site energy needs respectively. S.E. Nydick, *A Study of Inplant Generation in the Chemical, Petroleum Refining and Paper and Pulp Industries* (Cambridge, Mass.: Thermo Electron Corporation, 1976).

toward electric power generation in general. Attitudes influence not only how we act but how we think about issues. In the case of cogeneration, our general view of power production has encouraged us to frame issues in ways that have ignored cogeneration. For many years the common view of electric power production has been that it must necessarily be centered in large central station power plants owned by large publicly controlled monopolies that are interconnected in very large power grids. This view has made it difficult to ask questions that might provide answers favorable to cogeneration: Should there be competition in the generation of electric power? What types of new institutional arrangements can be designed to accommodate privately controlled, dispersed power generation? What equipment needs to be developed to enable small power producers to function efficiently? By failing to ask such questions, we have failed to devote effort to solving many of the problems that now stand in the way of cogeneration.

Utility Attitudes.   It is difficult to generalize about the attitudes of utilities toward cogeneration. Throughout the 1960s and early 1970s they actively opposed privately based power generation. For example, one of the nation's largest utilities conducted regular surveys of "competitive threats" from private power generators. Southern California Edison (SCE) included a provision in its rate schedules for large industrial users that prohibited cogeneration. The provision stated that:

> A ten-year requirements contract will be required for service under this schedule. A ten-year requirements contract is one in which the customer agrees to continue, during the term of the contract, to obtain from the utility all of the electrical energy needed to supply all of his electric utilization facilities existing at the commencement of the contract and all replacements, substitutions, and additions, at the premises served, made by the customer during the term of the contract. . . .[6]

Recently, however, SCE and others have begun to cooperate with industrial cogeneration projects. Many utility executives are still openly skeptical of the cogeneration concept. It is hard to predict how utilities will react to cogeneration in the next several years, although several factors appear to be encouraging cooperation. Cogeneration can in some instances assist financially troubled util-

---

6. Southern California Edison Company, *Schedule No. A-8, General Service Large*, California Public Utilities Commission Sheet No. 4724-E (October 13, 1976). This schedule has been replaced by schedule TOU-8.

ities in increasing their generating capacity without increasing their debt. It may provide a way around environmental and siting difficulties and offer a quick way of responding to changes in demand. On the other hand, when cogeneration equipment is owned by private industry, it adds nothing to the utility's rate base and thus nothing to the utility's permitted return. Privately based cogeneration may also be opposed by utilities that fear a loss in status or are unconvinced that industrial power can provide reliable service to the public. Finally, cogeneration is likely to be opposed or at least not supported in the next decade by many utilities that are faced with large reserves of excess capacity.

Industrial Management's Attitudes. Industry's interest in cogeneration has been increasing. In the past, industrial managers were not enthusiastic about cogeneration. Many took the position that "we are in the business of manufacturing widgets, not electric power." This resistance was probably due largely to the low cost of alternative power, to reports of industry problems in operating and maintaining generating equipment, to general uncertainty over future energy prices and policies, and to concern over the technical and economic risks associated with private power generation. Recently, industrial skepticism has appeared to fade as companies such as Dow Chemical have advertised their success with cogeneration.

Economic Barriers

Naturally, no industry or utility will participate in a cogeneration venture if it is unprofitable to do so. The major determinant of the profitability of cogeneration is the level of utility rates. In addition, an industry will invest in cogeneration only if the project meets its financial criteria. The setting of utility rates and industrial investment criteria have both discouraged cogeneration.

Utility Rates. The economic viability of cogeneration projects has been adversely affected by the rates at which utilities normally sell power to industry, the rates at which utilities sell backup or standby power to industry, and the rates that utilities are willing to pay for power generated by private parties.

Normal Industrial Rates. By charging average rather than long-run incremental costs, utilities have been providing misleading price signals to industry as to the value of cogeneration. An industry will not cogenerate at a cost of 2.5 cents/kWh if it can buy power from the utility at its average cost of 2.1 cents/kWh. The industry has no way of seeing (and no incentive to act even if it could see) that the cost to the utility of generating power from new power plants is over 3 cents/kWh.

Rates for Standby Power.   Industry has been discouraged from using utilities for standby power because demand charges, so-called ratchet rates, and special standby assessments make power that is used only occasionally several times more expensive than regular industrial rates.[7]

Standby rates are economically justified to compensate utilities for the cost of equipment that must be used to serve customers that demand power only occasionally. But present standby rates are obviously not pegged to the real cost of service to utilities since they do not take into account when the standby service is demanded. There is no economic justification for an industry to pay an additional standby charge if it demands power when the utility has generating equipment sitting idle. In general, standby rates need to be reformed consistent with the following principles:

1. Standby rates should be based on probabilistic analyses of when and where cogeneration facilities will require service. They should not be calculated on the assumption that all cogeneration facilities in an area will fail simultaneously.
2. Standby rates should be based on time of use pricing principles. Charges should vary with the time of day and the season of the year, since cogeneration standby service will require a utility to maintain additional capacity only when the use of that standby service corresponds to the utility's peak demand period.[8]

Two California utilities have recently reformed their standby service rates. Southern California Edison is offering an interruptible time of use rate schedule that allows cogenerators to obtain standby service on an interruptible basis at lower rates than regular standby. Pacific Gas and Electric Company is offering a standby schedule that provides different seasonal capacity charges, offers lower rates

7. A demand charge is a fee assessed an industry for the maximum amount of power that the industry used during the monthly billing period, usually measured as the highest level of consumption during any fifteen minute interval in the billing period. Ratchet charges carry over the demand charge into future months. Standby assessments are special charges for power that is demanded only occasionally.

8. These principles are suggested and discussed in F.X. Murray, *Where We Agree: The Report of the National Coal Policy Project*, vol. 1 (Boulder, Colo.: Westview Press, 1978), pp. 228-32.

for standby taken off-peak, and grants customers allowances for the reliability of their equipment and for standby taken on a scheduled basis.[9]

Rates for Excess Industrial Power. Utilities have traditionally offered minimal rates for power sold to them by industry. The Stauffer Chemical Company, for example, recently approached the Pacific Gas and Electric Company with an offer to sell power it was producing by using waste heat from a sulfuric acid plant. PG&E offered first to buy the power at 0.2 cents/kWh. After some negotiations it offered 0.3 cents/kWh and finally 1.4 cents/kWh. This compares with the company's present generating costs of about 3–3.6 cents/kWh for oil-fired generators and 2.4 cents/kWh for nuclear generators.[10] In general, utilities have been willing, when pushed, to pay an industry for the utilities' forgone fuel costs but not for any portion of their capital costs. The guiding principle for the purchase of industrial power, however, should be that the utility should offer to purchase "firm power" at a price equal to the costs that the utility would incur by generating additional amounts of electricity at that time of day and season of the year. If the use of cogenerated power saves the utility from having to build additional power plants or other equipment, then the rates paid to the industry should be appropriately higher. "Dump power" should be purchased by the utility at its running cost for that time of day and year at which the power is purchased. Overall, the rates for purchased power should be set so that they encourage cogeneration when it is the lowest cost alternative source of electric power supply for the utility system as a whole.

Industrial Investment Criteria. In many firms cogeneration projects compete at a disadvantage for limited investment capital. This is because many firms employ a two-tiered system of investment criteria whereby management demands that non-product-related investments such as cogeneration (or any conservation project) possess a return on investment (ROI) twice as high as product-related investments.[11] Thus, a chemical company may

9. See generally California Public Utilities Commission, "Staff Report on California Cogeneration Activities" (San Francisco, 1978). Unpublished.

10. Opening Brief of Environmental Defense Fund in Application of Pacific Gas and Electric Company No. 55509, California Public Utilities Commission, pp. 35–36.

11. G.N. Hatsopoulos, E.P. Gyftopoulos, R.W. Sant, and T.F. Widmer, "Capital Investment to Save Energy," *Harvard Business Review* 111 (March-April 1978).

require a 15 percent ROI on a new ethylene plant while demanding 30 percent for a retrofitted cogeneration unit.

Regulatory Barriers

Most of the present laws regulating power generation were written to accommodate the concept of large central station power generators owned by large publicly controlled monopolies. As such, many of these laws either do not account for the possibility of, or are openly hostile to, dispersed privately controlled power generators. Regulatory policies that inhibit cogeneration include the monopoly status granted to existing utilities, the regulation of industry as a public utility when it produces power, power pool agreements, policies toward public utility holding companies, state facility-siting statutes, licensing requirements for boiler operators, fuel allocation regulations, prohibitions on discriminatory practices by utilities, and environmental controls.

Monopoly Status of Existing Utilities.   One of the most formidable barriers to cogeneration is the monopoly status of existing utilities. In keeping with the widely held theory that the generation, transmission, and distribution of electric power is a natural monopoly, state legislatures and utility commissions have, almost without exception, granted monopoly status to existing utilities. In some states the monopoly status of utilities in providing retail service is enshrined in the statutes. More typically, the monopoly of incumbent utilities is a policy that has been developed by utility commissions acting under the general charge that they shall regulate "in the public interest." This policy is generally enforced through the utility certification process. In the majority of states, an entity desiring to initiate utility service in an area must apply to the state commission for a certificate of public convenience and necessity. Where an incumbent utility is capable of serving that area, the application for certification will generally be denied. This is because of the widely held rule that a utility in the field shall have the field unless public convenience and necessity require an additional utility. Even where an existing utility is providing deficient service or no service at all, it will often be given preference in a hearing on public convenience and necessity. If an existing utility is providing inadequate service, many public utility commissions (PUC) will give it a period of grace in which to remedy its deficiencies. And where an applicant seeks to serve an area not presently being served by any utility, many commissions will give preference to a nearby existing utility. This preferential treatment of incumbent utilities is not mandated by law. Indeed, a strong argument can be made that the "public interest" requires PUCs to examine the many benefits offered by cogeneration and to weigh those against any benefits of supporting an incumbent utility. Clearly, incumbent utilities have no legally enforceable right to protection of a monopoly acquired solely through the certification process.

Incumbent utilities, however, may have a legal right to protection of their monopoly status gained through the issuance of franchises. In most jurisdictions the state or local government (not the PUC) must issue a franchise before a power generator can cross, use, tunnel under, or in any way encroach upon public property, streets, or alleys. In roughly half of the states these franchises can be exclusive. Where they are exclusive, and where they have been held to be valuable property rights, a cogenerator may not be able to enter an area without receiving the permission of the incumbent or unless the government "takes" the franchise and compensates the incumbent.

Even where the incumbent utility holds a nonexclusive franchise, it may be able to seriously delay or even halt a cogeneration project. Recently, for example, an Oklahoma utility holding a nonexclusive franchise obtained an injunction (which was upheld by the state supreme court) blocking a housing development from generating its own power until the development obtained a franchise.[12]

Cogenerators may find it a burden to obtain a franchise. Since the franchise must usually be obtained from a local government, the process can be time consuming and costly and the outcome unpredictable. The legislature may seek to attach various conditions to the franchise, including the payment of special fees or taxes, the filing of reports, or the provision of special services.

Industry Fear of Regulation as a Public Utility. Many industrial executives have expressed a reluctance to cogenerate out of the fear that their companies will become subject to regulation by either the Federal Energy Regulatory Commission (FERC) or a state PUC. This fear is understandable; the consequences of regulatory jurisdiction are far-reaching. If an industry were declared by law to be a "public utility" it could be subject to:

• The need to apply for a certificate of public convenience and necessity. As discussed above, such an application may be denied

12. Oklahoma Gas and Electric Company v. Total Energy, Inc., 499 P. 2d 917. Okla. Sup. Ct. (1972).

if an existing utility is already serving the area in question. In addition, certification proceedings can be time-consuming and expensive.

- The need to apply for a franchise. If a cogenerator intends to made use of public property in any way or cross public property with power lines, it may have to apply for a utility franchise. (Note that in many states this duty may occur even where a company is not a public utility.)

- Rate regulation. If an industry is a public utility, its retail rates would have to be approved by the PUC and its wholesale rates by FERC. Industry fears that regulatory lag might prevent it from keeping pace with increasing costs and that its rate of return on cogeneration projects might be held below the industry's normal rate of return.

- Duty to serve. Traditionally, public utilities have been required to provide reliable service to all persons who demand such service. Industry fears that these duty to serve requirements could be invoked to require the industry to provide electricity to new customers.

- Inability to discontinue service. Utilities are not permitted under most state laws to discontinue service without permission from the PUC, even upon the expiration of service contracts with customers.

- Restrictions on the sale of securities. Typically, public utilities may not sell securities without the permission of the regulatory authorities.

- Mandatory accounts and reports. Both FERC and state PUCs would require a public utility to file extensive reports and accounts.

Neither federal nor state law is clear on when an industrial cogenerator will be subject to regulation as a public utility.[13] Many of the relevant statutory provisions are ambiguous or unclear and the courts have had little opportunity to interpret their applicability to industrial power generation. The "best guess" is that:

1. An industry that generates electricity for use solely on its plant site and whose transmission lines do not cross public property generally will not be subject to the jurisdiction of either FERC or the state PUCs. Where the plant's transmission lines cross

13. The question of the jurisdiction of the state PUCs and FERC over industrial cogenerators is explored in detail in Norman L. Dean, *Energy Efficiency in Industry* (Cambridge, Mass.: Ballinger, forthcoming).

public property, the industry may have to receive a local franchise and, in a few rare cases, may be subject to state PUC jurisdiction.

2. A cogeneration project that sells power to a select group of contract customers for their own use without holding itself out to serve the public generally will not be subject to PUC jurisdiction in the majority of states nor to the jurisdiction of FERC. There is a substantial minority of states, however, in which the cogeneration project might be subject to PUC jurisdiction.

3. A cogeneration project that sells power to a public utility risks subjecting its plant to the jurisdiction of FERC. In a minority of states it also risks subjecting itself to the jurisdiction of the state PUC (to the extent that FERC jurisdiction has not pre-empted state jurisdiction).

4. An industry that sells steam or heat to a utility for use in a cogeneration unit may be subject to PUC regulation in those few states that regulate the sale of heat or steam.

5. A cogeneration project that is owned jointly by an existing public utility and a private industry is likely to be subject to both state and federal regulatory jurisdiction.

Power Pools. One possible constraint to cogeneration that has received little attention is the state statutes authorizing utility participation in power pools and the regulations of the power pools themselves. Section 3 of the Massachusetts law relating to the New England Power Pool (NEPOOL), for example, authorizes NEPOOL members to enter into contracts for the purchase and sale of electric power from electric power facilities and states that nothing in this section is to authorize a sale of power except from a specifically designated generating unit which is an electric power facility. Electric power facilities, however, are defined so as to include only generating facilities rated 25 MW or above. After examining this law, the recent draft report of the Massachusetts Governor's Commission on Cogeneration concluded that "most, if not all existing cogenerators are specifically precluded from entering into contracts for the sale of electricity to a NEPOOL utility, which sale could then be counted toward a participant's capability responsibility."[14] Obviously, many utilities will be discouraged from purchasing power from cogenerators if they cannot use that power to fulfill their responsibilities to their power pool. Each power pool agreement and each state law

14. State of Massachusetts, "Draft Report of the Governor's Commission on Cogeneration" (Boston: June 8, 1978), 2-63. Unpublished.

relating to a power pool agreement needs to be carefully examined for its possible impact on industrial cogeneration.

The Public Utility Holding Company Act.   The ownership of cogeneration facilities by third party entities has been hindered by the threat that the industrial owner of the third party company would be subject to Securities and Exchange Commission jurisdiction under the Public Utility Holding Company Act. Companies that control the affairs of public utilities are subject to extensive SEC regulation unless they qualify for one of several statutory exemptions.

State Facility-siting Statutes.   Almost half of the states have now enacted large energy-facility-siting statutes that prohibit the siting of electric generating facilities without the prior hearing and approval of a state commission or board. These proceedings can be very expensive, requiring an industry to prepare long-range demand forecasts, submit detailed technical reports, and participate in public hearings. In order to mitigate the impact of these statutes on small power producers, many of the states have enacted legislative or administrative exemptions for generating plants below a certain size—with the cutoffs ranging from about 25 to 200 MW. These cutoffs are high enough, however, to require many, if not most, cogenerators to comply with the facility-siting act requirements.

Personnel Limitations.   Industrial firms that decide to cogenerate may have difficulty locating sufficient trained and licensed personnel to operate and maintain the necessary boilers and steam lines. Many states have stringent licensing and experience requirements for operators of high pressure steam equipment. The demand for competent steam operators is already apparently exceeding the supply. A significant switch to cogeneration could seriously exacerbate that shortage in the short run.

Fuel Allocation Regulations.   Under the existing set of fuel allocation priorities, industrial users have a lower priority than utilities. Consequently, industrially generated power has a lower reliability than utility-generated power since the regulations would cut back an industry's fuel supply before a utility's. This in turn lowers the economic value of power purchased from an industry. Consideration might be given to increasing the fuel allocation priority of those parts of an industrial facility that cogenerate power for export.

Prohibitions on Discriminatory Practices.   The great majority of state utility laws prohibit a utility from granting preferential treatment to a customer or treating similar customers in different ways. Arguably, these provisions could prohibit a utility from entering into a long-term contract for the sale of power from an industrial firm to the exclusion of other private firms that desired to sell power.

Environmental Constraints and Opportunities.   Cogeneration facilities face several environmental constraints worthy of note. While cogeneration plants may reduce overall air pollution, they will often require a cogenerator to burn more fuel than it would have merely to fulfill its needs for process steam or heat. As a result, cogeneration can increase local emissions of air pollutants. This may present serious problems, especially in nonattainment areas. The emission offset policy may well make it impossible for a cogenerator to locate in a nonattainment area. Moreover, a cogenerator may employ a different technology than a central station utility plant, thereby producing a different mix of pollutants. Diesel cogeneration plants, for example, discharge smaller quantities of particulates and may sometimes discharge smaller quantities of sulfur dioxide. At the same time, however, they produce considerably greater quantities of nitrogen oxides. Finally, cogeneration facilities are considerably smaller than central station utility plants, but may face similar environmental monitoring, modeling, and permitting costs. This means that it may cost more per kilowatt hour of electricity to secure a permit for a cogenerator than for a central station utility plant.

On the other hand, existing environmental laws may provide an opportunity for encouraging cogeneration. Under the 1977 amendments to the Clean Air Act, states are required to submit new state implementation plans (SIPs) by January 1979. These plans and state pollution control programs can be employed to increase the efficiency of energy use, including the use of cogeneration.

One method for encouraging increased energy efficiency would be through the preferential rationing of pollution rights. Federal law now "limits" the amount of air pollutants that can be discharged into the atmosphere in any particular region. In attainment areas, discharges are limited by the Prevention of Significant Deterioration (PSD) increments. In nonattainment areas, discharges are limited by the so-called emissions offset policy. In both situations states are free to develop schemes that allocate this scarce resource—the right to pollute. One obvious way of encouraging increased efficiency, including cogeneration, would be to give preference in the allocation of pollution rights to polluters employing the most efficient systems.

Another method of increasing energy efficiency through pollution control (and vice versa) is to base emissions limitations on the useful output of the steam plant rather than on the heat content of the fuel. Presently, emissions standards are based on the heat content of the fuel. In other words, a plant is permitted to emit x pounds of pollutant per million Btus of fuel burned. This puts more efficient plants at a relative disadvantage. For example, a new utility power plant is permitted under the new source performance standards to emit 0.012 pounds of SO_2 per kWh of electricity generated whereas a cogeneration unit would be permitted to emit only about 0.0072 pounds per kWh.[15]

PRESENT POLICY INITIATIVES

Surprisingly, neither FERC nor the state public utility commissions have the power to set aside many of these barriers, even those directly related to power generation, transmission, and sale. FERC appears to possess the authority to order a utility to sell backup power to, or to exchange power with, an industry, provided that the industry is engaged in the "transmission or sale" of electric power. FERC, however, cannot require a utility to purchase cogenerated power or to wheel power (i.e., to transmit power from one utility to another).

In general, state utility commissions do not have authority to require a utility to wheel power, buy cogeneration equipment, or purchase cogenerated power. Many PUCs have the authority to require that a utility sell backup power at reasonable rates, but most commissions probably have only limited authority to exempt cogenerators from certain aspects of utility regulation.

In short, the barriers to cogeneration cannot be dealt with solely at the administrative level but will require remedial legislation at the federal and state levels. In recognition of this fact, there has been limited action at both the state and federal levels to lift the barriers to industrial cogeneration. California and Massachusetts have been the most aggressive in attempting to encourage cogeneration. The Massachusetts governor appointed a Commission on Cogeneration that recently issued its draft report. That report reviews in great detail the barriers to cogeneration in Massachusetts

15. Murray, *Where We Agree*, p. 129. These figures assume that the utility plant has a heat rate of 10,000 Btu per kWh and that the cogeneration plant has a heat rate of 6,000 Btu per kWh.

and offers numerous legislative and administrative proposals, including establishment of a state "technical services group" to promote cogeneration and provide assistance to industry; changes in state law to limit utility commission jurisdiction over cogenerators; reductions in administrative burdens on cogenerators; and changes in utility rates that discriminate against cogenerators. The California Public Utilities Commission has ordered the state's largest utilities to provide specific rate proposals for cogeneration, to file status reports on utility and industry cogeneration projects, to submit guidelines for conditions under which the utilities will purchase cogenerated power and capacity, and to submit guidelines for the development of utility-owned cogeneration facilities. Georgia, New Jersey, Maine, and Ohio have completed or commissioned studies of the subject; and Hawaii recently enacted legislation exempting cogenerators from the jurisdiction of utility commissions.

At the federal level, the Federal Energy Agency, the Energy Research and Development Administration, and now the Department of Energy have funded research on cogeneration, mainly on the potential and technical feasibility of the concept. A federal interagency task force was formed to coordinate federal cogeneration efforts. FERC has been examining its possible role in cogeneration. Bonneville Power has taken steps to encourage it, and major utility groups, including the Electric Power Research Institute and the Edison Electric Institute, have undertaken examinations of the concept. Conferences on cogeneration are cropping up across the country, and there is now even a cogeneration society.

President Carter's National Energy Plan supported increased cogeneration. It proposed insuring that industrial firms receive a fair price for the power that they sell to utilities and for the backup power that they must purchase. In addition, the National Energy Plan proposed permitting the Department of Energy to exempt industrial cogenerators from federal and state regulations, providing an additional 10 percent investment tax credit for industrial investments in cogeneration equipment, and providing that industrial cogeneration facilities could be exempted from coal conversion requirements.

It now appears that there will be federal legislation on cogeneration sometime in the future, although the precise outlines of that legislation are cloudy. The congressional conference committee considering the National Energy Act reached the following agreement in December 1977: FERC will be required to prescribe rules requiring electric utilities to offer to sell to or buy power from qualifying cogenerators. Those rules shall ensure that the rates set by state regulatory commissions for these sales will be subject to specific limits and will not discriminate against cogenerators. FERC will also be empowered to prescribe rules exempting qualifying cogenerators and small power producers of up to 30 MW from state utility regulations, the Federal Power Act, and the Public Utility Holding Company Act if the secretary of energy determines that such exemption is necessary to carry out the purpose of the Act. A qualifying cogenerator will be defined as the owner of a cogenerating facility that meets size, fuel use, and fuel efficiency standards prescribed by FERC. One recent press report, however, indicates that this compromise may be breaking down. If this is true, federal legislation may be several years in the future.

As important as these federal and state policy initiatives have been, they have ignored several important areas of concern. The relationship of cogeneration to environmental controls has received minimal attention. Few have looked at the financial and regulatory conditions that may encourage or discourage utilities from cooperating in cogeneration ventures. Insufficient attention is being given to funding research on equipment that can assist in the widespread efficient use of cogeneration, including R&D on fluidized bed combustion, efficient small turbines, coal-burning combustion turbines and diesel engines, and low temperature bottoming cycles. Fuel allocation priorities, power pool agreements, personnel limitations, and state facility-siting statutes need additional examination. Finally, insufficient attention has been focused on the impact of the tax code on cogeneration. One commentator recently suggested that the 10 percent investment tax credit on utility investments gives utility power a subsidy that could be balanced only with a 30–45 percent industrial investment tax credit.[16]

THE QUESTION OF COMPETITION

Even more significant than these omissions, however, is the failure to examine the larger issue of possible competition in the electric power generation industry. Policymakers continue to view power generation from the perspective of large central station generating units controlled by large publicly controlled monopolies. Cogeneration is almost always seen as supplementing central station power rather than supplanting it. The proposed federal legislation, for example, specifically provides that aid will not be given to privately owned cogeneration facilities that provide retail electric power.

16. Williams, *Industrial Cogeneration*, p. 24.

Virtually all proposals for encouraging cogeneration have assumed that central station utilities will continue to assume primary responsibility for power generation. Missing from the policy debate has been any serious talk of the possibility that electric power generation should be deregulated—that the utilities should function as common carriers and that new institutions such as a futures market should be developed to assure the reliable future supply of electricity. Indeed, cogeneration appears to give the lie to the theory that electric power generation is a natural monopoly. As has long been argued by a number of economists, it appears that industry can compete for the right to supply electricity without the threat of economies of scale forcing the formation of large monopolies and without the unnecessary duplication of equipment. It does not stretch the imagination much to envision industrial firms vigorously bidding for the right to sell power to regional transmission and distribution monopolies with the government involved only in the regulation of transmission and distribution of power, of anticompetitive conduct, and of the safety of generating facilities. At the least we should begin discussing the possibility of such competition.

SELECTED BIBLIOGRAPHY

California Public Utilities Commission. "Staff Report on California Cogeneration Activities." San Francisco, January 17, 1978. Unpublished.

Dean, Norman L., *Energy Efficiency in Industry*. Cambridge, Mass.: Ballinger, forthcoming.

Murray, F.X., *Where We Agree: The Report of the National Coal Policy Project*. Boulder, Colo.: Westview Press, 1978.

Nydick, S.E., et al., *A Study of In-plant Power Generation in the Chemical, Petroleum Refining, and Pulp and Paper Industries*. Cambridge, Mass.: Thermo Electron Corporation, 1976.

Resource Planning Associates. *The Potential for Cogeneration Development in Six Major Industries by 1985*. Cambridge, Mass., 1977.

Spencer, R.S., et al., *Energy Industrial Center Study*. Midland, Mich.: Dow Chemical Company, 1975.

State of Massachusetts. "Draft Report of the Governor's Commission on Cogeneration." Boston, June 8, 1978. Unpublished.

Williams, Robert H., *Industrial Cogeneration*. Princeton, N.J.: Center for Environmental Studies, 1978. This paper will also appear in volume 3 of the *Annual Review of Energy*.

Preparing for an Oil Crisis: Elements and Obstacles in Crisis Management

Edward N. Krapels

INTRODUCTION

During the five-year span between the Arab oil embargo of 1973-74 and the Iranian oil workers' strike of late 1978, oil-importing nations launched a number of programs designed to diminish their collective and individual vulnerability to sudden reductions in oil supplies. Of the variety of steps taken, the two that will affect national oil supply security most directly are emergency petroleum stockpiles and the establishment of the emergency allocation program of the International Energy Agency (IEA).

The IEA emergency oil-sharing program entitles each member country to a predetermined amount of oil when an oil crisis is declared by the IEA Secretariat. The member countries also have made a commitment to acquire a given level of "energy self-sufficiency"—that is, resources that enable the country to replace all its net oil imports for sixty days (rising to ninety days by 1980). For most countries, this commitment requires maintaining emergency oil stockpiles.[1]

This chapter examines several aspects of national oil security programs. First, the emergency petroleum stockpiles of six importing

Parts of this paper are taken from the author's report, "Oil Supply Security: Emergency Petroleum Reserves in Six Oil-Importing Countries," prepared for the Rockefeller Foundation, 1978.
    1. Under IEA rules, other oil-saving or supplying measures—for example, fuel switching or shut-in oil production—can satisfy the requirement. Very few countries, however, have such programs on a large scale.

countries—the United States, Japan, West Germany, France, Italy, and the Netherlands—are examined. It is apparent that only the United States is aiming for an emergency reserve equivalent to ninety days' supply of its net oil imports—the "energy self-sufficiency" target of the IEA countries. Most other countries appear to be settling for an emergency stock equivalent to about forty-five days of net imports.

The next section of the report illustrates that even forty-five days of emergency stocks can provide substantial protection, if countries are willing to restrain their use of oil in an emergency so that the limited oil stocks will not be squandered on unessential uses. In addition, governments must ensure—in their dealings with the international oil industry and with other governments—that they receive their fair share of oil imports. The IEA emergency program, if it works, will produce a fair allocation, but governments are concerned about whether it will work.

The final section of this chapter briefly discusses the difficulties that the United States is having with various facets of its emergency program. Five years after the Arab oil embargo, the Department of Energy still does not have a finished emergency program—that is, one ready to be implemented—nor does it have any readily available emergency oil supplies. Given these factors, the United States will be among the least-prepared importing countries if an oil supply disruption occurs in 1979. Its vulnerability, however, should diminish in the 1980s as the government-owned strategic petroleum reserve grows to its billion barrel size. By 1985, the United States should be among the best-prepared countries, since its emergency reserve will be roughly twice the size, in proportion to the likely level of imports, of those of most other IEA countries.

EMERGENCY PETROLEUM RESERVE PROGRAMS IN SIX OIL-IMPORTING COUNTRIES

Table 6-1 summarizes the emergency petroleum reserve programs of six oil-importing countries. It shows that the French, Italian, and Dutch emergency reserves are "complete," meaning that total national stock levels are sufficiently high to comply with government targets. The American, Japanese, and German programs are incomplete in that oil is still being added to national stockpiles to achieve government storage objectives at some future date.

On the amalgamation-segregation issue, only the United States maintains its emergency reserve entirely separate from oil company

Table 6-1. Summary Description of Emergency Reserve Programs.

Country	*Status*	*Amalgamated with or Segregated from Oil Company Inventories*	*Ownership of Emergency Reserves*
United States	Incomplete	Segregated	Government
Japan	Incomplete	Both	Government Industry
Germany	Incomplete	Both	Government Industry "Third party"
France	Complete	Amalgamated	Industry
Italy	Complete	Amalgamated	Industry
Netherlands	Complete[a]	Both	Industry "Third party"

[a]The Dutch program is complete in the sense that there is no need to build additional stockpiles to meet government storage objectives. The stocks, however, are being "recognized" to create some segregated emergency reserves.

stocks. Its "strategic petroleum reserve" (SPR) is owned by the government. In Japan, Germany, and the Netherlands there are combined programs—that is, some but not all emergency reserves are held separately from commercial inventories. In Japan and Germany, the governments maintain some segregated emergency reserves (in Japan via the stock ownership of the Japan National Oil Company). In Germany and the Netherlands, "third parties"—namely, special storage corporations—own and maintain some of the emergency reserves.[2] In France and Italy, there are no segregated emergency reserves. The oil companies own, maintain, and finance the entire national stockpile.

Extensive discussion of the differences in these emergency reserve programs goes beyond the scope of this chapter. Instead, it is sufficient to present the difference between the nations' total oil stockpiles and their emergency reserve levels, as estimated elsewhere.[3] Tables 6-2 and 6-3 present yearly averages of month end stock levels as reported in government stock statistics. Table 6-2 presents volumetric data. Table 6-3 presents stocks in terms of the number of

2. These "third party" arrangements are recent innovations in Germany and the Netherlands. Their principal commercial impact is to take the "obligatory" (i.e., emergency) stocks off the balance sheets of the oil companies. From a security point of view, the main impact is to separate these stocks from commercial inventories, giving the government a clearer picture of and more control over emergency reserves.

3. Edward N. Krapels, *Oil Supply Security: The Levels and Uses of Emergency Petroleum Reserves in Six Oil-importing Countries* (New York: Rockefeller Foundation, 1979).

Table 6-2.   Average Stocks of Crude Oil and Principal Finished Products (in millions of barrels).

Country	1973	1974	1975	1976	1977
United States					
Oil company stocks	661.0	710.0	761.0	764.0	861.0
Strategic reserve[a]	0	0	0	0	8.0
Japan[b]	203.5	254.0	266.5	272.4	296.1
Germany					
Oil company stocks	128.8	146.3	153.6	164.4	194.6
Federal reserve[a]	0	3.0	12.0	26.0	33.0
France[b]	n.a.	217.3	222.3	197.3	206.7
Italy[b]	126.4	149.4	136.8	122.1	141.9
Netherlands[b]	58.9	73.0	72.4	66.3	70.5

Note: Average month end stock levels (except for U.S. and German government-owned reserves) for all countries, except Italy, for which only quarter end data are available for 1974 through 1977.

[a]Year end level of stocks.

[b]No government-owned stocks (other than military, which are not included in any of the national data).

Table 6-3.   Average Stocks of Crude Oil and Principal Finished Products (in days of previous year's net imports).

Country	1973	1974	1975	1976	1977
United States					
Oil company stocks	154	123	136	137	122
Strategic reserve	0	0	0	0	1
Japan	49	52	55	61	61
Germany					
Oil company stocks	50	52	60	68	73
Federal reserve	0	1	5	11	12
France	n.a.	88	92	99	97
Italy	71	77	69	71	77
Netherlands	108	129	138	159	134

Note: Net imports equal total imports less total exports less international marine bunkers. See Table 6-4 for net import data.

The figures are based on the amount of principal petroleum products and all crude oil in stock; if all products were included, the number of days of imports in stock would rise by two to ten days' worth, depending on the country. Therefore, these figures should not be used to determine whether or not countries complied with their storage obligations under the IEP or the EEC.

n.a. = Not available.

days of each country's net oil imports (i.e., total imports less total exports less international marine bunkers) during the previous calendar year.[4] Table 6-4 gives net import data.

Table 6-3 shows large discrepancies in the number of days of

4. This is the standard measure used by the International Energy Agency.

Table 6-4. Net Imports of Selected Countries, 1972-1976 (in thousands of bbl/day).

	U.S.	*Japan*	*Germany*	*France*	*Italy*	*Netherlands*
1972	4,273	4,136	2,599	2,191	1,776	541
1973	5,776	4,835	2,824	2,466	1,929	564
1974	5,604	4,871	2,580	2,427	1,976	525
1975	5,582	4,426	2,397	1,986	1,711	417
1976	7,059	4,789	2,665	2,123	1,848	526

Source: OECD, *Quarterly Oil Statistics* (Paris, various years).

imports in stock in the various countries. However, the table cannot be interpreted as providing a picture of the emergency reserve levels because the data include the working stocks (i.e., cycle stocks, "tank bottoms," seasonal stocks, and even pipeline fill in the case of the American data) that the oil industry must have to conduct its operations. (The reserve levels are shown in Table 6-5 and were obtained by subtracting estimated working stocks from the total stock levels.)

In Table 6-5, the discrepancies in the number of days of reserve stock in the various countries have narrowed. The United States, in fact, now has the least, properly indicating that most U.S. stocks are held by industry for commercial requirements. The Netherlands has the highest figure. This can be attributed to its high level of export

Table 6-5. Estimated Emergency Reserves (in days of previous year's net imports).

Country	*1973*	*1974*	*1975*	*1976*	*1977*
United States	32	31	40	38	37
Japan	21	29	31	35	38
Germany	21	28	31	40	45
France	n.a.	62	61	55	—
Italy	37	46	42	37	45
Netherlands	56	85	93	101	84

Note: Commercial inventories were estimated as follows: (1) For crude oil, ten days of average refinery throughput plus 5 percent of total stocks for tank bottoms, plus—for the United States only—30 percent of total stocks for pipeline fill (the data of the other countries already exclude pipeline fill). (2) For gasoline and distillates, 20 days of average domestic sales of each product plus the average seasonal buildup for the previous five years. For the United States only, 17 percent of gasoline stocks and 10 percent of distillate stocks were deducted to account for pipeline fill. (3) For residual fuel oil, ten days of average domestic sales plus international marine bunker sales, plus the average seasonal buildup for the past five years.

n.a. = Not available

operations, which requires Dutch refiners to hold "foreign" oil in Dutch storage tanks.[5]

It is important to emphasize that although the estimates in Table 6-5 provide a more realistic picture of emergency reserve levels than the "raw data" in Table 6-3, the estimates are only approximations—and they already are out of date. The fact that they are only approximations is repeated to emphasize that there is no firm dividing line between emergency reserves and commercial stocks in the amalgamated programs. The fact that they are out of date is stressed because in three of the six countries the total national stockpile and the emergency reserve levels are increasing as a result of government policy. The planned increases in American, German, and Japanese stock levels are noted in Table 6-6. These plans, if they come to fruition, will change the relative emergency reserve positions of the six countries, as Table 6-7 shows.

It is evident in the table that the American reserve will be the largest by far. The fact that it comes "on top of" an oil industry inventory already measuring a billion barrels makes it even more impressive, although the American government is unique among the six in deciding (at least thus far) not to consider commercial inventories as part of the emergency reserve.[6] Thus, whether or not the estimates of U.S. emergency reserves are reasonable,[7] the U.S. government will not treat commercial inventories as if they contain emergency reserves, but will rely upon the strategic reserve. Therefore,

5. Dutch refiners export and sell as international bunkers over 65 percent of their output. The principal purpose of the Dutch government in establishing the "third party" to hold emergency reserves is to separate some stocks for Dutch use during an emergency.

6. This is said in full knowledge of the government's periodic statements to the contrary to the IEA. The State Department has represented commercial stocks to the IEA as the emergency reserve whereby the United States has met its IEP obligation. For a critique of this inconsistency, see the U.S. General Accounting Office's "Issues Needing Attention in Developing the Strategic Petroleum Reserve" (Washington, D.C.: February 16, 1977). IEP stockpile definitions allow this to occur, but the U.S. Department of Energy does not treat commercial inventories as emergency reserves in its crisis planning. At most, oil company stocks will "bridge" the time lag required to deploy the SPR. John Lichtblau of the Petroleum Industry Research Foundation, in a study conducted for the U.S. Department of State (Contract No.1722-520004, September 1974) concluded that U.S. "excess stocks," defined as those that could be drawn down without causing major supply constraints, might permit the substitution of 21 days of total oil imports at the 1974 import rate of 6.1 million bbl/day.

7. And some Department of Energy officials claim that they are not. Their argument stems from the point that the oil industry has no incentive to maintain excess stocks under normal business circumstances. The rebuttal is, of course, that when circumstances become abnormal, steps can be taken to streamline the system to "liberate" some of the commercial safety stocks.

Table 6-6. "Real" Increments to 1977 Emergency Reserves.

Country	1977 Estimated Emergency Reserves in Days of Previous Year's Net Imports	Additional Quantities (millions bbls) Anticipated by		Emergency Reserves in Days of Forecast Net Imports		Target Completion Date
		1980	1985	1980	1985	
United States[a]	37	325	1,000	80–87	124–179	1985
Germany[b]	45	27	0	54	54	1980
Japan[c]						
Oil industry	38	72	0	48	48	1980
Japan National Oil Company (JNOC)	0	0	63 (189)[d]	0	8 (25)[d]	1982 (1985)
Total	38	72	63 (189)[d]	48	56 (81)[d]	

Note: "Real" increments means planned increases in the number of days of domestic sales or net imports in stock. French and Italian reserves will increase only insofar as domestic sales increase; the number of days in stock is not scheduled to rise.

[a]U.S. import projections: 1980 "high" level 7.5 million bbl/day, "low" level 6.4 million bbl/day; 1985 "high level 11.5 million bbl/day, "low" level 7.0 million bbl/day. 1980 projection taken from *Review of the Strategic Petroleum Reserve, Plan.* Hearings before the Senate Committee on Internal and Insular affairs, February 4, 1977 (Washington, D.C.: Government Printing Office, 1977), p. 28; 1985 projection taken from SPR, "Amendment No. 2" p. 9.

[b]German import projections: 1980 projected imports 2.98 million bbl/day, 1985 projected imports 3.01 million bbl/day. Projections taken from the International Energy Agency, *Energy Policies and Programmes of IEA Countries* (Paris: OECD, 1977, p. 28).

[c]Japan's 1980 oil industry emergency reserve addition estimated by subtracting MITI's March 1978 storage target from its March 1980 storage target. 1980 projected imports: 6.9 million bbl/day, 1985 projected imports: 7.6 million bbl/day. Projections from IEA's *Energy Policies.*

[d]Figures show JNOC's maximum stock target in parentheses.

Table 6-7. Forecast 1980 and 1985 Emergency Reserve Levels (in days of forecast net imports).

Country	1980	1985
United States	80–87	124–179
Japan	48	56–81
Germany	54	54
France	55	55
Italy	45	45
Netherlands	50–100	50–100

Note: Dutch level depends upon status of export stocks.

should an oil crisis go on long enough, the depletion of the SPR will be viewed as the "bottom of the U.S. tank."

A similar perception of the "bottom of the tank" could emerge in Germany and the Netherlands, if the "third parties" are believed to hold the entire national emergency reserve—that is, if the oil companies sell or lease most of their "excess stocks" to them. In France, Italy, and Japan, on the other hand, the "bottom of the tank" is far less visible; the governments may not know when emergency reserves are near depletion until distribution problems occur.

The difficulty of identifying emergency reserve levels is acknowledged by the governments and the oil industries of the countries with amalgamated programs. This problem was the principal topic of discussion at a meeting[8] held at the Royal Institute for International Affairs in London in November 1977. Although the participants did not endorse the particular commercial inventory requirement assumptions used in Table 6-5 (some thought they were too low; others, that they were too high), there was agreement that some such numbers do have to be used to represent realistically the amount of oil that can be painlessly removed from stocks during a crisis.[9]

Whatever the real level of emergency reserves in countries such as France and Italy, where emergency reserves are completely amalgamated with commercial inventories, an argument can be made that governments are unlikely ever to allow emergency reserve drawdowns to approach the "bottom of the tank." This is mentioned here only as an introduction to the discussion that follows, which deals with the likelihood that governments will find emergency reserve drawdowns more painful as the stock level decreases. The cost of running out of oil is high. In fact, it is significant that econometric models of oil inventory systems place an "infinite" cost on running out of stocks. The model is instructed to arrange swaps, exchanges, and diversions to get oil even if this is far more costly than usual. Al-

8. The meeting was attended by government officials from the United Kingdom, the United States, Germany, France, and the Netherlands; by officials from the International Energy Agency and the Commission of the European Economic Community; and by oil industry officials from the United Kingdom, United States, Italy, and France.

9. The U.S. Federal Energy Administration expressed a very pessimistic view of the "real reserves" in other IEA countries. It estimated that current "real estimates of actual usable reserves are only 20 days. Most countries would not be able to identify those quantities of stocks that could actually be used during an emergency." FEA memorandum to Senator Henry Jackson dated March 16, 1977, reprinted in *Review of the Strategic Petroleum Reserve Plan*, Hearings before the Committee on Interior and Insular Affairs, U.S. Senate, February 4, 1977 (Washington, D.C.: Government Printing Office, Publication No. 95-10, 1977), p.408.

though the analogy can be pushed too far, this computerized panic may not be an inaccurate representation of the behavior of governments faced with the depletion of their emergency reserves.

KEY EMERGENCY
MANAGEMENT PROBLEMS

Given that the United States and the other IEP member countries all have emergency reserves—although the level of protection that each country is acquiring varies—how will the governments use the reserves and manage oil supply problems in general? One possibility is that governments will follow demand restraint and stock drawdown schedules mentioned in the IEP agreement. As explained by a U.S. State Department spokesman, the IEP suggests the following responses to various levels of oil disruptions:

In a selective embargo, when at least one member loses more than 7 percent of its oil consumption, but the group loses less than 7 percent of its total consumption:

—The embargoed country absorbs its embargo loss up to 7 percent of its consumption. (This is the self-risk element under the program.)
—The other members share the remaining shortfall among themselves on the basis of their consumption.

In a general crisis, when the group as a whole loses more than 7 percent but less than 12 percent of its normal consumption:

—Each country restrains demand by 7 percent.
—The remaining shortfall is shared among all members on the basis of (net) imports.
—Countries draw down their emergency supplies as necessary to maintain their consumption at 93 percent of normal.

At the "second level" of a general crisis, when the group as a whole loses 12 percent of its normal consumption:

—Each country restrains demand by 10 percent.
—The remaining shortfall is shared on the basis of (net) imports.
—Countries draw down their emergency supplies as necessary to maintain consumption at 90 percent of normal.[10]

10. *Agreement on an International Energy Program, Hearings Before the U.S. Senate Committee on Interior and Insular Affairs* (Washington, D.C.: Government Printing Office, 1974), pp. 21–22.

This formula in effect makes members' demand restraint the first line of defense against an oil supply reduction and makes stock draw-downs—that is, emergency supplies—the second line of defense. Moreover, if every IEP member follows the formula perfectly, all countries will suffer the same level of demand restraint and will lower oil stocks by the same rate as the crisis progresses. It must be noted, however, that membership in the IEP does not constitute an obligation to restrain demand and use stocks in the manner prescribed in the agreement, unless the participating country chooses to make these target figures into national laws. Few, if any, members have chosen to commit themselves explicitly to the IEP targets. Instead, most governments have acquired broad powers to regulate domestic petroleum supplies as they see fit in a crisis.

A Simple Estimate of Stockpile Endurance

Although IEP countries are unlikely to follow identical demand restraint and stock drawdown policies in an oil crisis, it it useful to assume momentarily that they will do so. This assumption makes it possible to make a simple group endurance estimate. If IEA countries abide by the demand restraint recommendations, a 9 percent group supply loss—roughly the level experienced in the Arab oil crisis—would call for an emergency reserve drawdown equivalent to only 2 percent of IEA countries' normal consumption (demand restraint absorbing the first 7 percent). If the IEA countries each had a sixty-day emergency reserve—in terms of their net imports—a daily draw-down of 2 percent of consumption (equivalent to 3.3 percent of daily imports for the IEA as a group) would deplete the sixty-day emergency reserve in about eighteen hundred days—or nearly five years (the figure results from dividing 60 by 0.033).

To define the importers' abilities to endure larger oil supply losses that would require more substantial emergency reserve drawdowns, several calculations are needed. First, the emergency reserve draw-downs and the number of days required to exhaust thirty and sixty days of IEA stocks (equivalent to net imports) can be estimated as above. The results are presented in Table 6-8.

These calculations clearly show how emergency reserve drawdowns become more important as the size of the supply loss increases and how the number of days the disruption must last to deplete thirty and sixty days of stocks falls sharply once the supply loss exceeds 10 percent. What is the likelihood of supply curtailments greater than 10 percent? Although an assessment of the probabilities of oil supply losses goes beyond the scope of this chapter, the kinds of oil supply

Table 6-8. Effect of Various Levels of Oil Loss on IEA Stocks.[a]

Supply Loss (percent)	Demand Restraint (percent)	Emergency Reserve Drawdown Obligation		Days Required to Deplete Thirty and Sixty Days of Net Imports in IEA Stocks	
		Percent of consumption	Percent of imports	30 days	60 days
7	7	0	0		
10	7	3	5	600	1200
15	10	5	8	361	722
20	10	10	17	176	352
25	10	15	25	120	240
30	10	20	33	91	182

[a]Assuming that imports constitute 60 percent of IEA supplies, as they did in 1976.

reductions in the present market conditions that would cause the IEA to make large emergency reserve drawdowns can be defined.

IEA and OECD oil data for the period July 1, 1976 to June 30, 1977 (see Table 6-9) show that a 10 percent loss of the IEA's available supplies during this period would have averaged 3.6 million barrels per day; a 15 percent loss, 5.4 million barrels per day. IEA data on imports for the same period (see Table 6-10) show the levels of supply provided by specific producers. OPEC provided 74 percent of IEA's gross imports, or 20 million barrels per day; Arab OPEC countries provided 44 percent, or 12 million barrels per day; and Saudi Arabia, Kuwait, Libya, and the United Arab Emirates, who cut their production to initiate the 1973-74 oil crisis, provided 36 percent, or 9.8 million barrels per day. Combining the IEA supply and import data, it is possible to show the level of export reduction required to cause various levels of IEA supply loss.

These calculations define more precisely the impact of reductions in various OPEC subgroup exports on the IEA's emergency reserves. Table 6-8 showed that a 20 percent IEA supply loss would cause the IEA to deplete thirty days of oil stocks (defined according to the IEA agreement in terms of net imports) in one hundred seventy-six days; but Table 6-11 shows that, using 1977 oil flows as an indicator, Saudi Arabia, Kuwait, Libya, and the UAE would have to reduce their exports to the IEA by 73 percent to bring this about. This is a far greater reduction than they imposed in 1973. If the curtailment were a unified Arab effort, they would have to reduce exports by 60 percent. If it were a joint OPEC effort, the reduction would have to be 36 percent.

Table 6-9. OECD and IEA Oil Supplies, July 1, 1976–June 30, 1977 (in thousands of bbl/day).

	OECD	Non-IEA Members[a]	IEA
Indigenous production (crude, NGL)	13,142.4	438.6	12,703.8
Imports (crude, NGL)	26,108.0	2,936.9	23,171.1
Imports (products)	5,164.4	334.9	4,829.5
Exports (crude)	1,127.2	0	1,127.2
Exports (products)	2,635.2	328.4	2,306.8
International marine bunkers	1,324.2	109.2	1,215.0
Available supplies	39,328.2	3,272.8	36,055.4
Domestic consumption	33,727.0	2,901.2	30,825.8

Source: OECD, *Quarterly Oil Statistics* (Paris, second quarter, 1977).
[a]France, Finland, Iceland, Portugal, Australia. Norway is an associate member of the IEA and is included in the IEA total.

Table 6-10. IEA Crude and Product Imports, July 1, 1976–June 30, 1977 (in thousands of bbl/day).

Country	Crude	Products
Algeria	777	27
Iraq	1,125	—
Kuwait	969	67
Libya	1,768	29
Qatar	253	—
Saudi Arabia	5,394	110
UAE	1,510	—
Arab OPEC	11,796	233
Ecuador	60	—
Gabor	54	11
Indonesia	1,147	68
Iran	3,744	40
Nigeria	1,708	12
Venezuela	803	584
Non-Arab OPEC	7,516	715
Total OPEC	19,312	948
Norway	178	41
United Kingdom	196	273
China	133	—
USSR	212	206
Others	2,714	3,352
Grand Total	22,745	4,820
Less IEA Exports	1,016	2,374
Net IEA Imports	21,729	2,446
Combined IEA Crude and Product Net Imports	24,175	

Source: OECD, *Quarterly Oil Statistics* (Paris, third quarter, 1977).

Table 6-11. Percent Export Reduction Required to Cause Various Levels of IEA Supply Loss

Exporting Countries	IEA Supply Loss (percent)		
	10	20	30
Saudi Arabia-Kuwait-UAE-Libya	37	73	n.p.
Arab-OPEC	30	60	90
OPEC	18	36	54

n.p. = Not possible.

The Complex Context: Crisis-Management Variables

The simple endurance estimates in the preceding pages can be made more realistic by considering some obvious economic and political obstacles that are likely to exist in oil supply crises. These obstacles may include:

- Governments' unwillingness to impose 7 or 10 percent demand restraint,
- Governments' reluctance to use emergency reserves,
- Technical obstacles to emergency reserve use, and
- Differences in political perceptions and objectives.

The likelihood that these problems will arise, and their impact, depend naturally on the cause of the oil disruption, which will affect the political atmosphere in which governments will have to manage the crisis. A desire to avoid demand restraint may more likely appear in crises that a government believes will be short. Reluctance to use emergency reserves may crop up in crises that governments believe are open ended or deliberate applications of the oil weapon for coercion. Importing countries are more likely to have differing political perceptions in a deliberate embargo, because some importers may resent suffering because of the poor relations between the target country (for example, the United States in the 1973-74 embargo) and the oil producers.

The purpose of the following discussions is not to predict that these four obstacles must arise. Rather, it is to indicate that even though countries have stockpiles and there is an IEP, oil crises will be difficult to manage.

Demand Restraint

In the IEP emergency plan, demand restraint is to absorb the first 7 or 10 percent of the oil shortage. The 1973-74 crisis indicated, however, that few countries immediately lowered their demand for oil by such levels. This was partially because the crisis began in October, the beginning of the seasonal surge in demand. Even allowing for the seasonal increase in demand, however, there were clear differences in the degree of demand restraint. In Japan, consumption, as measured by inland sales statistics, increased by 7 percent in comparison with the same period a year before. At the other extreme, German oil consumption fell by 9 percent in comparison with that of the same period in the previous year. These differences in demand restraint were caused by a number of factors, including unequal growth in oil demand, differing domestic oil price policies, and variations in drawdowns of emergency reserves, all of which were connected to governments' perceptions of the level, duration, and impact of the oil crisis.

Since the IEP agreement has made demand restraint the first line of defense against future supply disruptions, the 1973-74 experience raises the question of how 7 or 10 percent demand restraint will affect an industrial economy. There is surprisingly little information about the effect of oil losses on economic growth. However, one assessment that has important implications is the analysis of the vulnerability of the American economy to sudden oil losses that was presented by the U.S. Federal Energy Administration in the *Strategic Petroleum Reserve Plan* of December 1976. The FEA estimated that a 7 percent loss of oil supplies would cause only a 0.9 percent decrease in the gross national product (GNP). However, 0.9 percent of a $2 trillion GNP amounts to an $18 billion loss.[11] In effect, the FEA believes that there is no "free" demand restraint. This reasoning is the basis for the Federal Energy Administration's comment that

it will be difficult to identify acceptable actions that will result in reductions substantially above three percent (of normal domestic oil demand) without severe economic impacts. . . . The attainment of seven and ten percent demand restraint levels (as called for by the IEA program) could only be achieved over an extended period of time. . . . Such reductions are likely to require gasoline rationing and other fairly severe measures.[12]

11. The assessment is based on an input-output model whose values were derived from the FEA's assessment of the cost of the 1973-1974 embargo. See FEA *Strategic Petroleum Reserve Plan* (Washington, D.C., December 1976), p. A-5; and S. Tani and D. Boyd, "Measuring the Economic Cost of an Oil Embargo" (Stanford Research Institute, October, 1976; available from the National Technical Information Service, Springfield, Va).

12. FEA, *SPR Plan*, pp. 25-26.

The FEA report mentions that the IEA agreement allows participating countries to "use emergency petroleum reserves held in excess of their emergency reserve commitment, rather than take the reductions in consumption" and suggests that U.S. consumption during a crisis be reduced "on a linear basis throughout the duration of the interruption to obtain a three percent reduction after three months, and a six percent reduction after six months."[13]

If the FEA's assessment is correct, even the "limited disruptions" requiring only 7 percent demand restraint could be quite damaging. Moreover, the United States is considered to use oil less efficiently—that is, to derive less GNP from its oil supplies—than most other importers. If so, Europe and Japan would suffer greater proportional GNP losses from oil shortages.

To avoid those losses, governments may be tempted to use emergency reserves even in a 7 percent oil disruption. Japan, as mentioned previously, is planning a 60 million barrel extra reserve by 1985, possibly to avoid demand restraint. The Japanese government is concerned about the costs of 7 or 10 percent demand restraint, not only because the Japanese are among the most efficient oil consumers, but also because Japan continues to have a higher oil demand growth rate than many other industrial countries. If the oil demand growth rate is 6 percent per annum when a disruption strikes, the 7 or 8 percent demand restraint imposed at the beginning of a crisis will effectively increase by 1 percent every two months.

These observations suggest that countries' ability or willingness to make a 7 or 10 percent cut in oil demand should not be taken for granted. Small decreases in the gross national product reverberate through the economy, causing politically troublesome increases in unemployment[14] and disruptions in international trade that can have far-reaching consequences.

Emergency Reserves that "Cannot Be Used"

If the demand restraint called for by the IEA program is considered unacceptable by some oil-importing governments, their only recourse to replace the lost supplies, short of dropping out of the IEA allocation program altogether, is to increase the rate of emergency reserve drawdown. The reserves, however, provide only a finite source of alternative supplies, and accelerating the

13. Ibid., pp. 25-27.
14. The FEA, for example, has estimated that the 1973–74 oil crisis caused 500,000 Americans to lose their jobs for varying lengths of time. See the *Project Independence Report* (Washington, D.C.: USGPO, November 1974). p. 288.

drawdown rate to avoid demand restraint will deplete reserves more rapidly than shown in Table 6-8.

Moreover, as reserve levels decrease, a new factor emerges to complicate collective emergency management. This may be called a psychological factor, or simple prudence, which militates against the depletion of emergency reserves and was referred to earlier in the observation that emergency reserves provide security only when they are still in the tank. As they are used up, security declines.

Some governments' reluctance to use emergency reserves was apparent in the 1973-74 crisis. The reluctance reappeared recently in the actions of American electric utilities in the coal strike of early 1978. Newspaper reports indicated that the Pennsylvania-New Jersey-Maryland "power pool" had an overall stock of coal equivalent to eighty days of their requirements, but a contingency plan was "to go into effect at a 45-day level . . . for conversions from coal to oil and halving output of coal-fired generators. At a 30-day level, coal-burning generators would be reduced to only plant protection [level of output]."[15]

In oil as in coal emergency management, it is inconceivable that the steady drain of emergency reserves would not affect governments' perceptions of and responses to the crisis. When some importers believe the disruption may last until emergency reserves are depleted, early confidence in the adequacy of reserves will give way to concern about the consequences of a large drop in stock levels. This concern is likely to appear first in countries whose emergency reserves are amalgamated with oil company working stocks. Uncertainty about when the decrease in stock levels will cause distribution problems, spot shortages, refinery closings, and other manifestations of inadequate stock levels will increase concern and anxiety. The fact that governments will find it difficult to predict when these things will occur may make them cautious about drawing down stocks well before emergency reserves are depleted.

The IEA agreement addresses this problem in Articles 15 and 20, stating that when "cumulative daily emergency reserve drawdown obligations . . . have reached 50 percent of emergency reserve commitments, . . . the [IEA Management] Committee shall report to the Governing Board . . . proposing measures required for meeting the necessities of the situation."[16] However, pressure for such a reconsideration is likely to come well before the 50 percent point specified in the agreement. In many countries, oil company working

15. *New York Times*, February 16, 1978.
16. IEA Agreement, Article 20, p. 7.

stocks are estimated to be about forty days of imports, so some countries will not want to wait until stocks are down to forty-five days of imports to reassess the level of demand restraint.

Technical Bottlenecks

The unwillingness to allow a large drop in emergency reserve levels is likely to be reinforced by the need to protect working stocks so that the oil distribution system can continue to operate globally as well as within national markets. A large decrease in stock levels resulting from emergency reserve drawdowns will create technical problems in the petroleum distribution systems, problems that will multiply as the crisis progresses and as the disruption begins to impinge on the types of crudes available to the refineries of importing countries. It is possible that the types of oil available will not match the types the refineries need to produce the mix of products desired by their customers. For example, a large decrease in "heavy" crude oils may make it difficult for refineries to produce enough residual oil in Europe, particularly if the crisis occurs during the winter. At the same time, the demand restraint programs in each country are likely to change the normal pattern or mix of products demanded from the refineries. For example, if most of the 7 percent demand restraint occurs in the gasoline market, it is possible that refineries will produce more gasoline than needed because they are engineered to transform a given fraction of crude into gasoline. In essence, a crude oil crisis can disrupt refinery operations from both ends—the quantity and mix of its crude supplies and the consumers' demand for its products.

The level and the composition of importers' stockpiles will determine how soon these technical bottlenecks emerge. Although the problem is too complex to be treated here, several illustrations can be offered that provide a part of the picture. In December 1976, the five nations in this survey that are members of the IEA had a combined crude stockpile of 662 million barrels and a refinery crude input level of 25.1 million bbl/day. Thus, they had about twenty-six days of refinery input in stock. Once a crude supply disruption strikes and the governments start using some of the crude stocks to meet their emergency reserve drawdown obligations, the number of days in stock gradually will decline. If the quantities of Abu Dhabi and Libyan "light" oils are substantially reduced, the mix of crudes in the American stockpile gradually will become "heavier." Within this general process, American refineries using light crudes will have less and less light oil in stock. As the level of these oil stockpiles declines, it will become necessary to distribute what light oils are available from remaining imports more quickly. Instead of receiving one tanker cargo with one week's supply of oil, a refiner may have to share the cargo with another refiner. The need to make smaller but more frequent deliveries, may in turn, put a strain on the logistics system of the industry, since it was not designed for this kind of delivery schedule.

If the crude oil stockpile in the IEA sinks to an "average" level of ten days of net imports, some refineries are likely to be down to only several days' supply and others will have been boosted to twenty days' supply. The use of averages in such a situation hides the low and the high numbers at individual sites—"an army can drown in a river that has an average depth of one foot"—and refineries can run out when the IEA countries have an average crude stock of ten days.[17]

There are scores of technical permutations of this sort in the supply management problem. Generally speaking, however, the lower the level of importers' stockpiles, the more likely it is that mismatches will occur between crude oil and refineries and product and demand. This is the essence of the need for working stocks and for close attention to the manner in which national markets, refineries, and stockpiles are connected. These technical uncertainties increasingly will have to be taken into account by governments and oil companies as a supply crisis evolves.

Perceptions of Crisis

If demand restraint of 7 or 10 percent is an unattractive response to a sudden oil loss and emergency reserve drawdowns become increasingly unattractive, how long can collective management survive? The willingness of societies to restrain demand or of governments to deplete emergency reserves is going to be influenced by their perceptions of the level, the duration, and the cause of the supply problem. An oil loss caused by an accident of a technical nature will produce a different reaction than one caused by a political crisis. Governments will expect an accidental disruption to have a limited duration. They can use emergency reserves in the expectation that there is no deliberate intent to weaken the nation's security. On the other hand, a deliberate supply disruption has a completely different aspect. First, although the exporters may intend to stage

17. An analogy used by a U.S. Department of Energy official commenting on the coal stockpile situation during the miners' strike of 1978. See "Accuracy of Figures on Coal Stockpiles is Open to Question," *Wall Street Journal*, February 27, 1978. It should be noted that several oil company experts who reviewed this paper indicated that IEA refineries would experience supply problems before the average IEA crude stock level reaches ten days.

only a "limited" crisis, it is unlikely that importers could afford to assume this is the case. Any deliberate disruption threatens to be open ended.

Second, deliberate disruptions can for political reasons be directed against specific importers and not the entire group. Membership in the IEA almost automatically involves many other importers in the management of the crisis,[18] but the automaticity of the IEA "triggers" does not assure automatic unanimity on the political issue. Importers who are "hostages" in a confrontation in which they have no strong political interest are likely to be less willing to endure economic losses or to deplete their emergency reserves for the sake of the foreign policies of other importers.

Third, although the automaticity of the IEP may cause importers to enter the crisis collectively, in later stages the risks inherent in drawing down reserves or continuing demand restraint may cause some importers to try to withdraw from the program. The difference in political positions causing the crisis may not matter in the early stages because initial drawdowns of emergency reserves may be considered painless. But when the importers least committed to the political cause come to believe that the crisis will last long enough to cause a large drop in reserves, the IEP is likely to becomes less attractive. In effect, the emergency reserves themselves become a more valuable asset than membership, and if there are ways to secure supplies outside the IEA framework, governments will find it less costly to drop out than to deplete the emergency reserves.

This attrition prospect among IEP members will be most directly a function of the political state of affairs during an oil crisis. Attrition is least likely in supply disruptions with an obviously limited duration or ones in which no individual member country is singled out. The musketeer attitude will be easier to retain in these circumstances simply because the political behavior of one member will not cause the damage incurred by the others.

Attrition is most likely in open-ended disruptions and in those aimed at individual countries. The key to the IEP's political cohesion in these circumstances will be the degree to which other IEP members are sympathetic toward the behavior (most likely a foreign policy posture) of the affected IEP member(s). Although judgments may differ over the strength of the loyalty of governments to the IEP in these circumstances, the relevant point here is that disinte-

18. For a more extensive evaluation of the implications of targeted embargoes, see Edward N. Krapels, *Oil and Security: Problems and Prospects of Oil-Importing Countries* (London: International Institute of Strategic Studies, Adelphi Paper No. 136, Summer 1977).

grative pressures will be maximized in this scenario and that governments' willingness to use emergency reserves, or to restrain demand, cannot be taken for granted. Neither stock drawdowns nor demand restraint is without costs.

In these most difficult political circumstances, the IEP countries may be compared to a group of labor unions united against a large industry.[19] The strike funds of the various unions may be compared to the IEP's emergency reserves. As the strike progresses, some unions are likely to deplete their strike funds before others. As depletion nears, the pressure on the leaders of these unions to settle is going to increase. Three outcomes are possible. First, the poorer unions may try to reach their own settlement with industry. Second, the poorer unions may put pressure on their wealthier fellows to settle the strike more speedily. Third, the poorer unions may demand that the richer unions share their more substantial strike funds.

A similar process is likely to evolve among the IEP countries in an open-ended disruption. The countries with the smallest emergency reserves may try to reach their own accomodations with the suppliers (this seems most likely in disruptions aimed at individual countries); or they may put pressure on the better prepared importers to settle the dispute with the suppliers; or they may demand that the countries with larger stocks provide more oil, either by modifying the IEP formula or by direct "subsidies" from emergency reserves.

The implication of this line of reasoning for the United States and Japan, the major IEP countries with the largest emergency reserves in the 1980s, is that they may not be able to enjoy unilaterally the benefits of their foresight. Like unions with large strike funds, their larger emergency reserves may cause others to impose larger responsibilities on them for the group's welfare.

THE U.S. GOVERNMENT EMERGENCY PREPAREDNESS PROGRAM

A nation's readiness for oil import disruptions is a function of the size and availability of its emergency petroleum reserve, of its willingness and ability to reduce oil consumption during a crisis, and of the skill of the government and the oil industry in managing the allocation of a reduced level of supply to consumers. Government obviously plays a critical part. In most countries, it is responsible not only for making very broad supply and demand decisions—the level

19. Thanks to Dr. Harald Leuba of Evaluation Research Corp. for this analogy. Dr Leuba attempted to get information on strike fund management from several unions but, not surprisingly, without success.

of demand restraint, the level of stock drawdowns, for example—but in many countries the government also becomes kind of an oil company, managing supplies from the refineries to the service station.

In the United States, five years after the Arab oil embargo, there is as yet no integrated oil supply and demand management program that is ready to be implemented should imports be disrupted. There are problems with the emergency supply program—that is, the billion barrel strategic petroleum reserve plan that was launched in 1975—and with the emergency conservation program.

To consider first the supply dimension, the SPR held only 70 million barrels in December 1978, instead of the 250 million barrels that were scheduled to be in place by this time.[20] Due to unanticipated difficulties in the preparation of the salt dome reservoirs, the SPR fill-up program has fallen behind schedule. The present fill schedule is as follows (in millions of barrels):

End of year	1979	1980	1981	1982	1983	1984	1985
SPR target	195	325	454	623	727	856	1,011

The delays in getting SPR oil in place have naturally delayed the date when SPR oil can be taken out for use in an emergency. Each annual increment in the SPR size requires that one or several new storage sites be prepared and filled. In the construction of most of these caverns, the Department of Energy gives priority to getting the oil into the ground. The ability to get the oil out of the caverns and into a pipeline network is, in most cases, a separate engineering task that is given a lower priority in the construction schedule. As a result, the 70 million barrels in storage in December 1978 could not be removed at that time. The removal facilities for these caverns will not be completed until the summer of 1979.[21] In general, the SPR drawdown capacity will build up slowly, and the United States will not have a readily available reserve of a size comparable to the emergency reserves of European countries and Japan until about 1983.

20. According to the "accelerated schedule" announced in March 1977 by the U.S. Department of Energy. See SPR "Amendment No. 1." The 70 million barrel figure for the end of 1978 was acknowledged by SPR project chief Joseph DeLuca before the U.S. House of Representatives Committee on Interstate and Foreign Commerce, Subcommittee on Energy and Power, on December 18, 1978.

21. This does not mean that the United States does not have access to some emergency supplies. If necessary, the amounts purchased for the SPR en route to the storage sites can be diverted for use in refineries.

Given the limited availability of SPR oil in 1979 and 1980, demand management must be the principal line of defense for the United States against sudden oil import reductions. "Demand restraint," a term coined in the IEP agreement, actually refers to a set of demand and supply management responses. Demand can be restrained by incentives—such as giving preferential parking spots to carpooling commuters—and by mandatory means—which can vary in severity from closing gasoline stations on weekends to outright rationing of gasoline. Or the government can simply order refineries to produce less gasoline and allow the price to increase in the hope that consumers will demand less.

Ideally, the U.S. Department of Energy would have emergency conservation plans on the shelf. These plans should provide directions for achieving the levels of demand restraint mentioned in the IEP agreement. They should identify those demand sectors where a decrease in oil supplies would have the least impact. Energy legislation required the department to submit such a plan to Congress by June 1976. When components of the plan were finally submitted in April 1979, Congress balked over approving those that would have produced the greatest energy savings.

The program that ran into the greatest congressional opposition was the gasoline-rationing plan. The Carter administration's original proposal was to give each carowner an equal number of gasoline-rationing coupons. Legislators from rural areas objected that the plan discriminated against their constituents. The House of Representatives refused to approve the standby plan, in spite of assurances by energy officials that it would only be used in drastic circumstances, prompting President Carter to suggest that Congress itself design the rationing program.[22]

The success of the department's apparently troubled crisis-planning programs will also be influenced by the quality of the information that the department receives on domestic and international oil developments. The quality of the international information is strongly influenced by the International Energy Program. If the IEP is activated when world oil supplies are disrupted, the United States and the other IEP members, as well as the major international oil companies serving these countries, will coordinate their oil supply information via the IEA Secretariat. The IEA staff will combine national and oil industry data to issue IEA-wide and national oil supply reports, including forecasts of imports in the upcoming two months. Although there is considerable concern about the reliability of the

22. See the *Washington Post*, May 11, 1979.

data going into the IEA procedure—some countries and some companies will submit better data than others—even a flawed IEA reporting system will be a valuable information resource, providing the most direct import forecasts available.

If the IEP procedure is not implemented, each government will have to assess on its own the impact of a general supply reduction on national oil imports. Since no national government can monitor the entire world oil industry by itself, import forecasts will have to be based on intelligence reports and analyses of the world oil market. The unavoidable inaccuracy of these methods of forecasting import losses is certain to hinder the domestic aspects of emergency planning.

To improve the government's ability to monitor both international and domestic supply developments during a crisis, the Department of Energy established in June 1978 an office to develop an Energy Emergency Management Information System (EEMIS). This office has issued a report that lists the department's information requirements during a crisis and its current capabilities to meet those requirements. There is a substantial gap between the two. In fact, the report estimates that two years will be required to build the management information system that meets the department's needs.

The Department of Energy does not appear to be well prepared to manage a petroleum import interruption. This conclusion is supported by a report from the department's own inspector general, who has stated that the department's emergency planning is "inadequate."[23] The United States will have neither an integrated emergency plan nor substantial emergency oil supplies before the 1980s.

CONCLUSIONS

This chapter has covered only a few of the principal elements of oil crisis management and only a few of the potential obstacles to successful management. Even this limited survey of the oil security question, however, has indicated substantial uncertainties about the abilities of governments of oil-importing countries to cope with certain types of supply disruptions.

It is clear that the next few years are most perilous. Stock-building programs in the United States, Japan, and West Germany will be proceeding. The United States will be catching up with the level of stockpile protection of its allies until about 1983. The delays in the

23. See *Energy Resources and Technology*, October 20, 1978, p. 416.

American SPR, plus the delays in completion of oil supply, demand, and information management systems, combine to make the United States extremely vulnerable to import disruptions in 1979 and 1980.

In this chapter an attempt also was made to account for some of the political and psychological aspects of crisis management. Even if all the technical preparations were perfect—and they are far from even being ready—collective crisis management would be hindered by differences in perceptions of the problem and in political objectives.

In short, the argument advanced here is that most government emergency programs, including the IEP, will be found inadequate to manage a substantial reduction in world oil supplies should one occur in the near future.[24] This assertion cannot be proven or disproven, but it seems prudent to caution government decision-makers to assume that it is true. If they assume otherwise, they may underestimate the threat that oil supply problems still poses for their countries.

24. The oil workers' strike in Iran, which broke out in early November 1978 and continues to disrupt supplies at the time this is being written—January 1979—may yet cause a reduction in world oil supplies. The gravity of the situation in 1979 will be determined by the Arabian Gulf countries.

Energy Prospects in Western Europe and Japan

Horst Mendershausen

THE OIL SHOCK AND BRAVE NEW VISIONS

The oil crisis of 1973 and the subsequent stock taking of oil supply prospects showed that the energy structures that Western Europe and Japan had built up in the preceding two decades of rapid economic growth were becoming untenable. From 1950 to 1973, France had raised its energy consumption threefold and its consumption of oil twelvefold, or from 20 to 72 percent of all energy consumed in the country. West Germany had raised its energy consumption threefold and its consumption of oil thirty-sevenfold, or from 4 percent to 58 percent of all energy consumed.[1] Japan, in the short span from 1960 to 1973 alone, had raised its energy consumption three and a half-fold and its consumption of oil eight and a half-fold, or from 32 percent to 76 percent of all energy consumed.[2] These energy structures, and the industrial, transportation, and space heating systems that rested on them, were found to be in jeopardy.

The peril was immediate as well as prospective. The oil on which both Western Europe and Japan had come to rely was almost entirely imported. In the early 1970s, the control of this oil supply fell to a

1. Horst Mendershausen, *Coping With the Oil Crisis, French and German Experiences* (Baltimore: Johns Hopkins University Press for Resources for the Future, 1976), p. 33.
2. *1977 IEA Reviews of National Energy Programs* (Paris: OECD, 1978), p. 164.

producers' cartel of oil country governments. The OPEC countries increased oil prices and limited production to sustain their inflated revenues. The oil-consuming countries, notably the industrial democracies, accepted the cartel's prices. This meant the disappearance of the cheap oil on which their energy economies had been based and supply uncertainty, which the Arab oil embargo of 1973 brought home. In the near term, European and Japanese oil supply was to be considerably more expensive and at the mercy of political troubles that these countries had virtually no power to control.

The longer term prospects appeared no less perilous. Given energy consumption patterns and continued economic growth worldwide, oil demand promised to outpace supply capacity within a decade or two. The "crunch"—large energy price increases and perhaps international conflicts over the limitation and allocation of oil supplies—might come sooner or later, depending on many things, but a deterioration of oil supply appeared inevitable to almost all forecasters before the end of this century or early in the next. They could not see a likely escape from the progressive exhaustion of technically accessible, politically available, economically affordable sources of crude oil. Western Europe and Japan regarded themselves as particularly vulnerable to supply shortages, more so than other parts of the world better endowed with energy resource materials.

Coping with the immediate energy peril and forestalling the more distant one became an urgent policy imperative that added to and for a while almost eclipsed the many other policy imperatives that the industrial societies of our time generate. The European countries' and Japan's search for ways to cope looked toward the following structural developments:

1. Oil import assurance from given sources; and
2. Oil import reduction from given sources, by way of (a) development of alternative sources for oil supplies (indigenous or new external), or (b) development of alternative sources of energy (indigenous or external), or (c) reduction of the energy inputs required per unit of gross domestic product (energy conservation).

Although the problems of bringing about major changes of this sort in a relatively short time were staggering and the uncertainty and confusion over suitable means of managing the transition were often great, the countries perceived opportunities for some progress in these directions. They believed it possible to assure themselves of preferential access to given sources of oil by offering, individually or through the European Community, attractive economic and political services to OPEC oil producers. Alternative oil supplies were not immediately available, but substantial oil finds in the North Sea were about to come into production, offering indigenous oil supplies to Britain and Norway and congenial import sources to other European countries. Elsewhere in the world, Alaskan oil, Mexican oil, and offshore oil in various places was beginning to promise supply relief that could benefit Europe and Japan directly or indirectly by filling some of the demands of other countries, notably the United States.

Among energy sources alternative to oil, coal, gas, and nuclear power seemed the most relevant for the remainder of the century. Coal, which oil had so largely replaced, was still plentifully available in the industrial world, at least in the ground, and if not under attractive cost prospects from European and Japanese mines, then from better placed potential exporters in North America, Australia, Poland, the USSR, and some other countries.[3] Dutch wells had just begun to produce natural gas, and a pipeline system to distribute the gas was nearing completion. North Sea wells could be expected to add more gas soon. Soviet, Iranian, and perhaps Algerian gas could be tapped with the help of other pipelines leading into Western Europe, and more gas could be moved in from various overseas sources through liquefied natural gas production, transport, and regasification. Finally, nuclear power seemed to be at the threshold of a surge to prominence in the countries' electricity production. Important reactor choices had been made (generally in favor of the light water reactor [LWR] type developed in the United States); industries in the United States, Western Europe, and Canada were gearing up to supply these reactors; and the economics of nuclear electricity compared favorably with fossil fuel electricity. Except for France, Sweden, and Spain, Western Europe and Japan had no significant indigenous uranium, but sufficient natural uranium and enrichment services seemed to be available from "friendly" sources.

Last, and first in sight during the emergency, were prospects for energy conservation. From the start, most European countries and Japan appeared frugal energy users in comparison with the United States—although an excellent study by Resources for the Future furnishes some important qualifications to this view[4]—but

3. See Chapter 8.
4. Joel Darmstadter, Joy Dunkerley, Jack Alterman, *How Industrial Societies Use Energy, A Comparative Analysis* (Baltimore: Johns Hopkins University Press for Resources for the Future, 1977). After analyzing the contributions of economic-structural and energy intensity factors to the differences in energy use per unit of output between the United States and Western European countries

under the pressure of uncertain and expensive energy supplies, they came to see opportunities for even greater frugality in industry, transportation, and space heating. During the winter of 1973–1974, drastic energy-saving measures were adopted in most countries, later to be relaxed.

The 1974 OECD Outlook

Even before these diverse opportunities were systematized in national energy programs and these programs brought together and stimulated in the new International Energy Agency (IEA),[5] a study by the Organization for Economic Cooperation and Development (OECD) reflected the profound change in expectations, which the oil shock had brought about, concerning the evolution of the countries' energy structure over the next decade. In 1974, an OECD study group presented two different sets of estimates of the countries' primary energy structure in 1985 (1) from the precrisis perspective of 1973 and (2) as seen from 1974. The first estimate, called "base projection," relied to a large extent on forecasts constructed by member country governments prior to October 1973—that is, mostly in 1971–1972. The second, a postcrisis projection, reflected national and OECD official judgments of progress along the line of the opportunities noted above, under the influence of higher oil prices.[6] The pre-1973 and 1974-based projections implied the same gross domestic product (GDP) growth rates as forecast before October 1973—that is, for OECD-Europe a little over 5 percent per year

---

and Japan in 1972, the authors concluded: "It is . . . our firm judgment that, in the comparative intercountry setting of this report, the assumed presence of an energy-conservation ethic and abhorrence of waste 'over there,' in contrast to the disregard for such things in the United States, is simply not supported by the facts and is simplistic in its view of the world" (p. 207).

5. Aside from its role in stimulating energy programs to reduce imports in the member countries and making contingency plans for sudden supply interruptions, the IEA system initiated in 1974 served to quiet down the countries' scurrying for preferential access arrangements (item 1). After the hectic and generally unproductive efforts of this kind in late 1973 and 1974, this endeavor settled down to a more cautious search for cooperative projects between oil consumer and producer countries and to competition for the growing volume of oil country imports.

6. OECD, *Energy Prospects to 1985, An Assessment of Long Term Energy Developments and Related Policies* (Paris, 1975). We are showing the projections "corresponding to a price of $6 (in constant 1972 U.S. dollars) per barrel of Arabian API 34° crude oil" rather than those based on the assumption of $9 per barrel, also presented in the source. No one knows of course what 1985 prices will be, or even what "constant 1972 U.S. dollars" will mean to different countries at that time, given the intervening exchange rate developments. The "$6-oil case" offers the more conservative forecasts of structural energy changes under the impact of higher than pre-1973 oil prices.

Table 7-1. OECD-Europe's Energy Prospects for 1985, from pre-1973, 1974, and 1976 Perspectives.

Energy Type	1974, Actual Quantities[a]		Prospects for 1985, as seen from					
			Prior to 1973[b]		1974[c]		Late 1976[d]	
	Million tons oil equivalent[e]	Percent composition	Million tons oil equivalent	Percent composition	Million tons oil equivalent	Percent composition	Million tons oil equivalent	Percent composition
Solid Fuels, Total	254	(22)	215	(9)	293	(13)	272	(16)
Production	206		183		241		216	
Net imports	36	(3)	32	(1)	52	(2)	56	(3)
Oil and Natural Gas								
Liquids, Total	668[f]	(57)	1,442[i]	(63)	1,121[i]	(51)	904[f]	(53)
Production	22		252		285		222	(13)
Net imports	708	(61)	1,190	(52)	836	(38)	738	(43)
Gas, Total	140	(12)	304	(13)	385	(18)	265	(16)
Production	132		249		288		196	
Net imports	9	(1)	54	(2)	97	(4)	70	(4)
Nuclear Electricity	20	(2)	236	(10)	273	(13)	159	(9)
Hydro and Other Sources	78	(7)	112[g]	(5)	112[g]	(5)	105	(6)
Total Primary Energy	1,160	(100)	2,308[h]	(100)	2,184[h]	(100)	1,704	(100)

[a]Source: OECD, *World Energy Outlook* (Paris, 1977), p. 91.

[b]Source: OECD, *Energy Prospects to 1985* (Paris, 1975), "Base Projection," p. 50.

[c]As in b, "$6 Case."

[d]As in a, "Reference Case."

[e]Subtotals reflect stock changes. One million ton oil equivalent (Mtoe) equals approximately 7.3 million barrels or 20,000 barrels per day.

[f]Excluding marine bunkers.

[g]Data in 1975 source adjusted to reflect same terawatt hours/Mtoe equivalent as for nuclear; roughly corresponding to treatment in 1977 source.

[h]Totals exceed source totals by 63 Mtoe, as a result of adjustment noted under g.

[i]Including marine bunkers.

Table 7-2. Japan's Energy Prospects for 1985, from pre-1973, 1974, and 1976 Perspectives.

Energy Type	1974, Actual Quantities[a]		Prospects for 1985, as Seen From:					
			Prior to 1973[b]		1974[c]		Late 1976[d]	
	Million tons oil equivalent[e]	Percent composition	Million tons oil equivalent	Percent composition	Million tons oil equivalent	Percent composition	Million tons oil equivalent	Percent composition
Solid Fuels, Total	63	(19)	77	(9)	89	(12)	38	(14)
Production	16		14		16		13	
Net imports	47[f]	(14)	63	(7)	73	(9)	75	(12)
Oil and NGL, Total	238[f]	(71)	622[i]	(72)	511[i]	(66)	411[f]	(67)
Production	1		2		6		3	
Net imports	263	(79)	620	(71)	505	(65)	422	(72)
Gas, Total	7	(2)	42	(5)	45	(6)	48	(8)
Production	2		2		6		8	
Net imports	5	(1)	40	(5)	39	(5)	40	(6)
Nuclear Electricity	5	(1)	102	(11)	102	(13)	49	(7)
Hydro and Other Sources	21	(6)	26[g]	(3)	26[g]	(3)	28	(5)
Total Primary Energy	334	(100)	869[h]	(100)	773[h]	(100)	625	(100)

[a]Source: OECD, *World Energy Outlook* (Paris, 1977), p. 92.
[b]Source: OECD, *Energy Prospects to 1985* (Paris, 1975), p. 53 "Base Projection,"
[c]As in b, "$6 Case."
[d]As in a, "Reference Case."
[e]Subtotals reflect stock changes.
[f]Excluding marine bunkers.
[g]Data in 1975 source adjusted to reflect same Twh/Mtoe equivalent as for nuclear; corresponding roughly to treatment in 1977 source.
[h]Totals exceed source totals by 14 Mtoe, as a result of adjustment noted under g.
[i]Including marine bunkers.

during 1971-1980 and about 5 percent per year during 1980-1985, and for Japan 8.1 percent in the first period and 7.4 percent in the second. The quantitative forecasts did not allow for a reduction in economic growth accompanying the oil price rise, although the likelihood of some reduction was discussed in the OECD study.

These early projections are shown in Table 7-1 for OECD-Europe and in Table 7-2 for Japan, in the two central sets of columns in each table. The reader may use the first set of columns on the left ("1974, actual quantities") as a reference base for the projections to 1985 but should for the moment disregard the fourth set of columns on the right ("late 1976"). We shall discuss them later on.

As one would expect, the precrisis projections for Western Europe in 1985 allowed for considerable increases in all types of energy consumption, except solid fuels, over 1974. These increases were relatively greatest for oil (especially oil produced in the region) and nuclear electricity. The early postcrisis projections envisaged even greater relative increases over 1974 for nuclear electricity and gas and absolute increases (but drops in the percentage shares) for oil and solid fuels. Comparing the two projections for 1985, the energy substitition expected to occur as a result of higher oil prices and available alternatives to imported oil focused on increased contributions of gas, nuclear electricity, and intraregional coal and oil, in that order of absolute changes. But even with the percentage share of expected oil imports in total energy reduced from 52 to 38 percent, the volume of these imports in 1985 were seen as substantially greater than in 1974.

In the precrisis projection, total primary energy consumption forecast for 1985 was more than double the 1974 level. It was a little less than double in the early postcrisis projection. The 5.5 percent cutback of total primary energy consumption between the two forecasts reflected the expected extent of energy conservation. The OECD authors considered a much higher rate of conservation (by 15 to 20 percent for OECD as a whole) possible, but unlikely in the absence of special conservation policies that would reinforce the market response to higher oil prices.

The picture drawn for Japan was similar, except in the following respects. Reflecting the much higher GDP growth rate postulated for this country, the foreseen growth of total primary energy requirements to 1985 was considerably greater than for Europe and affected all types of energy except domestic coal. The postulated energy conservation factor, reflected in the difference between the precrisis and the postcrisis total primary energy estimate, was greater too—that is, 11.2 percent. Comparing the two projections for 1985, one sees the expected change in Japan's primary energy composition go from oil to nuclear electricity, imported coal, and gas; but the increase in the shares of these three energy types, from the precrisis to the postcrisis perspective, was less for Japan than for Western Europe. On the whole, the change in perspective seemed to make less of a difference in the Japanese than in the aggregate Western European energy structure. Expected Japanese oil imports, while reduced in their predominant relative position in total energy supply (from 71 to 65 percent) were still almost twice as high in the postcrisis perspective for 1985 as the actual 1974 level.

Such was the outlook for our countries over the decade following the 1973–74 crisis. To the OECD projectors, this postcrisis vision appeared as a relatively conservative one with respect to the magnitude of the expected oil price change (the lower end of the range they considered realistic), with respect to nuclear power expansion (which some governments projected a good deal greater), and perhaps in other regards as well. If today one may characterize their postcrisis outlook of 1974 as a "brave vision," it is because we know a little more about factors that came into play affecting its realization, at least in the first half of the decade, and that also affected later projections to 1985 and 1990, as we shall see.

PROBLEMS WITH ENERGY POLICY

The sudden disappearance of cheap oil and the unlikelihood of its return gave rise to waves of public concern about energy availability and its use and to energy policy as a distinct new task of government. In all of our countries, energy agencies and programs sprang up and addressed the structural developments that seemed necessary to cope with the new situation. These differed from country to country. In the course of wide-ranging debates, during which the public was treated to much information as well as confusion, the mainstream of the public came to understand that the oil shortage was not a ploy of the international oil companies that could be dealt with by expelling and replacing them, that behind the short-lived energy crisis loomed a very large economic transformation and adjustment problem, and that governmental guidance was needed to cope with this problem.

But while governments in many of the parliamentary democracies were ready in a fairly short time to elevate a set of decisions and related implementation measures to the status of "official energy programs"—much more expeditiously so than the checks and balances government of the United States—they observed that the assumptions about needs and feasibilities on which these programs were based were put in question by events and new judgments almost as soon as the programs appeared. They also experienced unforeseen obstacles and risks, the competitive force of other political and economic concerns, and a need for flexibility and cautious experimentation that did not permit adherence to fixed time schedules.

This section will be devoted to a general discussion of the countries' experiences with the problems of energy policy during the few years that have elapsed since the oil shock. The discussion will refer to particular country situations only selectively and will focus on problems that concerned them all, albeit to a varying degree.

The 1976 OECD Outlook to 1985

Two years after the publication of *Energy Prospects to 1985*, OECD offered revised projections for 1985 in its *World Energy Outlook*.[7] As with the 1974 projection effort, we are using the relatively conservative variant of the projections that were offered in the 1976 study, the "reference case." This principal forecasting vehicle of the report rested on "continuance of present policies governing supply expansion and conservation" and on reduced rates of future GDP growth. In significant contrast to the earlier study, the new one did not offer alternative projections based on greater oil price rises, but it considered alternatives based on even lesser or not quite as much reduced GDP growth rates and on the adoption and presumed effect of more intensive supply expansion and conservation policies than currently in force.[8] The extent of growth retardation and the intensity of energy policy were now seen as the main variables.

The "reference case" projections from 1976 for Western Europe and Japan are shown in Tables 7-1 and 7-2 in the last set of columns on the right. Comparing them with the 1974 projections will lead us into some of the problems encountered by energy policies in

7. OECD, *World Energy Outlook, A Reassessment of Long-Term Energy Developments and Related Policies* (Paris, 1977). This study differed somewhat from the earlier one in scope, focus, and technique, but these differences will not hold us here. As the authors explained, the study drew "upon extensive reassessments completed by nearly all major energy consuming and some energy producing countries after the oil price increases of 1973–1974 [i.e., largely in 1976], but at the same time relies less upon member states' official forecasts than the first study [and more upon judgments of the secretariat]" (p. 8).

8. These alternatives were called the "low growth," "high growth," and "accelerated policy" cases, respectively.

the interval. The principal differences revealed by the comparison are as follows:

1. The new report reduced drastically the projected growth of primary energy. It expected OECD-Europe to consume some 1,704 million tons oil equivalent (Mtoe) in 1985 instead of the 2,184 Mtoe in the 1974 projection and Japan some 625 Mtoe instead of 773 Mtoe. These reductions resulted mainly from the scaling down of the assumed GDP growth rates, for Europe from about 5 percent to a little less than 4 percent per year and for Japan from close to 8 percent to somewhat more than 6 percent per year,[9] but the lesser growth of total primary energy used (TPE) rested also on greater allowances for energy conservation than in the postcrisis forecast, under policies by then in place. The prospective growth of TPE (and of oil imports) was cushioned by expected energy savings, measured from the basis of the crisis years, which for OECD-Europe amounted to an approximate equivalent of the expected total use of nuclear electricity and for Japan amounted to an approximate equivalent of the total use of hydropower and other sources.[10]

2. The new report cut back severely the projected growth of nuclear electricity from the levels that the earlier report had regarded as conservative for both Europe and Japan. The projected share of that type of energy fell back from 13 percent to 9 percent for Europe and from 13 percent to 7 percent for Japan. The new study placed much less hope in nuclear power as a substitute for oil in both regions by 1985.

3. For Western Europe, the new study also took a decidedly less optimistic view of the contribution of indigenous gas; it was more optimistic for Japan's gas supply but only on account of imported (LNG) gas. Coal imports were given more weight in both regions.

4. The reduction in oil's expected share in total energy that had occurred from the precrisis to the postcrisis projection in both regions was partly reversed in the move from the latter to the 1976 projection, the European percentage dropping now from 63 to 53 (not 51), and the Japanese percentage from 72 to 67

9. For OECD-Europe, 3.6 percent 1974–1980, 4.1 percent 1980–1985; for Japan, 6 percent and 6.6 percent, respectively.

10. See Table 7-6. This is based on 1977 IEA review material, not strictly comparable with the 1976 OECD forecast, and reflects, for Japan and several European countries, also the estimated effects of some conservation measures still to be introduced. The IEA material makes the TPE consumption (or oil saving) effect of conservation efforts by 1985 appear on the order of 172 Mtoe per year for Europe, 24 Mtoe per year for Japan.

(not 66). The share of oil imports likewise moved up again, in Japan's case even to the level of the precrisis projection. Still, in absolute terms, Europe's and Japan's projected demands for imported oil turned out to be lower than in the 1974 exercise.

Four important things had happened in the interval: (1) the recession, and in conjunction with it, a significant lowering of expectations for GDP growth; (2) encounters with various obstacles to the development of substitutes for imported oil; (3) diverse experiences with economic adaptation to the change in energy availabilities and prospects; and (4) some experience with the competition between oil saving and other imperatives in public policy. These things were reflected in the revision of the OECD projections, at least to some degree, and it would seem today, two years after the latest one was made, that the reflection was too weak rather than too strong.

These experiences, and the attending outlook revisions, also had an interesting effect on the enthusiasm with which the new energy programs were started in several countries. These had been encouraged by the international conference and bureaucratic frameworks of IEA and the European Community. The experiences cast doubt on the programmability of energy structure changes and made the governments back away from earlier commitments to specific national targets for energy quantities at specific dates and move toward indications of mere ranges for these quantities, conditional forecasts, and pronouncements of hopes and general orientations. Although adoption of an explicit energy program continued to count in the international forums as superior to vacillation over the composition of such a program, the difference between frustrated decisiveness and indecision narrowed. Some energy programming authorities, like the German, French, and Japanese, had unsatisfactory results to show because events did not follow the programs on schedule, and some who procrastinated like the Americans, looked bad because they had no, or perverse, programs.

Recession and Tempered
GDP Growth Expectations

The post-1974 recession in GDP growth, more pronounced in Europe than in Japan and in the United States, could be ascribed in part to rising energy prices and the siphoning off of income to the OPEC countries. It not only tempered immediately the growth of energy demands but also initiated a lowering of expectations for future growth of GDP and energy demand. Since the slackening of demand virtually stopped OPEC-decreed oil price increases and since non-OPEC oil from the North Sea, and shortly thereafter from Alaska, began to ease further the demand-supply tension in the world oil market, the threat of an immediate energy shortage that had made oil saving so urgent gave way to much more complex problems, including that of what to do with the oil available. Europe and Japan had ample oil, gas, coal, and electricity, and idle capacities in their oil refineries. Some OPEC governments were pressing the oil companies to ship more oil to Europe and Japan, and companies were asking the governments there to relieve the refinery situation by permitting greater consumption of fuel oil. The prospect of the "energy crunch" moved further into the future. Since the countries' higher bills for oil imports could also be met in one way or another,[11] the fear of an oil-induced international financial debacle dissolved for the present, and in more sober evaluations of things to come, it even seemed unwarranted for an indefinite time ahead. If there was to be trouble in international finance, it was not just because energy had become more expensive.

There was no rejoicing in the industrial countries over the fact that the easing of the energy pinch that they had wished for came mainly by way of energy savings resulting from slower growth and higher unemployment, but it did give them some time to reflect on the restructuring needed for their energy systems. One could perhaps live, at least for the next decade, with a somewhat higher share of imported oil in total energy than one had allowed in 1974. One might also have to—either because alternatives could not materialize fast enough for technical reasons; or because their financial attractiveness, which seemed unquestionable when OPEC price increases had been inflation leaders, became questionable when the costs of other energies began to escalate faster than oil; or for still other reasons to be examined presently. Thus, even if the sense of urgency did not abate among the energy specialists, European and Japanese decisionmakers felt induced, or compelled, to hesitate with big commitments and to pursue innovations with caution.

11. The ways in which countries met their oil bills differed. Some, like France, relied on capital imports in various forms. Germany covered its oil bill consistently with overall current account surpluses from 1974 on and even achieved, in 1977, a substantial current account surplus with the OPEC countries alone. Japan, Italy, and the United Kingdom proceeded like France in the earlier postcrisis years, but moved toward overall current account surpluses in 1976 or 1977. The decline of the dollar has lowered substantially the foreign exchange cost of imported oil for Japan and all European countries. The OPEC cartel still fixes its prices in U.S. dollars. Stable dollar prices of oil have meant declining yen, deutsche mark, and franc costs per barrel.

In a short span of time, the future energy structure for which they were to make commitments had become less clear cut. In 1974 they had been told to look forward to continued brisk oil price increases, with few questions asked about the persistence of recently experienced high rates of economic growth. In the later 1970s, they learned of prospects for sluggish economic growth and of a likelihood of "fairly stable oil prices in real terms" through the 1980s—and thereafter perhaps a big new spurt.[12] They might well wonder then what there was to be urgent about. The sense of urgency returned soon enough when at the beginning of 1979 the revolution in Iran initiated a new tightening of supplies. But answers to the quest for energy alternatives seemed no more readily available than they had been five years earlier.

Obstacles to the Development of "Secure" Energy Sources

In 1974, nuclear energy, coal-based energy, non-OPEC oil, and gas appeared to be "safe" sources of energy, technically and economically accessible in the years ahead. But it did not take long for all of them to run into obstacles as societies set about expanding their exploitation and for doubts to be raised about their "safety" in one sense or another.

Nuclear Power—Internal and External Problems. European and Japanese energy planners and industrialists met their greatest disappointments with their top choice for alternative energy development, nuclear electricity. The hindrances to its expansion came from unexpected quarters. In 1974, planners had been apprehensive that power plant producers might be unable to supply equipment fast enough to carry out the stepped-up expansion programs, or that a bad accident in a nuclear facility might upset the programs, or that financing might prove difficult. By 1978, European producers of reactors and related equipment (chiefly German and French) had excess capacities and kept production lines open largely with the help of foreign orders (in good part from the Middle East and Brazil, but some of these have been canceled in the meantime). The safety record of the nuclear industry had been quite good, and financing was no serious problem except in Italy and Spain. But governments that had been urging the expansion of nuclear

12. See in this connection the Trilateral Energy Task Force to the Trilateral Commission (authors: John C. Sawhill, Hanns W. Maull, and Keichi Oshima) *Energy: Managing the Transition* (New York: the Trilateral Commission, 1978), pp. 8–13.

capacity for years and were still devoting the lion's share of their energy R&D budgets to nuclear power (see Table 7-14) found themselves unable or unwilling to meet such requirements of its implementation as site selections, construction permits, approvals of startups or continued operation of finished power plants, determination and approval of waste disposal and spent fuel reprocessing facilities, and the protection of construction projects against outside interference. This loss of heart on the part of governments was brought about to some extent by the practical difficulties of industrial application not uncommon with a new technology and, as more and more reactors were put on line, by uncertainties with the back end of the fuel cycle—waste disposal and decommissioning of nuclear plants. But above all, internal and external forces made themselves felt. Nuclear power development per se was opposed, or attacked as the last and seemingly most risky encroachment of industrialization on the natural habitat and established ways of life; there were fears that nuclear facilities were vulnerable to terrorist attacks or that they might be used to manufacture nuclear weapons. New ("green") coalitions of such disparate groups as radicals, conservative farmers, and environmental organizations, operating locally, within nations, and across national boundaries, began to dog nuclear projects. They initiated law suits, organized refusals of landowners to sell land needed for the projects, held noisy demonstrations, and obstructed work at the sites. Most governments felt compelled to temporize and to wait for the storm to subside. They expected a slower rise in electricity demand and were sensitive to demands for environmental protection. They were also reluctant to engage in violent confrontations with bodies of citizens that often included their own political supporters and to risk their defection at the polls. Finally, difficulties regarding uranium supply and enrichment sources raised by potential suppliers did not help. They repudiated the guidance they had given to industry and industry had to lower its sights.

The sharp downward revisions by OECD in 1976/1977 of nuclear electricity estimates for Western Europe and Japan by 1985 understated the lowering of sights that occurred in both regions.[13] It certainly continued after 1976, as the course of unofficial projections by country in successive issues of the *Jahrbuch der Atomwirtschaft* indicates (Table 7-3). At present, the lower ends of the

13. The OECD projection for Japan, shown in Table 7-2, still reflected a capacity estimate of 35 GW operating in that country by 1985. That was well below the official (MITI) goal for that year, 49 GW, set in 1976. But today, even 35 GW seems too optimistic for Japan's nuclear capacity in 1985.

Table 7-3. Nuclear Electricity Capacity in 1985 as Seen from 1975, 1976, and 1977, by Country.

Country	1985 in the Perspective of			Low 1977 Expectation in Percent of 1975 (percent)
	1975	1976	1977	
		(gigawatt)		
Belgium	9.5	6-9	5-6	53
France	42.4	39-47	30-40	71
West Germany	45.2	34-42	19-29	42
Italy	24.3	12-18	5-10	21
United Kingdom	14.4	12-16	11	76
Other E.C.	5.9	2-3	1-2	17
Sweden	10.6	10-12	8-10	75
Switzerland	7.8	5	3-4	38
Spain	25.8	18-22	13-20	50
Other Western Europe	11.3	7-10	6-8	
Total Western Europe	197.2	145-184	104-138	53
Japan	49.3	35-45	25-34	51

Source: *Jahrbuch der Atomwirtschaft,* (Dusseldorf: Handersflatt) 1976 (for 1975), 1977 (for 1976), and 1978 (for 1977); Table 1 in each volume.

indicated ranges of the latest capacity projections appear the most realistic, and even they may not be reached. Italy furnishes a striking example. The revised national energy program of 1977 replaced the "minimum" nuclear electricity output forecast for 1985 in the program's earlier (1975) version—that is, 29 Mtoe—by a mere 10 Mtoe. But the IEA review found that even this capacity might not be realized due to siting delays and setbacks caused by antinuclear opposition.

Some capacity that will not materialize by 1985 may of course come into being later on. Between 1985 and 1990, the latest available (1977) IEA review of member country expectations projects an increase in European members' and Japan's nuclear electricity output roughly as great as during the nine-year period from 1976 to 1985 (Table 7-4). But if part of the performance projected for 1985 must be considered "at risk" today, the projections for 1990 certainly cannot be taken at face value. Unless the conditions of the industry improve significantly in the next few years, they will not be fulfilled. We shall examine in a subsequent section whether and where such an improvement appears on the horizon.

European Oil and Gas—Competing Imperatives. The substantial downward revision of European oil and gas production contained in the 1976 OECD outlook to 1985 resulted from different causes.

Table 7-4. Nuclear Energy Production by Country, 1973 and 1976, and Outlook to 1985 and 1990 (Mtoe).

Country	1973	1976	1985	1990
Austria	—	—	1.7	3.0
Belgium	—	2.2	7.7	8.0
Denmark	—	—	—	3.6
West Germany	2.8	5.7	34.9	58.2
Greece	—	—	—	3.0
Italy	0.7	0.8	10.0	35.0[a]
Luxembourg	—	—	3.0	3.0
The Netherlands	0.3	0.9	2.7	2.7
Norway	—	—	—	2.7
Spain	1.5	1.7	11.3	22.9
Sweden	0.5	3.6	11.5	13.7
Switzerland	1.4	2.0	4.1	5.2
United Kingdom	7.2	8.8	15.0	18.0
Turkey[b]	—	—	1.0	n.a.
IEA-Europe	14.4	25.7	102.9	180.0[c]
France	3.0[d]	n.a.	55.0[e]	n.a.
OECD-Europe	17.4		158.0	
Japan	2.4	8.3	46.0	83.7

Source: *1977 IEA Review of National Energy Programs.* For France: "Rapport de la Commission de l'énergie du VII[e] Plan," March 1976, pp. 5, 30. For Turkey: "OECD/IEA, 1975 Review of National Programmes," January 1976, p. 14.
n.a. = Not available.
[a]Lower end of range.
[b]1976 estimates.
[c]Including one for Turkey.
[d]1974.
[e]"Hard core" estimate. A later (1977) estimate of the commission placed the estimate at 45 Mtoe.

The earlier forecast assumed all-out development and exploitation of the North Sea and Dutch fields. For various reasons this is not happening. British and Dutch government regulations have given exploration a relatively free rein, although in the British case the decision to insert a governmental oil company, BNOC, into the process and the delays involved in establishing its place slowed down the action somewhat; but Norwegian exploration policy was one of slow growth from the start, and it significantly limited output prospects by 1985. Regarding the exploitation of fields found, neither the British nor the Norwegians—nor the German authorities for that matter—gave the private companies the maximum incentive possible under the umbrella of OPEC prices, but creamed off much of the potential economic rent through royalty and special tax impositions. British taxation is said to have raised the threshold

Table 7-5. Oil and Gas Production in Principal European Producer Countries, 1973 and 1976, and Outlook to 1985 and 1990 (Mtoe).

Producer Countries	1973 Oil	1973 Gas	1976 Oil	1976 Gas	1985 Oil	1985 Gas	1990 Oil	1990 Gas
United Kingdom	0	25	12	33	100–150	35–45	90–140	35–40
Norway	2	—	14	0	39	27	36	17
The Netherlands	—	55	—	75	—	69	—	51
West Germany	—	15	—	15	—	14	—	12
Italy	—	13	—	13	—	15	—	10

Source: *1977 IEA Reviews of National Energy Programs* (Paris: OECD, 1978).

field size for commercial development and barred the exploitation of smaller fields. Like the British, the Norwegians also favored a national "chosen instrument" company. This has undoubtedly affected the companies' development policies in the North Sea and will affect future output.[14]

In the Dutch case, the output prospect for 1985 is beginning to reflect the government's decision to stretch the availability of gas from presently known reserves for the benefit of Dutch consumers in later years, although there is hope that additions to reserves will induce a relaxation of the conservation policy. Meanwhile, the Dutch appear unwilling to renew gas export contracts with German, French, Belgian, and Italian consumers. Contracts for Norwegian gas supplies may help to replace some of the shortfall. Indeed, looking a little farther ahead to 1990, all European oil- and gas-producing countries (except Britain, for gas) now expect to enter into a period of declining outputs, with or without the application of specific conservation policies (Table 7-5). Known reserves are limited, and additions to them are not particularly encouraged under existing regulatory and fiscal policies in several countries. If governments—especially the Norwegian, but also the British— were to turn all appropriate signals to full speed ahead, reserve and output prospects might still be lifted above the levels now projected for the later 1980s.[15]

14. Peter Odell of the Netherlands and M. A. Adelman of the Massachusetts Institute of Technology have expressed themselves on this matter, the first, for example, in a paper read at the RFF/NSF Workshop on the Federal Energy Administration's National Energy Outlook, Washington, D.C., August 15, 1976, and the second in *Resources*, published by Resources for the Future, Summer 1976.

15. In its "accelerated policy scenario" for 1985, OECD allows for an addition of 26 Mtoe to Western Europe's volume of natural gas production, shown for the "reference case" (196 Mtoe); see *World Energy Outlook*, p. 54.

Here we observe a set of other imperatives competing with that of reducing the dependence on OPEC oil. The environmental protection imperative, which we found at work on the nuclear scene, reappears in the concern of the Norwegian government for established fisheries in North Norway. Offshore oil activity does not appear to mix well with fishing.

The imperative of national economic balance is at work in Norway's slow development policies in the form of efforts to avoid an inflationary overheating of the economy and excessive resource transfers to the oil sector. This imperative also motivates Dutch policy to reserve Dutch gas for the Dutch consumers and British policy to reserve British oil for British refineries, some of which are only partly built (which runs afoul of an optimum use of existing refining capacities, as oil companies see it). Furthermore, in the name of national economic balance, the appetite of governments for revenue and their concepts of fiscal equity lead to the taxing away of energy producers' economic rent. In this connection, it is worth noting that the frequent admonitions of governmental and international energy experts to rely on market-conforming prices in order to bring about appropriate energy developments are rarely directed at European fiscal discriminations against returns on capital invested in energy and are almost exclusively aimed at discriminations in favor of energy consumers. If undisturbed market price relations offer good incentives for energy savings, why should they not also be permitted to serve as guides for investment into energy projects, in Europe as well as in the United States? In various countries, holding down oil company revenue is seen as a requirement of national economic balance, or of politics.

The classic company imperative of maximizing returns on investment regardless of what or where, gears investment and activity to all the circumstances. There are indications that involvement in North Sea ventures was not always of the highest priority to the major companies and that their eagerness for such ventures has not grown as events developed and some governments showed preference for operators dependent on the national government. There are also indications that uncertainty about the future configuration of energy supply and demand conditions drives companies away from energy projects that promise a recovery of investment in the long term only.

Finally, political imperatives of various kinds appear to have dampened the North Sea and various other energy developments. They range from neomercantilistic preferences for certain arrangements for landing and disposing of North Sea output to a reluctance to initiate oil operations in the northern waters, in which the Soviet Union has strong strategic interests, or elsewhere, to proceeding with a breeder reactor project that displeases the United States. In Holland, opposition to nuclear industry cooperation with Brazil almost forced the government to repudiate a commitment to expand the Almelo uranium enrichment plant.

Coal—Home Produced or Imported? There are also considerable obstacles to turning the ample coal reserves of the Western world, even of Western Europe, into a growing supply and to implementing the economic use of coal in Europe and Japan. The postcrisis OECD projection of a rise in European coal production to 1985 (Table 7-1) and its absorption in the economies (in power generation and elsewhere) was based on the belief that higher oil prices would reverse the precipitous decline of the industry in previous years. Up to now, oil has not risen enough to produce this result. The later OECD projection for Western Europe reduced the expectations for 1985 and only failed to show a decline below the 1974 level because of expected increases in the outputs of Spanish and Turkish coal, chiefly lignite. Except for lignite, West European (and Japanese) coal remains a high cost fuel in relation both to oil and gas and to overseas coal where it is available. For this reason and others, its markets remain in doubt.

This presumptive alternative to imported oil therefore depends in the first place on continued and, in the face of stagnating oil prices, even increased protection and subsidization in the main European coal-producing countries;[16] second, on a slowdown in nuclear power expansion, the more economical alternative; third, on the availability of and on the will to admit substantially greater coal imports from lower cost regions; and finally, on technological developments that would raise the efficiency and environmental acceptability of coal fuel offered either in solid, liquid, or gaseous form.

The British and West German governments have been trying hard to create markets for this politically significant article, but this did not stave off further declines in demand and the appearance of surplus stocks of coal. The second condition was also fulfilled, but it turned out (for example, in Germany) that environmental protection that obstructed nuclear expansion also militated against a large new coal-fired power plant. The last two conditions may

16. German *Steinkohle*, selling for about DM 200/ton at the mine, appears to be subsidized to the extent of about DM 60/ton produced in 1978. *Der Spiegel*, February 20, 1978, pp. 81-82.

brighten the picture at a later time, perhaps in the 1990s, when stagnating gas output and fresh boosts in oil prices may widen coal's opportunities, and imports may flow more freely.

The near-term picture has been discouraging. The British National Coal Board and the government embarked on a large capital investment program in order to raise production, in both existing and new mines, from 135 to 150 million tons (Mt) in 1985, and more thereafter. West German ambitions, expressed in the wake of the energy crisis, were more modest, the plans of industry being mainly to maintain existing capacity and employment for the time being. From 1974 on, there was an upsurge of investment in the European coal industry. Capital expenditures in the European Community rose from 336 million units of account in 1973 to 851 million in 1976, with the United Kingdom in the lead. But in the interval, the overall demand for coal in the EC continued to decline, with only a small increase in the power plant sector, and EC production of hard coal fell from 270 to 248 Mt. Imports did rise and offset at least part of the decline. Western European hopes for an increase in the role of coal in the region's energy economy failed to materialize, at least over the few years following the 1973-1974 crisis.

In the medium term—that is, through the 1980s—the demand prospects are somewhat more hopeful, assuming moderate economic growth, coal-oil and gas price relations favorable to coal, and nuclear power delays redounding to the advantage of coal. In Gerald Manners' estimates (Chapter 8), on which this analysis relies in part, demand for solid fuel in Western Europe might increase from 418 Mt in 1977 to perhaps 423-463 Mt in the 1980s. But European coal ouput prospects are not hopeful. Experience with Britain's coal expansion plan since 1973, plus the labor, productivity, cost, environmental, and market problems of the industry, suggest that production is more likely to remain at the 1976 level of 120 Mt than to expand, and it may even slip back. German industry plans to stabilize hard coal output at about 90 Mt should be regarded as indicating the upper limit for the 1980s, and lignite output is not expected to grow. So the slight rise in demand is unlikely to be accompanied by a rise in domestic production, and it will be up to coal imports into Western Europe to sustain the modest increase in the European solid fuel sector's contribution which OECD (1976) forecast for 1985.

For Japan, the picture is rather similar. The domestic production base is, of course, small and likely to shrink further despite subsidies. The dependence on imports is far greater than in Europe. The more sanguine OECD expectations for the expansion of the

Japanese solid fuel consumption (Table 7-2) rest on the growth of imports. But such a growth would require, among other things, the development of a Japanese infrastructure for steam coal use.

Inasmuch as assumptions for the longer term, beyond the 1980s, can vary considerably, it is difficult to project a much better fate for the solid fuel sector at that time or a much worse one for that matter. Likely increases in demand in both regions will be met only if imports are forthcoming.

This is an important question on which a recent IEA report is focusing.[17] It does not expect a large increase in coal trading before the 1990s but considers it possible thereafter, provided potential exporters such as the United States, Canada, Australia, and South Africa will generate the output and commit themselves in good time not to restrict the flow of exports for national reasons and provided potential importers such as France, West Germany, the United Kingdom, and Japan make timely commitments to accept substantial tonnages steadily. The IEA report stresses the potential value of steam coal for the U.S. energy economy, notably the electricity-generating sector, but qualifies its optimism for coal's prospects in Western Europe and Japan. For Western Europe, the report estimates that imported steam coal from various sources, and even domestically produced coal, should be competitive with oil in electricity generation and that "steam coals imported from Poland and South Africa could possibly be competitive with nuclear power in base load operations in power stations near coastal areas or with easy access to water transport." In Japan, the study considers imported coal to be in a good competitive position in relation to oil but notes that "the high transportation cost of coal in Japan and the need to burn coal in an environmentally acceptable manner raises doubts about the competitive position of imported steam coal vis-à-vis nuclear power in future years."[18]

Consequences for Oil Imports

Calculated by OECD as residuals, the 1985 net oil import estimates for both Western Europe and Japan are absolutely smaller than the postcrisis estimates, but they constitute larger percentage shares of TPE, 43 and 72 percent, respectively, in the two regions (Tables 7-1 and 7-2). Compared with 1974, the forecast tonnages of net oil imports are significantly larger, but their percentage contributions to TPE are significantly smaller. The energy alterna-

17. International Energy Agency, *Steam Coal, Prospects to 2000* (Paris: OECD, 1978).

18. Ibid., p. 59

tives to imported (OPEC) oil are thus counted upon to replace a good part of the latter, especially in Western Europe, although not quite to the extent forecast in 1974. The dependence on gas imports from OPEC countries, however, is likely to increase, if not by 1985, then later.

Will the alternative energies do as well as expected? That will depend on whether the hindrances to their exploitation have been sufficiently allowed for in the estimates. If they have not, net oil imports will be higher, at least relative to TPE. Oil remains the swing fuel. If electric power and space heating requirements cannot be met to the hoped for degree by energy carriers other than OPEC oil, OPEC oil will quickly be called upon to avoid a shortage.

Will the alternatives continue to do well after the mid-1980s? According to the 1977 IEA reviews, most country "programs" expect net oil import-TPE ratios to decline further from 1985 to 1990, but with some (e.g., Japan, Germany, and Denmark) this expectation rests on nuclear power developments—and with Japan, also on LNG developments—of questionable certainty. The United Kingdom, Norway, Belgium, and Austria, however, expect their ratios to move even earlier—that is, from 1980 to 1985 (Table 7-6). Of course, all energy supply and conservation alternatives are involved. The tonnages of net oil imports in 1985 and 1990, forecast in the national programs and underlying the percentages of Table 7-6, are shown in Table 7-7. Except for Denmark and Sweden, all

Table 7-6. Net Oil Imports as Percent of Total Primary Energy, 1973, and Estimated for 1985 and 1990.

	Net Oil Imports in Percent of TPE		
Country	*1973*	*1985*	*1990*
Austria	41	40	43
Belgium	60	48	53
Denmark	91	48	45
West Germany	54	45	42
Greece	77	57	54
Italy	73	62	52–56
Luxembourg	36	24	23
The Netherlands	44	53	51
Norway	34	-98	-71
Spain	64	48	42
Sweden	59	46	44
Switzerland	64	50	49
United Kingdom	49	-10	-2
Japan	75	64	56

Source: *1977 IEA Reviews of National Energy Programs* (Paris: OECD, 1978).

Table 7-7. Net Oil Imports by Country, 1973 and 1976, and Outlook to 1985 and 1990.

Country	National Program Type[a]	Mtoe 1973	1976	1985	1990
Austria	B	10	10	13	17
Belgium	A	28	23	29	38
Denmark	A	18	16	10	10
France	n.a.	116	102	98	n.a.
West Germany	A	144	132	151	154
Greece	B	9	9	14	18
Ireland	B	6	5	11	18
Italy	A	97	92	126	126–136
The Netherlands	B	28	25	48	51
Norway	A	7	-6	-27	-22
Spain	A	37	46	47	52
Sweden	B	28	28	28	28
Switzerland	B	15	13	13	14
United Kingdom	A	110	79	-24	-4
Turkey	n.a.	9	10	34	n.a.
Japan		255	266	381	399

Source: *1977 IEA Reviews of National Energy Programs.* For Turkey: "OECD/IEA, 1975 Review of National Programs," January 1976, p. 17. Pertaining to 1974, 1975, 1980. For France: "Rapport de la Commission de l'énergie du VIIe plan," March 1976, pp. 5, 30. Oil Consumption 1973, 1975, and 1985 ("hard core").

n.a. = Not available.

[a]A: "Accelerated policy scenario." B: "Base case." See *IEA Review*, pp. 9, 10.

Table 7-8. Energy Consumption for Western Europe, Japan, and the United States, 1973 and 1977 (Mtoe).

Energy Consumption	Western Europe[a] 1973	1977	Japan 1973	1977	United States 1973	1977
Oil						
Gasolines	133	138	43	45	313	329
Middle distillates	248	241	51	56	201	220
Fuel oil	270	223	143	129	148	159
Other	98	94	33	31	156	158
Total consumption	749	697	269	260	818	867
(Net imports)	(726)	(627)	(268)	(259)	(361)	(459)
Natural gas	130	171	5	12	572	495
Solid fuels	270	264	62	60	340	363
Hydro and nuclear power	109	147	20	25	97	128
Total primary energy	1,258	1,278	356	358	1,828	1,853

Source: *BP Statistical Review of the World Oil Industry 1977* (London: British Petroleum Co. Ltd.).

[a]Including Finland, Yugoslavia, Iceland, Cyprus, Gibraltar, and Malta.

countries' net oil imports are expected to rise (net exports, to fall) from 1985 to 1990, regardless of whether or not the outlook presented by the country implies "program acceleration."

A Glance at the Recent Past

The reader may wish to supplement these prognoses and questions about future energy patterns with a summary of what actually happened to energy consumption in the four years following the oil crisis (see Table 7-8). In 1977, Western Europe, Japan, and the United States consumed about the same amounts of primary energy as they did in 1973. Western Europe consumed less oil—chiefly less fuel oil, but a little more gasoline—and it reduced its net oil imports twice as much as a result of North Sea production. Increases in the consumption of natural gas, hydro, and nuclear power slightly overbalanced the drop in oil and the lesser one in coal. Japan moved in about the same directions, but the gas-for-oil substitution was much weaker, and there was, of course, no domestic oil to replace imports. The U.S. development in this time span, which is shown for reference, contrasted significantly in the oil and natural gas sectors. Declining availability of gas here permitted no substitution of gas for fuel oil, and declining domestic oil production accentuated the increase in oil imports. Gasoline consumption increased only a little more, proportionately, than in Europe. It remains to be seen which of these changes in energy use patterns will be extended in the years ahead and which ones will be modified or reversed.

The Security of Supplies

Predictable availability, on reasonable terms, of energy materials from abroad is a concern of first rank with Japan and most Western European countries. For almost all of them, the failure of the oil supply system built by the international companies in the 1950s and 1960s to live up to that expectation was the starting point of energy policy. Because of the demonstrated unreliability of the principal sources of their oil, they have been trying ever since to turn away from them.

Now it is evident that this effort signifies entering into new supply dependencies, as well as staying in the old one, albeit to a somewhat lessened extent. Except for Norway, not one of the countries can expect to be self-sufficient in energy materials. They face an increasing dependence on imports of natural gas, coal, uranium, and attendant foreign services and a continuing one for oil, from OPEC and other sources. The new suppliers are other industrial or economically developed countries, outside Europe and within; or less developed ones, chiefly in Africa and Latin America; or Communist countries.

In 1974, everything that was not OPEC (or AOPEC) oil seemed secure. Therefore, the pursuit of supply security seemed to boil down to reducing dependence on the flow of OPEC oil and preparing for future interruptions by setting up national reserves and an emergency international oil-sharing system. The IEA was chartered to help the countries carry out these plans. Countries strove to diversify their imports, content, and sources.

By 1978, they knew that they had more things to worry about than another Arab oil embargo, and these were precisely the things that they were relying on to become less vulnerable to such an embargo. They had to worry about some of their allies (the United States, Canada, and fellow Europeans like the Dutch) not renewing or interrupting gas, oil, coal, and uranium supplies for a variety of political or national-economic reasons and about the unreliability for similar or different reasons of Australians, South Africans, newly independent states, and Communist countries. From the OPEC side, there were threats to make supplies of crude oil dependent on the customers' willingness to import much less desired refined petroleum products as well. The worries could not be put to rest with the thought that all these supply streams were most unlikely to fail at the same time and that therefore if one did, the others would see the country through.

In theory, diversified risk is lesser risk; but acting on this principle can prove futile when the diverse sources coalesce to present a unified threat, as Arab oil countries did in the past and as friendly uranium suppliers tend to do today. The principle is also of little help with decisions about investments in energy plants, equipments, and infrastructures. Many of them are specifically related to particular energy materials, kinds and qualities, and even particular sources from which these are expected to come. LNG import systems will not work for coal, nuclear power plants will not run on fossil fuels, oil refineries or gas distribution systems do not run well on any sort of oil or gas. For purposes of energy policy and investments, especially the big and long lead time investments called for by the reorientation of energy structures, the fear of exposure to new unreliabilities and blackmail is paralyzing, whether one thinks of their perpetrators as particular partners or coalitions.

With many Europeans and Japanese today, the fear of supply insecurity from non-OPEC sources has come to rival the apprehensions about Arab-OPEC sources. Rational or irrational, temporary or protracted, this fear encumbers energy policy and investment decisions, in particular long-term commitments, and it already makes some commitments made since 1973 look dubious.

The acute perceptions of energy vulnerability have also given national energy protectionism a new lease on life. It was waning during the time of conversion to oil, when support was gradually being withdrawn from national coal production in most countries. Now, despite the countries' strong commitment to international trade in general, they tend to maintain or create domestic energy resources regardless of their competitiveness in free international commerce, if it existed. German, British, and Japanese coal, reprocessed nuclear fuel everywhere, and some of the planned British and Norwegian oil facilities find their rationale in assuring at least a minimum of national energy self-sufficiency. Consumers and taxpayers bear the cost. The withholding of easily exportable energy materials from foreign users is another facet of this revived protectionism.

Limits of Energy Policy

The practical limits of energy policy that one can observe in Europe and Japan today are fairly narrow. They are drawn (1) by technological uncertainties and economic adaptation problems, on which the preceding discussion has not dwelt and of which energy planners are usually well aware; (2) by the entry into play of a multiplicity of political and economic imperatives regarding goals and means, which are espoused by powerful elements in the various societies and which energy planners tend to disregard or decry; and (3) by obstacles to energy-structural adaptation that countries create for each other, notably some industrial countries for other industrial countries, and that are often put·up in the name of mutually accepted, only differently interpreted, considerations of national interest, international order, economic stability, and environmental protection. They also constrain and upset energy plans.

Thus, energy policy in the countries studied here has become submerged in a broad spectrum of issues, and it may well continue so if no new energy-specific crisis occurs and raises it again in importance above other specific purpose policies. Declaratory policies of governments notwithstanding, oil import reduction is no longer the overriding motive of action anywhere. If energy reform is now an "equivalent of war," it is so in the sense of war's confusions rather than the fighter's single-mindedness. The United States is not unique in this regard.

SELECTED COUNTRY SITUATIONS

The preceding sections have dealt with general energy topics relevant to Western Europe and Japan. The emphasis was on energy supply aspects. Some particular country situations have been noted under the general topics. This section will give greater prominence to particular country situations, but since space does not allow us to discuss these one by one and across the whole spectrum of energy topics, the discussion will focus, first, on energy conservation, the hitherto slighted topic, and second, on nuclear industry developments. The latter is the most volatile element in the supply outlook, and our earlier discussion of them can usefully be pursued somewhat further. The question to be taken up will be whether the deterioration of its prospects is continuing or is beginning to be reversed. Third, we shall consider research and development efforts.

Energy Conservation: Growing, Slowing

The energy intensity of an entire national economy, as measured, for example, by the ratio of total primary energy used (TPE) to real GDP, depends on the energy intensity of particular pursuits and the relative weight of these pursuits—sectors such as industry, transportation, residential-commercial; subsectors such as the steel industry or passenger car transportation; and so on—in the total economy. An effort to conserve energy can address itself to reducing the energy intensity in particular pursuits and to restructuring the national economy by giving preference to relatively low intensity pursuits. The national government programs with which we shall be dealing focus almost entirely on energy conservation in particular pursuits, although some, like the Belgian and Italian, speak of encouraging expansion of non-energy-intensive industries, which will of course take a long time to show results.

The conservation developments that the various governments foresee for their countries in the years ahead and the policies with which they try to encourage these developments are being brought together in the energy program reviews of the IEA for all of our countries, except France. We rely here on the latest review data, published by IEA for 1977. The quantitative measures of overall development, expressed in the TPE-GDP ratios, are part of the national submissions. The IEA reviews expose the presentations of the various governments to evaluations and suggestions by their peers—that is, representatives of other IEA governments.

This review process is a bit like a beauty contest, in which governments usually enter policy specimens that they believe will please the judges (or explain why they cannot) and in which the evaluators bestow praise and criticism by certain standards. The standards favor good intentions, the fixing of firm targets, large R&D spending, almost anything that raises energy prices to the consumer, fiscal incentives, and quantitative regulation. Leaving developments to market forces is usually treated as insufficient, although "energy pricing in conformance with the world market" gets good marks. In comparison with the United States, the European countries and Japan, with few exceptions, get superior marks in the latter regard.

Projected Conservation in Various Countries. The energy conservation picture revealed by this process is the best approximation available to what is going on in this field in Western Europe and Japan. It is of course strong on projections, programs, and expectations and weak on what changes in energy intensities are actually under way. To learn of the latter, one would need much more factual reporting and analysis than is available today. In time, we shall know more, but knowledge on energy saving is inherently more difficult to come by than output and consumption figures.

Table 7–9 summarizes the TPE-GDP evolution described in the various country submissions. The figures for 1973 and 1976 are presumably factual. They indicate that in most countries somewhat less energy was consumed per unit of GDP in 1976 than in 1973, which may reflect the rush of savings that were made during and soon after the oil crisis. In Japan, Switzerland, and Greece, the ratios remained constant.

The projections to 1985 and 1990 are not based on uniform assumptions. In some countries they tend to show "base case" expectations—that is "expected results from energy policies already in place" (marked B in the first column)—and in other countries they tend to show "accelerated policy" expectations, "corresponding to policies formulated and enunciated but not yet enacted or implemented" (marked A in the first column).[19] This may explain the greater drops in the ratios, from 1973 to 1985, for some of the "A" countries.

Italy, Switzerland, Spain, Greece, and Ireland expect no lowering of their TPE-GDP ratios from 1973 to 1985; in the case of the latter three it even increases in that period or thereafter. The IEA review gives all of them low marks on their energy conservation efforts, but one may wonder whether the standards of more developed Euro-

19. *1977 IEA Reviews of National Energy Programs*, p. 9.

Table 7-9. TPE-GDP Ratios, 1973 and 1976, and Outlook to 1985 and 1990 by Country.

Country	National Programs Type[a]	TPE-GDP Ratios[b]					"Oil Imports Saved" (-: added) Under Forecast TPE-GDP Trend in 1985 Mtoe
		1973	1976	1985	1990	1985 (1973=1)	
Austria	B	1.39	1.28	1.30	1.30	0.94	2
Belgium	A	1.51	1.42	1.34	1.31	0.89	7
Denmark	A	1.13	1.04	0.78	0.71	0.69	7
West Germany	A	1.27	1.20	1.11	1.04	0.87	44
Greece	B	1.11	1.11	1.24	1.25	1.12	-3
Ireland	B	1.73	1.49	2.03	2.57	1.17	-2
Italy	A	1.28	1.24	1.27	1.25	0.99	2
The Netherlands	B	1.70	1.68	1.60	1.50	0.94	5
Norway	A	1.54	1.41	1.20	1.12	0.78	6
Spain	A	1.48	1.47	1.50	1.58	1.01	-1
Sweden	B	1.34	1.32	1.16	1.09	0.87	8
Switzerland	B	1.00	1.00	1.00	0.90	1.00	0
United Kingdom	A	1.67	1.52	1.32	1.24	0.79	51
France[c]	—	n.a.	n.a.	n.a.	n.a.	n.a.	46
Total OECD-Europe[d]	—	n.a.	n.a.	n.a.	n.a.	n.a.	172
Japan	A	1.33	1.34	1.28	1.26	0.96	24

Source: *1977 IEA Reviews of National Energy Programs.*

n.a. = Not available.

[a]A: "Accelerated policy scenario." B: "Base case." See *IEA Reviews*, pp. 9–10.
[b]Toe per $1,000 of 1970 purchasing power.
[c]According to "Rapport de la Commission de l'énergie du VII[e] Plan," pp. 4, 13.
[d]Without Turkey.

pean countries can fairly be applied to Ireland, Spain, and Greece, all of which look forward to great structural changes in their economies. Denmark, Norway, and Sweden project quite large drops in their ratios. This reflects in good measure the setting of low official targets for TPE growth in the three Scandinavian countries: 3 percent per year for Norway, 1.2 percent for Denmark, and 2 percent (in the 1990s, zero) for Sweden, all well below historical levels. All three get excellent IEA marks for their conservation efforts, but while the governmental campaigns in this direction are praised for their intensity, the reviewers observe that the achievement of the low growth rates is quite uncertain. We shall discuss below the rather good-looking German, British, and French expectations, as well as the quite modest one for Japan.[20]

West Germany.   The three successive energy program statements of the West German government of 1973, 1974, and 1977 have conservation rise from the seventh to the fifth and then to first place in the ranking order of tasks (Table 7-10). Its rise to prominence reflected growing frustration with the progress and prospects of output expansion (notably nuclear) and not a belated discovery that Germans were energy wastrels. On the whole, they deserve rather good marks for economical use of energy, before and after 1973, without benefit of much government programming and special conservation drives. The IEA review of 1977 acknowledged the good performance —more so than the 1976 review did—and it gave particular praise to the new high official priority rating for conservation.

But while the new intentions were promising more energy savings, their translation into specific measures met with limited success. For new buildings, stricter standards for space heating were enacted, but a federal program to spend some $2.2 billion on retrofitting existing buildings foundered on the opposition of the *Laender.* So did a proposal for setting more economy-oriented electricity rates. German industry is being asked to do more cogeneration of electric power, over and above what it is already doing; and IEA has recommended a number of new incentives, guidelines, and fundings and considers the German energy program now "potentially more balanced."

20. Incidentally, the comparable U.S. score on this account was 0.93 under energy policies in place as of January 1978 and 0.91 assuming enactment of the National Energy Plan. A recent document of the European Communities (*Energy Objectives for 1990*, November 16, 1978 Luxembourg: Eurostat) puts in question the continued decline of the Belgian and Dutch TPE-GDP ratios. It shows slight increases for both from 1977 to 1985.

Table 7-10. Phrasing and Ranking Order of Energy Policy Elements in the "Continuous" German Energy Program.

Original Energy Program (September 1973)	First Amendment to Energy Program (November 1974)	Second Amendment to Energy Program (December 1977)
(1) Reliable oil supply	(1) Assure supply and reduce share of oil	(1) Reduce growth of energy consumption through conservation
(2) Expand economically attractive substitutes, gas, nuclear, lignite	(2) Accelerate gas, nuclear, lignite	(2) Reduce oil's share
(3) German coal where appropriate and necessary	(3) Optimal use of coal (including exports)	(3) Preferential use for German coal and lignite
(4) Environmental protection	(4) Appropriate location of facilities	(4) Develop nuclear as necessary for electricity, provided security of population is assured
(5) Appropriate location of energy facilities	(5) Increased energy conservation	(5) Reduce import risks through diversification, agreements, international cooperation
(6) Research	(6) More research	(6) Research in the use of domestically available sources
(7) Rational use of energy	(7) Contingency planning for emergencies	

TPE Level Expected for 1985

610 Mtoe (official prognosis)	555 Mtoe (conditional prognosis)	482 Mtoe (private prognosis passed on as information)

Source: Energy program statements of the West German federal government, published by the Ministry of Economics.

The differences between the listings of German energy policy priorities are also interesting in other regards, and we shall return to them later. In view of the importance of the changes, it is somewhat surprising that the government emphasized, in the latest statement, the continuity of its program. The explanation may lie in the considerable difficulties it experienced in arriving at the latest version and the tenuousness of some of the compromises made. These may have invited a presentation of considerable program changes as program continuity.

United Kingdom. The progression of TPE-GDP ratios for Britain exhibited in Table 7-9 is remarkable, with a substantial decline from 1973 to 1976 and more promised for the future. What is behind the achievement is not too well known—and in most of the specific efficiencies for industry, at least, the United Kingdom still appears below average among IEA countries—but the IEA reviewers call it one of the best in IEA. The U.K. government places emphasis on voluntary saving rather than on mandatory programs, and it has phased out artificially depressed energy prices to that effect. In fact, as we shall see in Tables 7-11 and 7-12, the increases in U.K. energy prices since 1973—before and after taxes, in different energy categories, by themselves, or in relation to the general price level—have been among the strongest in the intercountry comparison. The U.K. program for the future stresses areas in which public bodies can set an example—for example, public buildings and state-owned dwellings where investments in energy economies are being planned and to some degree financed and information efforts directed at industry and the transportation sector. As in several other countries, revised building codes emphasize economies in heating new buildings.

France. If France's conservation efforts had come under IEA review in 1975-1976, the reviewers would have found them among the best. The VIIth plan projected progressive economies in energy use, rising by 1985 to the equivalent of 45 Mt of oil imports per year in comparison with 1973. The government created an Energy Conservation Agency in 1974, with broad authority to propose conservation programs. The agency proceeded to promote energy-saving measures and to propose interest rebates for loans on energy-saving investments, rules for fuel use in heating, income tax deductions for heat insulation, and premiums to energy-saving industrial investments, to be financed by a special tax on the energy consumption of the largest users. Twenty million tons of oil were to be saved by suppressing waste, and 25 million by specific investments. The plan projected a reduction in the annual TPE-GDP ratio from 1973 to 1985 of 20 percent (Table 7-9).

A number of the proposed measures were enacted, and there was also a good deal of spontaneous response to higher energy prices. The agency could report a buildup of accomplished energy savings to 5 Mtoe per year in 1974 and to 12 Mtoe in 1975 from the 1973 benchmark as the easiest targets were being picked off. But then the advance slowed so as to reach a level of 13 Mtoe in 1976 and 14.5 in 1977, with the domestic and service sectors contributing the bulk of

Table 7–11. Gasoline and Diesel Fuel Prices per 100 liters in Selected European Countries, January 1, 1973, and 1978.

Country	Unit	Gasoline, Regular			Diesel Fuel		
		1973	1978	1978 as percentage of 1973	1973	1978	1978 as percentage of 1973
West Germany	DM						
Retail price		61	86	141	63	87	137
Tax		45	52	—	43	50	—
Price before tax		16	33	211	21	37	176
France	Fr						
Retail price		112	219	196	78	143	185
Tax		80	132	—	48	71	—
Price before tax		32	87	275	30	72	242
Italy	Lit						
Retail price		15,200	48,000	316	8,000	16,400	205
Tax		11,701	34,560	—	5,182	4,412	—
Price before tax		3,499	13,440	384	2,818	11,988	425
The Netherlands	Fl						
Retail price		72	104	144	37	57	153
Tax		53	65	—	18	21	—
Price before tax		19	39	202	18	36	193
United Kingdom	£						
Retail price		7.37	17.16	233	7.48	18.26	244
Tax		4.95	8.51	—	4.95	8.97	—
Price before tax		2.42	8.65	357	2.53	9.29	367

Source: Eurostat, *Energy Statistics Yearbook 1976* and January 1, 1978 Supplement (Luxembourg).

Table 7-12. Energy Price Indexes for Selected Countries 1976. (1973 = 100)

Country	Gasoline		Household Fuel and Light		Industrial Fuel— Lubricants	
	Price at pump	Deflated by consumer price index	Index	Deflated by consumer price index	Index	Deflated by wholesale price index
West Germany	132	112	139	118	154	124
France	168	120	165	118	139	112
Italy	285[a]	176	169	104	266	143
The Netherlands	137	104	160	121	180	122
United Kingdom	228[a]	136	192	115	308	148
Japan	209[b]	121	189	111	222	155

Source: Unpublished estimates from Resources for the Future, based on national price statistics, except where noted. Annual averages.

[a]Derived from national price data as published in Eurostat, *Energy Statistics Yearbook 1976* and Supplement, using average of regular gasoline prices shown for January 1, 1976 and 1977 (Luxembourg).

[b]Derived from national price data submitted to IEA. For the several European countries, these data show very similar indexes to those presented in the table.

the savings throughout. The movement had come to a virtual halt, well short of the targeted level of 45 Mtoe per year.

One of the prominent failures of the program was the rejection by the council of ministers in 1977 of a package of conservation measures, including an energy consumption tax on large users, which was lobbied to death by industry, and proposed penalties on gas and electricity consumption that exceeded specified amounts. A project to form a combined public company for the marketing of heat and power foundered on opposition from Electricté de France (EdF). The rejections were confirmed and extended in successive decisions of the ministers in 1977 and 1978. Despite official hopes that new proposals will fare better, it is now likely that the French energy-saving effort will have smaller results than anticipated.

Japan. Energy planning in Japan has been and continues to be dominated by the intent to provide the growing economy with growing, reliable, and environmentally safe energy supplies. Energy conservation has of necessity taken second place to this concern. A recent listing of energy policy objectives by the president of Japan's Institute of Energy Economics does not even mention it. (He does mention the need for measures to stimulate internal demand).[21] The

21. *Energy in Japan*, March 1978, p. 16.

government's program submitted to IEA, although of the "accelerated" type, correspondingly promises only a slight reduction in the TPE-GDP ratio (Table 7-9).

IEA reviewers have vacillated in judging Japan's conservation effort. The 1976 review had Japan rated above average among all IEA nations in actual conservation results, exhibiting about average specific efficiencies in transportation and industry and having adopted a "comprehensive conservation program."[22] The 1977 review was disparaging. It noted a large potential for energy saving in industry, transport, and housing and called not only existing but also newly enacted conservation efforts insufficient for all economic sectors—namely, lacking targets, incentives, statutory standards (for buildings, appliances), financing, and information drives. Energy conservation, said IEA, should get higher priority in Japan. The problem is that the top of the country's priority list is crowded, and Japan's energy planners appear very nervous about which way to turn without running into trouble. Industrial firms, it is reported, will invest in energy saving only if it promises quick returns. For the longer pull, they bank on supply. So, it seems, does the country as a whole.

In sum, the achievement of lesser energy intensities in these countries is a highly complex business. Higher energy costs, usually passed through, have already induced industry and consumers to economize, and the potential for further movement is uncertain. To the extent that new automobiles have already been made more energy-efficient, that household thermostats have already been reduced, that industry has already turned to more efficient equipment and practices, it may be difficult to come up with encores.[23] Some of the changes in energy consumption by business and households will of course make themselves felt only gradually, as new installations and equipments come into use and so will the effects of new government regulations and information campaigns; but it is also possible that accelerated growth, changes in cost relations, or stricter pollution controls will counteract tendencies toward greater energy frugality. Developments in several countries have shown an interesting inverse correlation between the emphasis on energy conservation and the promise of nuclear power. The opposition to nuclear power development often

22. IEA, *Energy Conservation in the International Energy Agency*, 1976 Review (Paris: OECD, 1976) p. 29.

23. For a brief overall account that offers a number of details supplementing our discussion, see "Europe's Energy Conservation Efforts are Uninspired" in the London Financial Times' *European Energy Report* 14 (August 15, 1978): 9ff. For further details on conservation aspects and measures see IEA's published 1976 review (*Energy Conservation*) and the more recent *1977 IEA Reviews of National Energy Programs*.

stresses conservation as a preferable alternative. Governments that have found it necessary to curtail nuclear programs and impossible to come up with a good supply alternative have hit on conservation as seemingly the most attainable and politically palatable way of balancing the future energy budget. It remains to be seen whether this correlation would also work to the disadvantage of conservation strivings, should nuclear (or other) power supply grow more rapidly relative to consumption.

Energy conservation in Europe and Japan is growing, but its progress appears to be slowing. In several countries the future rate of improvement may well be lower than it has been in the last four years.

Consumer Prices. In connection with the preceding discussion of conservation, a review of price developments since 1973 at the energy consumer level is of interest. But a systematic analysis of these developments, country by country, for the relevant energy items would be a fairly complex matter and is not possible within the framework of this chapter. There are a number of different questions worth asking, and each requires a special preparation of data. The statistical base for some of the answers is not readily available. The following presentation is therefore limited to selected countries, prices, and price indexes; and the discussion of the information that the reader may gain from the material is organized by question.

How have certain energy consumer prices changed since the oil crisis in the several countries? Table 7-11 answers this question for gasoline and diesel fuel in five European Community countries by comparing standard retail prices at the pump on January 1, 1973, and 1978 (first line under each country). The gasoline prices, expressed in national currencies, rose by about 40 percent in Germany and the Netherlands, doubled or more than doubled in France and the United Kingdom, and tripled in Italy. Diesel fuel prices rose at about the same pace as gasoline, except for Italy, where they only doubled. We shall reserve the tax aspect for later discussion.

Broader answers to the same question can be found in Table 7-12, in the left column of each of the three sets shown there for motor fuel, household fuel and lighting, and industrial fuel and lubricants. This table shows national price indexes for the three categories, 1976 on a 1973 basis, and it gives data for Japan besides the five European countries. The indexes for gasoline correspond to those in

Table 7-11,[24] allowing for the difference in timing; the other two broaden the picture. Household heating and lighting prices appear to have risen somewhat more than gasoline in Germany and Holland, but somewhat less in France, and considerably less in Britain and Italy. The price developments of industrial fuels and lubricants show their own country-to-country pattern. Germany and France experienced lesser energy price increases than the other countries in both the household and industrial categories. Looking across all three categories, we see that the increases of the national indexes to 1976 fell somewhere between 32 and 208 percent of 1973. The increases in Britain tended to be relatively great, those in Germany relatively small.

How much have consumer prices of certain heavily taxed energy materials increased, when one abstracts from the tax element? Gasoline and diesel fuel are usually the most heavily taxed fuels. Table 7-11 shows that in all countries, their before-tax prices increased substantially more than after-tax prices. Taxes were raised everywhere, but at a much slower pace than before-tax prices. The prices of untaxed gasoline and diesel fuel rose within a range of 76 percent (German diesel oil) and 325 percent (Italian diesel oil), compared with a range of 37 to 144 percent for posttax prices.

How have energy prices in these countries moved in relation to other prices relevant to the same classes of consumers? Returning again to Table 7-12, the reader will see that for all of the countries and energy categories considered, energy prices rose faster than the relevant deflators—general consumer price indexes or wholesale price indexes. Energy prices appear to have been inflation leaders, or relatively strong deterrents to consumption, within the national price patterns. The country-to-country pattern, however, has been far from uniform in this regard. Japan did not show a particularly high value of the deflated indexes for gasoline, but the highest one for those of industrial fuel and lubricants; Italy showed the highest value for gasoline and the lowest one for household fuel and lighting.

Leaving aside other interesting questions (e.g., about comparative price developments considering different exchange rate developments for the national currencies), we find that the price data yield

24. For Italy and Britain, the gasoline price developments reported by Eurostat diverged substantially from those in the RFF material. The former were used in Table 7-12 as well. For Japan, data submitted by the Japanese government were used in place of the RFF figures.

different answers to the different questions. A summary of these answers across the questions would have little meaning.

Nuclear Power — Continuing Retreat?

The inability of European countries and Japan to follow through on the hopeful nuclear development programs of the early 1970s, and the setbacks suffered, were discussed previously. The question is now whether the retreat from nuclear power expansion is continuing or shows signs of being reversed.

In discussing this question, we shall make no allowance for changes in important parameters that may occur in the future—near or more distant. Obstacles to nuclear power development might be significantly lessened by an upturn in electricity demand and an appearance of power shortages, which the frustrated proponents of nuclear (and other) power expansion have been warning of for some time, or by a tightening of oil supply or an oil supply crisis, or by more single-minded cooperation among the industrial democracies precipitated by threatening events. In the near term, even ordinary government change could deblock, or stop significant nuclear projects in some countries. In Sweden, for example, the resignation of an antinuclear premier ushered in a minority liberal party government that, with the help of the pronuclear socialist opposition, may decide to allow fuel loading at two waiting power plants for a startup in 1979 and to permit completion of a third plant. In Austria, on the other hand, a plebiscite in late 1978 decided that the country's first nuclear power plant, all finished and ready to go, should not be allowed to go on stream. It remains to be seen what consequences the Kreisky government, which had favored the activation of the plant, will draw from the vote and what a future Austrian government will do about the matter. In what follows, we shall deal with other currently visible factors.

France. The center appears to be holding. In July 1978, the French government empowered EdF to order another 10 gigawatts of nuclear electricity capacity in 1980-1981.[25] It still hopes to have a 40 GW capacity in operation by 1985. This would be less than the 50 GW once projected, but it would still form the bulk of the country's planned electric capability. Given delays in the commissioning of EdF's first LWRs and the prevailing siting difficulties and construction delays, the realization of the program will probably slip;

25. This followed approvals of orders for 4.5 GW in the 1970-1973 period; 4.5 in 1974; 5.4 in 1975; 5.8 in 1976; 6.1 in 1977; and 10 in 1978-1979. *Nuclear Engineering International*, October 1978, pp. 12, 13.

but following its reinforcement in the March 1978 general election and the weakening of political opposition, the government feels more confident that it can overcome local obstacles with the help of incentives and local interests in economic growth. EdF will from now on have to pay more attention to environmental requirements in order to get its construction permits.

Reactor type choices are well in hand, and the commitment to the Phénix/Superphénix commercial breeder program appears firm, the latter buttressed by a multinational European development program. In oxide fuel reprocessing and permanent waste disposal, the French have moved into a leading position in Europe and worldwide, and they have discovered significant profit and foreign exchange earning possibilities flowing from that advantage. Japanese, West German, and other countries' utilities have now contracted for and undertaken to prefinance the new reprocessing capacity that is being built at Cap La Hague. The international network of interests thus mobilized naturally strengthens the French commitment to the commercialization of the back end of the fuel cycle. Last but not least, a relatively secure uranium supply from domestic and African mines and the coming on stream of the Eurodif enrichment plant in 1979 give France a degree of immunity from outside pressures against that commitment.

The difficulties that may lie ahead on technical, environmental, commercial, and political grounds should not be minimized. But meanwhile the French nuclear industrial program is moving forward and is in better shape than those of most other countries.

United Kingdom. Governmental indecision about reactor choices in this oldest nuclear power country in Europe has been protracted; it now seems on the way to being overcome. In January 1978, the government cleared the way for ordering two advanced gas-cooled reactors and for developing the option of building LWRs in the 1980s. Commercialization of the fast breeder reactor proposed by the U.K. Atomic Energy Authority, however, still has to await the results of public inquiries that are about to get under way. The nuclear industry faces the task of reestablishing itself after a period of about nine years without orders. Part of the problem is to ensure that fast breeder reactor technology will be available when needed, either through a U.K.-built demonstration reactor based on the Dounreay prototype or through collaboration with continental countries and imports of technology.

With respect to oxide fuel reprocessing, initiated by the government to make public support evident, the public inquiry on the expansion of the Windscale complex in late 1977 finally broke the protracted stalemate, and the parliamentary decision to go ahead came quickly in the spring of 1978. The prospect of large foreign exchange earnings, already being realized by France, greatly favored the decision. A Japanese reprocessing contract was waiting, equaling that of France in size; and Japan has agreed in the meantime to provide through prepayments $285 million for the construction of Britain's new plant, about one-fourth of the estimated cost of the project.

With some 8.5 gigawatts of nuclear electricity capacity now in operation, effective capacity is scheduled to rise to about 11 GW by 1985 (Table 7-3). Thereafter, the balance of new additions and the retirement of the older small Magnox reactors may yet provide more conspicuous growth. British nuclear forecasters expect to see a capacity of 40 GW by the end of the century. In the present perspective, a second takeoff for Britain's nuclear energy seems possible and, considering the long-term outlook for energy derived from coal, oil, and gas, reasonable.

West Germany. The German picture is murky. The rise and then the sharp drop in priority given to nuclear energy in the three successive governmental energy program statements is evident from Table 7-10. The program for a comprehensive power and fuel cycle development, to which federal government and industry remain committed, is still reeling under the convergent attacks of a rambunctious antinuclear movement at home and American opposition to (1) some of its critical features—namely, the attempts to close the fuel cycle within the country via oxide fuel reprocessing and the LMFBR; (2) technology transfers to other countries that in some instances, notably Brazil, are spearheading Germany's sustained industrial export drive; and (3) even technological developments in uranium enrichment believed to be too easily exploitable for weapons purposes.

The entire configuration of the nuclear program, in which large resources have been invested, is at risk. The federal government's effort to solidify public opinion in support of the nuclear program has fed arguments into the diffuse public discussion but has not yet led to the kind of authoritative public inquiries that seem to serve the British government so well in the pursuit of this end. In conjunction with an interim decision to proceed with the construction of a breeder reactor at Kalkar in early 1979, the government did promise to form a commission of inquiry to review the nuclear program as a whole.

Committed to greater self-sufficiency in reactor fuel in order to lessen the exposure of national industry to the whims of foreign fuel suppliers, committed to safe waste disposal at home in order to keep unprocessed waste from piling up and to assuage environmental fears, and anxious to satisfy the United States without capitulating to its idiosyncrasies and sacrificing large investments, the social-liberal government in Bonn has accepted compromises in all directions. The burden of many of the compromises falls on the prospects of developing an energy supply alternative to oil.

At this point, there are but few developments that promise an easing of these pressures. At home, the "green movement" has begun to split up along conservative-radical lines. Its capability to destroy the junior coalition party, the Free Democratic Party (FDP)—that is, push it below the threshold of parliamentary representation—seemed established in two Land elections in the early fall of 1978, but it was found wanting in two later ones. While this has averted the immediate threat to the FDP's survival and to that of the Schmidt-Genscher government, it made that volatile party seek its salvation in an espousal of antinuclear views. FDP ministers in the Land of North Rhine–Westphalia, where the Kalkar breeder reactor is requiring further permits,[26] have been openly obstructing the nuclear energy program to which the FDP economics minister in Bonn is committed. Federal Chancellor Schmidt remains committed to the program, but his party shows divisions between the pronuclear labor unions and antinuclear Land sections and left-wingers and also hesitates to cross the *t*'s. Faced with the bickering over the nuclear energy program within and between the political parties, executives temporize, the Bundestag does not give clear signals, and permits to proceed with numerous projects are hung up between federal and Land governments, legislatures, and courts. Some of the projects may yet be strangled.

The most conspicuous project requiring further Land and federal approvals is that for an integrated nuclear fuel disposal center (*Entsorgungszentrum*) that the principal German electrical utilities have set out to create at Gorleben in Lower Saxony. It is to combine

---

26. Germany's nuclear licensing procedure is tortuous. Federal agencies provide general directions and technical assessments, but Land governments have final responsibility for the issuing of licenses. Licenses are issued in stages, covering successive phases of construction and installation. In early 1979, the Kalkar project obtained the third partial construction permit, which covers wiring and instrumentation in the already completed concrete structure. Installation of the major reactor components will be subject to further (fourth and fifth) partial permits. The main reactor vessel, which was delivered to the site in 1976, sits in a shed awaiting these developments, although the concrete vault in the reactor building that is to receive it is completed.

a large reprocessing plant, on-site facilities for the permanent disposal of waste, and plutonium fuel fabrication for LWR and fast breeder fuel assemblies. The decisions on this big project are of vital importance for the German nuclear power program, since enlargement or even continuation of existing reactor capacity has been made contingent on definitive forward movement in spent fuel disposal. The critical issues at present are land acquisitions and permits for exploratory drilling into the salt stock beneath the site. By the hoped-for start of plant construction in 1980–1981, the utility companies expect to have invested about $1 billion in the Gorleben project.

In the international dimension, closer cooperation with France offers at least temporary solutions to the waste and reprocessing problems, and the enmeshing of German interests with those of European Community partners and Japan, both in the nuclear industry field and more generally, helps to strengthen the Federal Republic's hand in the tug of war with the United States over the nuclear program. The U.S. administration also seems to be somewhat more aware of the risks of discriminating in matters pertaining to civilian nuclear industry against the one member of NATO and the EC of whom it expects the most than it was when Congress laid down new nuclear trade rules without much regard to other aspects of international politics.

Thus, current domestic and international developments offer but few hopeful signs for German nuclear energy; and important decisions and agreements in support of it will have to be made before one can say that the retreat has been reversed. If it is not, one may yet find a future version of the German energy program that revises oil policy back to the September 1973 imperative: seek "reliable oil supply!"

Japan. In Japan as in Germany, governmental and industrial leaders remain committed to nuclear power development and fuel cycle closure, despite the setbacks suffered in the first regard and the recent difficulties with the United States in the second. Installed nuclear capacity in Japan (about 10 GW) presently exceeds Britain's (8.5) and West Germany's (about 8). The prospects for reversing the retreat from earlier high expectations appear somewhat better in Japan than in Germany.

The density of population and industry on earthquake-prone territory accounts for some of the most acute difficulties experienced by the nuclear power program today. Choice and acceptance of suitable sites for new nuclear plants constitutes one of these difficulties. Moreover, fishing interests are affected by the inevitably coastal locations. Relatively good sites along the coast, at a safe distance but not too far from population centers, have already been taken up; new ones are hard to find. To put the plants into remote spots of the chain of islands would raise difficult power transmission problems. It does not help nuclear power development that it shares the siting problem with the other prominent Japanese undertaking in oil-alternative energy—namely, reliance on LNG. The demands of the latter for coastal facilities and infrastructure development along with adequate provisions for the safe handling of this difficult substance bring it into competition with nuclear plants for sites. Uncomfortable decisions remain to be made.

Japan may, however, have one advantage over West Germany in arriving at such decisions—namely, the greater centralization of its political structure. The decisionmaking process in Japan is not complicated by a federal system in which authorities at lower levels and of different political complexion can frustrate the policies of the national government if they so choose. This makes a difference, although it does not eliminate local problems.

The low operational rate of existing nuclear power plants—for 1977, the Ministry of International Trade and Industry (MITI) put it at only 42 percent—also may reflect the locational constraint. According to some observers, earthquakes or overly cautious government regulations account for it, at least in part. According to others, however, the blame falls on borrowed foreign technology and obsolete equipment. Be that as it may, Japanese technological development, encouraged by the big program, seeks to overcome the low performance rate and to meet the necessarily stringent safety requirements, as well as to endow the country with more suitable reactor designs such as the advanced thermal reactor and a fast breeder. The bulk of new Japanese reactor equipment is now made in the country. The international framework in which the Japanese are pursuing these and other nuclear technological developments has shifted somewhat from collaboration with American partners to joint undertakings with European, notably French and German, partners.

Popular opposition to nuclear industry appears to be weakening gradually. This is reflected in public opinion polls—although a recent one, which showed a majority favorable in principle, also showed almost half of that group opposed to nuclear installations near their locality—and in a declining militancy of antinuclear citizens' initiatives. While in early 1977 the president of Japan's Institute of Energy

Economics still pointed with apprehension at Japan's "integrated antinuclear movement," which he considered unique,"[27] a Western European observer in mid-1978 reported that the majority of opponents appeared to be fishermen who are not satisfied with the compensation offered to them.[28] This European observer also noted that, in contrast to Europe, Japan does not have semiprofessional antinuclear agitators who turn up at one site after another and organize protests. Nuclear projects seem to be getting a more favorable hearing in municipal and judicial proceedings. Earlier this year, one municipal parliament and two district courts rejected opposition efforts to block the construction of three new power stations.

On the international plane, the country's affluence in foreign exchange helps with efforts to secure adequate future imports of uranium and enrichment services and to participate in overseas uranium prospecting and mining. The principal difficulty stems from the divergence of the Japanese and the current American policies regarding closure of the industrial fuel cycle. Japan seeks domestic fuel reprocessing and the recycling of spent uranium and generated plutonium into power reactors in order to create at least a partial domestic base for nuclear fuel. It must be borne in mind that the Japanese government had staked its energy program, including the choice of nuclear reactor technology, breeder development, and much of its energy R&D work, on the acceptance of American technology and of earlier American views favoring fuel cycle closure. The reversal of the official American position in 1975–1977 undercut the Japanese program and the confidence in the government's stewardship, and it encouraged both the antinuclear opposition in the country and opposition to reliance on the United States.[29] The turnaround in American policy, coming on the heels of the Liberal Democratic party's setback in the December 1976 lower house elections, shook the Japanese government profoundly and furnished one more upsetting experience of surprises sprung on the country by its principal ally.

The United States has now grudgingly agreed to the opening and temporary operation of the Tokai Mura reprocessing plant, but still makes continued American supply of enriched uranium, on which Japanese reactors fully depend at present, contingent on a

27. Toyoaki Ikuta in *Energy in Japan*, Quarterly Report #36, March 1977, Supplement 1, p. 12.

28. *Neue Zürcher Zeitung*, August 8, 1978. The government also offers financial inducements to local communities that agree to nuclear installations.

29. See Richard P. Suttmeier, "Japanese Reactions to U.S. Nuclear Policy," *ORBIS* (Fall 1978): 651–80.

complete reconfiguration of the plant to "co-processing," a proposition that the Japanese consider fraught with great expense, technological uncertainty, and program delays and that they therefore resist. Japan agreed to temporarily defer plutonium fuel fabrication and its use in LWRs, but it can be expected to continue pressing for acceptance of these activities by the United States. Reprocessing of the now accumulating quantities of Japanese spent fuel in France and Britain, for which Japan has contracted in the interim—and in the absence of U.S. reprocessing services—requires U.S. consent under the enrichment contracts, and such consent, while recently granted for the first two transactions, promises to require repeated difficult negotiations and demonstrations of "need." The return of the reprocessed fuel to Japan is also at stake.

In contrast to the Europeans, notably the French and British, the Japanese could not and did not meet with open defiance the recently imposed American strictures on industrial fuel cycle development and the conditioning of fuel supply on abstention from the plutonium economy. They appeal to the United States not to constrain and upset the Japanese nuclear program that American government and industry have in the past shaped and supported. But while they hope for suitable compromises that will sustain the traditional relationship, the Japanese increasingly look to Europe for enrichment services, facilitation of Japanese nuclear technological and industrial development, and diplomatic support in the near-term contentions with the United States.[30] Ironically, American nuclear policy, which is fraying the bilateral bonds with Japan in this area, is favoring attainment of an objective of American foreign policy—namely, to give more substance to European-Japanese collaboration so as to strengthen the hitherto weakest side of the U.S.-Europe-Japan triangle.

In its persistent quest for assured energy supplies and greater "energy independence," Japan is of course not looking to dependence on Europe as a permanent substitute for dependence on America. Besides its effort to expand domestic reprocessing, it is pushing construction of a uranium enrichment plant.

In sum, while energy saving, made possible in part by slower economic growth and in part by conservation efforts, offers some compensation for difficulties with nuclear power development in a

---

30. During a visit to Japan in October 1978, West German Chancellor Helmut Schmidt declared that Japan and Germany "jointly consider it very important that the peaceful use of nuclear energy, as envisaged in the nonproliferation treaty, be assured without any restrictions." *Los Angeles Times*, October 13, 1978.

number of countries, the more important ones are far from having given up on nuclear power. It remains, along its technically now manageable lines, one of their main hopes for coping with the disappearance of cheap, reliable oil from the energy scene over the next few decades and for gaining more control over their energy base. They are making great efforts to keep it going and, as the following discussion of R&D programs will show, to develop their technological capabilities in the nuclear field.

Research and Development Efforts

Reviews of member countries' energy research and development efforts, which the IEA conducted in 1977, produced a good overview of the governmental budget allocations in this field. The data do not cover industry-financed energy R&D, which may in some instances be quite important, but apart from that they give a comprehensive picture of the magnitude of the national expenditures and their distribution over energy R&D categories. Unfortunately, France is not covered.

Table 7-13 presents the 1977 budget data, expressed in current U.S. dollars, by country and category. The German and Japanese energy R&D budgets are by far the largest among the countries in our group, followed at a distance by the Italian and British ones and then by those of the smaller countries; but in relation to each country's GDP, the Japanese budget is well below the Italian, German, and British ones, as well as those of Belgium and Holland. In absolute terms, as well as relative to GDP, the energy R&D budgets of the governments of IEA Europe and Japan are dwarfed by that of the United States, and the rate of growth of the American budget from 1974 to 1977 was also larger than that of any country in our group. To the extent that R&D spending measures effort, this shows a general ranking order of national efforts.

The allocation patterns in the various countries' energy R&D budgets show interesting similarities and differences. The percentage shares of the principal categories in the national budgets tell the main story (see Table 7-14). In most of our countries, nuclear energy absorbs one-half or more of the R&D budget, in Japan as much as 85 percent, in the United Kingdom and Germany close to 80 percent. Most of this spending goes into "conventional nuclear" and fast breeder work.[31] Spending on nuclear fusion comes third; in Europe it is largely concentrated in European Community projects.

---

31. In Japan, one-third of total nuclear R&D spending is described as work on "common nuclear technologies" and shown in Table 7-13 under supporting technologies. The source does not offer information on nuclear-industry-related expenditures in other countries' entries for supporting technologies.

Given the current difficulties with nuclear power in Europe and Japan and the widespread doubts about its future, the continued heavy R&D investment in nuclear energy is noteworthy. To some extent, it reflects real persistence and the budget makers' hope that the industry will overcome the present adversities. To some extent it reflects rigidities in the budget-making process or in the R&D business itself. In Japan, for example, budgeting procedure makes it easy to reallocate R&D funds within but not between energy categories; and in various countries, the interests vested in particular lines of development may demand and get a more or less fixed share of the total R&D budget. Even where changes in emphasis are desired, the costs involved in canceling projects, disbanding staffs, and setting up new projects and teams militate against quick adaptations. Such rigidities make changes in R&D budget allocation lag behind changes in energy policy outlooks or skip fluctuations in such outlooks. We have observed above the considerable drop in the priority rating of nuclear energy in German energy programs from 1974 to 1977. During this period, the share of nuclear projects in the German R&D budget dropped only from 88 percent to 77 percent (the dollar amount rose by 33 percent). Nuclear energy still gets the lion's share of German R&D money, while in the talk of the government parties today it is presented as the last resort.

But not everywhere did the share of nuclear energy R&D prove so resistant to energy policy variations. In Sweden, nuclear projects took 81 percent of energy R&D money in 1974, but in 1978 they got only 28 percent. This takes us to the countries that do not allot the bulk of their R&D money to nuclear. Of these, Sweden is perhaps the only one that could readily have allotted a large share to nuclear energy in 1977 but chose not to do so. Instead Sweden allotted 39 percent of its budget to energy conservation (against only 10 percent in 1974), by far the highest conservation share of all countries. Other countries were not as well equipped for nuclear R&D. Norway devoted more than half of its energy R&D budget to its newly found oil and gas wealth; Turkey and Ireland allocated substantial proportions of theirs to their coal resources (combustion, conversion, and supporting technologies).

The shares of nonconventional energy projects are inconspicuous. On the whole they are smallest in the countries with large energy R&D budgets and largest in the countries with small ones. Solar and geothermal energy projects stand out in this category (see Table 7-13), the former particularly in Europe, the latter in Japan. In 1977, these new (or perhaps better, old) energy sources attracted much more public comment than R&D money in Europe and Japan.

Energy conservation likewise drew fairly small shares of the R&D

Table 7-13. 1977 Government Budgets for Energy Research, Development, and Demonstration (in U.S. $ million.)[a]

Category	Germany	United King-dom	Belgium	Nether-lands	Ireland	Den-mark
Conventional Nuclear	270.7	85.1	12.0	31.2	—	8.4
Fast Breeder	158.1	92.3	33.3	32.2	—	—
Nuclear Fusion	35.1	11.5	2.9	6.1	—	0.8
Total Nuclear	463.9	188.9	48.2	69.5	—	9.2
Oil and Gas	5.5	22.3	0.6	4.1	—	—
Coal	72.0	2.9	5.8	3.1	0.5	0.2
Solar	11.0	1.9	0.5	2.4	0.1	0.8
Wind	2.5	0.2	—	2.4	0	1.2
Ocean	—	1.7	—	—	0	—
Biomass	—	0.4	0.3	0.4	0.1	0.1
Geothermal	0.9	0.3	—	0.1	—	0.4
Total Nonconventional	14.4	4.5	0.8	5.3	0.2	2.5
Other	0.6	5.8	—	0.6	—	0.1
Supporting Technologies[e]	22.9	3.4	23.0	14.0	0.6	3.0
Conservation	22.0	11.8	8.7	13.5	0.2	2.0
Total Energy R&D Budgets	601.2	234.6	87.1	109.7	1.5	16.9
R&D Budget Dollars per $1,000 GDP	1.16	0.97	1.12	1.04	0.17	0.40
Percent Change in R&D Budget, 1974 to 1977[g]	+30	-16	-13	+86	+100	+64

Source: *1977 IEA Reviews of National Energy Programs,* Report on 1977 Reviews of National Energy R,D and D Programmes, Tables 2, 3, 5.

n.a. = Not available.

[a]Using 1977 exchange rates.

[b]Italian figures include personnel and infrastructure costs.

[c]EC member country budget data do not include their contributions to EC programs. French contributions are included.

[d]Without Austria and Greece, for lack of data.

[e]This includes "a wide range of energy related technologies varying from coun-

budgets, although generally more than the nonconventional energies. The outstanding position of Sweden has been noted; it reflects the conservation emphasis in current Swedish energy policy. In other countries, however, the declared policy emphasis on conservation is not reflected—or at least not yet—in conspicuous R&D spending. The top priority item in Germany's 1977 energy policy statement (see Table 7-10) drew only 4 percent of 1977 R&D spending, up from 2 percent in 1974. Spain too declared conservation the most important policy task and spent 8 percent of its R&D budget on it. But one should not make too much of these discrepancies. The costs of R&D projects vary widely, and a significant effort in one field may be sup-

Nor-way	Sweden	Switzer-land	Italy[b]	Spain	Turkey	EC[c]	IEA Europe[d]	Japan	United States
3.8	12.9	6.0	80.3	19.0	1.9	60.2	591.5	178.6	358.6
—	—	—	67.0	1.2	—	—	384.1	89.0	594.4
—	3.8	1.9	21.2	1.4	—	52.7	137.4	30.3	328.5
3.8	16.7	7.9	168.5	21.6	1.9	112.9	1113.0	297.9	1281.5
12.4	0.4	—	0.4	2.9	1.6	32.2	82.4	0.5	48.8
—	2.4	—	0.2	2.8	6.4	16.4	112.7	13.1	395.0
0.1	2.5	0.9	2.5	2.9	0.6	11.3	37.5	5.7	146.8
—	1.8	—	0.1	0.3	—	—	8.5	0	15.0
0.1	.3	—	—	—	—	—	2.1	0.6	9.5
—	1.4	—	—	.3	0	—	3.0	0.3	4.5
—	0.7	—	5.0	2.7	1.4	4.2	15.7	11.1	53.4
0.2	6.7	0.9	7.6	6.2	2.0	15.5	66.8	17.7	229.2
0.9	1.4	1.2	0.4	1.8	—	9.0	20.8	2.1	—
2.8	8.2	0.9	76.2	3.9	1.0	4.2	164.1	156.9[f]	782.0
1.8	23.1	0.1	10.8	3.6	0.9	3.5	102.0	41.9	63.5
22.0	58.6	11.0	264.2	42.8	13.7	193.7	1661.8	529.9	2800.0
0.61	0.75	0.18	1.36	0.37	0.34	n.a.	1.09	0.77	1.50
+69	+173	+17	+81	-1	+94	n.a.	n.a.	+48	+181

try to country. The common denominators [sic!] are those related to electric power conversion and transmission, energy storage, environment protection and safety, energy systems analysis and basic energy research. In some cases, however, also included are such matters as transportation of fossil fuels, supporting research on nuclear and fossil technologies, and information services for energy R, D and D" (*IEA Review*, p. 50).

[f]Including $154.4 million for common nuclear technologies.

[g]Based on amounts in national currencies.

ported with much smaller funds than one in another field. One must keep this in mind when comparing the budget shares of development and demonstration work on, say, conservation on the one hand and nuclear energy—in particular fusion and breeders—on the other. For the same reason, one should not simply conclude, as the IEA review sometimes does, that relatively small R&D expenditures in one or the other category, in one country or another, indicate insufficient efforts or neglect. Such a judgment, or a judgment of "balance" in an R&D program generally, cannot be based on the budget arithmetic alone.

Table 7-14. Percentage Shares of Energy Categories in 1977 RD&D Budgets

Country	Fossil Fuels	Nuclear Energy	Noncon-ventional Energy	Other and Supporting Technologies	Energy Conser-vation
Germany	13	77	2	4	4
United Kingdom	11	81	2	2	5
Belgium	7	55	1	26	10
The Netherlands	6	63	5	13	12
Ireland	33	0	15	39	13
Denmark	1	54	14	18	12
Norway	56	17	1	17	8
Sweden	5	28	11	16	39
Switzerland	—	72	8	19	1
Italy	0	64	3	30	4
Spain	13	50	·14	13	8
Turkey	58	14	14	7	7
EC	25	58	8	7	2
IEA Europe	12	67	4	11	6
Japan	3	85[a]	3	1[b]	8
United States	16	46	8	28	2

Source: Table 7-13.

[a]Including nuclear-related supporting technologies.

[b]Excluding nuclear-related supporting technologies.

PROBLEMS OF COOPERATION AMONG THE INDUSTRIAL DEMOCRACIES

Will the industrial democracies cooperate or conflict in their energy and energy-related policies? Evidently there are opportunities either way. Cooperation is sought, and open conflict avoided, on all sides, but this does not necessarily make the first exclude the second. Everyone has to take care of his own and country situations differ, as do perceptions of desirable cooperation.

The national governments make the decisions on which collaboration or conflict depend. They must meet and weigh the competing imperatives that domestic and external forces present to them. Their decisions will often favor a collaborative outcome because mutually compatible imperatives hold similar priority levels in the different capitals, or because they can strike bargains over a suitable range of things, or because regard for the others' interests comes cheap. But this cannot be taken for granted. Given the leaders' general preference for cooperative behavior, it is most important for them to remain aware of the dangers of collisions arising simply from the insensitivity of one complex governmental system to the perceptions of facts and goals that move another governmental system at the same time, dangers that Richard Neustadt traced so well in his path-breaking study of the "Skybolt Affair" of the early 1960s.[32]

The principal fields of energy concern, conservation, supply development, R&D, and trade invite different dispositions. Energy conservation tends to evoke the most cooperative response: everyone wishes the other fellow luck with his efforts to save energy and often has some good suggestions for him, too. Most energy supply and R&D development efforts are also mutually favored. One country's companies seek to participate in interesting developments in other countries, and admissions are on the whole more frequent than exclusions. But nuclear energy developments, notably in the fuel cycle industries, have come to form an exception, at least between the United States and the others, since official U.S. emphasis in this field has turned from cooperating in industrial ventures with others to efforts to police foreign ventures. The others now tend to coop-erate more among themselves—Europeans with Europeans, Euro-peans with Japanese—although a good deal of cooperation with Americans continues, notably in R&D. Conflicts over possession of territories rich in energy materials have fortunately become a thing of the past among these countries.

International trade in energy materials is the most contentious area. Steady availability of goods or services for export, reliance on their imports, and the terms and conditions of transactions furnish the greatest opportunities for conflict and for withdrawals from interdependence into self-dependence. Correspondingly, efforts to achieve practical cooperation or noninterference are most needed in this area.

It is not the task of this chapter to investigate the furtherance of energy cooperation and the avoidance of conflict among the indus-trial democracies in their manifold aspects or to present a record of accomplishments in these regards since the oil crisis. This would presuppose introducing American energy developments, and some others, into the picture. But our discussion of European and Japa-nese developments has led to a number of things that these countries regard as important fields for cooperative action by the United States; and for symmetry's sake, another set of things can be listed on which the United States is appealing for European and Japanese cooperation.

In discussing these mutual appeals, we leave aside the wishes on

32. Richard E. Neustadt, *Alliance Politics* (New York: Columbia University Press, 1970).

both sides that regard the general economic and political environment in which energy matters are embedded, such as the partners' policies in international finance, inflation control, and economic growth adjustment; their role in peacekeeping in the Middle East and Africa; and so on. We focus on the more directly energy-related policies.

The most urgent European and Japanese demand on U.S. energy performance is for this country to lower its demand for imported oil. They do not ask as much for our dealing with them as for leaving them a bigger slice of the supply that comes into the world market. It is consequently a demand levied on our energy economy across the board, including domestic energy price policy, and one that is very difficult to bargain about. European and Japanese spokesmen like to shame Americans into greater efforts, but that does not have much influence on our decisionmaking processes. Leaders do make mutual commitments in OECD-IEA to limit their countries' oil demand, and some, particularly the French, propose that each country impose a ceiling on its oil imports. But such commitments have not been and probably will not be very solid. Best efforts politically possible will often produce the import reductions promised. In any event, there is no specific quid pro quo.

Next in importance today are European and Japanese demands for more cooperative U.S. dispositions in nuclear industry and trade matters. As subscribers to—or in France's case, cooperators with—the Nuclear Nonproliferation Treaty, they agree with the United States on combating the use of nuclear fuels for explosives—as President Carter put it in his press conference of April 7, 1977[33] —but they do not agree with banning the use of explosion-capable materials for industrial fuel, as our Nonproliferation Act of 1978 demands. The critical request for cooperation addressed to the United States is that it act as a reliable supplier of enriched uranium without imposing strictures of this kind on the fuel cycle programs of other industrial democracies. The matter is too complicated to be dealt with in a few sentences.[34] The statutory restrictions of the president's discretion under the NPA have made it more difficult for the United States to respond to the demand. But the importance of arriving at some understanding has by now been recognized on all sides and some quid pro quos may be found, as will be discussed below.

Another important possibility for cooperation lies in U.S. exploi-

33. *Department of State Bulletin*, May 2, 1977, p. 433.

34. For a broader discussion, see Horst Mendershausen, *International Cooperation in Nuclear Fuel Services: European and American Approaches*, (Santa Monica, Calif.: The Rand Corporation, P-6308, December 1978).

tation of its rich deposits of coal, not only for its own energy economy but also for Western Europe's and Japan's through a reliable stream of exports. It would be too much to say that this has crystalized into a demand on the United States, at least from the European side. As we have already pointed out, European thinking about a renaissance of coal as an energy source is closely linked to ideas of creating and protecting markets for British, German, and perhaps other European coal. Europeans who would like to see the United States commit itself to coal exports have not yet resolved among themselves whether their countries, or the European Community, want to commit themselves to large coal imports. One seems as necessary as the other, and all kinds of difficulties will have to be overcome on both sides in order to make the timely dispositions and structural investments that would permit this cooperation in future years. This applies to Japan as well.

The most urgent demand that the United States has addressed so far in the energy performance of Western Europe and Japan is that they continue the course of energy conservation and of shifting their demand for energy materials away from OPEC oil. This wish shares the theme of, and also the problems connected with, the reciprocal European-Japanese wish addressed to the United States. As the preceding discussion has shown, these countries have done much to set the course in the desired direction, but to what extent they will continue in it remains to be seen. Perceptions of the necessary direction, extent, and speed of the shift are not firm, and reevaluations are being made and will be made time and again.

In the presently conflict-ridden matter of nuclear energy, American expectations addressed to the Europeans and Japanese are somewhat contradictory. At the Bonn summit in July 1978, President Carter and the other leaders subscribed to the declaration that "the further development of nuclear energy is indispensable, and the slippage in the execution of nuclear power programs must be reversed." But we do wish their spent fuel reprocessing and commercial breeder programs, which they regard as essential for further development, to slip. In several countries, Germany being an outstanding example, building and operating permits for reactors have been made contingent on the execution of waste disposal programs and international contracts. These comprise reprocessing and fuel fabrication for thermal and breeder reactors. This contradiction will have to be overcome if we want to reverse the slippage—and in some countries the paralysis—of this important sector of energy policy.

One related U.S. demand has already been largely met by our partners in the framework of the London Suppliers' Group—namely, the demand to restrain the exportation of sensitive nuclear technology to other countries. Another, perhaps more critical, American demand has not yet been stated in a forthright fashion. It is that the partners put the separation and industrial use of plutonium which occurs on their territories and therefore within their sovereignties, under a form of management that provides a high degree of assurance against diversion to the manufacture of explosive devices and that international transfers of plutonium fuel to third parties meet this requirement as well. For this demand to become explicit would require our acquiescence in the conduct of these activities. Such acquiescence was suggested at least in part by President Carter in his aforementioned press conference of April 1977, but was also largely taken back by the subsequently passed NPA. There are, however, reasons to believe that if the United States focused its demand on collaborative management rather than interdiction (or denationalization) in this field, arrangements could be worked out with the Europeans and Japanese, weapon as well as nonweapon states. No easy matter, but in my judgment no utter impossibility.

A third U.S. demand in the nuclear energy field, rather traditional but recently sharpened, is that Western Europe and Japan accept us as reliable suppliers of enriched uranium and other services related to the industry. This amounts to a desire that they restrain their tendency to achieve nuclear independence from us, a tendency that also is not new but that has been reinforced in the last few years. This is somewhat parallel to the situation with coal. This chapter cannot go into details, but it may point out that collaborative dispositions in this direction would be facilitated by understandings on the governance of plutonium.

"Going it alone" in energy economics and breaking up or restricting some of the collaborative arrangements would be an expensive and unpromising course for all of the industrial democracies. Since they do not want to take such a course, one should hope that they will find ways to avoid it.

CONCLUSIONS

The energy situation of our principal allies toward the end of the century will depend on evolutions, events, and decisions (theirs and ours) that cannot be predicted with much confidence. In the five years since the oil crisis, perceptions of the state of affairs that will exist in 1985 in Western Europe and Japan have changed considerably. There have been surprises, and there may well be more surprises before and after 1985.

Early postcrisis forecasts looked toward large substitutions of other energy sources for OPEC oil in order to satisfy continued undiminished growth of energy demands. Later forecasts look toward considerably lower contributions of the alternatives to OPEC oil— from nuclear power to coal and non-OPEC oil and gas—satisfying slower economic growth and, with the help of energy conservation efforts, much more slowly growing energy demands. In these revised perceptions, slower GDP growth and energy conservation replace much of the previously projected mobilizations of energy alternatives to OPEC oil, and that has happened not because slow economic growth is wanted—it hardly is, outside Scandinavia at least—or because Europeans and Japanese have discovered that they are wasting energy conspicuously. It has happened because all of the contemplated substitutions for OPEC oil have run, or are seen as soon running, into difficulties.

In part, these disappointments can be attributed to the difficulties inherent in a great conversion process, under the best of management. But this is far from being the whole story. The industrial democracies are responsible for considerable hindrances to the conversion process, hindrances that they are creating for themselves in their internal political processes and hindrances that they are creating for each other.

Whether and for how long these countries can get along with one foot on the accelerator (for energy development) and another, heavy, foot on the brakes will depend largely on continued slow economic growth and on a helpful price-supply performance of the Middle East oil countries. If the industrial democracies want to lessen these problematical dependencies, they will have to ease up on the brakes. If they cannot do that, they will take their chances with slow growth and Middle East oil.

The industrial democracies can make it easier or harder for each other to develop energy resources alternative to OPEC oil. Pledges and initiatives to cooperate notwithstanding, they are making it harder in some respects. Cooperative dispositions should be mutual. For instance, the United States might facilitate nuclear energy development in some European countries and in Japan by supporting their programs rather than adding to their difficulties. In return, these countries might cooperate in practical dispositions to make their systems of fuel cycle closure more proliferation resistant. In this fashion, the nuclear sector, which continues to absorb the bulk of energy-related R&D efforts, might make a better contribution to total energy supply toward the end of the century than seems likely at present.

Prospects and Problems for an Increased Resort to Coal in Western Europe, 1980-2000

Gerald Manners

COAL IN THE CONTEMPORARY ENERGY ECONOMY OF WESTERN EUROPE

For more than two decades, the energy economy of Western Europe has been undergoing a major transformation: its traditional and heavy reliance upon domestic supplies of solid fuels has been replaced by a new and substantial dependence upon imported oil, plus a growing exploitation of domestic and imported natural gas. The recent discovery and production of North Sea oil only slightly modifies this picture. The lower costs and the greater convenience of the new sources of energy forced upon the region's solid fuel industries both a relative and an absolute decline. Their output fell from nearly 800 million tonnes of coal equivalent (Mtce) in 1960 to 316 Mtce in 1974 (Table 8-1). By 1974, solid fuels met only 19 percent of the region's energy needs, compared with 62 percent fourteen years earlier.

The national economies of Western Europe retreated from coal at varied speeds. By 1977, the largest users of solid fuel were the United Kingdom (123 Mtce) and West Germany (119 Mtce), although the relative dependence upon solid fuel was highest in Turkey, where 46 percent of the country's energy needs were supplied by coal and lignite (Table 8-2). In the same year, by contrast, the Italian economy used solid fuel to meet only 7 percent of its energy requirements, and the counterpart Netherlands' figure was less than 5 percent. This pattern of consumption reflected in considerable

267

Table 8-1. Western Europe: Consumption and Production of Solid Fuels, 1960 and 1974.

	1960		1974	
	Mtce[a]	*% of need*	*Mtce*	*% of need*
Total Energy Consumption	875.0	(100.0)	1991.1	(100.0)
Solid Fuel Consumption	540.4	(61.8)	375.3	(18.8)
Solid Fuel Production	798.7	(91.3)	315.6	(15.9)
Net Imports	31.0	(3.5)	35.7	(2.7)
Stock Change	−11.7	(1.3)	−6.0	(0.3)

Source: United Nations, Series J Statistics.
[a]Mtce = million tonnes coal equivalent.

Table 8-2. Western Europe: Dependence upon Solid Fuels, 1977.

Country	Total Energy Consumption Mtce	Solid Fuel Consumption Mtce	Solid Fuel as a Percent of Total Energy Consumption	Solid Fuel Production[a] Mtce	Production as a Percent of Solid Fuel Consumption[b]
Austria	41.08	6.01	14.6	1.8	30.0
Belgium and Luxembourg	83.00	15.70	18.9	7.5	47.8
Denmark	34.24	6.51	19.0	—	—
Finland	38.58	10.35	26.8	—	—
France	308.78	47.26	15.3	24.2	51.2
Greece	25.22	6.68	26.5	—	—
Iceland	3.67	—	—	—	—
Eire	12.86	3.01	23.4	2.0	66.4
Italy	241.81	16.53	6.8	0.4	2.4
Netherlands	124.5	6.01	4.8	0.6	10.0
Norway	47.93	1.50	3.1	0.4	26.7
Portugal	17.03	0.84	4.9	—	—
Spain	119.24	20.54	17.2	12.8	62.3
Sweden	85.34	7.35	8.6	—	—
Switzerland	42.42	0.84	2.0	—	—
Turkey	59.12	27.22	46.0	7.7	28.3
United Kingdom	354.37	122.58	34.6	127.7	104.2
West Germany	434.87	119.41	27.5	129.4	108.4
Total	2073.81	418.34	20.2	337.8	80.6

Sources: *B.P. Statistical Review of the World Oil Industry* 1977 (London: British Petroleum Ltd.). United Nations, Series J Statistics.
[a]Refers to 1975.
[b]Production 1975/consumption 1977.

measure the geography of Western European coal production. In 1975, West Germany (129 Mtce) and the United Kingdom (128 Mtce) were by far the largest producers of solid fuel in the region, supplies from France (24 Mtce), Spain (13 Mtce), and Belgium (8 Mtce) being quite small by comparison. Domestic supplies of solid fuel were supplemented by net imports of 54 million tonnes of coal in 1974. Throughout the 1950s and 1960s, these imports were mainly high quality coking coals from the United States. More recently, however, Poland has become a significant source not only of further metallurgical coals but also of steam coals for power stations. Additional imports are received from the USSR, Australia, and South Africa. The principal recipients of these imported coals are France and Italy (Table 8-3).

While the solid fuel industries of Western Europe at one time met a diversity of energy demands, by 1976 their markets were strikingly concentrated both sectorally and geographically. Out of a total market for 293 million tonnes of hard coal within the European Economic Community, nearly half was provided by power stations. (The greater part of lignite production, which is highly localized in West Germany—37 Mtce out of the region's 68 Mtce—was also used for the generation of electrical energy.) A further 101 million tonnes of hard

Table 8-3. Origins and Destinations of Coal Imports into the EEC, 1973 and 1976 (million tonnes).

	1973	*1976*
Origins of Imports:		
United States	10.1	14.2
Poland	12.3	16.0
USSR	3.7	4.1
Australia	2.2	4.5
South Africa and others	1.5	4.9
Total	29.8	43.7
Destinations of Imports		
Belgium	3.4	3.5
Denmark	3.0	4.2
France	5.4	13.8
Ireland	0.7	0.5
Italy	8.6	10.0
Luxembourg	—	0.1
Netherlands	2.9	3.8
United Kingdom	1.4	2.4
West Germany	4.5	5.4
Total	29.8	43.7

Source: Committee of European Communities, *Twenty-five Years of Common Market Coal* (Brussels, 1977), pp. 178-79.

coal were used by the iron and steel industry (excluding its power stations) and the closely associated coking industry. Outside these two sectors, the solid fuel market for industrial, domestic, patent fuel, and transport uses (plus the mines' own consumption) was a mere 50 million tonnes, some 17 percent of the whole, and contracting rapidly (Table 8-4). Disaggregating these markets geographically, over half (53 percent) of the EEC's power station demand for hard coal originated in the United Kingdom, and over 93 percent came from the United Kingdom (64 Mtce), West Germany (34 Mtce), and France (15 Mtce). This was 113 Mtce in all out of an EEC consumption of 121 Mtce in 1976. The markets for metallurgical and coking coal were only slightly more dispersed geographically; out of a total European Community coke consumption of 65 million tonnes, nearly 80 percent was used in West Germany (22 mt), France (12 mt), the United Kingdom (10 mt) and Italy (7 mt).

The contemporary market for solid fuel in Western Europe is by no means the outcome of market forces alone. Over the years, the consumption of coal in Britain and West Germany especially has been sustained by a plethora of public policies designed to protect their indigenous coal industries and to restrain their rate of contraction. These policies have sought to limit the impact of competition from alternative fuels (taxes on fuel oil, for example), to restrict the entry of low cost coal imports (quotas and duties), to subsidize the use of coal (payments to the electricity industry to maintain or increase its use of coal), and to subsidize the costs of production (capital writeoffs and grants in aid). The policies have been pursued particularly at the national level, but also supranationally through the European Coal and Steel Community and the EEC Commission. In Britain, the emphasis of government policies since the late 1950s has been to provide production subsidies and to alleviate the industry's

Table 8-4. Coal Markets in the European Economic Community, 1973 and 1976 (million tonnes).

	1973	1976
Power Stations	127.2	141.2
Coke Plants and Gas Works	109.4	101.1
Industry	28.8	21.7
Domestic	27.2	20.3
Other	11.7	8.2
Total	303.3	292.5

Source: Committee of European Communities, *Twenty-five Years of Common Market Coal* (Brussels, 1977), p. 145.

social costs in contraction; protection against oil and low cost coal imports and measures to increase the electric industry's use of coal have also been provided. In West Germany, the policy emphasis has been upon import quotas plus a user subsidy, the so-called *kohlepfennig*, payable by electricity consumers to support the use of domestic coal rather than imported fuel oil in the country's power stations. In France, the domestic coal industry never had the political force of its counterparts in Britain and West Germany, and although coal imports from non-EEC countries have at times been restrained, both the market for coal and the domestic industry have been allowed to contract persistently. At the EEC level, attempts have been made to coordinate state aids and subsidies to the coal industry. The principal achievement of supranational policy has been to preserve a market for supplies of relatively high cost, Western European coking coal by means of subsidies both from national sources and from an EEC fund for metallurgical coking coals sold in intra-EEC trade.[1]

IN THE WAKE OF THE ENERGY CRISIS

The transformation of real energy prices in the wake of the 1973–1974 energy crisis, plus a newly perceived vulnerability of the Western European economy to energy supply disruptions, predictably generated a reinterpretation of policy objectives at both the national and the EEC levels. A desire to reduce the region's dependence upon imported oil was given prompt expression in a series of hastily forged and highly ambitious programs of nuclear power station construction. The crisis also generated an interest in reversing the decline and extending the role of coal in Western Europe's energy economy.

At the national level, the most ambitious response came, not surprisingly, from the region's largest producer of hard coal, the United Kingdom's National Coal Board (NCB). The board and the British government laid plans to halt the contraction of the domestic coal industry and to embark upon a major capital investment program in order to increase production substantially in both existing and new mines. The *Plan for Coal* called for production to be raised from 130 million tonnes, the previous year's output, to 135–150 million tonnes in 1985.[2] Three years later, *Coal for the Future*

---

1. N.J.D. Lucas, *Energy and the European Communities* (London: Europa Publications, 1977), p. 39.
2. National Coal Board, *Plan for Coal* (London, 1974).

proposed a production target of 170 million tonnes in the year 2000.[3] Both of these objectives have been endorsed by the more recent consultative document on *Energy Policy*, which accepts that such tonnages can be both produced and marketed.[4] In West Germany, by contrast, the expressed ambitions of the coal industry in the wake of the energy crisis were more modest and cautious. The plans of the industry in the first instance were designed to check its historical decline and essentially to maintain its existing capacity.[5] Suggestions have been made, however, that the industry could increase its total output from the 129 Mtce in 1975 to 145–150 Mtce in the year 2000.[6] In France and Belgium, minor adjustments were made to production and investment programs, but overall it was accepted that in both countries coal output would continue to decline as the industry concentrated its activities on the best mining prospects in the Nord and Kempen coalfields respectively.

In May 1974 the EEC published a new energy strategy with a central objective of seeking to reduce the Community's dependence upon imported oil.[7] Arising out of it, the *Medium Term Guidelines for Coal* proposed that Community consumption could increase by 25 percent, or 30 Mtce, between 1973 and 1985; and of the 300 Mtce of solid fuel consumed in the latter year, it was hoped that domestic producers would supply 250 Mtce.[8] In effect, this was a call to maintain rather than expand Community production. Within this total, it was recognized that the British and German industries would have to raise their output by about 8 percent in order to offset the inevitable decline of production in France and Belgium. More specifically, the commission suggested an increase in British production to 120 Mtce (equivalent to 140 mt, and 5 mt in excess of the National Coal Board's target). Subsequently, a *Second Report on the Achievement of Community Energy Policy Objectives for 1984* accepted that production in the EEC by the middle 1980s would only be 220 Mtce and that Britain would produce only 115 Mtce

3. Tripartite Group, *Coal for the Future* (London: Department of Energy, 1977).

4. Secretary of State for Energy, *Energy Policy—A Consultative Document*, Cmnd. 7101 (London: HMSO, 1978).

5. D. Ezra, in House of Lords, *Report on Coal*, Select Committee on the European Communities, Session 1978–78, 1st Report (London: HMSO, 1978), p. 146.

6. H.D. Schilling, in House of Lords, *Report on Coal*, p. 140.

7. European Economic Community, "Towards a New Energy Policy Strategy for the European Community," *Bulletin of the European Communities*, Supplement 4/74 (Brussels, 1974).

8. European Economic Community, *The Medium Term Guideline for Coal* (Brussels, 1974).

(135 mt).[9] The Community assumed coal imports from third countries would increase from an existing 30 Mtce in 1973 to 50 Mtce in 1985 and took the view that policy should seek to ensure that all energy users had access to world coal supplies, at the same time as measures were taken to foster the domestic industry.

In the wider forum of the OECD, the view was also taken immediately after the 1973–1974 energy crisis that the production of solid fuel in Western Europe could be increased by some 7 percent from 329 Mtce in 1972 to 352 Mtce in 1985. A slightly higher "potential output" of 360 Mtce was discounted in *Energy Prospects to 1985* because it was felt that "there is not sufficient absorptive capacity of markets in the period under review."[10] In its later *World Energy Outlook*, the OECD saw Western Europe's coal production growing rather slower at less than 5 percent between 1974 and 1985 (from 417 to 436 mt).[11] Consumption, on the other hand, would, it estimated, grow from 468 to 516 mt in its reference case and to 553 mt with accelerated policy measures to reduce oil imports. Net imports, standing at 51 mt in 1974, would increase to either 80 mt or more than double to 117 mt, depending upon policy assumptions.

From 1974 on, there was an upsurge of investment in the European coal industry. Capital expenditures in the Community rose from 336 million units of account in 1973 to 851 million units of account in 1976 (on collieries, coking plants, and patent fuel facilities). By far the largest investments were made in the United Kingdom.

Despite the objectives, investments, and hopes of the OECD, the EEC, and at least two national governments, however, there are legitimate doubts as to whether the Western European coal industry will be able to rise to the opportunities that have been envisaged for it. The new investment in the industry may have stabilized deep-mined production capacity and permitted a small increase in surface mining output, but after 1973 the demand for domestic coal perceptibly weakened. Between 1973 and 1976 the overall demand for coal in the countries of the EEC continued to decline (from 304 to 293 mt). The demand for coking coal in particular fell from 109 to

9. European Economic Community, *The Second Report on the Achievement of Community Energy Policy Objectives for 1985*, COM(77)395 (Brussels, 1977).

10. Organisation for Economic Cooperation and Development, *Energy Prospects to 1985* (Paris: OECD, 1974).

11. Organisation for Economic Cooperation and Development, *World Energy Outlook* (Paris: OECD, 1977).

101 mt as the steel industry of the Community faced its most severe postwar crisis of weak demand, intensified foreign competition, global overcapacity, and weakened market discipline. The general industrial market, the domestic market and other smaller users of coal collectively reduced their demands by 18 million tonnes—from 68 to 50 mt. The only increase in coal consumption came in the power station sector where demand grew by a mere 14 mt from 127 to 141 mt. Meanwhile, EEC hard coal production fell from 270 mt in 1973 to 248 mt in 1976, while imports rose substantially from 30 to 44 mt. Most of the increase was in steam coal. See Table 8-5 for EEC solid fuel demand.

The commission of the EEC rightly observed in a letter to the council of ministers in 1976 that a cyclical contraction of the coal market was being borne exclusively by the Community's own coal industry and that failure to stabilize its markets was likely to prejudice its ability to respond to the expected future growth in demand—the Community's declared ambition. In consequence, the commission sought to impress upon member governments the need to provide short-term assistance to the EEC coal industry. In 1976 it proposed three possible measures. First, it urged the desirability of providing financial assistance for holding excess stocks of coal. Second, it proposed the use of financial mechanisms to increase the amount of coal used in Community power stations. And third, it advocated additional support for the coking coal industry in particular, proposing an extension of the existing subsidy scheme both in its size

Table 8-5. Demand for Solid Fuel in the EEC, by Sector and Country, 1976.

	Power Stations		Iron and Steel	Other Industry		Domestic		
	Coal	Lignite	Coke	Coal	Coke	Coal	Coke	Lignite
	Mtce		mt	mt			Mtce	
Belgium	2.8	—	6.1	0.7	0.3	1.9	—	—
Denmark	3.4	—	—	—	—	—	—	—
France	15.0	1.3	11.0	1.3	1.1	5.8	0.3	0.1
Ireland	—	1.0	—	—	—	0.6	—	0.3
Italy	1.2	0.5	6.4	0.2	0.4	0.2	0.2	—
Luxembourg	—	—	2.2	—	—	—	—	—
Netherlands	1.0	—	2.1	—	0.1	0.1	—	—
United Kingdom	63.6	—	9.8	5.9	0.3	13.9	2.9	—
West Germany	33.9	32.9	18.1	2.3	1.5	2.8	2.4	2.6
Total	120.9	35.6	55.7	10.9	3.8	25.4	5.9	3.1

Source: Committee of European Communities, *Twenty-five Years of Common Market Coal* (Brussels, 1977), p. 148-55.

(from 15 to 18 million tonnes per year) and in its duration. In the following year, three further measures were proposed. A 30 percent subsidy was suggested for coal burnt in new coal-fired power stations or modernized older thermal stations, with the subsidy applying to all coal, but with priority being given to EEC coal. A stocking subsidy of up to 20 million tonnes of coal was urged. And a transport subsidy of $12 per ton was suggested for all steam coal entering intra-EEC trade. On all these proposals, the council failed to agree, with the exception of an extension to the coking coal subsidy to 1981—and this measure remains the only aspect of EEC coal policy to which all members are financially committed. Through its directives, however, the council has insisted that the commission's permission be given before any new power station burning either oil or natural gas is constructed and before any existing contract to burn those fuels is renewed.

It has been particularly at the national level that additional assistance to the domestic coal industry has been forthcoming. In West Germany, investment aid, assistance to increase stocks, and the *kohlepfennig* subsidy have all been increased, and a ten-year sales agreement has been reached between the coal- and electricity-producing interests. In Britain, stocking aid, subsidized planning agreements for electricity supplies from Scottish and Welsh coals, increased coal burn subsidies for the Central Electricity Generating Board, and skilled labor subsidies are measures of increased public support. Aid to cover the losses of the French and Belgium industries has also been increased.[12]

In sum, the position in 1979 was that in the very short term after the energy crisis, despite considerable public support, the collective hopes of Western Europe to increase the role of coal in the region's energy economy had failed. Moreover, in addition to the overall decline in the market for coal, there had been an even greater decline in the region's production of coal and a rapidly rising level of coal imports from other parts of the world. It is against this background that the future must be assessed.

The lead time required to open up large, new markets for coal is considerable. For example, a 2,000-MW power station capable of burning 5 million or so tons of coal on base load and of absorbing the output of several large traditional coal mines takes between six to eight years to build and bring onstream. It can take even longer if it runs into environmental or other planning objections. It takes just

12. European Economic Community, *Investment Projects in the Electricity Sector of the Community*, COM(78)98 (Brussels, 1978).

as long, or even longer, to develop entirely new production facilities for deep-mined coal (and most of Western Europe's indigenous reserves are only capable of deep mine extraction); and an entirely new pit might take eight to twelve years before it is brought up to capacity production. It is logical, in consequence that "the next twenty years" should be analyzed in two phases. The first is a medium-term period of ten or so years, a period for which most major investments, both to consume and to produce coal, have already been made or are at an advanced stage of being planned. The implications of these investments can be specified and to a degree quantified. Given the recent and currently low levels of economic activity in Western Europe, plus the surplus of energy-using facilities (particularly the surplus of power station capacity) throughout the region, plus the prospects for a relatively slow takeup of those facilities in the next few years, the medium term might be loosely regarded as the 1980s. During this decade, the market for coal is substantially constrained by decisions already taken. Undoubtedly there remain a number of noteworthy uncertainties about the coal industry's prospects, and a place certainly exists for policy initiatives to influence the outcome of events, but the range of possibilities is far narrower than those to be associated with the subsequent decade. During the longer term, essentially the 1990s, there exists a very much wider range of market opportunities, production alternatives, and political options for coal. In consequence, the situation lends itself to a less quantified style of analysis and suggests the need to identify those key developments and crucial decisions that will significantly affect the coal industry's prospects.

MARKET PROSPECTS FOR COAL IN THE 1980s

For the purpose of this analysis, several initial assumptions must be made concerning broad macroeconomic trends and energy market developments. First, it is assumed that the Western European economy will emerge slowly from the present recession and that overall growth of gross national product in the 1980s will be within the range of 3–3.5 percent per annum. Second it is assumed that coal prices on the international market will remain constant in real terms. Third, it is (perhaps rashly) assumed that oil prices will fall slightly in real terms until the early 1980s, will have stabilized by the middle of the decade, and will reach some 20 percent above present levels in real terms by 1990. Fourth, it is assumed that gas prices will harden and rise in advance of oil price increases throughout the region, with the possible exception of the United Kingdom, and that gas sales will be increasingly concentrated upon premium markets. Fifth, it is assumed that present nuclear power objectives will be achieved. And sixth, it is assumed that public policies will remain broadly unchanged —namely, that there will exist a variety of national energy policies reflecting perceived national self-interests, but that there will be little effective policy of a supranational (especially EEC) nature. The effects of altering these assumptions will be considered later.

The largest market for solid fuel in Western Europe is that provided by power stations. In the EEC it stood at 157 Mtce in 1976. And by far the largest user of power station coal within the Community is the United Kingdom, which consumed 64 Mtce out of a total coal burn of 121 Mtce—some 53 percent. Official forecasts suggest that, in actual tons, this figure will increase from 73 million tonnes in 1975 to 88 mt in 1985 and 103 mt in 1990. However, there are good reasons for believing that the demand for power station coal in the latter two years will be considerably lower. The recent tendency for the coal burn at British power stations to increase (from 64 mt in 1973 to 80 mt in 1977) is likely to be reversed in the next few years as the relative prices of coal and fuel oil continue to narrow and as the merit order of power station utilization is adjusted accordingly. Moreover, once the 19,000 MW of new generating capacity currently under construction is completed within the next few years, the role of coal could be substantially reduced. Of the new capacity, plans for which were laid in the early 1970s in a quite different energy environment, some 50 percent is either oil- or oil-and-gas-fired plant, 30 percent is nuclear (the last stations of the second nuclear program based on advanced gas-cooled reactor (AGR) technology), 14 percent is oil- or hydro-based peaking plant, and only 5 percent is coal-fired.[13] In terms of its output capacity, the public electricity supply system in Britain will increase its dependence upon oil and nuclear capacity substantially between now and the early 1980s. The relative importance of coal-fired plant, in contrast, will fall from 65 percent of capacity in 1976 to perhaps 50 percent in the early 1980s—and even less if, as is widely expected, some old coal-fired power stations are retired in the meantime (Table 8-6). Given that the nuclear stations will substantially command the generating system's base load, the actual level of coal burn in British power stations to meet middle and peak load demands in the 1980s will be essentially a function of the relative delivered price of alternative fossil fuels. If the coal–fuel oil price differential were to widen

13. G. Manners, "Alternative Strategies for the British Coal Industry," *Geographical Journal* (July 1978): 224-34.

Table 8-6. Output Capacity of Power Stations in Britain and Power Stations Under Construction, 1976.

	1976 Capacity		*Under Construction*		*Total*
	MW	*Percent*	*MW*	*Percent*	*MW*
Coal-Fired	43,540	65.1	1,000	5.2	44,540
Coal-Oil; Coal-Gas	4,946	7.4	—	—	4,946
Oil; Oil-Gas	9,615	14.4	9,580	50.2	19,195
Nuclear	4,221	6.3	5,752	30.2	9,973
Others	4,597	6.9	2,736	14.3	7,333
Total	66,919	100.0	19,068	100.0	85,487

Source: Gerald Manners, "Alternative Strategies for the British Coal Industry," *Geographical Journal* (July 1978): 224–34.

to 25 or 30 percent in favor of coal, the generating board's coal burn could well reach the level of the official forecasts—that is, 88 million tonnes in 1985. If, on the other hand, oil were to regain its price advantage over coal and stand at, say, a discount of 10 or 15 percent per useful therm, then the coal burn of the British system could fall below 50 million tonnes in the medium term. This range of possibilities, confirmed privately by industry sources, was indicated in evidence to the House of Lords European Communities Committee.[14] Taking the initial assumptions of the present analysis, recognizing that British coal is priced domestically at levels nearly 50 percent higher than international values, and postulating that oil and coal prices per useful therm in the mid-1980s will stand approximately equal (a relativity that probably implies a rising level of subsidy to the coal industry), it would not be unreasonable to expect that the coal burn of the British generating system will lie somewhere between 65 and 75 million tonnes in the medium term. It is interesting to note that data supplied by the British government to the International Energy Agency, contrary to official policy, suggest a fall in the electricity coal burn from 77 mt in 1976 to 60 mt in 1985.[15] The Economist Intelligence Unit has also suggested that demand for coal from the generating boards will be well below official figures.[16]

The second largest user of power station coal is West Germany. In 1976 it burned 34 Mtce. In addition, West Germany consumes con-

14. J.A. Jukes, in House of Lords, *Report on Coal,* p. 89.
15. International Energy Agency, *The Electricity Supply Industry in OECD Countries* (Paris: OECD, 1978).
16. A.W. Gordon, *Steam Coal and Energy Needs in Europe to 1985,* Economist Intelligence Unit, Special Report No. 52 (London, HMSO 1978).

siderable quantities of lignite for electricity generation—for example, 33 Mtce in 1976. It is the intention of the German authorities at the very least to stabilize this level of solid fuel consumption and possibly to increase it by several million tons. In 1977 an agreement was reached between the coal industry and electricity interests whereby the latter will be supplied annually with 30–33 mt of power station coal over the next ten years.[17] And in its reports to the IEA (which assume that nuclear capacity will increase from 6,000 MW in 1976 to 26,300 MW in 1985, a slightly lower expectation than was espoused in the country's new energy program of 1977, but still a highly optimistic figure), the government indicated its expectation that there will be a modest increase in coal consumption by the electricity industry, suggesting 35 mt in 1980 and 40 mt in 1985. There appears to be general agreement, however, that the present level of lignite consumption (about 124 million tonnes) will not be increased.

Throughout the rest of Western Europe the market for power station coal and lignite is currently quite small. The largest consumer is France, which burned 21 million tonnes of high and low grade coal in 1976 (15 Mtce). In their reports to the IEA[18] and on the assumption that the country's extraordinarily ambitious plans to expand its nuclear capacity from its present 2,800 MW to 42,300 MW will in fact succeed, the French government takes the view that the coal burn of the electricity industry will decline to less than 16 mt in 1985 and 13 mt in 1990. Italy on the other hand, which in 1976 consumed a mere 1.3 mt of coal in its power stations, has recently embarked upon a major program to convert several of its larger coastal power stations to dual-fired capacity. The expectation is that coal consumption will increase to 5 mt in 1980 and perhaps twice that figure in the subsequent five years. Spain also expects to increase its coal burn from 6 mt in 1976 to 11 mt in 1985 and 14 mt in 1990. The Benelux countries plan to increase their coal burn by 3 or 4 mt, and it would not be unreasonable to expect some small increase in consumption in countries such as Denmark, Sweden, and Greece. The changes that are anticipated in the use of lignite are geographically quite specific. As reported to the IEA, between 1976 and 1985 the major developments will be in Turkey and Spain, where consumption will increase by 41 and 14 million tonnes, respectively.[19]

Pulling these country-by-country findings together, the picture that emerges is one of declining consumption in Britain and France

17. I. Fells, "The Energy Future of West Germany," *Energy Policy* (December 1977): 341–44.

18. International Energy Agency, *Electricity Supply Industry*.

19. Ibid.

being more than offset by the prospect of increases elsewhere in Western Europe, particularly in West Germany, Italy, and Spain. The net effect is an increase in demand for power station coal of some 10–20 million tonnes in the medium term. In considerable measure, these figures reflect the hopes of Western European electric utilities that a considerable capacity of nuclear power plant will become available in the 1980s, plus the fact that decisions to build oil-fired plant—decisions taken before 1973–1974—cannot be reversed. Only one-fifth of the thermal power station capacity under construction or planned in the EEC in January 1978 was capable of burning coal,[20] and only 16 percent of new conventional power stations completed or likely to be completed in the EEC between 1976 and 1981 will be fueled by coal or lignite (Table 8–7).

The second major market for the coal industry in the medium term is that of coking coal and is provided largely by the iron and steel industry. In 1976, the demand for such coal in the EEC was 101 million tonnes. The uncertainties surrounding the Western European steel industry today have already been noted. Its medium-term future will be shaped as much by political as by economic factors. This complicates forecasts. However, assuming with Wright that the economy of Western Europe between 1974 and 1990 will grow at a rate some 50 percent below that achieved in the 1960s;[21] that like the United States, Western Europe will become a net steel importer as international trade in finished steel increases and as low cost producers elsewhere erode away many of the European industry's traditional overseas markets and some of its markets at home; and that the coke rates of the Western European steel industry, which are currently well above those of the average practice (let alone the best practice) in Japan, will move down toward and match current Japanese figures (about 0.40–0.45 tonnes of coke per ton of pig iron), an intensity of use model produces the following projection. Between 1974 and 1990 the demand for steel in Western Europe will increase from 161 million to about 232 million tonnes. Assuming 10 percent net imports, production will stand in 1990 at 210 million tonnes. This yields a demand for about 100 mt of coking coal—approximately the same as the EEC demand in 1976. With rather more optimistic assumptions about economic growth, this figure might be increased by perhaps one-tenth.

Despite its prospective lack of overall growth, the market for

20. European Economic Community, *Investment Projects in the Electricity Sector.*

21. S. Wright, Non-Renewable Materials Project, University College London. Report submitted to the Social Science Research Council, 1978.

Table 8-7. Breakdown of New Conventional Thermal Power Stations (above 200 MW) to be Completed Between 1976 and 1981 in the EEC, by Type of Fuel (percentages).

| Country | Solid Fuel | | Others | | | | Total |
	Lignite	Coal	Coal/Oil	Oil	Oil-Gas[a]	Natural Gas	
EUR-9	1	12	3	58	24	2	100
Belgium	—	—	—	—	100	—	100
Denmark	6	36	15	5	38	—	100
Eire	—	—	—	74	—	26	100
France	—	—	—	100	—	—	100
Italy	—	—	3	97	—	—	100
Luxembourg	—	—	—	—	—	—	—
Netherlands	—	—	32	—	52	16	100
United Kingdom	—	13	—	76	11	—	100
West Germany	—	—	—	51	49	—	100

Source: Union of European Electrical Producers, The European Community Committee, *Target Program of the Electrical Sector Up to the Year 1981* (Paris, May 1976), p. 21.

[a]Natural and blast furnace gases.

coking coal in Western Europe will nevertheless undergo certain important changes in the medium term. An analysis of the prospects for steel demand at the national level reveals a relative shift of growth away from the high income countries of West Germany and France in particular—where the intensity of steel use is already relatively high—toward the countries of southern Europe. The share of Western European steel demands originating from Mediterranean Europe appears likely to increase from approximately 30 percent in 1974 to 36 percent in 1990. With a country like Spain having both a high proportion of new plant and not improper ambitions to expand its steel industry in line with national demands, there is likely to be a growth of coking coal requirements in southern Europe. This in turn implies an almost certain decline of demand in the countries of northern Europe and has important implications for the pattern of coking coal supply.

The other markets for coal in the medium term lie in the industrial and domestic sector especially and to a small extent in the conversion (patent fuel) industry. These markets have been contracting in recent years. In 1973 they stood at 68 mt in the EEC; by 1976 they had fallen to 50 mt. The opportunities for reversing this decline in the 1980s will vary from country to country and, particularly, with the availability and price of alternative fossil fuels. In Britain, for example, which provides the largest industrial and domestic markets within the EEC— representing 54 percent and 55 percent of the Community's demands in each case—the prospects are bleak. There, the likely availability of low-priced natural gas in increasing quantities from the North Sea suggests that these markets will remain highly competitive and that coal will continue to give ground. The U.K. Department of Energy, an optimist in these matters, has forecast that coal demand in these sectors will fall from 28 mt in 1975 to 18 mt in 1990; others have put the latter figure within the range of 10-15 mt.[22] Elsewhere in Western Europe the price position of coal might be slightly more advantageous and competition from natural gas less intense. But the basis for expansion is smaller, and the psychological foundation is weak. The price advantage that coal requires in the industrial market in order to offset its lower bulk density, its higher handling and storage costs, and the need to install new coal-burning equipment is already available in those parts of the region that have physical and political access to low cost imports. But the downward drift of fuel oil prices in 1977 and 1978 and the tendency still to regard coal as an "old" fuel militate against sales. As long as oil prices continue to drift downward or even remain stable in real terms, the prospects are for a continuing decline in the industrial and domestic markets for coal in Western Europe. After several years of increases in the price of oil, however, and aided by the development of fluidized bed technology, the industrial market in particular could begin to grow. Demand in 1990 could stand between 45 and 50 million tonnes.

Western Europe in 1977 consumed 418 Mtce of solid fuel. On the initial assumptions of this analysis, this demand will increase by only 5 to 30 million tonnes in the medium term. With quickened economic growth, this prospect would be achieved by the middle rather than the late 1980s, and the considerations that govern the longer term (discussed later) would then begin to apply.

Were the price of oil to harden and then begin to increase in real terms somewhat earlier than was initially assumed—a more likely prospect following the 1979 revolution in Iran—the role of the coal-fired power stations in the generating systems of Britain, West Germany, France, and Italy would be adjusted to burn more coal. The room for maneuver would be greatest in the British and West German cases, but would be constrained by the capacity and age of

---

22. G. Manners, in House of Lords, *Report on Coal*, p. 192 ff.; and Manners, "Alternative Strategies for the British Coal Industry."

their coal-burning plant. The coal burn of the region might be increased by some 20 million tonnes.

Were there to be a substantial slippage in the region's nuclear power program—and this is a highly likely prospect (see Chapter 9 on nuclear energy in Western Europe)—then fuel oil and coal would be required to make up the deficiency. As noted above, the French nuclear program is the largest and is perhaps most vulnerable; Brookes has recently suggested that 31–35 GW of nuclear generating capacity might be available in 1985 compared with the target of 42 GW.[23] Fells has cast serious doubts on the practicality of West Germany having available the 30 GW of nuclear capacity planned for 1985, in particular because of the delays imposed by environmental objections,[24] while in its report to the IEA,[25] the West German government suggested 26 GW as its likely nuclear capacity in 1985, yet a figure as low as 18 GW is by no means out of the question. In the EEC as a whole, the December 1974 objective for 1985 of 160 GW had shrunk by 1977 to a set of national programs that estimated (1985) capacity at just over 100 GW; and further slippage in construction timetables could mean that the mid-1980s will only see 65–70 GW operational. Outside the EEC, the story is the same. Western Europe's third largest program, that of Spain, has been delayed, and uncertainties surround any further construction in Sweden. Together, the governments of Western Europe individually submitted to the IEA[26] their expectations that nuclear electricity capacity would increase from 18 GW in 1976 to 102 in 1985. Assuming that only 80–90 percent of this is completed and that alternative base load capacity has to be found, the output of some 10–15 GW of capacity will need to be provided from conventional sources of energy. Equivalent to some 25–35 million tonnes of coal each year, this would be shared between oil and solid fuel. Coal's share could be 10–15 mt, and even higher if there was a political will for it to be so. Certainly the EEC commission has lost no opportunity to press upon member governments the desirability of increasing the coal burn of the Community. To date, however, their response has been lukewarm.

Should higher real oil prices and delays in the nuclear program coincide, it would be improper to assume that the additional demand for coal would be the sum of their individual effects, for there are

23. L.G. Brookes, "Role of Nuclear Energy," *Energy Policy*, June 1978.
24. Fells, "The Energy Future of West Germany."
25. International Energy Agency, *Electricity Supply Industry*.
26. Ibid.

obvious limits to the quantity of coal that can be burned in the power stations of Western Europe in the medium term. A published figure is not available, but an upper limit of 25 mt might be taken as a reasonable approximation.

In sum, the demand for solid fuel in Western Europe in the medium term could increase by between 5 and 50 mt above its 1977 level—namely, to 423–468 Mtce. This range is considerably lower than the 516–553 mt forecast by the OECD in 1977; it reflects both a fuller appreciation of the weakened market for coal outside the power station sector in recent years and a somewhat more pessimistic view of the region's economic growth prospects in the medium term. It is against this background that the supply options for solid fuel in the same period will be considered.

SUPPLY ALTERNATIVES FOR COAL IN THE 1980s

With higher energy prices after 1973, the profitability and the prospects of the Western European coal industry were transformed. Coal resources, which had previously been judged uneconomic, appeared overnight to become attractive commercial prospects. And as was noted earlier, there was a political will to assist in their exploitation. At the same time, exploration and development investment in new coal mines outside the region began to quicken and to widen the sources from which Western Europe might meet its coal requirements through imports. The domestic industry and the overseas industry need to be examined in turn.

Of the 270 mt of hard coal produced in the EEC in 1973, some 219 mt, or 81 percent, came from the mines of the United Kingdom and West Germany. The British coals were substantially steam coals and were won at somewhat lower average costs than the largely metallurgical coals of West Germany.

United Kingdom

In its plans, the National Coal Board responded ambitiously to the energy crisis. It sought to stabilize its shrinking capacity at about the 130 mt level produced in 1973, increase output to 135 mt by 1985, and increase it yet further to about 145 mt by 1990. The intention initially was that new investment would result in the creation of an additional 43 million tons of annual capacity by 1985, including 10 mt from the exploitation of a new coalfield centered on Selby in Yorkshire and 10 mt from other new pits; the inevitable loss of capacity through the exhaustion of old mines would thereby be offset. The most recent ambitions of the board are for an output of only 10 mt from new mines by 1985. However, they are planning for a compensating increase in production from their existing (but modernized) pits. The target is still 135 mt in 1985, of which 120 mt will be deep mined and 15 mt surface mined. Although it is only a few years (1969) since the British industry produced more than 150 mt of coal, the problems of returning toward that level of production are more difficult than they might first appear. This is partly because existing capacity is being steadily exhausted at a rate of about 2 mt per year. Moreover, the industry has been in general decline for over sixty years, with only brief periods of revival such as the immediate postwar period. During the subsequent years of the oil surplus, there was very little investment in the industry. Its labor force was run down rapidly (773,000 in 1956; 250,000 in 1976), and its workers now have a high average age. Productivity, which rose steadily in the late 1960s, has in recent years been tending to decline. Yet only by markedly increased productivity will it be possible to win a larger tonnage of coal without placing considerable burdens upon possible labor supplies and bidding up the price of mining labor in the process. There will, of course, be considerable productivity gains in the modernized and new pits. At Selby, for example, it is expected that coal will be produced at five times the present average. For this reason especially, it has been claimed that the total cost of coal from the new mines will be below the operating costs of existing mines,[27] an expectation that draws attention to the enormous range of costs that are carried by the industry in its different production facilities. The best (about one-third) are, without doubt, highly competitive sources of energy. But another 60 percent or so of the industry comprises units that were first developed over sixty years ago and carry very high production costs. To remain reasonably competitive, the NCB in theory needs to lose this old capacity as quickly as possible, but there are powerful social forces that seek to resist such a course of action. Indeed, it is a moot point whether the total economic and social costs of winning coal from many of the old mines are in fact higher than the economic and environmental costs of opening up new fields. Moreover, the environmental problems facing the production phase of the industry are noteworthy in their own right. Although there was little delay over starting work on the Selby coalfield (approved in the shadow of the energy crisis), many more formidable objections have been raised in the case of the second major proposal for mining in Leicestershire (Vale of Belvoir); at best

27. Secretary of State for Energy, *Energy Policy.*

such objections will slow, at worst (for the coal industry) they could deny the development of a further 8 million tonnes of capacity.

A large question mark hangs over the expansion plans of the National Coal Board. This was underlined by the Central Electricity Generating Board, its major customer, which in its 1978 *Corporate Plan* drew attention to the inability of the British coal industry to meet its production targets in the postwar years and boldly reasserted the generating board's preference for building additional nuclear and oil-fired power stations when the growth of demand eventually requires the construction of further generating capacity.[28] Moreover, insofar as the National Coal Board has had difficulty in recent years in placing all its production, and there is the clear prospect of a contraction of the British need for coal in the medium term, the market environment in the immediate future is alien to the expansion program.[29] The institution of an EEC subsidy on the transport costs of steam coal traded within the Community might help a little in this context, but would still not guarantee an appropriate stimulus. In sum, the experience of the British coal industry's expansion plans since 1973, plus the labor, productivity, cost, environmental, and market problems of the industry, suggest that production is more likely to remain at about 120 mt rather than expand and that it could well slip back to 100 mt in the 1980s.

West Germany

Although the coal industry in West Germany produces an inherently more highly valued product than that of the National Coal Board, the deeper and less favorable seams, together with the higher unit costs of the industry, combine to necessitate various forms of public support; and this support has had to be increased in recent years. There has also been a deliberate curtailment of production in the wake of weakened demand, and hard coal production has fallen from 104 mt in 1973 to 96 mt in 1976. The plans of the industry are to stabilize production within the range 90–95 mt throughout the medium term, assuming that its protection and the public subsidies will continue, that domestic demand from the power stations and steel industry will be sustained, and that the subsidized export of coking coal to other Community countries will persist. Insofar as the German industry shares with its British counterpart many of the same problems associated with reversing decades of contraction, with an aging labor force, with low productivity by international

28. Central Electricity Generating Board, *Corporate Plan* (London: CEGB, 1978).

standards, and with environmental problems, these production expectations should be regarded as upper limits, and an even lower figure of perhaps 85 mt is more likely. In addition to hard coal production, of course, West Germany has a substantial lignite industry, the largest in Western Europe. Tied to the electricity industry for its markets, there are no plans for its expansion, and in the medium term its output of 124 mt (33 Mtce) is not expected to increase.

Other EEC Countries

Elsewhere in Western Europe there are only limited prospects for the expansion of coal production. In France, Charbonnages de France have a production target of 20–21 mt in the 1980s, compared with 26 mt in 1973; their expectations are to concentrate production on their lowest cost (but still internationally very expensive) mines in the Nord. Belgium coal production stood at 9 million tons in 1973 and has since fallen to 7 mt; as the industry becomes concentrated on the Kempen coalfield, it is hoped to stabilize production at 8–9 mt. Coal production in the Netherlands has ceased. There appear to be no plans for a significant expansion of the modest coal production currently achieved in such countries as Austria (2 mt), Norway (1 mt), and Portugal (1 mt). The only countries where there are plans for a substantial increase in production, both of hard coal and lignite, are Spain and Turkey. In the former, output is planned to increase to 17 Mtce, and in the latter the expectations are for a production of 25 Mtce in the medium term. In all, solid fuel production outside the United Kingdom and West Germany stood at 84 Mtce in 1973; it had contracted to 76 Mtce by 1976. In the medium term, however, it seems likely to increase once again and to stand within the range of 90–95 Mtce.

The supply of coal and lignite from domestic sources in Western Europe in the medium term, in sum, appears likely to lie within the range of 308–343 Mtce. Set alongside the demand for 423 Mtce that was generated under the initial assumptions, the need for substantial imports is clear. Considered against the higher level of demand for 468 Mtce generated under the altered assumptions, the import needs of Western Europe will be substantially greater in the medium term. This import range of 80–155 Mtce compares with the OECD 1977 estimates of 80 mt under its reference scenario and 107 mt under its accelerated policy scenario for 1985.

Imported Coal

Imports of coal into Western Europe have increased and originated from a wider range of sources in recent years. Net imports stood at

45 Mtce in 1973. In the following four years, imports into the EEC alone increased by 15 Mtce. The traditional exporters to Western Europe (the United States, Poland, and the USSR) have recently been joined by Australia and South Africa.

The attractions of imported coal stem from its lower price compared with its domestic counterpart, which in turn reflects (in the case of imports from the market and mixed economies at least) substantially lower delivered (production and transport) costs. Table 8-8 indicates that compared with average British and West German production costs of $43 and $47 per ton, the costs of mining underground coal in Australia are between $18 and $25 per ton, whilst South African costs are as low as $15 per ton for deep-mined coal (in 1977 dollars). Surface-mined coal is even cheaper. In the United States the cost is reported to range between $6 and $12 per ton; in Australia it can be as low as $8 and in South Africa a figure of $8 per ton has also been quoted. These figures compare with British surface-mining costs of nearly $32 per tonne. Transport charges of perhaps $12-15 per tonne have to be added to non-European production costs—or perhaps even lower charges if purchases of coal are made long term, since this would allow lower priced contracts of affreightment to be negotiated with shippers. Imported coals, in other words, can be landed profitably in Western Europe at prices substantially lower than the domestic industry's average costs. Their advantage is considerable in both Britain and West Germany—the Central Electricity Generating Board recently noted that Australian coal, double handled via Rotterdam, was still cheaper than the domestic product delivered to Thames-side power stations.[30] Imported coals have an even stronger market position in countries away from the major Western European coalfields.

While substantial coal imports into Britain and West Germany are unlikely to be permitted given the existence of their domestic coal industries, other countries in Western Europe will find imports increasingly attractive. And the coal exporters are increasing their capacity accordingly. South Africa, for example, plans to increase coal production from 65 mt in 1977 to 125 mt in 1985 and to increase its exports from 2 to 27 mt.[31] Although the development of Australian coal reserves has proceeded largely in the light of prospective Japanese demands to date, Australian coal will undoubtedly find

29. See Manners, "Alternative Strategies"; Manners, in House of Lords, *Report on Coal;* "What Future for the Miners?" *New Statesman,* July 7, 1978, pp. 8-10; and *The Economist,* July 29, 1978, pp. 65-66.

30. Central Electricity Generating Board, *Corporate Plan.*

31. *World Coal* (April 1978).

Table 8-8. Comparative Costs of Mining Coal, 1977 (U.S. dollars per tonne).

Country	Underground Mining	Surface Mining
France	36[a]	—
West Germany	47[a]	—
United Kingdom	43–47[a]	32[a]
Australia	18–25[a,b,c]	8–24[b,c]
India	10–16[b]	—
South Africa	13–21[a,b,c]	8–10[c]
United States (Western States)	—	6–12[d,e]

Sources: [a]W.L.G. Muir, *Review of the World Coal Industry to 1990* (Wembley, U.K.: Miller Freeman, 1975).
[b]Industrial Research Institute, *Technical and Economic Study on the Availability of Coal, Nuclear and New Energy* (Tokyo: Government Publishing Co., 1976).
[c]International Energy Agency, *Steam Coal Prospects to 2000* (Paris: OECD, 1975).
[d]U.S. Bureau of Mines. *Basic Estimated Capital Investment and Operating Costs for Coal Strip Mines* (Washington, D. C.: Government Printing Office, 1976).
[e]C.E. Mann and J.N. Helle, *Coal and Profitability: An Investor's Guide* (New York: McGraw-Hill, 1978).

a growing market in Western Europe, as might coal from India as well. The Polish coal industry is being expanded primarily with domestic and COMECON needs in mind, but some increase in its exports can also be expected as its production rises from 186 mt in 1977 to the 240 mt planned for 1990 and as the country's need for increased earnings of hard currencies remains unchecked. There would not appear to be a likelihood of any nonpolitical supply constraints upon the import of coal into Western Europe in the medium term.

The question arises as to whether, in the event of an EEC transport subsidy for steam coal being made available, domestic supplies could seriously displace imports. The scheme as proposed by the commission, but to date rejected by the council of ministers, is quite modest and envisions putting in the first instance some 12 mt of steam coal into intra-Community trade. However, the level of subsidy currently proposed does not completely cover the difference between the price of British coal delivered to the Continent (Britain is the principal source of Community steam coal) and present spot prices of third country imports. This suggests that, unless the NCB were willing to price its export coal in relation to its lower cost mines rather than its average costs, the prospects for sales are not particularly promising. If the NCB were to adopt such a pricing policy, however, its relations with its largest home consumer, the CEGB, would become increasingly difficult. Moreover, in consequence of the supply disruptions in 1972 and 1974, the British industry lacks some credibility as a secure supplier of power station coal in the EEC. Lucas reports the attitude of north German importers.[32] By contrast, the new association between international oil interests— including 'domestic' companies such as Shell and BP—and the coal industry overseas gives to many import arrangements a dimension of apparent security that will undoubtedly further the growth of international trade in coal in the coming decades. A significant increase in intra-Community trade in steam coal currently does not appear to be a likely prospect.

The existing EEC coal transport subsidy on coking coal has been extended until 1981, although attempts to increase its magnitude have recently failed. As the location of steel production moves toward Mediterranean Europe in some measure, it is clear that the present subsidy will be insufficient to cover the transport costs on the longer haul from West Germany. In consequence, imports seem likely to displace some domestic production unless there is a clear Community desire to minimize coking coal imports and preserve the capacity of the West German industry.

In the medium term, therefore, the prospects are for a modest increase in Western European solid fuel demands—13 percent over 1977 requirements at the most. This implies that solid fuel will continue to serve a declining share of the region's total energy requirements. At the same time, the likelihood of a substantial increase in domestic coal and lignite production is quite bleak, and there may even be a decline compared with the output of the mid-1970s. In consequence, there will be in the 1980s a rising level of coal imports into Western Europe, and they will represent an increasing share of solid fuel consumption there. The magnitude of these imports could significantly exceed the levels currently being proposed in EEC and IEA reports.

THE LONGER TERM PROSPECTS FOR COAL

Beyond the medium term, the basic scenario of the earlier analysis must change. It is assumed that oil supplies will become scarcer in relation to demand; their price in consequence will rise in real terms. Western Europe's domestic supplies of natural gas will also at some point reach a plateau and then begin to fall; again, their value in the

32. Lucas, *Energy and the European Communities*, p. 124.

market will increase. Assuming a persistent growth in demand for energy and in the absence of supply constraints, Western Europe will become increasingly dependent upon nuclear power and coal. This dependence is seen as complementary, as well as to some degree competitive. In the longer term it is initially assumed that the nuclear option will be fitfully embraced throughout much of Western Europe. It is also assumed that supplies of coal will be available at costs significantly below the market price of oil and natural gas.

The longer term supply price of coal mined opencast appears likely to increase only slowly. Competitive forces in the international market for coal are currently not blunted by producer cartels, and given the geographically dispersed reserves of steam coal, their abundance in relation to prospective demands, the lack of corporate concentration, and the likelihood of many new entrants into the industry, the evidence suggests that competition will remain a feature of international coal markets in the 1990s. Simultaneously, it is expected that the technologies available for coal mining, transport, and use will lower unit costs and at least equal, if not exceed, the rising costs of environmental regulations that the industry will have to meet.

Whether the increasing quantities of coal used in Western Europe will be transported to their final markets as electrical energy or as a synthetic natural gas need not concern us here. The latter mode has an advantageous adaptability to variations in the energy load, plus the merit of greater thermal efficiency.[33] A view of this last uncertainty has a considerable bearing upon the actual magnitude of the future demand for coal in Western Europe. However, given the earlier analysis of a medium-term stagnation in the domestic production of coal, it is to the supply side of the market that attention must first be turned.

Of the two largest producers of coal in Western Europe, the British industry has the clearest ambitions concerning the longer term.

By the end of the century if our plans come to fruition, we should be producing, compared with the 120 million tons all-told today, including opencast, something of the order of 170 million tons. What is underlying those figures is no less than 100 million tons of the 150 million which will be the deep mine component of that total tonnage will (sic) have been capacity newly created in the twenty five years from 1975 to the year 2000. We shall end up with an industry that is two-thirds new.[34]

Providing this new capacity will be a considerable achievement.

33. Ibid. p. 134 ff.
34. Ezra, in House of Lords, *Report on Coal,* p. 146.

The NCB has admitted that "We will be fully stretched indeed in bringing forward and approving and commissioning year by year the equivalent of two 2 m.t.y. mines every year from now to the end of the century. To do more than that would be an enormous task."[35] One hundred and seventy million tons, therefore, must be regarded as the upper limit of possible British outputs at the end of the century. In all reality, a much lower figure is more probable. The problems facing the British coal industry in the medium term—problems of labor supplies, productivity, costs, and environmental constraints—will be equally present in the longer term. If anything, the environmental constraints upon the industry will increase with time, partly because the need to develop mining facilities in areas without a mining history will grow and will meet a predictable opposition, and also because the longer term will additionally involve the construction of new coal-using facilities. Finding new sites for power stations and gas works has never been an easy task in the past twenty five years; it will become more fraught with difficulties in the future as concern about environmental quality increases and the institutional mechanisms to delay (if not stop) developments are more fully exploited. There is a further problem, too. The long-term program of the British coal-mining industry to increase its productive capacity will demand a sustained flow of investment throughout the medium term, when the industry is having considerable difficulty in finding markets, when its production could well be contracting, and when its profitability is likely to be in question. The investments might also coincide with the early closure of some of the industry's high-cost pits and with the doubts being raised about the longer term market for British coal, which is not totally assured. "The Community coal industry has sought firm assurance of its long-term markets. No guarantee of any market can be given without a similar guarantee of competitive prices, reliability and quality."[36] The long-term objectives of the National Coal Board will demand the sustained support of the British government and national energy policy if they are to have any chance of being realized. That support cannot be taken for granted.

There are no comparable long-term plans for the West German coal industry. Private observers, however, have suggested that production might be raised to 145–150 million ton by the year 2000, provided that long-term contracts can be arranged between the producers and consumers.[37] These might need more than a little public support,

---

35. M.J. Parker, in House of Lords, *Report on Coal*, p. 106.
36. Central Electricity Generating Board, in House of Lords, p. 84.
37. Schilling, in House of Lords, *Report on Coal*, p. 140.

however, given the relatively high costs of German mines. Lignite production might also be increased, but there are considerable land use constraints on how much might be achieved, and a 20–30 percent increase is the most that can be realistically contemplated.[38] Although the environmental costs of lignite production and use are considerable—as indeed are those of hard coal production and use—the view can be taken that their amelioration is within the resources of an advanced economy, and as a result, "General environmental considerations are not a limiting factor to coal expansion."[39] As in Britain, however, there is no doubt that environmental concerns are likely to delay the response of the solid fuel industry to market opportunities, as has happened recently with two coal-fired power stations in the Ruhr,[40] and there will be a recurring need, at particular times and places, for society to strike a working compromise between its needs for energy and its environmental preferences. Elsewhere in Western Europe, only Turkey and Spain appear to have the reserves of solid fuel upon which a small expansion of production might be based.

Overall, it has to be stressed that the Western European coal industry is substantially a deep mine industry. This contrasts with the world industry, which uses surface mine technology for about half of its output today and is likely to be 80 percent opencast in the future.[41] Irrespective of geology, deep-mined coal is relatively expensive coal. In Western European geological conditions, deep-mined coal is particularly expensive. Given this reality, and while lower cost imports of coal are available in sufficient quantities, market forces would undoubtedly encourage a further contraction of Western European coal production in the longer term. Provided these imports were drawn from a diversity of sources, and assuming the institutions and facilities capable of handling a substantial trade in coal came to be developed, such a reliance would hold only limited strategic risks— and the environmental costs of production would be carried outside Western Europe. On the other hand, such a growing dependence upon coal imports would have adverse consequences on the balance of payments of many countries within the region, and it would be quite contrary to the political desire of Western Europe to increase its self-sufficiency in energy supplies. The equation has both economic

38. Peters, in House of Lords, *Report on Coal*, Session 1978-78, 1st report, p. 142.

39. K.J. Brendow, "Coal demand and supply in 1985" (Paper presented to the International Institute of Applied Systems Analysis, Conference on Energy Resources, Moscow, 1977), p. 11.

40. Fells, "The Energy Future of West Germany."

41. A.T. Shand, in M. Portillo, ed., *National Coal Conference '78*, verbatim report of proceedings, pp. 26-27.

and political components. At the supranational (EEC) level, it has to be recognized that the effectiveness of policy ambitions in the energy field has been very limited to date. The prospect (under the initial assumptions about the longer term), therefore, is for Western Europe to become increasingly and heavily dependent upon coal imports. The quantities involved will be essentially a function of the rate of growth of Western European energy demands in general and electricity demands in particular. Numerical forecasts, however, would be highly speculative.

The assumptions underlying this longer term prospect can, of course, be varied. Three alternative elements in the scenario need to be considered. The first concerns the future availability of oil and natural gas, particularly from domestic reserves within Western Europe. If, in the context of very low rates of demand growth, the supply of these two fuels were to remain adequate if not plentiful throughout the present century—and there is room for disagreement about the magnitude of prospective supplies[42] —then the demand for coal in Western Europe would grow more slowly than was originally postulated. At the same time, the strength of the political arguments to support a domestic coal industry in Britain and West Germany would be substantially weaker. The growing dependence on imported coal would, in consequence, proceed unchecked.

The second alternative assumption concerns the availability, and hence the price, of coal exchanged in international trade. In the context of growing demands for coal in North America and Asia, it cannot automatically be assumed that supply will always be sufficient to meet the import needs of Western Europe at highly competitive prices. A tightening of supply in international trade would tend to harden prices and in time bring them nearer to Western European coal production costs. Given the lead time between mine investment and sustained coal production, however, it would be some time before such a set of circumstances made an impact upon domestic coal supply. A challenge facing the Western European coal producers—and, indeed, the governments of Western Europe, singly and collectively—is to judge effectively if and when such a set of circumstances might arise and to plan their investments accordingly. In the absence of confident foresight, however, the case for maintaining a subsidized

42. P.R. Odell, "Indigenous oil and gas developments and Western Europe's energy policy options," *Energy Policy* (June 1973): 47-64; "Western Europe's natural gas resource system" (Paper presented to the IGU Commission on Industrial Systems, Krakow, Poland, 1977); B. de Vries and J. Kommandeur, "Gas for Western Europe: how much for how long?" *Energy Policy* (March 1975): 24.

industry in the meantime is rather more compelling, although its size would be subject to endless debate.

The third alternative assumption concerns the future role of nuclear power in Western Europe. The public opposition to nuclear power in Western Europe, as elsewhere in the world, is well known and increasingly documented. It is unlikely to abate completely, and it could well increase (see chapter 9). Were this to be the case and were the nuclear programs of Western Europe to be scaled down substantially and permanently, then the need to construct additional conventional power stations would occur both earlier and on a very much larger scale. The demand for coal would be increased substantially, and the political support for the coal industry of Britain and West Germany would be enhanced, at least within those two countries. But given the production constraints and costs of Western European coal production, in the first instance at least it would be international supplies of coal that would be sought to satisfy the greater part of increased demands.

In sum, all the indications are that Western Europe in the longer term will become increasingly dependent upon imported supplies of coal. As this occurs, there is no reason to believe that the necessary port and other transport investments will not be forthcoming. Questions could well arise, of course, about the political security of the emerging supply pattern and whether the magnitude and geography of import dependence was becoming too great and insufficiently diverse. It is more difficult to judge the probable magnitude of environmental issues that might surround a major resort to imported coal. With coal-fired power stations posing distinctive problems of large stockyards and ash disposal, there will be siting problems for most utilities wishing to construct new plant. There will also be concern over the health risks of combustion, some of which (such as carbon dioxide and heavy metal emissions) are still unclear. Nevertheless, such concerns are more likely to delay and increase the cost of a resort to coal than they are to arrest what appears to be an almost inevitable trend in the Western European energy economy.

SUMMARY

Three contrasts and one conclusion emerge from this survey of the prospects for an increased resort to coal in Western Europe over the next twenty years. There is, first, an acute contrast between the prospects for coal in the medium term, when demand growth is likely to be small and coal will continue to serve a declining share of the region's energy market, and in the longer term. In the 1990s, the evidence suggests that coal will once again enlarge its role in the Western European energy economy, and a considerable increase in demand will occur.

There is, second, a vivid contrast between the prospects facing the domestic coal industry of Western Europe, which faces at best the likelihood of output stability and possibly a continuation of its recent tendency to contract, and the prospects for imports. The latter will both increase in volume and take a larger share of the Western European market, slowly in the 1980s and then more decisively in the 1990s.

Third, there is a contrast between the energy interests and politics of Britain and Western Germany on the one hand, each with a large and relatively high cost coal industry to protect, and the rest of Western Europe on the other hand. This divergence of interest will undoubtedly constrain the ability of the EEC to form an articulate policy toward the role of coal in Western Europe's energy economy, leaving market forces and perceived national interests as more dominant influences upon the outcome of events. It could also mean that in the 1990s the resort to coal will be fastest in those countries without domestic reserves, but with an unrestrained access to low cost imports.

The one conclusion that emerges from this analysis is the almost certain reappearance of a substantial world trade in coal, tentatively in the medium term, but more forcefully in the 1990s. Dominated in all probability by large transnational corporations, many of them simultaneously or previously involved in the production and distribution of oil, it will be worldwide in scope. There can be little doubt about its relationship to the American energy economy. The corporations will be in part American owned or American controlled. The mining, transport, and utilization technology will rest in part upon American experience and research and also upon American equipment manufacturers. And the trade will be both from and to the United States. While some Appalachian coals will doubtless continue to serve Western Europe, other suppliers of coal to the Western Europe market will be looking for market opportunities elsewhere, including those in the United States. Coal shipments from South Africa to Florida, or from Australia to California, come immediately to mind. They could well affect the supply and demand relationship of the domestic coal industry in the United States.

Prospects and Problems for an Increased Resort to Nuclear Power in Western Europe, 1980-2000

Gerald Manners

NUCLEAR POWER IN THE CONTEMPORARY ENERGY ECONOMY OF WESTERN EUROPE

Construction Programs

Before the oil price increase of 1973-1974, the nuclear power industry in Western Europe could claim notable achievements in both research and energy production, achievements that afforded a solid foundation for future progress. In 1976 the region had about one-third of OECD nuclear power capacity, with West Germany (6.1 GW), Britain (5.4 GW), Sweden (3.2 GW), and France (2.8 GW) having made the largest investments in nuclear generating plant.[1] By 1977 some 10 percent of EEC electricity supplies were coming from nuclear facilities.

The most precocious development of civilian nuclear power had been in Britain where, immediately after the 1955 Suez crisis and the temporary disruption of oil supplies, the first major nuclear power station program based upon the Magnox gas-cooled reactor was launched. It resulted in the construction of nine stations, with a combined capacity of some 5 GW, which were all operational by 1971. A second program, announced in 1964 and based on an advanced gas-cooled reactor design, is currently adding a further 6

1. International Energy Agency, *The Electricity Supply Industry* (Paris: OECD, 1978).

GW of capacity in five stations and should be completed by 1980–1981. Although representing less than 7 percent of the generating capacity of the public supply system in 1976, the nuclear power plants delivered base load energy and in fact met some 13 percent of the country's electricity needs in that year, a share that is expected to rise to over 15 percent by 1980.[2]

In West Germany, the exploitation of nuclear power began on a much more modest scale in the 1950s, but gained considerable momentum from the middle 1960s. The first nuclear program of 1956 yielded only one small plant of 252 MW, which began production in 1966. A second program, however, launched in 1963 and revised several times, was much more ambitious. By the mid-1970s it had resulted in the completion of nine stations using both boiling water (BWR) and pressurized water reactor (PWR) technologies, and it had an output capacity in excess of 6 GW. In 1976 these stations made up nearly 8 percent of the country's generating capacity and were rapidly increasing their contribution to energy supplies. Although they produced only about 7 percent of West Germany's electricity in that year, by 1980 their contribution is expected to have increased to 16 percent.[3]

The first program of nuclear power station construction in France was started in 1957. It comprised 1,360 MW of capacity at Marcoule and Chinon and, once again, was a modest beginning by British standards. A second program launched in the 1960s and substantially based upon gas-cooled technology, was equally tentative; its total capacity was only 1,860 MW and was completed by 1972. The third French program, however, which was initiated in 1970 and based upon PWR technology, was much bolder. Initially comprising 8 GW of planned capacity, it was later substantially expanded to become currently the largest nuclear power program in Western Europe. Its first reactors were scheduled for completion in 1978 and 1979. Representing some 6 percent of total generating capacity, the potential of Electricité de France's (EdF) nuclear power plants was only 2.8 GW in 1976, when they met 8 percent of electricity demands. By 1978, however, the contribution of nuclear power, with the completion of the first plants of the third program, had increased to 13.4 percent of EdF's supplies, and further increases were expected in subsequent years.

Swedish use of nuclear power, after major technical difficulties with a Swedish-designed heavy water reactor in the 1960s, was eventually based upon 'standard' BWR and PWR technologies, and

2. Ibid.
3. Ibid.

the country's first commercial plant came on stream in 1972. During the next four years, another four reactors were completed. In consequence, by 1976, a total of 3.2 GW of nuclear plant—over 13 percent of Sweden's electricity generating plant—was available and produced more than 18 percent of the country's electrical energy.

Elsewhere in Western Europe in 1976, nuclear power stations had a combined capacity of just under 5 GW (Table 9-1). Their national importance varied considerably. In Belgium, for example, the contribution of nuclear power to the national supply of electrical energy was outstandingly large; 1.7 GW of capacity met some 25 percent of the country's electricity demands. In Switzerland, installed nuclear capacity of 1 GW (representing 8 percent of the country's generating facilities) satisfied 18 percent of the nation's electricity needs. In other countries, however, the role of nuclear power was more modest, the 1.1 GW of Spain contributing less than 6 percent, and the 0.6 GW and 0.5 GW of Italy and the Netherlands meeting just over 2 percent and rather less than 7 percent respectively of their countries' electricity needs.

As with conventional generation, some of the nuclear power stations of Western Europe are international in ownership and purpose. The Tihange (870 MW) plant in Belgium, for example, is jointly owned by Belgium and France. The Tricastin (4 units of 925 MW) plant in France is 12.5 percent owned by Belgium, an investment made in exchange for future supplies of enriched uranium to be supplied by Eurodif. The ownership of the BWR and PWR reactors at Fessenheim (France), Bugay (France), Leibstadt (Switzerland), and Naiseraugst (Switzerland) is shared in different proportions between the utilities of France, Germany, and Switzerland. The fast breeder reactor at Kalkar in West Germany is jointly owned by Germany, Belgium, and the Netherlands, and the larger 120 MW Super-Phénix fast breeder at Creys-Malville in France is jointly owned by France, Italy, and Germany.[4] Not only do these plants reflect shared solutions to the need for electricity supplies and shared investment in nuclear research, they also underline the international dimensions of nuclear power developments in Western Europe, a characteristic that was first signaled by the creation of Euratom in 1958 and later endorsed with the development of international arrangements for uranium enrichment, spent fuel storage and reprocessing, and waste disposal.

International cooperation has long characterized the arrangements

4. Union of European Electrical Producers, *Programmes and Prospects for the Electricity Sector 1978–1983 and 1985–1990* (Paris, 1978).

Table 9-1.   Nuclear Power Capacity, Existing and Estimated, in Western Europe 1976–1990 (GW).

Country	Recent Official Estimates[a]			Alternative Estimates	
	1976	1985	1990	1985	1990
Belgium	1.7	5.4	5.4	5.4	5.4
Denmark	—	—	2.6	—	2.6
France	2.8	42.3	65.3	31.0	40.0–45.0
Germany	6.4	26.3	40.8	18.0	28.0
Ireland	—	—	—	—	—
Italy	0.6	11.4	40.9	2.0	5.0
Luxembourg	—	—	2.1	—	—
Netherlands	0.5	0.5	1.9	0.5	0.5
United Kingdom	6.2	9.7	13.5	9.7	11.0
EEC-9	18.2	95.6	172.5	66.6	92.5–97.5
Austria	—	0.7	2.1	0.7	0.7
Finland	—	3.2	3.5	2.7	3.5
Greece	—	—	2.1	—	0.6
Iceland	—	—	—	—	—
Norway	—	—	1.9	—	—
Portugal	—	—	1.0	—	—
Spain	1.1	11.7	18.5	7.7	12.6
Sweden	3.2	3.6–7.4	3.6–7.4	3.6–7.4	7.4
Switzerland	1.0	2.8	3.6	1.8	2.8
Turkey	—	0.3	0.6	—	0.6
Total	23.5	117.9–121.7	209.4–213.2	83.1–86.9	120.7–125.3

[a]From International Energy Agency, The Electricity Supply Industry (Paris: OECD, 1978).

for the preparation of nuclear fuels—natural (purified) uranium for the Magnox reactors and enriched uranium for the advanced gas-cooled (AGR) and water-cooled reactors. An agreement between Britain, the Netherlands, and West Germany led to the creation of URENCO CENTEC, intially with two enrichment plants in Britain and the Netherlands. Later, under French leadership, the Eurodif project was launched, associating France, Italy, Spain, Belgium, and Iran in the use and expansion of enrichment facilities in France. In addition, several European countries have contracts for the supply of enriched uranium from the U.S. Department of Energy and from Techsnabexport of the USSR.

Storage and Disposal

Short-term storage facilities for spent nuclear fuels are normally provided adjacent to the power stations themselves. Longer term storage and reprocessing facilities, on the other hand, have been and are being provided centrally. They are not yet available in every country. In Britain the principal reprocessing facilities for both the Magnox and AGR power stations are in Windscale (Cumbria), where the fission products are removed for disposal and unused uranium and plutonium are prepared for future reuse. Belgian, German, Italian, and Japanese utilities have taken advantage of these facilities in the past. Permission has recently been given, after an extended public enquiry, for a substantial extension of these facilitites in the form of an enlarged thermal oxide reprocessing plant (THORP); like earlier Windscale facilities, this will be available to overseas users, Japan in particular. To date, West Germany has met its reprocessing requirements outside its borders—in Britain and France especially—and for some years this is likely to continue, since plans for a major West Germany reprocessing plant at Gorleben are unlikely to be realized before the early 1990s. In France there are two reprocessing facilities, a small one at Marcoule and a much larger one at Cap le Hague. The latter has contractual obligations not only with the German utilities, but also with utilities in Switzerland and Spain. Belgium currently relies mainly upon France for its reprocessing needs, but is planning to restart an old reprocessing facility at Dessel to cater to some of its own requirements.

The handling of low level wastes in all countries is constrained by both national government rules and authorizations and the standards set by the International Commission on Radiological Protection. The disposal of high level wastes has been temporarily solved in Western Europe through the storage of the fission products and actinides in tanks containing acidic solutions. A more permanent method of storage involving the solidification of the high level nuclear wastes in a borosilicate glass has been practiced in France since 1969, and a comparable British facility will be completed in 1979. But the questions surrounding the most appropriate places in which to dispose of this glass remain unresolved.

Present achievements in the production of nuclear energy in Western Europe, plus the associated international arrangements for cooperative research, technical assistance, and commerce, reflect only one aspect of the region's resort to nuclear power. Since 1973 both national and international initiatives have sought to make a much greater use of nuclear energy in the late 1970s and the 1980s. Progress toward this goal is examined in the next section.

RESPONSE TO THE ENERGY CRISIS

An implied assumption of the plans that were drawn up in the months immediately after the 1973-1974 energy crisis was that the considerable progress already achieved in the development of civilian nuclear power in Western Europe in the 1950s and 1960s could be speedily exploited to construct a large number of additional nuclear power plants that would substantially reduce the region's dependence upon imported crude oil. Quite apart from the strategic advantages of such a development, the higher level of energy prices after 1973 appeared to remove any doubts that might have remained in the minds of utility managements in particular about the economic advantages of nuclear energy. The plans at one stage were exceedingly ambitious. In its *Energy Prospects to 1985*, the OECD suggested that the capacity of Western Europe's nuclear plant might be increased from the 15 GW of 1973 to 175 GW in 1985 and 345 GW in 1990—or even, under an accelerated program to reduce the region's dependence upon oil, to 227 GW and 480 GW in 1985 and 1990 respectively.[5] These hopes must be set alongside what might now be regarded as the very much more modest scale of generating capacity that is likely to be commissioned in Western Europe in the next decade or so—a capacity of perhaps 85 GW in the middle 1980s and no more than 120-125 GW in 1990 (see below). This downward revision of nuclear prospects is regionwide.

France

With Britain having recently discovered a considerable domestic abundance of fossil fuels, especially offshore oil and natural gas, and with West Germany having a substantial (albeit in part a high

5. Organisation for Economic Cooperation and Development, *Energy Prospects to 1985* (Paris, 1974).

cost) solid fuel industry, it is not surprising that the most ambitious and sustained national nuclear power program in Western Europe is that of Electricité de France. The scale of existing and prospective balance of payments' problems in France, in the absence of any large domestic energy reserves, plus the strategic vulnerability of such a situation for an economy with considerable ambitions for further manufacturing growth, precipitated the decision to accelerate and substantially extend the country's third program of nuclear power station construction based upon PWR technology. The initial objective was to complete 42 GW of capacity by 1985 and 65 GW by 1990. Given the relatively small base of nuclear experience in relation to these ambitions upon which the country had to build, this program is surprisingly well advanced. Although there has been some slippage in the timing of the construction program, the national utility and the government still (officially) hope that 40 GW of capacity will be commissioned by 1985. However, the capacity of those stations currently under construction, plus further stations that are planned and for which there are no apparent licensing or other administrative obstacles to delay their completion, is only 31 GW. Given the delays that could face the authorities in obtaining further permissions, therefore, it seems likely that EdF will not have nuclear generating capacity in excess of that figure by the mid-1980s. By 1990, on the other hand, nuclear capacity in France could have increased by a further third or more and have reached 40 or 45 GW.

West Germany

German plans have met with much more serious delays. For a brief while after the energy crisis, there was talk of building 45 or even 50 GW of nuclear generating plant by 1985, but by 1976 these plans had been scaled down to a more realistic goal of 30 GW by the mid-1980s. In their 1977 submission to the IEA,[6] the West German authorities suggested a likely capacity of 26 GW in 1985. The latest UNIPEDE report includes figures of 22.6 GW for 1985 and nearly 38 GW for 1990.[7] However, with the construction of 4.4 GW of nuclear plant halted by various court procedures and with 1.3 GW of the 1985 program still unlicensed, a more realistic estimate of West German capacity in the mid-1980s is only 18 GW, with perhaps a further 10 GW being completed by 1990.

Spain

The third largest nuclear program to be announced after the energy crisis was that of Spain. Once again there have been a variety

6. International Energy Agency. *Electricity Supply Industry.*
7. UNIPEDE. *Programmes and Prospects for the Electricity Sector.*

of delays in implementing these plans. In its *Plan Energetico Na-cional* (1975), the government proposed the construction of nearly 23 GW of nuclear plant, to be completed before 1987. In its sub-missions to the IEA, these hopes had been scaled down to a current official expectation of less than 12 GW being available in 1985.[8] Private estimates, however, based upon the firm administrative decisions and legal permissions for plant construction, suggest that it is more likely that under 8 GW will be completed by that date and that it could be 1990 before 12 GW are available to the Spanish utilities.

Italy

There was a time when Italian ambitions for a major nuclear power program were comparable to those of Spain. In the govern-ment's 1975 energy program, 24 GW of nuclear capacity were proposed for the 1980s. Within two years, however, a new plan had reduced this goal by 50 percent, and 11 GW came to be regarded as the target for 1985. The 1990 objective, as reported to the IEA, remains a highly improbable 41 GW.[9] The implementation of the most recent Italian plans has been sufficiently delayed for there to be considerable uncertainty about whether the Ente Nazionale per l'Energia Elettrica's (ENEL) immediate goal of commissioning 6 GW of nuclear plant by 1985 will in fact be realized. It rests upon the adoption of "emergency measures for granting admin-istrative authorizations," and it appears likely that the persistent opposition of local authorities will seriously hamper the progress of the industry. Possibly only 2 GW will be finished by 1985.[10] Although 11 GW in theory is still feasible by 1990, a more likely achievement is only 5 GW.

United Kingdom

Elsewhere in Western Europe, nuclear power programs have from the outset been rather more modest. Nevertheless, they too have been characterized by both technical and political delays. In Britain, for example, although extravagant talk in the immediate wake of the energy crisis urged a major expansion of nuclear capacity, by 1975 it was widely recognized that for a number of years, the Central Electricity Generating Board and other power authorities would be faced with a considerable surplus of generating plant. In consequence, much of the subsequent planning in the electricity

8. International Energy Agency. *Electricity Supply Industry.*
9. Ibid.
10. UNIPEDE. *Programmes and Prospects for the Electricity Sector.*

sector has been concerned with completing the (technically delayed) AGR power stations and then ensuring the survival of a nuclear construction industry through to the time in the 1980s when it is expected that a further expansion of nuclear capacity will be required. By the early 1980s, therefore, British generating boards should have access to 10 GW of nuclear capacity, but on the basis of existing plans, this will be increased by only 1 or 2 GW by the end of the decade.

Sweden

In Sweden, in contrast, it has primarily been serious political delays that have held back the further use of nuclear power. A government recommendation for a substantial expansion of nuclear generating capacity was first proposed in 1972 and—after much debate and consultation—was approved in 1975. However, the decision to go ahead with a thirteen-reactor program was set aside following a change of government in 1976. A moratorium on plant construction and the further use of nuclear power was imposed. Disagreements about the future place of nuclear generation in Sweden's energy economy within the Falldin coalition government, however, led to its October 1978 collapse, and the prospects for a further resort to nuclear energy now look brighter with the return to power of the Social Democrats. The disagreements within the Swedish body politic are sufficiently deep rooted that the matter is likely to remain unresolved for some time. Nevertheless, there is now a possibility that earlier plans will be taken up once again and the Swedish nuclear capacity will be increased to more than 7 GW by the middle 1980s. Still, the present evidence is so uncertain that is is equally likely that no further additions will be made to present nuclear power capacity, which would leave Sweden with just over 3 GW of generating plant from this source.

Other European Countries

Swiss plans for the expansion of nuclear electricity to 3.4 GW by 1980 have been held back by delays at three large stations, and 2 GW must now be regarded as the most likely outcome by 1985. Finland, whose program is based upon Soviet technology, fuel, and reprocessing, has plans for 3.2 GW of power by the mid-1980s; some slippage in the construction program, however, suggests that 2.7 GW is a more likely outcome in 1985. In a recent (November 1978) referendum in Austria, a small majority voted not to authorize the operation of the Zwentendorf plant (0.7 GW). Whether and when this decision will in time be reversed is a matter for speculation—

but there is little chance of further nuclear plant being completed before 1985. In the Netherlands, too, there are no plans for additional nuclear power stations to be commissioned before 1985, when the present 0.5 GW of capacity will be the sole contribution of nuclear power to the country's electricity supplies.

It has therefore been Belgium that, almost alone. has been able to adhere substantially to its early postcrisis plans for nuclear power expansion. In 1975 proposals were made to add 4 GW to the country's existing capacity of 1.7 GW, with the intention of providing 50 percent of the supply of electrical energy from this source by 1985. Present expectations are that a total of 5.4 GW of nuclear plant will in fact be commissioned by 1985 and that a further 1.4 GW will be completed by 1990.

Some countries in Western Europe, of course, have temporarily forgone the nuclear option. Ireland, for example, has decided upon a nuclear power station site, but has no firm plans to build a plant. Denmark has decided to wait until 1980 at least before committing itself to nuclear power—by which time it is hoped that many of the concerns about the disposal of high level waste will be set aside. Norway has ample supplies of conventional energy. Greece, Portugal, and Turkey are planning on small investments in nuclear power, but these will not be available until the late 1980s at the earliest.

Summary

In sum, although in its 1974 energy statements the commission of the EEC suggested that its nine member countries should aim at installing 200 GW of nuclear power plant by 1985, there has subsequently been a steady erosion of formal ambitions and realistic expectations. Late in 1974, the sum of the plans of the member governments of the EEC was for 160 GW of capacity by 1985. By 1977, these programs had been formally revised downward to 103 GW, a figure that the EEC commission later came to regard as too ambitious; it suggested that 90 GW was more probable.[11] By late 1977, in fact, member governments submitted to the IEA a set of nuclear expectations for the end of 1985 that summed to 96 GW.[12] A year later, in October 1978, informed private opinion within the commission had once again revised downward the probable level of nuclear electricity generating capacity in the mid-1980s, and figures between 65 and 70 GW were being proposed as the most

11. European Economic Community, *Second Report on the Achievement of Community Energy Policy Objectives for 1985*, Comm/77/395 (Brussels, 1977).
12. International Energy Agency, *Electricity Supply Industry*.

likely amount of commissioned nuclear plant. Such an achievement will rest heavily upon steady progress in the construction and commissioning of new stations in France in particular, a country that could well have nearly half of the Community's nuclear capacity by that date (see Table 9-1). Outside the EEC, governments were expecting to have available at least 22 and possibly 26 GW of nuclear plant by 1985 when they reported to the IEA in 1977. More recent private estimates for the mid-1980s, however, range between 16 and 20 GW, the range resting substantially upon the eventual attitude of the people and government of Sweden to the further use of nuclear power in that country. In Western Europe as a whole, therefore, it would be unrealistic to expect nuclear generating capacity to exceed 90 GW in 1985. It could well be only 83 GW; and if there are further unexpected technical or political delays, the figure could be lower still. By 1990 the best current estimate is an installed capacity ranging between 120 and 125 GW (Table 9-1).

ANATOMY OF THE DELAYS TO THE NUCLEAR PROGRAMS

While each country in Western Europe has distinctive energy problems and plans and a specific approach toward the exploitation of nuclear power, there are certain common denominators to the delays that have characterized the use of nuclear energy in recent years. These are worth specifying and relate to six factors in particular: the changed expectations of the future levels of electricity demand; the unexpected problems posed in financing the building of nuclear plants; technical difficulties encountered in the construction process; obstacles presented by slow and cumbersome consent procedures; site-specific objections to the alleged environmental impact of nuclear power stations; and a series of concerns related to the safety aspects of nuclear technology.

Reduced Demand for Electricity

The first—but by no means the most important—reason for the delayed exploitation of nuclear power is the effect upon the electricity utilities and energy policy planners alike of the initial fall in the demand for electrical energy following the 1973–74 energy crisis. This has been followed by a persistent sluggishness in the growth of electricity demands, partly as a consequence of higher energy prices and partly as a result of the enduring world economic recession. In most countries the slow recovery of the market has led to a downward revision in electricity demand forecasts, and it has necessitated substantial changes in the scale and timing of both conventional and nuclear power station construction programs. The base case of the OECD's *Energy Prospects to 1985* assumed a growth rate of 7.2 percent per annum in Western European electricity demands between 1972 and 1985. By 1977 the OECD's *World Energy Outlook* adopted in its reference scenario a 5.6 percent annual growth of electricity demands until the mid-1980s.[13] In May 1976, UNIPEDE forecast that the 1980 electricity consumption of the EEC was likely to lie within the range of 1,244-1,359 TWh (reflecting annual growth rates of 5.3 percent and 7 percent between 1975 and 1980); by September 1978, however, the forecast for 1980 by the same organization had been narrowed to the range of 1,244-1,279 TWh (assuming annual growth rates of 4.9 percent and 5.8 percent).[14] By 1978, in fact, UNIPEDE forecasts were acknowledging the prospect of a steadily falling growth rate in electricity demand within the EEC, and the current forecasts (compared with the range of 5.2-5.8 percent per annum between 1975 and 1980) are for growth rates of 4.9-5.9 percent between 1980 and 1985 and 4-5 percent between 1985 and 1990. Utilities and governments—and the French government in particular—have in recent years espoused the hope that increases in the price of competitive energy sources (in excess of those charged by the electricity industry) will lead to an increase in electricity's share of the total energy market. But in fact, any substitutions of this nature seem likely to be offset for some years by the effects of a low rate of gross domestic product (GDP) growth throughout the region. The need for nuclear power, in consequence, has been considerably reduced, and this has been reflected in national construction programs.

Financial Difficulties

A second reason for the slowdown in nuclear programs has been the financial difficulties presented to the utilities as a result of inflation and the various sources of construction delay. Nuclear power stations involve the commitment of large sums of capital and long gestation times. These in turn require carefully managed financing. The rising costs of building nuclear power stations, however, in current dollars and sometimes in real terms, have been paralleled by the inability of most utilities to adjust their rates upward at the same speed. The result has been that their internal funds have been

13. Organisation for Economic Cooperation and Development, *World Energy Outlook* (Paris, 1977).

14. UNIPEDE, *Target Programme of the Electricity Sector up to the Year 1981* (Paris, 1976).

squeezed and that there has been a need to resort to further borrowing. This has sometimes taken time to arrange and has delayed the agreement of construction contracts.

Technical Difficulties

Technical difficulties have been a third and persistent factor delaying nuclear programs in most countries. While the experience of the Central Electricity Generating Board at Dungeness in England might be somewhat extreme—the construction time of the first AGR there now appears likely to be some sixteen years—the speed of technological innovation and the complexity of the civil engineering in the nuclear power industry were undoubtedly underestimated in many of the earlier plans of the utilities. There has been a need, therefore, to rephase much construction work to schedules more consistent with the performance of the civil and the power engineering industries. As Brookes put it, "We really ought not to have expected rapid progress in the earlier years when bringing a new technology into practical application. We should have expected the typical 'S' curve pattern of a slow-growing initial stage leading to a steep penetration rate in the middle period and later a flattening as penetration into the base load power plant market nears completion."[15]

Consent Procedures

The fourth reason for delay has been the inadequacies and uncertainties that surround the legal consent procedures for the construction of nuclear power plants. To the extent that there is disquiet about the safety of nuclear power, it is imperative that clearly defined procedures should be provided for the consideration of the issues and the evaluation of alternative risks. Yet this has not always been the case. The inadequacies of procedures have probably been at their most acute in West Germany, where the federal constitution allocates responsibilities between the Land governments and, in an overseeing role, the government in Bonn. The latter is required to lay down—and has specified—broad environmental standards. But these have been sufficiently imprecise for individuals, or groups of individuals, to dispute them and to apply successfully in the courts for restraining orders on the utilities. Construction work in consequence has been held up for several years. Again, through its Ministry of the Interior, the federal government has decided that

15. L.G. Brookes, "The plain man's case for nuclear energy," *Atom* (April 1976): 99.

no further nuclear stations should be built until a "safe" method of storing nuclear wastes has been found; but the Land governments and the courts have been given no precise means of interpreting the meaning of the word "safe." There have also been many instances—in West Germany and Italy especially—of an apparent conflict of interest between the municipalities and the licensing authorities "above" them, and once again there has been no ready means for their speedy resolution.

Environmental Concerns

The local environmental impact of nuclear power plants—both real and imagined—has led to a cluster of essentially site-specific delays to the construction program. Once again, this has been particularly noticeable in West Germany, where the utilities have sought to locate a number of nuclear plants at the focus of the 380 kV grid system and near the confluence of the rivers Main and Rhine. This is an area with considerable electricity demands in such industrial centers as Frankfurt, Mannheim, and Ludwigshafen, but one that also includes some important vineyards; in consequence, environmental opinion has been particularly sensitive to local fears about such matters at the local microclimatic effects of heat discharged from cooling towers (a problem that is not peculiar to nuclear power, of course). More generally, however, as Surrey and Huggett point out, the impact of nuclear power stations tends to be negative from the point of view of the local community.[16] They offer only limited long-term employment; they generate only a limited local income; they tend to lower local property values; they undoubtedly intrude visually in the local environment; and they are associated with fears of local pollution. It is not surprising, therefore, that local interest groups have sought at least to delay, and at best to prevent, the construction of nuclear plants. And to some degree they have succeeded.

Safety Aspects

The last, and most important, reason for the delays and the reduced size of Western Europe's nuclear power programs is a complex of concerns about various safety aspects of its further exploitation. There are two principal dimensions to this problem. The first is specific to the technology of nuclear power and relates to the health hazards, the risks of accidents, and in recent years, the un-

16. J. Surrey and C. Huggett, "Opposition to nuclear power," *Energy Policy* (December 1976): 286-307.

certainties surrounding the back end of the nuclear fuel cycle. These matters have been central to the delays imposed upon the nuclear industry in Austria, Denmark, Sweden, and West Germany especially. The innocence of the early years of nuclear technology, when the "peaceful atom" was often seen as a clean, safe, and economical panacea for an energy-hungry world, has been overtaken by a range of doubts about the technical risks that are being taken by the nuclear industry. A balanced public evaluation of these risks, particularly those associated with the recycling of spent nuclear fuel and the disposal of nuclear wastes, has been hampered by both the sheer complexity of the processes themselves and, at times, the unwillingness of industry spokesmen to admit openly and fully some of the problems that are being faced. The resulting suspicions have limited the ability of society to judge the balance of risks that might reasonably be associated with nuclear power compared with alternative energy futures. It is clearly impossible to say whether the psychological and cultural forces that regulate the thresholds of risk acceptability, which in the case of nuclear energy are apparently very high by comparison with many other risks in modern life,[17] are tending to move higher or lower.

Opposition to Nuclear Expansion

Another dimension to the questions surrounding the safety aspects of nuclear power is the emergence of an articulate and increasingly international lobby that reflects, and arguably exaggerates, deep-seated public anxieties about its use, particularly because of nuclear weapons. Although it was scarcely mentioned in the recent Austrian debate regarding the Zwentendorf reactor, much was made of the proliferation issue by the Town and Country Planning Association[18] in their evidence to the Windscale inquiry. Indeed, many authorities in the industry would share with Hill the view that "The problem of proliferation of nuclear weapons is . . . far and away the most worrying aspect of nuclear power."[19] While proponents of nuclear power go on to argue that the solution to the problem is political and international and that it will not be overcome by banning the construction of further nuclear reactors,

17. See J. Lenihan, "Public attitudes to nuclear energy," *Atom* (November 1977): 319–23; and Lord Rothschild, Richard Dimbleby Lecture 1978, abstracted in *The Times*, November 24, 1978, p. 14.

18. Town and Country Planning Association, *Planning and Plutonium* (London, 1978).

19. J. Hill, "Nuclear power—the real problems and the emotional issues of the public debate," *Atom* (July 1977): 126–31.

others disagree. They take the view that despite the progress that has been made through the International Atomic Energy Agency, the Non-Proliferation Treaty, and the heightened awareness of the problems involved at a national level, and whatever agreements are reached following the current International Nuclear Fuel Cycle Evaluation discussions, the risks will rise with a further resort to nuclear power—and that it should therefore be opposed.

The expression of public disquiet about the safety of nuclear power has varied from country to country, and it is not always easy to isolate peoples' anxieties about nuclear safety with any degree of precision since they are so frequently interlocked with many other concerns, such as the desirability (or otherwise) of economic growth, the wider energy debate, broader environmental issues, and specific arguments within political parties or between politicians. Nevertheless, it is noteworthy that a common denominator of European experience has been the greater visibility of nuclear concerns and debates in those circumstances of coalition politics where a minority party with a positive antinuclear viewpoint holds—or threatens to hold—the balance of political power. In West Germany, for example, the Social Democratic and Christian Democratic parties have on occasion had to give way to the smaller Free Democrats, who have been much more equivocal on nuclear issues and whose vote has been threatened by the so-called "green parties." Had not the votes for the larger parties been so finely balanced, it is possible that nuclear concerns would not have achieved so much prominence in the 1978 local and state elections. The same applies to both Swedish and French politics.

A further noteworthy feature of the European nuclear safety debate is that where a vote or opinion poll has been taken on a specific nuclear issue, the electorate on balance appears to have favored a cautious exploitation of nuclear power. The Swiss referenda in 1979 are a case in point. The extended Swedish debate between 1974 and 1975 revealed a large majority "in favor of" energy conservation and "against" the expansion of nuclear power, but many participants expressed their continuing uncertainty, and in a (Swedish Institute of Public Opinion Research) poll only 13 percent were wholly against nuclear power, while 31 percent were in favor of building more than the existing program of eleven reactors. In Baden Württemberg, a local referendum in connection with the Whyl nuclear plant produced a majority in favor of the plant (although the license was subsequently withdrawn following repeated site occupations, violence, and confusion). In a series of local referenda in France in 1975, on the other hand, three localities voted against nuclear power, while one voted in favor of a plant. In the 1978 Austrian vote, the balance of opinion was finely against the commissioning of a new station (50.5 percent versus 49.5 percent of those voting, but the turnout was so small (60 percent of the electorate compared with the normal figure of 90 percent) that it is clear that other matters were also on the voters' minds. A somewhat earlier opinion poll conducted in Britain found that while 32 percent of those canvassed were against nuclear power, 49 percent were in favor of its further exploitation, and it appeared to be largely in the area of waste disposal that public concern was substantial.[20]

Summary

Despite the persistence and the complexity of the various factors that have delayed the construction of nuclear power plants in Western Europe, two points are worth noting to place matters in perspective. First, in the medium term (that is, throughout the 1980s, there is the prospect of nuclear power making an increasing contribution to the satisfaction of the region's energy demands. In 1974, nearly 15 GW of nuclear capacity met nearly 6 percent of Western Europe's electricity needs. By 1980 it is expected that nuclear capacity will have risen to at least 30 GW, which will be able to meet some 11 percent of electricity requirements. The 85 GW of capacity forecast for 1985, employed on base load generation, could be supplying at least one-quarter of Europe's electricity needs by that date. Second, despite the delays, there is little apparent weakening in desire of the utilities and most governments in the region to press on with their commitments to exploit nuclear energy in the 1980s and 1990s.

LONGER TERM PROSPECTS
FOR NUCLEAR POWER

Given recent experience, any search for useful insights into the longer term prospects for nuclear power must begin with an examination of the most likely restraints upon its extended use. One of the most important of these is likely to be the (disputed) economics of nuclear energy.

Economics

The decisions to embark upon a major program of nuclear power station construction in the early 1970s were based upon the assumed

20. D. White, "Nuclear power: a social survey," *New Society*, March 31, 1977.

economic advantages of nuclear technology, especially in light of the fourfold increase in oil prices in 1973–1974. Subsequently, however, oil and (some) solid fuel prices have fallen in real terms, while the costs of nuclear power have increased substantially, not only with inflation but also following the effects on the industry's capital charges and cash flows of the extended delays in the construction programs. Uranium prices too have increased severalfold, although this does not have a particularly serious effect upon the overall economics of the technology. This is not the place to debate the question of nuclear power costs. Three points, however, are worth noting. First, many genuine doubts surround the assumptions most commonly employed by the utilities, the industry itself, and governments in the evaluation of nuclear power economics. Sweet, for example, has recently questioned the assumptions and data normally employed in official British analyses, drawing attention to the greater validity of alternative load factors, fuel costs, capital costs, and research and development expenditures in the assessment of nuclear power costs—and hence a somewhat different view of the industry's benefit-cost relationships.[21] His conclusion that the supposed [economic] benefits have yet to be demonstrated is not new. Nor need it be regarded as a major obstacle to further nuclear programs. But it is the most recent, and most timely, reminder that the balance of economic advantage in the longer term might be seen by some utilities in some places to be the use of energy sources other than uranium. Second, it can be demonstrated that new coal-fired power stations, operating on base load for about five years and with a lifetime load factor of 50–55 percent, offer cheaper electrical energy than nuclear stations, provided that coal prices are modest (6–7 mills/kWh) and do not increase significantly over the life of the plant.[22]

While such circumstances look a highly unlikely prospect for power stations utilizing British or German deep-mined coals, imported coal from such countries as South Africa, Australia, and India might well be negotiated and supplied on that basis. Should a world trade in steam coal begin to develop strongly in the late 1980s and 1990s and should that trade be characterized increasingly by long-term supply agreements, it is possible that many utilities in Western Europe with an easy access to modern, deep water, coal import facilities will judge nuclear power to be a relatively expensive source of energy (although it could still be an attractive investment

21. C. Sweet, "Nuclear Power Costs in the U.K.," *Energy Policy*, June 1978.
22. U.K. Department of Energy, *Coal and Nuclear Power Station Costs*, Energy Commission Paper no. 6 (London, 1978).

for noneconomic reasons). Third, it is widely recognized that for satisfying energy demands in the middle load, and particularly for providing heat,[23] nuclear power is an inherently unattractive technology. In sum, to the extent that there are advantages in diversifying the sources of electrical energy, it is clear that utilities and governments in the future will quite properly regard nuclear and conventional generation to a large extent as complimentary, rather than as competitors. For electricity demands that in a technical sense might equally well be served by either mode of generation, however, the economics of conventional generation based upon low cost coal imports could be a significant restraint upon the longer term size of Western Europe's nuclear program.

Uranium Supply

A second restraint upon the future expansion of nuclear power in Western Europe stems from a number of questions concerning the longer term supply of uranium. The most recent comprehensive study of uranium resources (outside the planned economies) is *Uranium: Resources, Production and Demand.*[24] It concludes that the world's "reasonably assured" and "estimated additional" resources of uranium showed only a modest 40 percent increase between 1973 (when an earlier study was completed) and 1977, even though the cost-price assumptions employed in the definition of those resources were increased by over 500 percent. This is a matter of some European concern. Estimates of the rate of growth of uranium demand throughout the world are necessarily speculative, given the uncertainties that surround economic growth prospects and the questions that overhang the nuclear industry's future role in overall energy supply. Nevertheless, assuming no nuclear fuel recycling, the total resources of uranium would cover the world's requirements only up to about the year 2010. In consequence, given the lead time in power plant construction, very soon after 1990, fears could begin to arise concerning the ability of the mining industry to satisfy uranium demands throughout the lifetime of new nuclear stations.

The geography of the firm uranium discoveries is highly concentrated in the more developed world. The United States, Canada, Australia, and South Africa have the greater part of known resources. Only France among the countries of Western Europe has a signifi-

23. N.J.B. Lucas, *Energy and the European Communities* (London: Europa Publications, 1977).

24. Organisation for Economic Cooperation and Development, *Uranium: Resources, Production and Demand* (Paris, 1977).

cant, albeit still quite limited, domestic supply. This particular distribution of known uranium resources is in considerable measure, of course, a function of the political evaluation by the transnational mining corporations of the risks (relating to exploration and development) likely to be encountered in different parts of the world. There is good reason to believe, therefore, that within the developing world especially, considerable resources of uranium have yet to be discovered, and that the reestablishment there of a favorable investment climate for exploration and mineral development could dramatically alter both the size and the geography of uranium reserves. Nevertheless, questions still arise about the political security of future supplies. Even in the politically stable developed countries in recent years, there have been serious delays in the development of uranium-mining operations, and temporary embargoes have been placed upon uranium deliveries from Canada and Australia (and upon enriched uranium from the United States). Such interruptions have been short lived, and the reasons for them are understandable. But collectively they have raised questions about the long-term reliability of uranium supplies. In consequence, the immediate objective of most European utilities is to ensure the greatest geographical diversity of uranium supplies. More important, there is a widespread consensus in the region, shared by the industry, most governments, and the EEC, that every effort must be made to ensure a greater self-sufficiency in nuclear fuels. To achieve this, the cases both for more nuclear fuel enrichment and reprocessing facilities and for the development of the fast breeder reactor are highly persuasive.[25] While technical and safety problems are recognized in such a course of action (see below), little sympathy appears to exist for the position of U.S. policy initiatives in these matters.

The technological uncertainties that overshadow the future role of nuclear power in Western Europe primarily concern the reactor types that might be chosen, the reprocessing facilities that will be employed, the methods of waste disposal that are likely to be arranged, and the transport of radioactive materials. A powerful answer to the uncertainties of future uranium supplies lies in the development of the breeder reactor. By burning not only uranium but also the plutonium that arises as a by-product of thermal reactors and by converting depleted uranium that can not be used in thermal reactors into additional plutonium, they can extract fifty to sixty times more energy from their fuel than the thermal reactors now in operation. The U.K. Atomic Energy Authority claims that the 20,000 tonnes of depleted uranium already in Britain could

25. T. Price, "The uranium market—economic and political factors," *Atom* (November 1978): 290-94.

produce energy equivalent to 40,000 million tons of coal if it were to be used in breeder reactors. The appeal of such claims is considerable, and the technology is well advanced into the development phase. The first experimental breeder reactor was built in Britain in 1954; a 15 MW plant operated at Dounreay from 1959 to 1977, and a 250 MW reactor has been operating on the same site since 1974. In France, at Creys-Malville, the region's first "commercial" breeder reactor, the 1,200 MW Super-Phénix, is being built with French, Italian, and German funds; it is scheduled to be commissioned in 1981. However, it could be the late 1980s before enough experience has been gained with a reactor of this size to justify its widespread introduction into the European energy system and more than a decade later before orders placed at that time could be translated into operational facilities. Moreover, there could well be delays—even serious delays. Given the pioneering nature of the technology, some of these will be essentially technical. Others, however, are likely to stem from the articulate, if not necessarily widespread, public concern about the risks and dangers inherent in the extensive exploitation of plutonium as a source of energy. The point that has to be made here, however, is that there is very little likelihood that breeder reactors will make a significant contribution to the satisfaction of Western Europe's energy demands in the next twenty years. Rather, this will be a period when decisions are taken that will affect the contribution of the breeder to energy supply in the twenty-first century. The contribution of nuclear technology to the satisfaction of Western Europe's energy demands in the 1980s and 1990s will be in the form of the conventional thermal reactor.

The supply of enriched fuel to the region's reactors poses political rather than technical uncertainties. The technology is well proven. Policies are in hand, therefore, that seek to reduce the dependence of Western Europe upon the United States and the USSR for the enrichment of natural uranium. The capacity of URENCO is being extended in Britain and the Netherlands, while a third plant, under construction at Gronau in West Germany, is scheduled for completion in 1983. And the facilities of EURODIF are in due course to be complemented by those of COREDIF, another international consortium under French leadership.

Reprocessing and Disposal

The extent to which it will be possible for Western Europe to reprocess in future the spent fuels from its nuclear reactors is now becoming clearer. Self-sufficiency is in sight. Within the OECD in general, it has recently been argued that in light of the best current estimates of future reprocessing capacity, facilities will be insufficient to meet the projected demands.[26] Such are the delays in the nuclear power station construction program in Western Europe, however, that on the basis of the generating capacity forecast noted earlier (circa 85 GW in 1985; 120-125 GW in 1990), there will in fact be more than enough reprocessing facilities in Western Europe to meet the region's needs well into the 1990s—and ample opportunity to meet some of the needs of Japanese utilities as well. Even the OECD's low estimate of Western Europe's reprocessing capacity in 1990 (5,100 tonnes) far exceeds the 2,740 tonnes required for 125 GW of thermal reactors. Much of the capacity will be concentrated in France, where the facilities of COGEMA could reach 1,600 tonnes by 1985, and in Britain, where after a major planning enquiry, permission has recently been given for the construction of a new thermal oxide reprocessing plant at Windscale in the 1980s (see Table 9-2). If there is to be a shortage of reprocessing capacity in the next twenty years, it is unlikely to be in the 1980s—and probably not in the 1990s unless there are particularly serious delays to West Germany's proposed *Entsorgungszentrum* at Gorleben. There the world's first industrial center to take care of every aspect of spent fuel reprocessing, storage and reuse of plutonium, and ultimate disposal of all radioactive wastes is in an advanced stage of being planned. The central features of the complex will be a reprocessing plant for thermal reactor fuel, a spent fuel storage pond, fuel fabrication facilities for (breeder) plutonium, underground storage facilities for high level radioactive waste, and additional storage facilities for low level wastes. Present plans are to start construction in 1981, to have the reprocessing plant ready by 1990, and to receive high level waste in the middle 1990s.

The major unresolved technical question for thermal nuclear power in the longer run concerns the disposal of high level radioactive wastes. An interim solution—the use of storage ponds provided centrally or adjacent to the power stations—bears longer term technical risks. On present evidence, it would appear that the vitrification of high level wastes would have considerable technical advantages. However, the first commercial scale plant using such a process only started operation at Marcoule in July 1978. And a joint European (EEC) effort to discover the most suitable geological structures within which the vitrified waste might be safely stored is still in its early stages.[27]

26. Organisation for Economic Cooperation and Development, *Reprocessing of Spent Nuclear Fuels in OECD Countries* (Paris, 1977).

27. N. Chapman, D. Gray, and J. Mather, "Nuclear waste disposal: the geological aspects," *Atom* (July 1978): 186–88.

Table 9-2. Estimated Nuclear Fuel Reprocessing Capacity in Western Europe, 1985 and 1990 (thousand tonnes U).

Country	1985	1990
France	0.9–1.6	1.6–2.4
Britain	0.8–1.0	2.0
Germany	—	1.4
Belgium	0.3	0.4
Spain	—	0.0–0.6
Italy	—	0.1–0.8
Total	1.7–2.9	5.1–7.6

Source: Organisation for Economic Cooperation and Development, *Reprocessing of Spent Nuclear Fuels in OECD Countries* (Paris, 1977).

Such is the geography of nuclear facilities that quantities of enriched and spent fuel and of nuclear wastes demand transport both within the region and between Western Europe and the rest of the world. Within Europe, two specialized transport companies have been formed—one with British, French, and German participation for the international transport of spent oxide fuel within the region, the other as an association of a British company with Japanese companies for the transport of spent fuel from Japan to Europe. To date, these companies have moved some 600 tons of spent fuel to Windscale and the Hague from European reactors and 100 tons from Japan to Windscale, using all modes of transport (road, rail, and sea) at a very high level of safety. As the volume of fuel and waste transport increases, the purely technical problems appear to be small as flask design is improved and standardized.[28] The uncertainties lie in the field of risk assessment and public perceptions of safety and the security measures to be adopted.

CONCLUSION

From the (occasionally complacent) viewpoint of the nuclear "establishment," and against the background of the past twenty years of considerable achievements in nuclear understanding and engineering, any technical problems associated with the enrichment, reprocessing, storage, and transport of nuclear fuels and wastes appear capable of solution. The safety aspects of these technologies, however, as interpreted both by governments and by other observers, leave some causes for concern. At the level of governments this

28. H. Keese, "Nuclear transportation, today and tomorrow" (Paper presented to the International Conference on the Nuclear Cycle, London, September 26–29, 1978).

concern has led regularly in most countries—most recently following the accident at Harrisburg—to rigorous reviews of the national regulations and safeguards concerning the behavior of the nuclear industry. In addition, full cooperation has to be accorded to a mounting complex of international agencies, agreements, and enquiries such as the International Atomic Energy Agency, the Non-Proliferation Treaty and the International Nuclear Fuel Cycle Evaluation. There is every reason to believe that over the next twenty years, regular reviews of national safeguards will continue, and that safety standards will thereby be increased. Similarly, international intergovernmental cooperation will doubtless persist and increase, with the goal of the nonproliferation of nuclear weapons particularly in mind: this cooperation will be designed to ensure political measures that make it disadvantageous to excite the suspicion of others in the matter of nuclear weaponry, technical measures that will isolate the sensitive parts of the nuclear fuel cycle, and institutional measures that will vest in international ownership the most sensitive parts of that cycle.[29]

At the same time, and at an entirely different level, the objections raised by individuals and groups of individuals to the safety aspects of specific nuclear proposals and developments and, indeed, the exploitation of nuclear power as a whole also appear likely to persist. The balance of argument and emotion—in which a variety of conflicting interests, environmental lobbyists, radical antigovernment groups, and opponents of high technology all combine to oppose in different degrees the further exploitation of nuclear power—does not appear to be shifting one way or the other. In West Germany the effectiveness of the tactics used by these groups to delay nuclear developments could be reduced by the clarification of consent procedures at the interface of federal and state responsibilities. In France on the other hand, the opposition to nuclear power could become more effective in future, since much of the present program was launched before the opposition became effectively organized. Throughout Western Europe as a whole, therefore, it would be a mistake to assume that the deep-felt concerns and the delaying tactics of those individually or collectively opposed to nuclear power, who are now increasingly international in their information and inspiration, will diminish to any significant degree.

Today, many governments in Western Europe are disinclined to make estimates of their nuclear power capacity in the 1980s, let

29. Sir H. Bondi, "Non-Proliferation: A U.K. View" (Speech delivered to Atomic Industrial Forum/British Nuclear Forum International Conference on the Nuclear Fuel Cycle, London, September 26–29, 1978).

alone the 1990s.[30] The International Energy Agency has suggested that Western Europe's nuclear capacity will be within the range of 84-96 GW in 1985, within the range of 123-155 GW in 1990, and within the range of 268-363 GW in 2000.[31] France, Germany, Spain, Britain, and Italy would be the five largest producers at the end of the century. Given the economic, technical, and safety constraints on the expansion of nuclear power, it is highly unlikely that the lower figures in these ranges will in fact be exceeded. Indeed, reality could fall short of these figures, particularly after 1990.

The implications of these prospects vary substantially with the assumptions made about the future rate of economic growth in general and the development of energy demands in particular in the next twenty years. A slow rate of growth in energy demand in Western Europe, including a sluggish expansion of electricity requirements, would mean that the somewhat measured pace of nuclear power expansion that is currently in prospect would in general be acceptable. Faster rates of economic growth and energy demands, on the other hand, would undoubtedly necessitate a more vigorous approach toward the exploitation of alternative sources of energy—perhaps the greater use of (oil-fired) gas turbines in the short term, but coal in the longer run.

In any case, from the late 1980s on, coal could become a significant beneficiary of the delays already encountered in the resort to nuclear power. A perceptible quickening in the rate of growth of Western European energy demands would, therefore, accelerate the emergence of a significant international trade in steam coal (see Chapter 8). To the extent that coal is an alternative to nuclear energy (as opposed to oil), this diversion of demand is likely to be more readily embraced in southern and coastal Europe—and most vigorously resisted by utilities in those parts of the region that might be denied access to low cost coal imports for reasons of either politics or transport costs.

Whatever the rate of economic growth, however, it is clear that Western Europe has embarked upon a course of nuclear power development that places a premium upon regional energy self-sufficiency. This is the notion that explicitly underlies both national and EEC policies—and that is used to discount the doubts that remain about the economics of nuclear power. In every aspect of the nuclear power industry therefore, except the exploitation of

30. International Energy Agency, *Electricity Supply Industry.*
31. International Energy Agency, *Steam Coal Prospects to 2000* (Paris: OECD, 1978).

uranium resources—the geography of which is substantially beyond the region's control—a set of arrangements is beginning to emerge that seeks to minimize the vulnerability of Western Europe to external political acts and, in particular, to the perceived risks that flow from the region's relatively poor energy resource base.

Energy Policy in the Soviet Union and China

Marshall I. Goldman

    If it is difficult to ascertain the energy policy of a capitalist country like the United States, it is even more difficult to analyze the energy policies of the Soviet Union and China. In addition to all the usual difficulties, such as trying to describe how large energy reserves are and at what price, the Soviets and Chinese compound the problem by classifying as state secrets much of the information that we are otherwise accustomed to working with. Thus, in addition to banning data on petroleum reserves, in 1978 the Soviets even classified all foreign trade statistics showing the physical volume of petroleum imports and exports. The Chinese classify almost all of their economic data, including information on reserves, the physical volume of production, and foreign trade.

Given the absence of key statistical information and the inaccessibility of production sites for most outside observers, it is no wonder that there are dramatic, but sometimes diametrically opposite, points of view about Communist capabilities and intentions. Thus in April 1977, the U.S. Central Intelligence Agency (CIA) predicted that by 1985 the Soviet Union and its East European allies will be net importers of 3.5 to 4.5 million barrels of oil a day (mbd). Only a year later Petrostudies, a Swedish oil consulting group, asserted that on the contrary, Soviet petroleum output will soon soar. Instead of the 1 million barrels per day it presently exports, by the mid-1980s the Soviet Union will be exporting 3.7 mbd (l85 million tons) or almost four times as much to the hard currency world.[1]

1. *International Herald Tribune,* September 14, 1978, p. 4.

Depending on how one weighs what scanty evidence there is, both arguments have some merit. As spelled out by the CIA in April 1977 and in a more detailed supplemental July report, the Soviets face serious engineering problems.[2] Production is diminishing sharply in their older and at one time major producing fields in the Baku region and the Volga area.

In addition, the giant producing fields in West Siberia have peaked earlier than expected so that in a short period of time it will be difficult, if not impossible, to rely on these fields to compensate for falling production elsewhere. Indicative of what lies ahead is the growing Soviet practice of injecting water into the West Siberian fields. This is the favored Soviet method of secondary recovery. But this method has failed to halt the decline of output elsewhere, and the fact that such large quantities of water are being injected in West Siberia has led the CIA to predict that output will decline sharply here as well. As more water is injected into the well, more water also comes out of the well with the oil. In some cases, the amount of water now being extracted equals the amount of oil lifted out of the well. This method also requires large quantities of semisubmersible pumps, some of which must be imported because of insufficient production capability in the USSR itself.

Finally, the CIA points out that the Soviets have failed to expand the size of their proven reserves enough to compensate for the ever-increasing growth of petroleum production. In part this is because of their failure to expand their exploratory work as much as planned and in part because much of the geological exploration has focused on supplemental drilling in already producing fields rather than initial exploratory drillings for new fields. And even when new fields are discovered, all too often they are located in remote and hostile portions of the USSR which make it difficult and expensive, if not economically unfeasible, to utilize this petroleum.

The Swedes, in contrast, argue that the CIA has mixed up its data.[3] According to the Swedes, the CIA is confused over which field is being flooded. It is the Romashkino field in the Volga region that has had excess water injection, not the giant Samotlor field in West Siberia, which alone constituted about one-quarter of total Soviet

2. The Central Intelligence Agency, *The International Energy Situation: Outlook to 1985*, ER77-10240 U, (Washington, D.C., April 1977); The Central Intelligence Agency, *Prospects for Soviet Oil Production*, ER77-10270 (Washington, D.C., April 1977); The Central Intelligence Agency, *Prospects for Soviet Oil Production: A Supplemental Analysis*, ER77-10425, (Washington, D.C., July 1977).

3. *European Energy Report*, London, September 26, 1978, p. 15.

output in 1977. Moreover, the Soviet Union is "systematically under-producing its wells by up to 30%."[4]

Because they take such an extreme position, there are some who suspect that the Swedish report is more disinformation than solid analysis. But just as the Swedes appear to be unduly optimistic about Soviet prospects, so the CIA may be too pessimistic. The remainder of this chapter will analyze the arguments about Soviet energy policy followed by a similar, although considerably more abbreviated, explanation of Chinese energy policy.

To understand the present, it is necessary to go back a bit and see how Soviet energy policy has evolved over the years. The most notable characteristic of Soviet energy policy over the past several decades is that the Soviet switch from an emphasis on coal to liquid fuels came very late compared with the United States. Whereas in the 1940's the United States, like almost every country relied on coal for over 50 percent of its energy, by 1950 coal's share in the United States had dropped to under 40 percent (see Table 10-1). Petroleum and natural gas in the United States rapidly supplanted coal, so that not only was there a fall in the relative share of coal consumed, but also in the absolute amount consumed. The quantity consumed in tons increased again only in the late 1960s, but until very recently the relative share of coal in the United States has continued to diminish. Offsetting that, oil's share has remained consistently over 40 percent since the 1950s. By 1976, it accounted for approximately 47 percent of all energy consumed in the United States. The growth in the use of natural gas has been even faster, at least until about 1972. Whereas gas made up only 11 percent of all energy consumed in 1940, by 1960 it supplied more energy than coal. In 1971, at its peak, it was the source of 33 percent of all the energy consumed in the United States.[5] While there was a lag of a few years, for the most part the other OECD countries have made a similar shift.

In contrast to what happened in the United States, coal remained the main source of energy in the Soviet Union for a much longer period of time. In 1940 Soviet coal accounted for about 75 percent of all Soviet energy consumed (see Table 10-1). Reflecting the different trends in the two countries, coal continued to predominate in the Soviet Union, so that until at least 1957 coal supplied over 70 per-

4. *International Herald Tribune*, September 14, 1978, p. 4.
5. U.S. Bureau of the Census, *Statistical Abstracts for the United States; 1977*, 98th edition (Washington, D.C., Government Printing Office, 1977), p. 594.

Table 1-10.   Consumption of Energy in the United States and the USSR by Major Energy Source (percent).

	U.S.			USSR		
Year	Coal	Oil	Gas	Coal	Oil	Gas
1940	52	31	11	75	23	2
1945	51	30	13	—	—	—
1946	—	—	—	78	19	3
1950	38	40	18	77	20	3
1955	29	44	23	75	23	3
1960	23	45	28	62	29	9
1965	22	44	30	50	32	18
1970	19	44	33	41	36	23
1971	18	45	33	39	36	25
1972	17	46	32	38	38	24
1973	18	47	30	37	39	24
1974	18	46	30	36	39	24
1975	18	46	28	35	40	25
1976	19	47	27	34	39	27

Sources: United States: U.S. Bureau of the Census, *Statistical Abstract for the United States: 1977,* 8th ed. (Washington, D.C.: Government Printing Office, 1977), p. 594. Soviet Union: A.M. Nekrasov and M.G. Pervukhin, *Energetika SSSR v 1976-1980 Godakh* (Moscow: *Energia,* 1977): 146; Tsentral'noe statistichesko upravlenie, *Narodnoe khoziaistvo SSSR v 1959* (hereafter *Nar khoz*) (Moscow: *Statistika,* 1959): 176; *Nar khoz* 1970, p. 183; *Nar khoz* 1977, p. 204; Ministerstvo Vneshnei Torgovli, *Vneshniaia Torgovlia SSSR v 1976 g* (Moscow: *Statistika,* 1977 and for earlier years).

cent of all energy consumed. In sharp contrast, coal's relative importance was falling in the United States, and in 1955 coal was the source of less than 30 percent of America's energy. The relative swing away from coal in the Soviet Union began only in 1955. However, it was not until l966 that coal's relative share was less than 50 percent. Thereafter coal's relative importance fell rapidly, so that by 1976 it accounted for less than 35 percent. Offsetting this, the relative importance of oil and gas rose sharply. Nonetheless, the consumption of natural gas in the Soviet Union never exceeded that of coal, as happened in the United States, and even now Soviet domestic consumption of oil is not much larger than coal (Table 10-1). Of the three fuels, oil made up 39 percent of Soviet energy consumption in 1976 and coal 34 percent. The contrast with the United States and its heavy dependence on petroleum is striking.

When analyzing the Soviet fuel balance and determining how dependent the Soviet Union has become on petroleum, Western specialists frequently confuse Soviet production with consumption.[6] This is

6. Iain F. Elliot, *The Soviet Energy Balance* (New York, Praeger, 1974), p. 7; *Review of Sino-Soviet Oil* (January 1976): 21; *Soviet Power Reactors, 1974,*

Table 10-2. **Production of Energy in the USSR by Major Energy Source (percent).**

Year	Coal	Oil	Gas
1940	59	19	2
1945	62	15	2
1950	66	17	2
1951	66	18	2
1952	66	19	2
1953	66	20	2
1954	65	20	2
1955	65	21	2
1956	63	23	3
1957	61	25	4
1958	59	26	6
1959	56	28	6
1960	54	31	8
1961	51	32	10
1962	49	34	11
1963	46	35	12
1964	44	35	14
1965	43	36	16
1966	41	37	17
1967	39	38	17
1968	38	39	18
1969	37	40	18
1970	35	41	19
1971	34	42	20
1972	34	43	20
1973	32	44	20
1974	31	44	21
1975	30	45	22
1976	29	45	23
1980 plan	26	43	24

Source: Nekrasov and Pervukhin, *Energeti kaSSSR*, p. 146. *Nar khoz* 1959, p. 176; *Nar khoz* 1970, p. 183; *Nar khoz* 1977, p. 204.

because the Soviets usually publish only the relative production statistics (Table 10-2).[7] By relying only on the production figures, Western observers sometimes conclude that the relative use of petroleum in the Soviet Union approximates that in the United States. Since the relative share of Soviet petroleum in total energy production in 1976 was 45 percent, it does indeed approximate the American

Report of the United States Nuclear Power Delegation Visit to the USSR, September 19-October 1, 1974, USERDA, ERDA-2 (Washington, D.C., Dept. of Energy, 1974), p. 10; Zbynek Zeman and Jan Zoubek, *Comecom Oil and Gas* (London, The Financial Times, 1977), p. 64.

7. Tsentral'noe statisticheskoe upravlenie, *Narodnoe khoziaistvo SSSR za 60 let* (hereafter *Nar khoz 1977*) (Moscow) *Statistika* (1977): 204.

figure for consumption.[8] What is often neglected, however, is the fact that the Soviets are net exporters of 25 percent to 30 percent of their oil production, but only 3 percent of their coal and 4 percent of their gas. This means that the percentage of petroleum in the consumption fuel balance will be much smaller than the same percentage in the production fuel balance. Those who neglect to make the distinction may be misled into believing that Soviet reliance on petroleum for domestic consumption of energy is much greater than it actually is.

Economists ridiculed Soviet planners for their backwardness and failure to switch to oil and gas from coal. At the time it was universally agreed that this lag only confirmed the inadequacy of the Soviet price system. Presumably, or at least so Western economists argued, a better price system would have provided better signals and a clearer mandate to join the rest of the world in switching from coal to liquid fuel. Instead, Soviet prices were held relatively constant, so there was no incentive to change.

When change did come, the pressure to reduce the burning of coal stemmed as much from the desire to reduce pollution as from the discovery of new oil and gas fields in the Volga and West Siberian regions. The level of particulate and sulfur fallout in the 1950s was considered a serious health hazard.[9] Fortunately, the decision to reduce the burning of coal could be implemented because of a series of important new geological finds. With the opening of the gas fields in Siberia, the Soviet Union found itself with the largest gas reserves in the world. With time it has become the world's second largest producer of natural gas after the United States.[10] While information about petroleum reserves is classified, the exploratory work in the mid-1960s in West Siberia has provided the wherewithal for the Soviet Union to become the world's largest producer of petroleum. Obviously, without domestic gas and petroleum, the Soviets would have probably been unable to import enough gas and petroleum to make the switch from coal. But basically the motivation to turn to gas and oil for electrical generation and heating was due more to the desire to reduce pollution than to any response to a change in price signals.

The Soviet price system is not a good mechanism for transmitting the proper energy signals. After all, the only major change in the

8. This is calculated in terms of million tons of standard fuel equivalent; standard fuel is equal to the heat value of 7,000 kilocalories per kilogram.

9. Marshall I. Goldman, *The Spoils of Progress: Environmental Pollution in the Soviet Union* (Cambridge, Mass.: MIT Press, 1972), p. 127.

10. *Petroleum Economist* (September 1978): 362–63.

wholesale price of Soviet coal, oil and natural gas came in 1967. While there have been minor adjustments since that time, the Soviet Union made no major change at the wholesale level to reflect the 1973 upheaval in world prices. Indeed, wholesale fuel prices as of 1976 were even a bit lower than the 1970 prices.[11] Even if prices were to change more frequently, the Soviet system would continue to send out false signals, because the Soviets do not make provisions for royalty payments for mineral rights. Since inclusion of such charges would violate Marxist ideology, this means that prices for minerals are inevitably understated.

Perhaps the biggest shortcoming of the Soviet pricing system is what the Soviets profess to see as one of its most important advantages—its immunity to outside fluctuations. This isolation makes it possible for the Soviets to maintain relatively fixed prices regardless of what is going on in the capitalist world. This in turn ensures relatively stable prices that encourage Soviet managers to make long-range plans without having to worry about confusing and distorting price adjustments. Such a system, however, is also based on the assumption that there is no fundamental change in demand and supply relationships similar to the one we have seen in the mid-1970s. Even so, it is conceivable that since the USSR is isolated and relatively unaffected by the world economic system, the radical changes that have taken place might have been of little consequence to the Soviet economy. Since the ratio of exports as a percentage of gross national product (GNP) is less than 4 percent in the Soviet Union, one of the lowest percentages in the world, such a policy is probably feasible when applied to most goods. But while this may hold for the economy in general, it does not apply to petroleum and natural gas. World fluctuations do affect the liquid fuel industry in the Soviet Union, because not only is the Soviet Union the world's largest producer of petroleum, it is also the world's third largest exporter after Saudi Arabia and Iran. As mentioned earlier, it has exported between 25 percent and 30 percent of its total petroleum production during the past few years. In the case of natural gas, the Soviet Union is the world's second largest producer and the third largest exporter. On a gross basis, it exports about 10 percent of its production.

Given the relative importance of world trade to the ultimate disposal of Soviet liquid fuel, it is illogical for Soviet price makers to ignore the fourfold increase in prices that took place in 1973. No wonder that with the Soviet wholesale price virtually the same as it was in the late 1960s, the Soviet Ministry of Petroleum Industry's

11. *Nar khoz* 1977, p. 198. *Nar khoz* 1974, p. 212.

(MPI) profitability rate had fallen from 63 percent to 23 percent by 1976.[12] As Soviet oil production teams have been forced to move further north and east, the rate of profit has continued to fall. For the same reason, the rate of profit in the coal ministry fell from 6 percent in 1970 to 0.8 percent in 1976. A more recent report indicates that the Ministry of Coal operated at a loss and required a subsidy.[13] Profitability for all energy industries is reportedly down to 6 percent. Obviously, if wholesale prices of energy in the Soviet Union were allowed to reflect world prices, the rate of profit of the various production ministries would be much higher, but Soviet planners would be tempted to divert all of their output to foreign markets. At the same time, if prices were higher, Gosplan—the Soviet planning agency—might be more willing to increase the amount of investment allocated for the development of new, but seemingly unprofitable, oil fields.

Of course, it is entirely possible that if the Soviet price system had been more responsive, the Soviet Union, like most Western nations, would have switched to liquid energy much earlier if the price had been cheaper and thereby would have consumed even more petroleum. From a long-run point of view, maybe it is just as well that the switch was belated. Because they have not had a chance to move as far away from coal and to become as dependent on petroleum as we have, it should now be less difficult for the Soviets than it is for us to switch back to coal. (The Soviet experience also raises the question of just how superior the Western capitalist pricing mechanism is, at least for energy.)

On the whole, however, economic mechanisms in the Soviet bloc do complicate the task of utilizing resources effectively. For example, the Soviet incentive system all but guarantees that the Soviet petroleum industry will operate inefficiently. Soviet geologists, for instance, strive not so much to increase the amount of petroleum they discover, but the number of meters they drill. Only in this way can they fulfill their output targets, which are based on meters drilled rather than on petroleum found. Naturally, the harder and deeper the rock, the slower they drill, so drillers try to avoid such places and concentrate on softer and shallower ground. As described by one Soviet observer, it sounded more like a smallpox than a mining report. "In some places the land is becoming increasingly pitted with shallow,

12. These figures were provided to me by a Soviet economist in Moscow in late 1977. See also *Nar khoz* 1977, p. 638

13. Iu. Iakovets, "Ekonomicheskie rychagi i povyshenie effektivnosti mineral' no-syr' evogo kompleksa," *Planovoe khoziaistvo* (January 1978): 69-70.

exploratory holes drilled in incessant pursuit of a larger number of total meters drilled."[14] It comes as no surprise, therefore, that "there are geological expeditions in the Republic of Kazakhstan that have not discovered a valuable deposit for many years, but are counted among the successful expeditions, because they fulfill their assignment in terms of meters. The groups that conscientiously "turn up" deposits are often financial losers."[15]

Another shortcoming of the Soviet planning system is that many of the production functions that in this country are clustered within a single corporation are split among several ministries. This in part explains why the geologists have their own production goals separate from those of the MPI. In the same fashion, the MPI is separated from the Ministry of Gas Industries. The MPI is preoccupied almost solely with petroleum production. As a result, it is usually not over-concerned with the gas that is a by-product of petroleum output. (For each ton of oil extracted, there is usually an associated 150 to 200 cubic meters of gas.)[16] Consequently, as recently as 1975, 20 billion cubic meters of gas—the equivalent to 7 percent of total natural gas output—were flared as waste.[17] In fairness to the Soviet Union, Saudi Arabia and Iran also flare much of their by-product gas, because there is no industry in the country available to consume it. That is not the case in the Soviet Union, but because oil, not energy, is the responsibility of the MPI, it is not particularly concerned about making that gas available to other sectors of the Soviet economy.

Energy output is negatively affected by other features of the Soviet planning and economic system as well. Just as the land and mineral rights are treated as free goods, so are geological and exploratory work. In effect, the site is a free good. And as mentioned earlier, mineral rights are also not counted in determining the value of oil fuel. Thus, the MPI is more likely to move on to another site whenever labor costs at an existing site begin to rise.[18] As a result, there is less incentive to extract as much petroleum out of the ground than there would be in societies with other types of incentive and ownership systems. Some Soviet economists are aware of the problem and

14. *Pravda*, January 27, 1978, p. 2.
15. *Ibid.*
16. T. Khachaturov, "Ekonomicheskie problemy ekologii," *Voprosy ekonomiki* (June 1978): 6.
17. CIA, *The USSR: Development of the Gas Industry*, ER78-10393 (Washington, D.C., July 1978), p. 48. *Current Digest of the Soviet Press* (February 8, 1978), p. 2.
18. Marshall I. Goldman, "Externalities and the Race for Economic Growth in the USSR: Will the Environment Ever Win?" *Journal of Political Economy* (March-April 1972): 314.

criticize the existing process.[19] This does not deny that the system of private well ownership also results in waste—only the Soviet problem generally seems to be more serious.

Petroleum production problems in the Soviet Union are not confined to the MPI. They are a part of a whole system. Access to high quality steel and drill bits, for example, is critical if drilling is to extend beyond 2,000 meters in depth. But Soviet steel and drill bit makers are even today rewarded more for quantity than quality of production. Hence it is not surprising that Soviet drilling pipe has major threading defects, when the main indicator for the pipe manufacturer is not the quality or even the length of the pipe he produces but the tonnage.[20] This reinforces the Soviet drillers' tendency to concentrate on shallow onshore drillings. More than that, it is not unusual to find that as little as 15 percent of the drillers' time is actually spent on drilling. The rest is spent on taking out and reinserting drill pipe to attach new drill bits and to repair and replace the pipe.

Because the Soviet Union is the world's leading producer of petroleum and because it is acknowledged to be the world's second largest industrial power, it would be logical to assume that the Soviets would have relatively sophisticated technology in the petroleum production field. However, innovation in the Soviet system suffers. Consequently, except for the turbodrilling process, the Soviet Union lags behind in almost all areas of petroleum technology.[21] Soviet shortcomings in petroleum technology can be remedied with imports. But without foreign drill bits, oil logging equipment, and secondary and tertiary technology, overall Soviet petroleum output, not to mention output per well, would be far below its maximum potential.

Production is, of course, only part of the process. The efficiency with which the Soviets consume their energy resources is also important. Some decisions have been made that attempt to minimize energy consumption. The Soviets have a system of regional heating that obviates the need for each apartment house to have its own furnace and hot water heater. Since much of this heat is cogenerated with electricity, it also serves to utilize what otherwise would be regarded as thermal pollution. In the same way, the automobile stock in the

19. Khachaturov, "Ekonomicheskie," p. 10; T. Khachaturov and M. Loiter, "Ekonomicheskaia tsenka prirodnykh resursov pri proektirovanii i stroitel' stve," *Vestnik AN SSSR* (March 1973): 59.
20. *Pravda*, February 28, 1978, p. 2.
21. Robert W. Campbell, "Technological Levels in the Soviet Energy Sector" (East-West Technological Cooperation Colloquium, 1976, NATO-Directorate of Economic Affairs, Brussels, 1976), p. 253.

Soviet Union is the lowest per capita of any industrial state, and the Soviet public transportation system is one of the most efficient. This is clearly a result of the Soviet Union's moving late from coal to liquid fuels. If the USSR had made the move at the same time as the rest of the world, its automobile population would undoubtedly be larger than it is today.

While the Soviets may spend less energy on household heat per degree day and on per capita use of automobiles, there are other sectors of the system where energy is squandered.[22] For example, building insulation is poor, and drafts are endemic. Because of sloppy work habits, much waste also takes place in Soviet factories, particularly in metallurgical and ore refinery enterprises. Similarly, because drivers in most of the Soviet Union's motor pools are rewarded premiums on the basis of kilometers driven, not tasks performed, the drivers, both in the cities and on the farms, are constantly criticized for wasting gasoline. This explains the incredible sight of herds of elephantlike water trucks roaming Moscow streets with spray spewing from their trunks regardless of the fact that it is raining. Other drivers tamper with their speedometers to show that they have covered the assigned distances and then illegally sell their gas on the black market.[23]

Discouraging and even frustrating as such waste may be, most of the Soviets' problems discussed thus far stem from human or systemic failings rather than from nature's. These shortcomings may be correctable, which would not be the case if they were due solely to nature. Of course, nature does impose some limitations. For example, there are only so many oil deposits in readily accessible areas, and sooner or later (depending on the intensity of extraction) it will be necessary to look elsewhere. Unfortunately, that elsewhere is to the north and east and offshore, the region of the Soviet Union where the natural conditions are most extreme, living and working conditions accordingly, most rigorous, and the population most sparse. The seriousness of this disparity is indicated by the fact that 75 percent of the Soviet population and 83 percent of its industrial production is located west of the Urals, whereas only 10 percent of the mineral fuel reserves are there to service that population.[24]

This imbalance in total reserves has always been inconvenient, but until recently there were still reasonably abundant reserves west of the Urals. Thus, even as late as 1975, the European sector of the

22. *Petroleum Economist* (September 1978): p. 363.

23. *Selskaya Zhizn*, February 28, 1978, p. 3.

24. A.M. Nekrasov and M.G. Pervukhin, *Energetika SSSR v 1976-1980 Godakh* (Moscow: Energia, 1977), p. 144.

Soviet Union provided 50 percent of the country's fuel and energy.[25] However, by 1980, as the western reserves are depleted, it is anticipated that the European portion of the Soviet Union will supply only 37 percent, the Urals 7.4 percent, and the eastern part of the Soviet Union 55.6 percent of Soviet energy. Based on present knowledge of existing resources, there is every reason to believe that this trend will accelerate in the future. That means that Soviet workers must be moved east to extract and process Siberian raw materials and that most of those raw materials in turn must be sent to the west over thousands of kilometers of railroad and pipeline.[26] Moreover, the Soviet Union has committed itself to be the major supplier to Eastern Europe of a large variety of raw materials, particularly petroleum and natural gas. This extends the journey even further and also limits the exportable surplus that can be sold in the hard currency market. In the past this has been a political problem, but the extra transportation required makes it a physical matter as well.

Clearly, the Soviets have some significant obstacles to overcome if they are ever to meet their production targets for 1980 and if they hope to be able to sustain their 1 million barrels per day of petroleum exports to the hard currency countries. The CIA report was not exaggerating then when it called attention to most of these matters. But while the CIA report was excellent as an engineering survey of current petroleum field conditions, it is not a good economic study, nor does it allow for any creative solutions by the Soviets. In particular, the CIA assumes that the Soviets will be unable to find adequate energy substitutes for petroleum , that they will not be restrained by a shortage of foreign currency needed to pay for imports, and that they will be unable to solve the technology problem.

As we shall see, all three assumptions are at best only partially correct. Ironically, one reason is the very issuance of the CIA report. MPI officials who have been bemoaning their difficulties for many years now find themselves armed with a potent weapon (the CIA report) in their battle to win priority support for their efforts from both Gosplan and Gosbank. Requests for internal and external resources are now more likely to be heeded, whereas before they were sometimes ignored. In a sense the CIA report may be a nonselffulfilling prophecy.

25. Ibid., p. 149.
26. Ibid., p. 148.

Table 10-3. Composition of Fuel Used in Boilers and Furnaces (percent).

Fuel	1970	1975	1980 (Plan)
Coal	37.9	32.9	29.5
Coke	7.6	6.6	5.9
Oil	15.5	18.3	14.7
Natural Gas	25.4	29.6	34.8
Peat	1.7	1.2	1.2
Shale	0.7	0.7	0.6
Wood	2.0	1.4	0.9
Liquefied Gas	0.8	0.9	1.1
Coke Oven Gas	1.9	1.7	1.5
Blast Furnace Gas	2.5	2.2	1.9

Source: Nekrasov and Pervukhin, *Energeti kaSSSR*, p. 149.

As elsewhere in the world, the Soviets are making a determined effort to find substitutes for the domestic use of petroleum. As mentioned earlier, because of the belated Soviet switch in the fuel balance, petroleum is not as deeply entrenched in Soviet energy life as it is elsewhere in the world. Already the Soviets are stressing the need to revert to the use of coal to heat boilers.[27] This is particularly true in the Ural and Volga regions. However, until at least 1980, the relative importance of coal used for boilers (Table 10-3) and in the fuel balance will continue to diminish.[28] In the far northeast, where coal is unavailable, and in West Siberia, where gas is abundant, the second best solution is to burn gas. Indeed, it is anticipated that the use of natural gas will increase significantly both absolutely and relatively. Thus, its use as a source of boiler and furnace fuel is slated to grow from 29.6 percent in 1975 to 34.8 percent in 1980. Natural gas and, to a small extent, liquefied gas are the only fuels whose use with boilers is due to increase over the five year period (Table 10-3). In the same way, natural gas as a percentage of overall energy production is to increase from 21.2 percent to 24.5 percent (Table 10-4; see also Table 10-2).

In the populated areas of the western Soviet Union, where almost all fuels are in short supply, the Soviets have embarked on a major drive to utilize atomic energy for electric generation and, eventually,

27. Ibid., p. 147.
28. Leslie Dienes, "The Soviet Union: An Energy Crunch Ahead?" *Problems of Communism* (September-December 1977): 43; John P. Hardt, Ronda A. Bresnick, and David Levine, "Soviet Oil and Gas in the Global Perspective," *Project Interdependence: U.S. and World Energy Outlook through 1990* (Washington, D.C., Congressional Research Service, Library of Congress, November 1977), p. 803.

Table 10-4.   Fuel Balance Production of All Energy Forms (percent).

	1975	1980 (Plan)
Oil and Gas Condensate	43.0	43.1
Gas Natural and By-product	21.2	24.5
Coal	30.0	26.0
Peat	1.1	0.9
Shale	0.7	0.5
Hydroelectric	2.6	3.0
Atomic	0.4	1.4
Wood	1.0	0.6

Source: Nekrasov and Pervukhin, *Energeti kaSSSR*, p. 149.

for household heating. While the overall share of atomic energy will continue to be small, the share of atomic energy in the European part of the Soviet Union is due to increase from 3.1 percent of all energy generated in the western Soviet Union in 1975 to 10 percent in 1980.[29] During the five year period from 1976 to 1980, 35 percent of all the new electric capacity to be opened in the European part of the Soviet Union is supposed to be produced by atomic reactors. However, the plan is running behind schedule.[30] The Soviets also hope to increase the absolute amount of energy produced by hydroelectric plants and to develop long distance transmission of electricity from power plants located at the mouths of the Siberian coal mines and at dams. There is also hope that more processing of all energy materials will take place near the mining sites in Siberia. This should result in the increased use of raw materials, particularly flared gas that would otherwise be lost forever. It should also reduce the transportation costs, because less of the waste associated with the unprocessed raw materials will have to be carried by the Soviet transportation system.[31]

The impact of these various measures should be to reduce the domestic use of petroleum or at the least to halt what had been a tendency to move to an ever-increasing reliance on petroleum. If

29. Nekrasov and Pervukhin, p. 114.

30. Ibid., p. 114; CIA, *The Soviet Economy in 1976-77 and Outlook for 1978*, ER78-10512 (Washington, D.C., August 1978), p. 6. *Time*, October 30, 1977, p. 69.

31. N.K. Baibakov, "Soglasovannyi plan mnogostornnikh integratsionnykh meropiiatii—novaia stupen' razvitiia sovmestnoi planovoi deiatel'nosti stran—chlenov CEV," *Planovoe khoziaistvo*, September 1975, pp. 11, 12; D.V. Belorusov, I.I. Pafilov and V.A. Sennikov, *Problem' razvitiia i razmeshchenie proizvoditel'nykh sil zapadnoi Sibiri* (Moscow: Mysl', 1976), pp. 259-60; N. Mel'nikov and V. Shelest, "Toplivno-energetichekii kompleks SSSR," *Planovoe khoziaistvo* (February 1975): 15.

Soviet plans are implemented, the use of fuel oil as a source of boiler fuel should fall from 18.3 percent in 1975 to 14.7 percent in 1980 (Table 10-3). The significance of the shift is made even more impressive when it is realized that in 1970 fuel oil constituted 15.5 percent of all boiler and furnace fuel. Thus, while the trend five years ago was to increase the use of petroleum for boilers and furnaces, now it is to decrease it. The same trend is reflected in the move away from petroleum as a source of electrical power.[32]

The intent of all these measures is to ensure that with existing production prospects the Soviets will have enough petroleum to satisfy their export needs. One of the most significant shortcomings of the original April 1977 CIA report is that it ignores the economic implications of annual imports of 3.5 to 4.5 mbd by the Soviet Union in the mid-1980s. If this were to happen and Soviet demand was added to the already existing world demand, petroleum prices would increase sharply. Even at existing 1977 prices, the Soviets would have to pay $18 to $24 billion a year just for petroleum imports. In addition, of course, the Soviet Union would presumably want to continue to import an amount somewhat comparable to its regular hard currency imports, which came to something like $12 billion in 1977. That would make a combined total of $30 to $36 billion.

The obvious question, which the CIA has only belatedly begun to ask, is: How would the Soviets pay for all this oil? Total Soviet exports to the hard currency countries amounted to only about $10.4 billion in 1977. However, since approximately 51 percent, or $5.3 billion, of that consisted of petroleum exports of 1 mbd, and since the CIA assumes that the Soviet Union will no longer have this petroleum to export, that would mean that it would have hard currency earnings of only about $5.1 billion to pay for $30 to $36 billion worth of imports. There are not many countries that can sustain that type of annual trade deficit.

The CIA has apparently responded to this type of argument. It now concedes that the Soviet Union itself will not be a net importer of petroleum, although it still insists that the Council for Mutual Economic Assistance bloc (CMEA-Eastern Europe, Mongolia, Cuba, and now Vietnam) as a whole will need to import approximately 2.7 mbd.[33] This may still be high. The fact remains that the Soviet Union

32. Nekrasov and Pervukhin, *Energetika SSSR*, p. 153.
33. CIA, *Soviet Economic Problems and Prospects*, ER77-10436U (Washington D.C., July 1977), p. 22.

has little else in the way of substitutes to make up for the petroleum exports. Timber exports, the second largest earner, brought in only $1 billion in hard currency in 1977. Next was natural gas, which earned about $570 million in hard currency. While natural gas exports are due to increase in the near future, it is unlikely that they will grow enough to amount to more than $1 billion or $1.5 billion in hard currency.

The CIA is not the only one to recognize these limitations. Soviet planners are aware of the problems. This accounts for their effort to husband petroleum domestically and to substitute other fuels wherever possible, particularly for use as boiler and furnace fuel. It also explains the Soviet decision to double the price of gasoline and the fact that in the past year many drivers and petroleum consumers reported a shortage of fuel at the gas pumps and fuel depots.[34] As a result of such efforts, the Soviets were apparently able to increase exports in 1977 to both the hard currency countries and Eastern Europe (see Table 10-5). It remains to be seen how long the Soviets will continue this policy. Should their trade balance move from deficit to surplus, as it did in 1974, then the Soviets may curb their petroleum exports. All things being equal, they would prefer to consume domestically or to save rather than to export. But as long as they have a large foreign trade deficit, they must at least try to sustain their exports.[35] Interestingly, in a study released in 1974, the CIA predicted the Soviet oil exports would peak in 1976 and then decline. As a minimum they are off by at least one year.

The Soviets are not relying solely on conservation and substitution to assure a flow of exports. They are also moving vigorously to increase output. Their efforts are impressive. It is true that the location of the new fields is most inconvenient and that the working conditions are intolerable. But we sometimes forget that the Soviets are used to working under such circumstances. After all, petroleum was first discovered at Tiumen in West Siberia only in 1959.[36] The first exploitation of the field took place in 1964, when 200,000 tons of oil were produced.[37] Yet by 1977, despite the mosquitos, swamps,

---

34. Information was gained from personal discussion in Moscow in the fall of 1977. See also *Pravda*, March 7, 1978, p. 3; March 18, 1978, p. 2; March 19, 1978, p. 2.

35. Joint Economic Committee, *Allocation of Resources in the Soviet Union and China, 1975* (Washington D.C.: Government Printing Office, April 12, 1974), p. 24.

36. *Review of Sino-Soviet Oil* (May 1977): 21.

37. *Ekonomicheskaia Gazeta* 17 (April 1978): 2.

Table 10-5. Soviet Oil and Natural Gas.

| | | Petroleum (million tons) | | | | | | Natural Gas (billion cubic meters) | | | | |
| | | | Export | | | | | | | Export | | |
Year	Output	Total	CMEA	Hard Currency	Crude	Refined	Output	Total	CMEA	Hard Currency	Hard Currency Import
1972	400	107	57	34	76	31	221	5	3	2	11
1973	429	118	63	36	85	33	236	7	4	2	11
1974	459	116	67	31	80	36	261	14	5	5	12
1975	491	130	72	38	93	37	289	19	11	7	12
1976	520	149	78	49	111	38	321	26	13	11	12
1977	546	155–159	81–85	51			346	32–34	15–16	17	12

Source: *Nar khoz 1972–1977* and *Vneshniaia Torgoulia SSSR 1972–1977.*

permafrost, cold, and impossible supply conditions, production exceeded 200 million tons. Moreover, virtually the entire effort was carried out with existing Soviet labor and technology. The Soviets have been equally impressive in exploiting their extremely challenging natural gas fields.[38]

Whenever it will help, the Soviets in recent years have brought in outside experts and technology. For the most part, they turn first to the United States, but if necessary, when they encounter obstacles they turn to another source. The fact that it may be second best deters them only for a time. The important question is whether or not the new technology is superior to existing Soviet practice.

Illustrative of what can happen when export licenses are either slow or not forthcoming is the Soviet search for the use of gas injection secondary recovery equipment. Originally they had agreed with a handshake to purchase the equipment from an American company. When the American export license was slow in coming, the final contract for $220 million was signed instead with the French company, Société Technip.[39]

How far the Soviets are prepared to go is best illustrated by what is happening on Sakhalin Island. There the Soviets have actually entered into a joint venture (on Soviet territory) with Japanese and American partners for the exploration of oil.[40] While there were a variety of joint ventures with foreign companies in the 1920s, the Soviets, at least until Sakhalin, had subsequently taken a determined stand against all such ventures on their soil. Undoubtedly, those who supported this ideologically heretical action must derive some comfort from the fact that the Japanese-led effort has discovered oil.[41]

Other examples of Soviet use of foreign technology include the purchase of offshore jackups, the Dresser drill bit plant, semisubmersible pumps, well logging equipment, vast quantities of drilling and pipeline pipes, and secondary and tertiary recovery equipment. All of this helps to increase Soviet productivity and to extend the pumping life of a well beyond what critics like the CIA have anticipated. Such equipment can make a big difference, and since it will serve to increase Soviet production and to postpone the day when the Soviets will find it necessary to compete with the United States

38. *Izvestiia*, February 24, 1977, p. 2.
39. *Review of Sino-Soviet Oil* (August 1978): 42; *International Herald Tribune*, October 6, 1978, p. 9.
40. *Review of Sino-Soviet Oil* (January-February 1977): 51.
41. *Business Week*, October 17, 1977, p. 52; *Foreign Trade*, (July 1978): 64; *Moscow Narodny Bank Bulliten*, August 23, 1978, p. 6; *Review of Sino-Soviet Oil* (August 28): 42–43; *Wall Street Journal*, September 11, 1978, p. 6.

on world energy markets for petroleum, the U.S. government should facilitate, not hinder, the export of petroleum technology to the USSR. The contemplated purchase of a secondary recovery procedure from one American company would make it possible to increase the yearly output of some of the older Baku wells threefold, from 300,000 to 1 million tons.[42] Such spectacular improvements are not possible everywhere, but they do indicate that it is necessary to allow for foreign technology when drawing up estimates of future Soviet output.

Of course, there is much the Soviets can do to increase oil and gas output based entirely on their own efforts. The best thing would be to alter the incentive system to eliminate the shortcomings described earlier in this chapter. That is more easily promised than performed. Presumably it could be done only as part of a reform of the overall Soviet planning and production system. It could have far-reaching consequences that so far the Soviet leadership has been unwilling to face. Yet even within that framework, the Soviets can and apparently are doing more to improve their exploration efficiency. For example, as of August 1978, they have consolidated all offshore exploration and drilling under the Ministry of Gas Industries. They can also turn to other promising sites. They are already beginning to extend their drilling beyond the Mesozoic strata to the Paleozoic layers and to East Siberia.[43] Furthermore, there are some geologists who feel that the Soviets will find additional oil deposits under some of their very bountiful gas deposits in West Siberia.[44] While the CIA is correct in that most of these new fields so far seem to be much smaller in productive capacity than the giant field at Samotlor, there remain vast expanses of Soviet territory that are as yet unexplored.[45] Finally, they are now beginning to increase their exploration of offshore sites. Until recently, they have lacked the technology to drill very deeply offshore. Some of their newly imported equipment now makes it possible, not only in the deeper regions of the Caspian but in the Barents, Kara, Okhotsk, and East Siberian seas. As in the case of Sakhalin, there is even the possibility that some of this work will be undertaken jointly with foreign firms.[46]

42. Discussion with American manufacturers.

43. *Review of Sino-Soviet Oil* (April 1977): 20-21; *Review of Sino-Soviet Oil* (August 1978): 20.

44. *Literaturnaia Gazeta*, January 18, 1978 p. 10.

45. M.M. Odintsov and A.A. Bykharov, "Mineral'nye resursy zony," *Vestnik A.N. SSSR*, (September 1975), 47.

46. *New York Times*, July 16, 1976, p. D-6; *Petroleum Economist* (May 1977): 192; *Moscow Narodny Bank Bulletin*, April 5, 1978, p. 2; *Moscow Narodny Bank Bulletin*, August 2, 1978, p. 3.

The effectiveness of Soviet policy can be judged by the way the Soviet Union plans to satisfy the energy needs of Eastern Europe. While, as we saw in Table 10-5, they have managed to increase exports to both Eastern Europe and the hard currency countries in 1977, there are many who question whether the Soviets will be able to continue to do this in the 1980s.

In an interesting analysis, Edward A. Hewett calculates that the East European energy deficit will grow by 60 percent from 1975 to 1980 (or from a deficit of 95 MTSF [million tons in standard fuel equivalent] in 1975 to 152 MTSF by 1980).[47] This is predicated on his assumption that East European energy production will grow at 2.5 percent a year from 1976 to 1980, while consumption will increase by 4 percent a year. Hewett questions whether the Soviet Union will be able to satisfy this growing shortfall, presumably with petroleum, and still export to the hard currency market. He calculates that the Soviets will have an energy surplus in 1980 of about 211 MTSF. That would leave a bloc surplus of only about 60 MTSF, not the approximately 105 MTSF that existed in 1975.[48] The presumption is that the surplus would diminish even more in subsequent years and that the bloc as a whole might soon become net importers.

While Hewett's analysis may be correct, there are some offsetting factors. The first is that the ratio of energy consumed to GNP seems to have fallen slightly in the Soviet Union, just as it has in the United States.[49] That does not mean that Soviet production is unaffected by the growing shortage of energy, but it does mean, as we have seen, that the Soviets are striving to conserve on energy consumption. The same reduction in energy consumption relative to GNP may be occurring in Eastern Europe. Second, while Hewett in his analysis properly focuses on the shortfalls that the Soviets seem to be suffering in coal and oil production, he neglects the success they seem to be having in gas production and in the substitution of gas for oil. Not only is gas becoming more important within the USSR, but it is also becoming increasingly important in Eastern Europe now that the Orenburg or Soiuz pipeline has opened. In 1979, the pipeline will carry 8 to 9 billion cubic meters of gas to Eastern Europe, and in 1980 its planned flow is to be 15.5 billion cubic meters.[50] That would provide 2.8 billion cubic meters of gas a year for Bulgaria,

47. Edward A. Hewett, "The Soviet and East European Energy Crisis: Its Dimensions and Implications for East-West Trade" (Austin: Center for Energy Studies, University of Texas at Austin, August 1978), Mimeographed. pp. 22-23.

48. Ibid., pp. 22-24.

49. CIA, *Soviet Economy in 1976-77*, p. 6.

50. *Review of Sino-Soviet Oil* (August 1978): 56.

Czechoslovakia, East Germany, Hungary, and Poland. Romania will receive 1.5 billion cubic meters. In addition, since the pipeline has a capacity of 28 billion cubic meters a year, there is a good chance that the original quotas will be supplemented. Finally, it should also be noted that Czechoslovakia is due to receive a transit fee of 3.6 billion cubic meters of gas a year for their willingness to participate in the complicated Iran-Soviet Union-Western Europe natural gas deal. The first gas in this undertaking will be shipped in 1980.[52]

The significance of these gas shipments is that they will reduce the energy deficit in Eastern Europe from 152 to about 130 MTSF, assuming that Hewett's somewhat pessimistic assumptions are correct. More important, the deficit will be reduced, not with petroleum, but with the shipment of natural gas, which is already allocated. This reduction should be taken into account before any supplementary amounts of natural gas are added and before the East Europeans and Soviets have to haggle over increasing the allotment of oil and coal exports. Of course, this increase in natural gas output in the Soviet Union, except for the Iranian transshipment, is included in the calculation of Soviet energy surplus, but the significance here is that this is above and beyond any petroleum exports and before the Soviets begin to provide for their own needs.

Although it is not of the same magnitude, Hewett also neglects to allow for the Soviet shipment of electricity in the East European electrical grid. In 1977, the Soviets exported 11.5 billion kilowatts of electricity or 1 percent of their total production. Except for Finland, all of this went to Eastern Europe. With the opening of a new transmission line in 1978, the Soviets expect to supply another 6.4 million kilowatts and more later.[53] The first stage alone should add another 2 MTSF. Just as with natural gas, the increased export of electricity will substitute for petroleum.

Thus, while there seems little doubt that the Soviets are having some significant production problems, they are beginning to take some far-reaching steps to reduce the drop in output and to ensure that they have an exportable surplus. They are seeking to restore output in some of the older wells by using foreign technology and to sustain or increase output in some of the newer wells with the same techniques. In addition, they are belatedly increasing their exploratory work in as yet untapped areas both on and off shore. In all of

51. *Sotsialisticheskaia Industriia*, September 29, 1978, p. 3.
52. *Moscow Narodny Bank Bulletin*, November 24, 1976, p. 9; *Moscow Narodny Bank Bulletin*, June 14, 1978, p. 13; *Review of Sino-Soviet Oil*, (March 1978): 63.
53. *New Times*, no. 39 (1978): 13.

these efforts, the United States should seek to facilitate the flow of petroleum extraction technology to the USSR. True, this will enhance Soviet output capabilities and thus Soviet economic as well as political and military strength, but it will also postpone the day when the USSR will find it necessary to compete with countries like the United States for world petroleum and prolong the flow of Soviet petroleum onto the world market. However, even if such technology is made available to the USSR, it is unlikely that the Soviet Union will ever be able to do enough to increase output on the scale predicted by the Swedes. And just in case the CIA is right and overall production does begin to fall, the Soviets are beginning to substitute gas, coal, and atomic energy to generate power that formerly was produced by petroleum. In large part this is necessary, because the Soviets need the petroleum to provide them with the hard currency to finance their hard currency imports. They also must continue to help supply their East European allies who otherwise will encounter serious economic and political problems if they have to go to the hard currency market for the bulk of their petroleum. Obviously, the day when Soviet supplies run out cannot be postponed forever, but that day seems further off than the CIA report would indicate. It is entirely conceivable, therefore, that the Soviet Union will be able to maintain and even increase its flow of energy resources to Eastern Europe and still be able to maintain its sales of petroleum to the hard currency countries into 1980 and possibly 1985.

In some ways, petroleum plays the same role in Chinese economic policy as it does in the Soviet Union. First, there are some serious gaps in the information about reserves and production, and second and most important, the Chinese have become very dependent on petroleum exports to finance their foreign trade imports. One estimate shows that oil exports will constitute 90 percent of Chinese foreign trade earnings.[54] With the death of Mao and the downfall of the Gang of Four, increased industrial efficiency has become a priority target. This in turn means increased reliance on foreign technology, which in turn means that there must be exports. In what follows, however, it is necessary to remember that the Chinese are even more mercurial in their attitudes toward foreigners than the Soviets and, consequently, that while trade and technology are up today, it would not be too surprising if they were down tomorrow.

The Chinese have come a long way in a relatively short time. Prior

54. *Review of Sino-Soviet Oil* (March 1978): 71.

Table 10-6. Production and Export of Petroleum in China (million tons).

	Production				Export		
	1	*2*	*3*	*4*	*5*	*6*	*7*
1955	1.						
1956	1.2						
1957	1.5	1.8					
1958	2.3						
1959	3.7	3.7					
1960	5.1	4.6					
1961	5.2	5.5					
1962	5.7						
1963	6.4						
1964	8.7						
1965	11.0	10.					
1966	14.1	13.5					
1967	13.9	12.7					
1968	15.2	13.9					
1969	20.4	16.					
1970	28.2	25.					
1971	36.7						
1972	43.1						
1973	54.8	53			2.4		
1974	65.8	65			6.1		
1975	74.3	80			11.4		
1976	83.6	88					
1977			93-94	100		7.5	8
1978							
1979							
1980				200			

Source: Column 1: Central Intelligence Agency, *China: Oil Production Prospects,* ER 77-1003 OU (Washington, D.C., June 1977), p. 9.
Columns 2 and 5: *Total Information* (Geneva) 69 (Spring 1977): 6.
Columns 3 and 6: *Review of Sino-Soviet Oil* (February 1978): 60; (March 1978): 70; (April 1978): 65; (July 1978): 67.
Columns 4 and 7: *Washington Post,* October 16, 1978, p. A3.

to 1960, they were dependent almost solely on the Soviet Union for virtually all of their petroleum. Of course, the Chinese lead a spartan life and therefore manage to operate on a very small per capita energy basis. That means that as their own domestic oil production has increased, they are able to set aside a larger than usual share for export.

Estimates of Chinese petroleum production vary. Table 10-6 presents a range of estimates. There are even greater differences as to predictions about further production. The CIA, as in the Soviet case, takes one of the more pessimistic lines.[55] The CIA predicted that by

55. CIA, *China: Oil Production Prospects,* ER77-1003 OU (Washington D.C., June 1977), pp. 1, 23.

1980, the Chinese would produce 2.4 to 2.8 mbd (120 to 140 million tons annually), of which only 200,000 to 600,000 barrels a day (10 to 30 million tons annually) would be available for export. At the lower range that would be less than what was exported in 1976. In fairness it should be noted that the CIA report was written when China was in the "clutches" of the Gang of Four. There was considerable hostility to the outside world. Other specialists, especially given China's present willingness to import technology, put potential production and exports much higher. For example, the U.S. Bureau of Mines reports that 1977 production was 100 million tons (2 mbd).[56] One estimate equates China's reserves with those of Saudi Arabia.[57] Some Japanese project output at 440 million tons by 1985, with exports equaling 200 million tons.[58]

Assuming no further political shifts, there is reason to believe that the Chinese will indeed export substantial quantities of petroleum. Particularly impressive is the way the Chinese have increased their production and exports in recent years. Moreover, output seems to keep growing at rates that exceed 10 percent.[59] Exports appear to be keeping pace. The Chinese now export not only to Japan, but to the Philippines (6 million tons over five years), Brazil, Hong Kong, and North Korea, and now even to Romania, Italy, and the United States.[60]

China's export to Japan has been and promises to be particularly important, especially in the wake of the Japanese-Chinese peace agreement. Japan imported 6.6 million tons in 1977. This is expected to grow to at least 15 million tons by 1982 and possibly to 30 million tons.[61] Moreover, the Chinese have begun to negotiate actively with Japanese and American companies for joint undertakings offshore. Like the Soviet Union, China is also seeking to increase its production of other energy sources. This is done at least in part to enable the Chinese to set aside petroleum for export. They are building a huge hydro-electric project on the Yangtze Kiang River, with total capacity of 25,000 megawatts. They have also signed a $4 billion

56. *Washington Post,* October 10, 1978 p. 13; *New York Times,* November 8, 1978, p. 5.

57. Selig S. Harrison, "China: The Next Oil Giant, Time Bomb in East Asia," *Foreign Policy* 20 (Fall 1975): 4.

58. Ibid., p. 25; Choon-ho Park and Jerome Alan Cohen, "The Politics of the Oil Weapon," *Foreign Policy* 20 (Fall 1975): 33, 40; Wang Kung Ping, *The Peoples Republic of China—A New Industrial Power with a Strong Material Base* (Washington, D.C.: U.S. Bureau of Mines, 1975), p. 38.

59. *Review of Sino-Soviet Oil* (August 1978): 75.

60. Ibid.; *Wall Street Journal,* November 10, 1978, p. 43.

61. *Review of Sino-Soviet Oil* (March 1978): 70.

contract with West Germany to open up two strip mines and six underground mines in order to boost cost production to 1 billion tons by 1988.[62] If these projects are built as planned, the Chinese should be able to meet their more ambitious export targets.

It is risky to generalize too much for two countries as different as China and the Soviet Union. Yet there are some common tendencies in both countries that must be noted. Both have production problems. Both have been analyzed by the CIA, which takes a dim view of their future production and export expansion possibilities. But if China and the Soviet Union are to pay their import bills, both countries need petroleum exports badly. Moreover, both countries have vast territories on land and off shore that are as yet not fully explored, but that are thought to have potential for gas and oil production. Finally, both have embarked on a drive to bring in both foreign technicians and technology to help increase production. For that reason, the pessimists may be unduly conservative. While certainly production increases will not come easily, the likelihood is that they will come and that both countries will have exportable surpluses through 1980 and possibly 1985.

62. *Business Week*, October 9, 1978, p. 56.

Energy in Non-OPEC Developing Countries

11

Dennis W. Bakke

INTRODUCTION

The status of non-OPEC developing countries in the world energy situation is frequently overlooked. The fact that developing countries (LDCs) use only 9 percent of the world's commercial energy[1] too often leads to the conclusion that their role is negligible. In addition, the scarcity of credible data on this subject makes analysis of energy needs difficult. However, LDC commercial energy consumption is growing rapidly; it increased 250 percent between 1970 and 1974. Several studies project that LDC oil consumption

---

1. James W. Howe et al., *Energy Problems of Developing Countries: Implications for U.S. Policy*, Final Report to the Council on Environmental Quality Contract #EQ-7AC016 (Washington, D.C., July 1978).

I am indebted to Jim Howe and his staff of the Overseas Development Council for their constant education on LDC energy issues during the past eighteen months and for significant research upon which this paper was based. The same is true of Bob Nathans, Phil Palmedo, and the work of the Brookhaven National Laboratory. In addition, my work was made much easier by a draft of the very excellent literature search and study by Joy Dunkerley, William Ramsay, Elizabeth Cecelski, and Emmanuel Mbi of Resources for the Future entitled, "Preliminary Study on Energy Consumption and Supply of the Urban and Rural Poor in Developing Countries." Comments and advice on an earlier draft from John Sawhill were also extremely helpful.

Much of the material for this section and other parts of the paper was included in the Report on Energy for Developing Countries of the 18th Annual Stanley Foundation's Strategy for Peace Conference held at Airlie House, October 5-8, 1978. Jim Howe served as chairman, and Dennis Bakke, rapporteur of the group that created the report. Also participating were Vladimir Baum,

will rise from 15 percent of the world's total in 1985 to 25 percent in the 2000s. Whether or not those projections are accurate, LDCs will be major consumers in the world petroleum markets in the years ahead.

It is in the U.S. interest to be concerned with the energy needs of LDCs. Energy is an integral part of development, and LDC development can enhance the future economic growth of the United States. Forty-one percent of the world's population live in non-OPEC LDCs. Exports to developing countries have grown from $14 billion in 1960 (1977 dollars) to $43 billion in 1977.[2] These emerging nations can provide markets for future American products and services. For these reasons, among others, we describe the basic energy characteristics of non-OPEC developing countries and outline the energy problems facing them. We also discuss the alternatives for dealing with their energy problems and recommend possible ways to alleviate some of their negative aspects.

Both modern commercial energy sources (oil, coal, hydropower) used in modern sectors of LDCs and traditional resources (firewood, charcoal, wastes, and animal draft power) used in most LDC rural areas and among the urban poor are considered when we discuss energy in developing countries. Both are important. An estimated 70 percent of energy consumed in Brazil is derived from commercial sources, but only 31 percent in Bangladesh, and even lower percentages in other LDCs.[3] In modern sectors of the developing nations, oil is the primary energy source. Since these sectors are growing

---

director, Centre for Natural Resources, Energy and Transport, United Nations; Jay A. Conger, director, International Marketing, Solarex Corporation; C. Richard D'Amato, legislative director, Office of Congressman James M. Jeffords; Alfredo del Valle, staff member, United Nations Development Programme; Lawrence Ervin, al Dir'iyyah Institute; Stephen Klein, energy policy advisor, Agency for International Development; William J. Lanouette, staff correspondent, *National Journal*; Francis A. Luzzatto, director, International & Special Assistance Division, Office of Voluntary Citizen Participation, ACTION/Peace Corps; Philip Palmedo, director, Energy Policy Analysis Group, Brookhaven National Laboratory; Anthony Pryor, visiting research fellow, Rockefeller Foundation; Phactuel Rego, chief, Unit of Applied Sciences, Department of Scientific Affairs, Organization of American States; Gregs G. Thomopulos, vice president; head, International Division, Stanley Consultants, Inc.; and Ishrat H. Usmani, senior energy advisor, Centre for Natural Resources, Energy & Transport, United Nations.

2. *U.S. Statistical Abstract, 1977.* (Washington, D.C., Government Printing Office, 1978).

3. Edward Beardsworth, Samuel Hale, Jr., Robert Nathans, Philip Palmedo, et al., *Energy Needs, Uses and Resources in Developing Countries* (Upton, N.Y.: Policy Analysis Division, National Center for Analysis of Energy Systems, Brookhaven National Laboratory Associated Universities, 1978).

rapidly, oil consumption is also growing rapidly. In addition, among the 2.4 billion people that currently depend on traditional energy sources in LDCs,[4] there appears to be a shift away from such fuels toward the use of petroleum products. Oil use is thus increasing steadily in both sectors. The expanding use of commercial energy in the modern sector and the shift toward its use in the traditional sector results from several factors:

1. The modernization process (the attempt to improve human welfare through the application of science and technology) that is occurring among the urban higher income groups increases the demand for modern industry, transportation, higher agricultural production, and new housing. Fulfilling these needs requires additional commercial energy. A nation cannot industrialize without substantial amounts of nonhuman energy.
2. The modernization process also affects the rural and urban poor by stimulating demand for a "better life." Through education, mobility, and improved communication, the poor learn of the comforts and life-enriching innovations of modernization and seek to obtain what they perceive as desirable. Commercial energy is needed in this case both to support new ways of doing old things less onerously (e.g., tractors in lieu of labor) and to operate new innovations (e.g., radios).
3. The disappearance of traditional fuels caused by increases in population and urban energy needs also leads to increased demands for commercial fuels.

These are the pressures creating an expanded use of modern energy forms, but why is oil almost always chosen as the source of this energy? Five reasons can be cited:

1. Oil, until recently, has been relatively inexpensive and abundant.
2. An entire oil-related infrastructure has developed in most LDCs that is superior to other distribution systems developed for competing forms of energy.
3. The most widely used technologies are based on oil. This is especially true in the transportation sector, which consumes a high percentage of the commercial energy used in many developing countries. To a lesser extent this is also true for lighting, cooking, and irrigation systems.

4. Private discussion with James Howe, Overseas Development Council, Washington, D.C., 1978.

4. Some multinational corporations, international organizations, and developed nations have steered development in LDCs toward petroleum use. The switch from coal to diesel in India's railroads, strongly urged a few years ago by the World Bank, and the construction of petrochemical fertilizer plants in many LDCs by multinational corporations are examples of this phenomenon.
5. Tradition is difficult to overcome. Choosing an alternative fuel means overcoming inertia and shifting from familiar options to unknown ones.

It is clear that the expansion of oil consumption in both the modern and traditional sectors is caused by powerful economic and institutional factors not easily countered. One of the central energy problems facing LDCs is that expanding petroleum consumption and the accompanying development of an oil-based infrastructure come at a time when some experts predict world oil production could peak and begin to decline within the next two decades.

Even if supplies of oil and other conventional fuels were abundant, however, the financial burden of following this path would be exhaustive for most LDCs. In the next twenty to thirty years, LDCs must deal with a fourfold problem. First, like developed nations, LDCs face the dilemma of shifting their existing modern economies away from substantial dependence on petroleum. Second, unlike developed countries, they must also contend with the increasing oil needs of a rapidly expanding modern sector. Third, LDCs must provide energy for those who are making the transition from noncommercial to commercial energy. This transition is taking place because of the demands of modernization and because traditional energy sources are disappearing. Finally, many developing nations must contend with the environmental degradation and the reduction in the quality of rural life caused by diminishing supplies of wood and other noncommercial fuels. Certainly, an important part of the overall LDC energy problem involves deforestation and the resulting loss of rich agricultural topsoil and hardships for those whose way of life depends on wood fuels.

The magnitude of the crisis is overwhelming when one realizes that developing countries face this transition with all the handicaps characteristic of their plight. Typically, they suffer from a lack of capital, insufficient skilled personnel, inadequate transportation and communication networks, and weak policymaking institutions that are unable to make a strong response to the energy crisis.

One footnote to assessment of this problem concerns the relative economic impact on LDCs of the rapid oil price increase in 1973–

74. The pervasive recessions among industrialized nations are well documented. By comparison, LDCs did not fare quite as badly. The external public debt of non-oil-exporting LDCs did increase 83 percent from 1973 to 1976 as opposed to only 56 percent from 1970 to 1973.[5] However, gross national product (GNP) grew 18 percent in nonoil LDCs from 1970 to 1973 compared with only 3.5 percent for the same years among industrialized countries. During the four years prior to and including 1973,[6] both groups of countries had essentially the same 16–17 percent GNP growth. The reasons for this smaller, negative impact among LDCs are not documented. However, there could be two reasons. The first is that a relatively smaller percentage of commercial fuel (especially oil) is used where infrastructure is limited. Or, second, the high cost of transporting and marketing oil and the oil markets within LDCs meant that these countries had a higher baseline retail price before the OPEC price increase than did industrialized nations. Because distribution costs did not rise as much as oil prices, the percentage increase in oil prices was greater for industrialized nations than for LDCs.

ASSESSMENT OF LDC
ENERGY CHARACTERISTICS[7]

The methodology for analyzing alternative solutions to the problems described above should avoid the analytical pitfalls that can easily enter discussions of energy problems and policies of developing countries. Specifically, four pitfalls should be guarded against.

1. LDCs are not at all homogeneous, even though they are commonly lumped together into one group. Some developing countries, for example, have a per capita commercial consumption twenty to thirty times greater than other developing countries.[8] Many of these countries, like Brazil, Taiwan, and South Korea, are more similar to second tier industrial nations than they are to many LDCs. These countries have over 50 percent of their population in cities, while others have less than 10 percent in urban areas. Some of the countries are almost totally dependent on subsistence agriculture for their economic base, while others have a fairly highly developed industrial

5. World Bank, *World Debt Table*, vol. 1 (Washington, D.C., October 20, 1978).
6. World Bank, *World Economic and Social Indicators* (Washington, D.C., October 1978).
7. Some of the ideas for this paper's structure and analysis methodology emanate from a private communication from Lincoln Gordon, February 28, 1978.
8. Private discussion with James Howe.

economic structure. Thus, a special way of dealing with these essential dissimilarities must be implemented.

2. LDCs will not remain in their current state of industrialization or development. The modernization process may be the most powerful factor operating in the world system today. Whenever people from the developed world have interacted with those living in traditional settings, modernization has changed life substantially. While it is true that peoples differ in their willingness to pay the price or in their capacity to make the changes required, no significant number of people over an extended period of time have rejected the opportunity provided by modernization for basic comforts, improved health, and reduced physical drudgery. Hence, even though it proceeds at various speeds, the process appears universally inevitable and irreversible.[9] The question is not whether nation states will seek to develop, it is how fast, and what will be the consequences? This must be taken into account when assessing the energy future for developing countries.

3. Solutions to LDC energy problems will not necessarily be found in small-scale, decentralized, or renewable resource technologies, nor should the immediate future of these countries be void of petroleum. The search is not for renewable strategies, conservation strategies, or even strategies for expanding indigenous supply. The goal should be supplying the country's energy needs for development at the least possible cost. The emphasis should be on energy productivity, and that may well mean that some countries will stay almost totally dependent on centralized oil or other conventional systems for many years to come while others use substantial amounts of renewable resources.

4. One of the least recognized pitfalls is the tendency to concentrate the search for solutions to LDC energy problems on energy supply alternatives rather than on improving energy efficiency. The argument is made that per capita energy consumption in LDCs is inconsequential and, therefore, that efficiency improvements are not important. It is true that per capita energy consumption is low. However, it is not as low as one might first assume if both commercial and traditional energy are considered. In addition, much of the commercial energy goes to modern sectors to fuel cities and industries. There are at least as many opportunities for saving energy in these sectors as there are in countries like the United States. Use of energy

9. Dennis W. Bakke, "Developing Countries and United States Domestic Policy in the Context of a Changing International System" (Paper presented to the National War College, Washington, D.C., May 1, 1977).

in the rural sectors is also extremely inefficient, and one of the fastest ways to improve the energy situation may be through increasing energy efficiency in this sector.

However, these pitfalls are not easily avoided. Useful data on energy demand and supply in LDCs are incomplete. Details on use of both commercial and noncommercial fuels are almost nonexistent. Some studies have been undertaken—notably a study on energy in Bangladesh; Department of Energy work in Egypt and Peru; activities of the Institute for Energy Research (Stony Brook) in Mexico; and work by Peace Corps volunteers in selected villages sponsored by the Overseas Development Council, the al Dir'iyyah Institute, and the Agency for International Development (AID). Currently, however, the data are restricted primarily to work by the World Bank and the United Nations and to national studies by a few countries such as India and Korea.

Using the data that do exist, Table 11-1 classifies LDCs according to their similarities and differences. It is a rather simplistic approach, presented only to indicate the LDC environments for which alternative strategies must be found. There are numerous ways to build developing country classification schemes. The most popular is to group them by gross national product or income.[10] Several studies have used other characteristics. For example, the Overseas Development Council uses its physical quality of life index in conjunction with GNP. The excellent Brookhaven study classifies the countries according to their economic structure—industrial, balanced economies, agricultural exporters, oil exporters, and other agriculture.[11]

Table 11-1 supplements these schemes. On one axis of the matrix the countries are divided into three groups (high, medium, low) according to the amount of commercial energy consumed and the degree of urbanization. On the other axis, the countries are classified by their conventional energy resource potentials based on U.N. series J data.[12] What is sought is a simple way of capturing the essence of both the supply and the demand environment. On the demand side this means identifying those characteristics that best portray both the amount of energy used and the way that that energy is used. The per capita commercial energy figure is helpful in that it is a rough indicator of industrialization and also shows the quantity of energy

10. Carroll L. Wilson et al., *Energy Global Prospects 1985–2000* (New York: McGraw-Hill, 1977).

11. Beardsworth et al., *Energy Needs, Uses and Resources in Developing Countries.*

12. *World Energy Supplies 1972–1976* United Nations Series J Statistical Papers no. 21 (New York: United Nations, 1978).

Table 11-1.   LDC Energy Characteristics.

	Rich in Energy Resources	Poor in Energy Resources
I High Commercial Energy Consumption/High Urbanization/Industrialization	Turkey Argentina Brazil Colombia Guyana Mexico Peru Trinidad and Tobago Yugoslavia South Korea	Cyprus Lebanon Singapore Jamaica Taiwan Chile Panama Surinam Uruguay
II Medium Commercial Energy Consumption/Medium Urbanization/Industrialization	Congo Egypt Eq. Guinea Gabon Liberia Mozambique Rhodesia Syria Tunisia Papua New Guinea Malaysia Oman India Bolivia Costa Rica Nicaragua Paraguay	Ivory Coast Mauritius Morocco Zambia Jordan Philippines Thailand Dominican Republic El Salvador Guatemala Honduras Fiji
III Low Commercial Energy Consumption/Low Urbanization/Industrialization	Angola Botswana Cameroon Central African Republic Madagascar Senegal Swaziland Upper Volta Zaire Afghanistan Bangladesh Pakistan	Benin Burundi Chad Ethiopia Gambia Ghana Guinea Kenya Lesotho Malawi Mali Mauritania Niger Rwanda Sierra Leone Sudan Tanzania Togo Uganda Nepal Somalia Sri Lanka Viet Nam Haiti Burma Southwest Africa Yemen

Source: *World Energy Conference Survey of Energy Resources, 1974* (New York: U.S. National Committee of the World Energy Conference, 1974).

used. Unfortunately, interpretation of the quantity of energy consumed is often clouded by the fact that many countries use substantial amounts of noncommercial fuels. However, even if a country with a low per capita commercial energy consumption and high noncommercial usage has a combined consumption equal to a country with the opposite characteristics (e.g., high commercial energy use and relatively low noncommercial use), the energy environments and available solutions in those two countries would be very different. Hence, a matrix that places them in different categories is useful.

The other factor used in the demand side of the matrix is the degree of urbanization. In every nation where modernization and industrialization are initiated, people begin to leave the countryside and move into cities. Even though rapid urban growth has certain negative economic and social consequences, the amount of urbanization in a country remains one of the best indicators of its degree of modernization. This classification provides an indicator of the degree of industrial development, but more important, it indicates the amount and type of infrastructure development (e.g., roads and communication systems). Both are important factors in determining usage patterns for commercial energy.

To determine a country's energy supply statistics, the resource potentials were compared with a derived demand figure calculated by raising actual commercial energy consumption figures to a level where per capita commercial energy consumption is equal to the lowest level of those in the high urbanized group (actual consumption figures were used without adjustment for countries already in the high urbanized group). This was done to correct what could be a misleading conclusion that a country at an early stage of development with a low consumption figure might have sufficient energy resources to meet its current energy demands. However, it may fall short as development occurs and energy consumption rises significantly. (See the appendix for a country-by-country comparison of energy demands.)

Obviously, this approach has shortcomings. For one thing, many of the LDCs, especially the larger ones, are not internally homogenous. A country like Brazil, for example, could place one of its regions within each of the six categories. In other words, problems and solutions that apply to a country classified in the low energy consumption, resource poor category might be similar to a particular region within a country located in the high consumption, resource rich category. The second difficulty is the quality of data on the resource side. In many of the countries listed as resource poor, very little exploration of energy supplies has taken place and their resulting classification may be incorrect.

There are a number of similarities among the countries listed in Table 11-1. Almost all are plagued with relatively low life expectancies. People in East African nations, for example, have a life expectancy of forty-five years.[13] The comparable figure for Western Europe is seventy-nine. In spite of the short life span and high infant mortality rates in most LDCs, there are generally extremely high population growth rates. The rate for South America is 3 percent per year, while the figure for North America and Europe is about 0.5 percent. Most of the nations do not have transportation systems, communication devices, and sanitary and medical services adequate for their rapidly growing population. Energy is important in maintaining and expanding these services.

Another characteristic that affects energy needs and the strategies for these countries is the great diversity in income and infrastructure. Almost every LDC—even the most poverty stricken—has at least one or two urban areas where modern commercial energy is available and where services are provided that are similar to those in developed nations. Yet even LDCs classified in group I in the matrix will have a significant portion of their population without access to these modern services and with exceedingly low incomes. In these areas, whether they be urban slums or rural subsistence agriculture areas, human muscles with hand implements still dominate the energy picture. Water is still pumped and carried by hand; cooking is done on fires generated by wood, dung, or crop residues; transportation is by animal or by foot; and artificial light is generally provided by kerosene or fire.

CHARACTERISTICS OF HIGH ENERGY USE/URBANIZATION—GROUP I

Table 11-2 lists some of the basic statistics for each of the LDCs grouped according to the matrix in Table 11-1. Both the countries rich in energy resources and those poor in resources that fall into group I exhibit many similar characteristics. For example, they both have median per capita commercial energy consumptions of approximately 1,000 kilograms of coal equivalent (kce)[14] and 55 percent of the population lives in urban areas. The median per capita GNPs for

13. Thomas T. Kane and Paul F. Myers, *1978 World Population Data Sheet of the Population Reference Bureau, Inc.* Urban Population Percent Statistics (Washington, D.C.: Population Reference Bureau, 1978).

14. Beardsworth et al., *Energy Needs, Uses and Resources in Developing Countries.*

Table 11-2. Characteristics of Developing Countries.

Country	Per Capita GNP U.S. $[a]	PQL I[b]	Percent Urban Population	Per Capita Commercial Energy Consumption[c]
Energy Rich				
Highest Urbanization				
Turkey	990	54	45	630
Yugoslavia	1680	85	39	1930
Argentina	1550	84	80	1754
Brazil	1140	68	60	670
Colombia	630	71	64	671
Guyana	540	84	40	1114
Mexico	1090	75	64	1221
Peru	800	58	55	682
Trinidad and Tobago	2240	88	49	3132
South Korea	670	—	43	1038
Energy Rich				
Medium Urbanization (36-59 percent)				
Congo	520	25	40	209
Egypt	280	46	44	405
Eq. Guinea	330	28	45	101
Gabon	2590	21	32	—
Liberia	450	26	28	404
Mozambique	170	23	6	186
Rhodesia	550	42	19	—
Syria	290	33	20	—
Tunisia	840	44	50	447
Malaysia	860	59	27	552
Oman	2680	—	5	334
India	150	41	21	221
Bolivia	390	45	34	303
Costa Rica	1040	87	41	544
Nicaragua	750	53	49	479
Paraguay	640	74	37	153
Papua New Guinea	490	34	13	278
Energy Rich				
Low Urbanization (below 36 percent)				
Angola	330	15	18	74
Botswana	410	38	12	—
Cameroon	290	28	29	104
Central Republic Africa	230	18	36	34
Madagascar	200	—	16	71
Senegal	390	22	32	195
Swaziland	470	36	8	—
Upper Volta	110	17	4	20
Zaire	140	28	29	78
Afghanistan	160	19	15	52
Bangladesh	110	33	9	28
Pakistan	170	37	26	183
Energy Poor				
Highest Urbanization				
Cyprus	1480	87	42	1278
Lebanon	—	80	60	928

Table 11-2.   continued.

Country	Per Capita GNP U.S. $[a]	PQL I[b]	Percent Urban Population	Per Capita Commercial Energy Consumption[c]
Singapore	2700	85	100	2151
Taiwan	1070	88	63	693
Chile	1050	77	79	765
Jamaica	1070	87	41	1427
Panama	1310	81	50	865
Surinam	1370	85	50	2063
Uruguay	1390	88	83	942
Energy Poor				
Medium Urbanization				
Ivory Coast	610	28	20	366
Mauritius	680	75	44	279
Morocco	540	40	38	274
Zambia	440	28	36	504
Jordan	610	48	42	408
Philippines	410	73	32	326
Thailand	380	70	13	284
Dominican Republic	780	64	47	458
El Salvador	490	67	39	248
Guatemala	630	53	36	237
Honduras	390	50	31	232
Fiji	1150	83	38	582
Energy Poor				
Low Urbanization (below 36 percent)				
Benin	130	23	14	52
Burundi	120	23	2	13
Chad	120	20	14	29
Ethiopia	100	16	12	39
Gambia	180	22	16	66
Ghana	580	31	31	182
Guinea	150	20	20	92
Kenya	240	40	10	174
Lesotho	170	50	3	—
Malawi	140	29	10	56
Mali	100	15	13	25
Mauritania	340	15	23	108
Niger	160	14	9	35
Rwanda	110	27	4	14
Sierra Leone	200	29	15	116
Somalia	110	19	28	36
Southwest Africa				
Sudan				
Tanzania	180	28	7	70
Togo	260	28	15	65
Uganda	240	33	7	55
Nepal	120	25	4	10
Sri Lanka	200	83	22	127
Viet Nam, O.P.R.	—	60	22	—
Burma	120	51	22	51
Haiti	200	31	23	30

these groups ranges between $1,100 and $1,400.[15] They also have similar average physical quality of life indexes (PQLI) of 74-84.[16] However, differences appear on the energy supply side. The countries rich in energy resources import on the average 36 percent of their total commercial energy consumption, while the nations poor in resources import 88 percent.[17] This is the case even though much of the fossil fuel and hydro potential that exists in resource-abundant countries is relatively unexploited.

MEDIUM ENERGY USE/URBANIZATION
—GROUP II

The medium group of energy resource rich and poor countries also exhibits similar characteristics. A total of between 34 and 36 percent of their population lives in urban settings. The median GNPs for the groups are $520-540 and the average PQLI indexes fall between 40 and 50. Furthermore, the per capita energy consumption for both groups is approximately 300 kce. On the supply side, the energy resource—abundant countries import an average of 48 percent of their total commercial energy consumption while the resource poor import an average of 95 percent.

LOW ENERGY USE/URBANIZATION
—GROUP III

The low commercial energy use, urbanization groups have 90 percent of their real populations in rural settings and average a commercial energy per capita consumption of 70 kce. Although statistics are not available for verification, it is estimated that commercial energy use

15. Kane and Myers, *1978 World Population Data Sheet of the Population Reference Bureau, Inc.*
16. John W. Sewell et al., *The United States and World Development Agenda 1977* (New York: Praeger, 1977).
17. UNCTAD, *Handbook of International Trade and Development Statistics* (1976).

Source: Thomas Kane and Paul Myers, *1978 World Population Data Sheet of the Population Reference Bureau, Inc.* (Washington, D.C.: Population Reference Bureau); John W. Sewell, *The United States and World Development Agenda 1977* (New York: Praeger, 1977).
[a]1976-1975 data.
[b]PQLI = physical quality of life index.
[c]Kilograms of coal equivalent.

is only 10–30 percent of total consumption in these countries.[18] The median GNPs for these two groups are between $160 and $230, and PQLI indexes are between 28 and 30. With the exception of Nepal, Sri Lanka, Burma, Haiti, Yemen, and Viet Nam, all the resource poor countries in group III are in Africa.

ENERGY DEMAND PROJECTIONS

Commercial energy consumption in developing countries was approximately 9 million barrels per day equivalent in 1975 or 9 percent of the world's commercial energy consumed during that year. As mentioned earlier, these figures do not include noncommercial energy used in developing countries, and noncommercial energy use is significant. For example, in one study of India, these energy sources accounted for about 58 percent of the total energy consumption. This figure is even higher if animal draft energy is included among the noncommercial energy forms.[19] Therefore, to gain a truer perspective on energy consumption in countries like India, and probably other countries found in the medium energy use, urbanized category (group II), the commercial energy per capita use needs to be multiplied two to two and a half times. Since countries in the low group probably have from 60 to 90 percent of their energy supplied from noncommercial sources,[20] their commercial energy figures need to be multiplied three to nine times to accurately portray energy usage levels. Furthermore, group I countries probably obtain less than 50 percent of their energy from noncommercial sources, and so their figure would be multiplied one and one half to two times. However, this great uncertainty about baseline consumption levels in these countries is one of the factors that make generating energy projections so risky.

Another major factor affecting demand is the changing size of the industrial sector. Energy use per capita is likely to rise more rapidly than income as a whole if industrialization, especially energy-intensive industrialization, takes place. There have been indications that some developed countries will attempt to reduce their oil use by exporting energy-intensive industries to developing countries. However, in comparing developing countries with the developed nations, LDCs presently are found to be generally low producers of energy-intensive

18. D.E. Earl, *Forest Energy and Economic Development* (Oxford: Clarendon Press, 1975).

19. Howe et al., *Energy Problems of Developing Countries.*

20. Earl, *Forest Energy and Economic Development.*

materials.[21] It is likely that if there is a transition to energy-intensive industries, it will occur in those countries that are relatively energy rich. Hence, their energy consumption will probably grow considerably faster as they develop than those countries that are poor in energy resources.

ENERGY/GNP RATIO

One of the often discussed characteristics of energy in the industrialized nations is the relationship between energy consumption and GNP. The necessity of a one-to-one relationship of energy to GNP growth suggested by some analysts has pretty much been discounted because of the wide variance in GNP to energy consumption levels among highly industrialized nations. While there is generally an increase in per capita energy consumption as GNP rises, the differences are so great at almost every income level (energy consumption varies by a factor of three to five at almost every income), so as to render the statistic by itself more misleading than helpful in energy policy analysis.

Another element to be considered in making demand projections is how fast the shift from traditional fuels will take place. Table 11–3 shows the estimated commercial energy demand for the year 2000 provided by several recent studies that attempt to take such factors into consideration. The Workshop on Alternative Energy Strategies (WAES) and Strout projections use economic growth projections and energy GNP correlations as the basic tool for estimating future demands.[22] The Brookhaven projection utilizes sets of LDC country groups and places technical limits on the ability of an LDC to substitute alternative fuels for oil in any of its major energy sectors. This tends to reduce the demand projections compared with those of other studies. The Overseas Development Council (ODC) has added a twist to the recent projections by estimating the energy required to meet basic human needs in developing countries. Their estimates are two or three times as much as the Brookhaven projections and probably will not be achieved by LDCs. However, their analysis is significant in that it shows the incredible pressure that could be placed on oil as an energy source if third world countries are able to develop rapidly. Hence, ODC and others offer four alternative outcomes:

1. Developed countries might have to reduce their oil consumption to a greater extent than is economically prudent to allow for the

21. Beardsworth et al., *Energy Needs, Uses and Resources in Developing Countries.*
22. Wilson et al., *Energy Global Prospects 1985-2000.*

greatly expanded third world needs. Most would agree that this is highly unlikely.

2. LDCs will have to abandon their targets of rapid industrialization and substantial improvements in the quality of rural and urban life for their citizens.

3. Developing countries, realizing the hopelessness of significantly increasing their share of world oil, may seek to develop energy strategies that depend less on petroleum.[23]

4. Major new petroleum or other commercial fuel supplies will need to be found in many LDCs.

Great uncertainties surround these projections, including the transition toward industrialization, energy intensiveness of industry and mechanization of agriculture, the shift from traditional to modern fuel sources, and the growth in GNP. These uncertainties make judgment about the validity of the projections in Table 11–3 impossible. It does appear that energy demand in LDCs is supply-limited. Whether the eventual consumption rate in the year 2000 is in the range of 25–26 million barrels of oil equivalent per day as projected by Brookhaven and in the low WAES projection or, alternatively, is much higher, as indicated by the World Energy Conference and ODC, depends on the ability to obtain affordable energy supplies that support the development process.

ENERGY USE AND EFFICIENCY ALTERNATIVES

Future energy demand projections like those in Table 11–3 are often taken as immutable premises in LDC policy discussions. These projections in essence become goals that determine the amounts of supplies that must be secured. Seldom is much attention given to reducing demand through improving the efficiency of energy use. In each of the brief descriptions of energy use sectors below, attention is given to the opportunities for efficiency improvements. Conservation investments represent a rich source of energy in both the modern and traditional sectors between now and the year 2000. Because of its widespread applicability and the short lead times possible on some of the efficiency investments, conservation can make an even larger contribution to the energy needs of many LDCs than most, if not all, of the nonconventional energy supply alternatives.

23. James A. Bever, James W. Howe, William E. Knowland, and James J. Tarrant, "Energy for Developing Countries, A Report to the Rockefeller Foundation" (Washington, D.C., October 31, 1977), preliminary draft.

Table 11-3. Commercial Energy Demand Projections for the Year 2000.[a]

		Millions Barrels Per Day *Oil Equivalent*
WAES	High	35.6
	Low	26.5
Brookhaven		25.9
World Energy Conference		
Constrained		40
Unconstrained		50
Strout		38.7

[a]The WAES high projection assumes a constant oil price in 1975 dollars through 2000. Their low projection assumes a gradual increase to $17.50 per barrel in 1975 dollars. Brookhaven assumes the price will increase in real terms 50 percent by 1990 and 100 percent by 2000.

Rural

In developing countries, cooking accounts for most of the rural household energy use. In fact, in most rural settings, cooking accounts for 35-50 percent of the energy consumed.[24] Estimates indicate that more than half of the cooking needs are met with firewood, with the remainder supplied by charcoal, crop residues, cow dung, and in some countries, a commercial fuel such as kerosene. In the rural parts of India, Pakistan, and Bangladesh, for example, noncommercial or traditional fuels account for about 90 percent of the total household or domestic consumption,[25] which in turn accounts for 65 percent of total per capita energy use.[26] Firewood, which fuels the economies of most rural developing countries, is the poor man's oil.[27] In this situation, wood and other traditional or noncommercial fuels may be extremely expensive even though they never enter the market. Wood is now scarce in many countries, and families have to devote several man days per week to gathering sufficient quantities of wood for cooking fuel.[28]

The massive use of wood and its derivative, charcoal, have non-energy implications of great magnitude, a fact vividly portrayed by

24. Roger Revelle, in Norman Brown, ed., *Renewable Energy Resources and Rural Application in the Developing World* (Washington, D.C.: American Association for the Advancement of Science, 1977).

25. Beardsworth et al., *Energy Needs, Uses and Resources in Developing Countries.*

26. Howe et al., *Energy Problems of Developing Countries.*

27. Arjun Makhijani and Alan Poole, *Energy and Agriculture in the Third World* (Cambridge, Mass.: Ballinger, 1975).

28. Eric Eckholm, *Losing Ground: Environmental Stress and World Food Prospects* (New York: Norton, 1976).

Eric Eckholm in his monograph, "The Other Energy Crisis" and his book, *Losing Ground*.[29] Analysts find it difficult to pinpoint the exact cause of the scarcity of wood. It has been attributed to rapid rural population increases, high oil prices in urban areas that cause city dwellers to switch to wood or charcoal, and a per capita consumption increase among rural citizens. However, population pressure on the land is probably the major cause of deforestation, erosion, and the loss of rich agricultural land. This is not a problem isolated in any one group of developing countries. It has more or less reached crisis stage in South Asia, the Caribbean, African countries surrounding the Sahara, Central America, and the mountain countries of South America.[30]

Although data are limited, energy appears to be used inefficiently in the traditional sector. Use of wood for cooking in open fires is often cited as an example of significant inefficiency. Indeed, it does take three to six times more energy to cook a meal with wood in an open stove than it does to cook the same meal on a modern gas range in the United States.[31] However, the level of efficiency may be underestimated in certain cases where the fire is also used to provide ancillary benefits such as space heating, protection from animals and insects, light, and hot water. In spite of this, there is considerable room for improvement in cooking practice. Roger Revelle has indicated that two times more energy is required to cook a meal than is actually contained in the meal itself.[32] A study of Mexico City concludes that per capita energy consumption among the poor was lower in the city than it was in the rural areas.[33] One of the reasons for this is probably the relative efficiency of the commercial fuels available in cities as opposed to the traditional fuels used in the rural areas.

Urban

Table 11-4 lists the world's major LDC metropolitan growth areas, their 1978 population, and the expected increase by 1995. While these increases in city sizes may be inevitable, they are not necessarily desirable, and many countries are taking actions to slow migration to urban areas. To the extent that they are unsuccessful,

29. Ibid.; and Eric Eckholm, "The Other Energy Crisis" (Washington, D.C.: Worldwatch Institute, 1975).

30. Eckholm, *Losing Ground*.

31. Makhijani and Poole, *Energy and Agriculture in the Third World*.

32. Revelle; *Renewable Energy Resources and Rural Application in the Developed World*, Howe et al. *Energy Problems of Developing Countries*.

33. Richard L. Meiers, Sam Berman, and David Dowell "Urbanism and Energy in Developing Regimes," Report to Brookhaven National Laboratory (Berkeley, Calif., March 1, 1978).

Table 11-4. Population Projection for the World's Largest Metropolitan Growth Areas.

Urgan Region	1978 Population (in millions)	Settled Population to be Added to 1995 (in millions)[c]
"Paulo-Janeiro" (Sao Paulo, Rio de Janeiro)	21	22
Nile Delta (Cairo, Alexandria)	20	20
Mexico City	13	15
Calcutta (Kharaqpur, Haldia)	10	12
Shanghai	9	11
Bombay	8	11
Jakarta	7	11
Delhi	6	11
Manila	7	10
Karachi	4	9
Bangkok	4	8
"CalSouth" (Los Angeles-San Diego-Tijuana)	11	8
Moscow	12	8

Source: Edward Beardsworth, Samuel Hale, Jr., Robert Nathans, Philip F. Palmedo, et al., *Energy Needs, Uses and Resources in Developing Countries* (Upton, N.Y.: Policy Analysis Division, National Center for Analysis of Energy Systems—Brookhaven National Laboratory Associated Universities, 1978).
[a]Populations in 1978 are subtracted from those anticipated in 1995, with appropriate adjustments for megalopolis formation, and rounded to the nearest million.

the energy implications for LDCs are significant. Energy use in these rapidly expanding cities is principally commercial in nature. Table 11-5 provides information for Mexico City on the uses of energy, including that consumed in public services and transportation. Mexico is in the high urbanization, industrialization category (group I). Hence, a higher percentage of its energy consumption tends to be commercial fuels, especially for the urban poor, than would be the case with developing countries within groups II or III. But in every country, the urban poor tend to use considerably more commercial energy than their rural countrymen. In spite of this use of commercial energy, the slums of most cities in developing countries are without the basic energy services for household use or business.

On the other hand, the middle and upper income groups in LDC urban settings use energy in ways surprisingly similar to comparable groups in the developed world. In other words, energy use by the urban affluent in LDCs is very similar to that of urbanites in developed countries.[34]

34. Howe et al., *Energy Problems of Developing Countries.*

Table 11–5. Per Family Energy Consumption for Mexico City (Btu $\times$ 10^6).

Fuel Use Categories	*0–1,000*	*1,000– 2,500*	*2,500– 5,000*	*5,000– 10,000*	*10,000 or more*
Food	12.5	19.	27.	40.8	57.8
Transportation	5.9	27.	68.	145.	223.
Residential Uses	22.7	27.9	32.6	51.4	58.6
Cooking	10.0	9.8	10.0	10.0	10.0
Water heat	8.6	7.9	6.2	13.9	18.1
Lighting	2.0	4.3	5.4	7.6	10.0
Appliances	2.1	5.9	9.7	17.6	18.0
Heating	—	—	1.3	2.4	2.6
Public Services	3.7	7.5	9.0	9.6	10.5
Lighting	—	3.4	4.2	4.2	4.2
Water pumping	0.7	1.0	1.5	1.9	2.8
Garbage collection	0.1	0.2	0.4	0.6	0.6
Schools, offices, hospitals	2.9	2.9	2.9	2.9	2.9
Housing	3.3	13.2	19.4	26.8	33.9
Total	48	95	158	272	382
Households $\times$ 10^3	375.4	989.7	500.5	250.3	159.3

Source: "Urban Energy Use Patterns in Developing Countries: A Preliminary Study of Mexico City." Prepared by Gordon McGranahan and Manuel Taylor, Urban and Policy Sciences, State University of New York at Stony Brook, p. 54.

Note: These data apply to the consumption of energy embodied in the various fuel use categories.

Opportunities for efficiency improvements abound in the urban sector. Steel and glass buildings account for 10–20 percent of the commercial energy consumption in cities. The construction of these buildings was often influenced by Western architects whose designs reflect low energy prices of times past. However, there may be opportunity for building retrofits, (e.g., insulation and heating and cooling system controls) to improve the efficiency of these structures.

Even more potential for conservation exists in new buildings. In an LDC city growing at 6 percent per year, 60–70 percent of the residential and commercial buildings that exist in the year 2005 will be built after 1975. U.S. studies indicate that buildings can be cost effectively constructed to be two to three times more energy efficient than they were prior to 1973. LDCs might consider standards or other methods to ensure energy-efficient new buildings, even if initial construction costs are greater.

Food Production

Food production is crucial to the development process. A non-oil-exporting economy that cannot feed its rural farm population as well as its teachers, road builders, doctors, researchers, and government workers from indigenous sources will find economic development extremely difficult.

There are numerous reasons why many LDCs are having difficulties meeting the minimum nutritional needs of their people (e.g., population pressure on the land, lack of technical skills, lack of incentive because of land ownership, insufficient credit). Energy is also a major factor, and energy-based fertilizers, pest controls, and fuel for transporting crops to market are also important. Moreover, there is a need to find energy to reduce the labor peaks that occur in subsistence agriculture, especially at planting and harvesting times. Without energy-fueled technologies, massive amounts of human labor are needed during these concentrated periods. However, during the remainder of the year, the laborers cannot find work. Also, the peak labor phenomenon encourages people to have large families to cope with such intense labor needs and thus adds to overpopulation problems. Energy to run tractors can reduce these labor needs during critical times of the year. Maybe even more important is energy to run irrigation pumps that will allow a second or third crop and spread the labor requirement more evenly throughout the year. In addition, present subsistence agriculture may also be energy inefficient. Makhijani and Poole estimate that it takes three times more energy to produce a ton of rice in a developing country like India than it does in the United States.[35]

Transportation

Transportation, so critical to development, is inadequate in most LDCs. The use of energy to transport goods and people, especially in rural areas, will have to increase for modernization to occur. It is the most difficult sector to deal with from an energy perspective. With the possible exception of Brazil's use of methanol from wood and crop residues, no adequate substitute for petroleum-based fuels exists to supply motor vehicles. This is why LDCs in the low urbanization, energy use category (group III) can require as much as 40–60 percent of their commercial energy budget for the transportation sector.[36]

Efficiency improvements in this sector will be difficult, but there is room for improvement, especially within cities. Rapid urban growth provides an opportunity for national land use planning that locates production facilities, residential areas, and markets in ways that reduce the need for scarce transportation fuels. This is, of course,

35. Makhijani and Poole, *Energy and Agriculture in the Third World.*
36. Conversation with Lawrence Ervin based on his research at Donovan, Hamester and Rattien, Inc.

a difficult task in the environment of uncontrolled migration that presently exists in many LDCs.

Another dimension of the transportation problem worth discussing stems from consideration of system versus vehicle productivity. There is an obvious trade-off to be made between an efficient vehicle that requires imported oil and less efficient vehicles that can use domestic coal or lignite. The trade-off becomes less clear when system efficiencies are considered, particularly during periods of growth. For example, a country having a supply of coal might adopt policies aimed at the development of a transportation network that is predominately electrified rail rather than highway. At maturity, such a network could be superior to a highway network in terms of both economic and energy productivity. At the early stages, however, the low transportation demand would not justify electrification on either basis. A staging strategy that included, during the early period, a very inefficient vehicle—for example, coal-fired steam—might be justified.[37] This transition or staging problem is a complication that arises in all sectors.

Industry

The industrial sectors of many LDCs use energy in a fashion similar to industrialized sectors in the developed world. They have the same need for steam, motor power, and process heat, primarily because their manufacturing processes and operating systems are usually designed in developed nations. Hence, even without detailed studies of efficiency, one can assume that current use is probably as inefficient—if not more so—than it is in the developed nations.

The opportunity for future improvements in efficiency is even greater in LDCs, however, since their industrial sectors are growing more rapidly. If present trends continue, 60–70 percent of the industrial plants and equipment in the year 2000 will be installed after 1978. Programs should be considered that improve industrial energy efficiency. New plants and equipment should be designed and installed with the future realities of high energy prices in mind. Consideration should also be given to steering development away from energy-intensive industries, especially in nations with poor energy resources, unless they can be shown to be competitive on the world market despite high cost imported energy. The opportunities for improving energy productivity in the new industrial sectors of these countries should be given top priority.

37. Conversation with Richard H. Shackson.

ENERGY SUPPLY ALTERNATIVES

Supply alternatives are even more country-specific than demand alternatives. Options that may be appropriate for one country will not necessarily apply to another because of topography, climate, and indigenous resources. The supply strategies of those LDCs in Table 11-1 classified as rich in energy resources will probably be very different from those in the other group. Generally, however, the situation in most LDCs demands that any promising alternative be explored for potential local application in spite of barriers that may be associated with its implementation.

Many supply alternatives have potentially negative environmental consequences. Deforestation problems associated with firewood use, safety concerns with nuclear, ecological difficulties with hydro, and CO_2 problems with coal all become issues when discussing supply strategies. However, the energy environmental concerns are usually secondary to energy productivity concerns and are not typically a barrier to developing energy resources.

Oil and Gas

Oil has become the primary source of energy. Almost every LDC has depended on oil to fuel its development process regardless of indigenous supplies of alternative energy sources. As pointed out earlier, this trend may have to change in the years ahead.

Because of domestic oil supplies, some LDCs can depend on oil much longer than others. The WAES study, for example, projects annual production of oil from non-OPEC LDCs to increase from 3.5 million barrels per day to 6–12 mbd by 1985, but it estimates that three developing countries, Mexico, Brazil, and Egypt, could account for as much as 40 percent of the total production. This oil will obviously benefit these three countries. However, it is not likely to have a major impact on other developing nations, since any exported oil would probably go to developed countries at high world market prices.

On the other hand, reliable estimates of actual oil reserves in LDCs are not available. Table 11-6 illustrates the striking difference in drilling density between developed countries such as the United States and LDCs such as the Congo. There are an estimated thirteen million square miles of potential petroleum-yielding areas in non-OPEC developing countries (compared with three million in the United States and four million in OPEC countries). Yet the number of wells drilled per square mile of potential petroleum acreage in

Table 11-6. Drilling Density in Oil-exporting LDCs.

	Petroleum Prospective Area (thousand square miles)	Wells Drilled to End of 1977 (thousands)	Wells per Prospective Square Mile	Percent of U.S. Density
Mexico	435	18.6	0.04	5
Oman	60	0.5	0.008	1
Tunisia	83	0.3	0.004	0.4
Egypt	355	1.4	0.004	0.5
Malaysia	91	0.4	0.004	0.6
Syria	40	0.3	0.008	1
Angola	45	0.6	0.013	2
Trinidad-Tobago	13	9.2	0.71	90
Congo	31	0.1	0.003	0.4
Bolivia	254	0.9	0.004	0.5
Bahrain	0.3	0.2	0.67	85

Source: Gordian Associates, Inc., Washington, D.C.

LDCs is only a small percentage of the U.S. drilling density. For example, in Africa, the density is 0.01 percent of the U.S. total, while in Latin America it is only 3 percent. Strategies to increase drilling rates will benefit both LDCs in energy rich categories and those in energy poor groupings. Unfortunately, for the less endowed nations, the major benefits are likely to go to countries already classified as energy rich, primarily because finding rates in those nations are generally higher than those in the resource poor group.

In addition, in a number of the non-OPEC LDCs natural gas is geographically located in roughly the same distribution pattern as oil. However, much of it is located far from population centers, thus requiring investment in capital-intensive pipeline systems to bring the gas to market. Only in those countries such as Mexico, Egypt, and perhaps Argentina that have both a large supply of natural gas and substantial domestic urban markets is the development of gas as a major supplier of energy foreseeable.

Coal

Coal is the forgotten fuel in the LDC energy picture. Exploration for this energy source has been almost nonexistent until recently. Only in India and Korea are significant amounts of coal used. Only 10 percent of the world's known resources are in LDCs, and 94 percent of these are in India and China. However coal does exist elsewhere in both high and low grade deposits, and a recent study by the International Energy Agency advocates the substitution of coal for oil on a massive scale to balance energy requirements with supplies over the next two decades.[38]

One of the problems with coal is that the technology for producing and using it was developed in the Western nations under very different conditions than exist in LDCs. For example, the extraction technology for coal is geared to high labor costs and large high grade coal deposits. Large central plants have been designed to convert the resource to useful energy. None of these technologies may be particularly appropriate for developing countries. In addition, there is the question of finding the capital to develop the necessary transportation system and infrastructure. New ways to produce and consume coal are needed if LDCs are to exploit this and similar resources to their fullest economic extent.

Electricity

For the most part, electricity is not a source of energy, but is generated by the sources of fuel discussed in this section, on either a centralized or a decentralized basis. Electricity is also considered to be a central part of any development effort. It not only can provide light, communication systems, and refrigeration to villages, but also can increase productivity by providing shaft power to pump or grind and to perform other similar functions. During the past twenty years, much of the focus in development aid has been on electrification projects. Since electricity is so versatile, annual growth during the past ten years in LDCs has been just under 10 percent per year. Estimates show that the demand for electricity will grow at a rate of 11 percent annually in the years ahead.[39] A note of caution is appropriate in the face of this expected demand. Even though conventional wisdom is that electricity plays a major role in developments, it may not be the cheapest way to meet significant portions of LDC energy needs.

In spite of major efforts in rural electrification, only 12 percent of the people in developing countries live in areas that have been provided with electricity. This average includes a range of figures from 4 percent in sub-Sahara Africa to 15 percent in Asia, North Africa, and the Middle East, to 23 percent in Latin America.[40] If the trends of the past fifteen years are followed, the Overseas

38. International Energy Agency, *The Electricity Supply Industry in OECD Countries* (Paris: OECD, 1978).

39. Beardsworth et al., *Energy Needs, Uses and Resources in Developing Countries.*

40. A World Bank Paper, *Rural Electrification,* October 1975.

Development Council predicts that only 25 percent of the people living in LDC rural areas in 2000 will reside in villages that are connected to an electric grid.[41] This does not mean that they will use electricity in their home or workplace, only that they will reside in a village that has access to the energy source. The situation for other fuels such as gasoline or diesel would probably not be much better. Even if electricity and other commercial fuels were available, it is unlikely that most people in the rural areas could afford to put them to use.

Hydro

Generally, water power is the most attractive source of electricity in developing countries (44 percent of all LDC electricity is generated by hydropower). LDCs contain 70 percent of all the world's major hydro potential, with only a small fraction of this energy source exploited. However, the development of dams and related facilities depends on more than just topography. Hydro sites need to be close to population centers or industries requiring electricity. Dam sites can also be limited by navigational needs. In addition, the length of time required to build hydroelectric facilities with their accompanying distribution network may discourage many developing countries from such projects.

Hydro is unique among major supply options in that the rationale for its installation may result more from the desire to control floods and irrigation than to provide power. In such cases, power may be only a by-product used to help finance the project. In any case, where appropriate sites do exist, major hydro can be an attractive energy source.

Nuclear

Nuclear energy in LDC development is even more complicated than in places such as the United States. It is faced with the problems of high foreign exchange and capital requirements, the need for skilled personnel, uncertainty of enriched uranium supply, and safety risks. More important, however, is the size of the interconnected electric grid that must exist before a nuclear plant is technically feasible. For example, most experts believe a single generating source (e.g., one nuclear plant) should supply only 10-15 percent of the electricity for a grid. The smallest plant now available has a capacity of 600 megawatts. Thus, following the 10-15 percent rule, a nation or group of nations should have an interconnected

41. Conversations with Jim Howe.

electric grid of 5,000–6,000 megawatts (MW) before a nuclear plant would be technically feasible. Only six non-OPEC LDC countries appear to have interconnected grids of this size (Brazil, Mexico, India, Taiwan, Argentina, and Pakistan),[42] although ten to twenty nations could have interconnected grids as large as 5,000–6,000 MW by the year 2000. There is some possibility that a smaller plant (e.g., 400 MW) could be developed, but questions remain about its economic viability. No cost figures for a smaller plant are available, but the current trend has been toward larger plants for economic reasons. Under these conditions, development of economic smaller plants does not appear encouraging.[43] In general, the nuclear option is worth serious consideration only by a few LDCs, primarily those in group I.

Biogas

Organic wastes that contain carbon and oxygen can be used to produce biogas, principally methane, for use as an energy source. As part of the process, nitrogen is produced as a fertilizer. Biogas development has taken place principally in India and China. In India, biogas units are fueled primarily by cow dung. In China, Smil estimates that there are more than four million biogas units.[44] The gas is used primarily for cooking and lighting. Consequently, biogases from both dung and waste vegetation appear useful for rural settings. Their eventual widespread application awaits large-scale demonstrations and commercialization projects throughout the LDC world.

Fuel Wood

In some countries, especially those blessed with tropical forests, it is technically feasible to supply much of the energy requirements from the forest. Earl calculated that only 10 percent of the tropical forest in Africa would provide enough fuel to meet the household needs of that continent for the next twenty years.[45] Again, however, there are great differences among the resources available. In those energy poor countries where forests are rapidly disappearing, a major effort is needed to increase the supply of wood, not for fuel purposes only, but to maintain the productivity of the land

42. U.S. Office of Technology Assessment, 1978.

43. Private discussion with Philip F. Palmedo, Brookhaven National Laboratories.

44. Vaclaw, Smil, "China Claims Lead in Biogas Energy Supply," *Energy International*, June 1974.

45. Earl, *Forest Energy and Economic Development.*

so severely threatened by deforestation. In those places blessed with abundant forests, such as Brazil and tropical Africa, these resources can provide substantial amounts of energy to support modernization.

Minihydro

While centralized large-scale hydro has a number of drawbacks mentioned in the previous section, the same problems are not as acute with minihydro developments. Decentralized hydro installations have excellent potential for providing electrical power for irrigation and lighting and other applications of village and rural use within LDCs. The infrastructure requirements are much less for these kinds of installations, and appropriate sites are abundant.[46] The cost for minihydro range from as low as estimates of 6-7 mills per kilowatt to 45-100 mills.[47] Even at the higher levels, however, this source of electricity would be competitive in many situations in LDCs and should be considered as a source especially by resource poor countries.

Other Renewables

Two other renewable resources that have potential are wind and direct solar energy. Wind energy—especially to pump water and to generate electricity—has promise in areas where there is consistent wind of over 10 kilometers per hour. Unfortunately, dependence on wind energy is limited because of its irregularity in time and velocity. Much more data and research are required to determine economic and technical applicability of wind power in LDC settings. Because of its site-specific nature, widespread application will probably progress slowly.

The technology receiving the most attention over the past several years is direct solar. Because of the overwhelming need for cooking fuel in developing countries, the possibility of using solar energy for cooking has become immensely popular. Unfortunately, the demonstrations to date have been largely unsuccessful.[48] However, it is important to remember that these demonstrations have been

46. Beardsworth et al., *Energy Needs, Uses and Resources in Developing Countries.*
47. David French, "Renewable Energy for Africa: Needs, Opportunities, Issues," prepared for AFR/DR/SDP U.S. Agency for International Development (Washington, D.C., July 14, 1978).
48. J.D. Walton, Jr., A.H. Roy, and S.H. Bomar, Jr., *A State of the Art Survey of Solar Powered Irrigation Pumps, Solar Cookers, and Wood Burning Stoves in Sub-Sahara Africa* (Atlanta: Georgia Institute of Technology, January 1978).

few in number, narrow in scope, and poorly designed. But until technology advances to the state where there is some kind of storage system that will allow cooking indoors and when the sun is not shining (cloudy days, early morning, and nights), solar cooking will remain limited in use. Thermal solar technologies may have more agricultural potential in pumping water and supplying low grade heat for crop drying. Even with the addition of these applications, however, thermal solar technologies are not likely to become a major source of energy during the next thirty years.

Photovoltaic cells hold greater promise for widespread use than thermal technologies if cost reductions continue on their present course. Even now they are competitive for isolated installations such as telephone and other communication systems. They also have the desirable attributes of operational simplicity and almost no maintenance. The U.S. Department of Energy has estimated that costs will decrease by a factor of 10 to 50 cents a peak watt by 1985. If this happens, photovoltaics could become a major source of electric power to villages and rural areas of LDCs.

When reviewing these technologies, there is a tendency to become enamored of one or more of them simply because the technology is workable in the LDC context or the resource is available. The critical question we must continue to ask, however, is: Which source of energy (from the supply or demand side) or mix of sources meets the needs of the particular LDC at the minimum total cost? Appropriate technologies and abundant energy resources are not ends in themselves. The crucial question is: Which system delivers the needed energy services to the consumer at the least cost?

LDC ENERGY PROPOSALS

Objectives

Evaluating the demand and supply alternatives to form conclusions about LDC energy futures must be done in the context of other development issues and objectives. At least seven development-related objectives can be used to measure the effectiveness of potential energy programs:

1. Provide adequate energy supplies to meet the basic human needs of all the nation's people;
2. Increase national independence and improve national security;
3. Provide energy for industrial, commercial, and agricultural development;

4. Protect the environment and maintain the productivity of agricultural lands;
5. Apply energy resources to maximize employment;
6. Design energy supplies to reduce the rate of urbanization and/or the number of people emigrating from the nation; and
7. Save precious foreign exchange by reducing oil imports.

Each LDC will weigh the importance of these objectives differently. For example, country X, a resource poor nation in group III suffering from deforestation, may rank objective 4 as most important, while country Z in group I may place more importance on objective 3. Another country may at the moment be in transition from group III to group II, and the time factor could be critical to its objectives. These differences in developing priorities could be major determinants in the country's eventual energy strategies. Again, country X might concentrate on regenerating wood supplies and the adoption of more efficient cookstoves. Country Z might focus on a major hydro development to provide electricity for several of its urban and industrial centers. Each country needs to weigh its own objectives and to design energy policies and programs that best reflect these priorities.

Policy and Actions

The alternatives for attacking LDC energy problems are enmeshed in difficulties. Thus, identifying actions that will even partially overcome the dilemma facing these countries is a formidable task. This section first outlines some generic actions required to ameliorate the energy situation in developing countries and, second, suggests possible U.S. actions for implementing those alternatives.

Development of Energy Policy Institutions. Throughout the chapter, references have been made to the need for better assessments of individual LDC energy problems. As important as energy is in developing countries, it has not become the major subject of debate within those countries that it has in industrial nations.[49] Food, agriculture, and related development problems continue to hold first priority among LDC policy analysts and planners. There are relatively few scholars and even fewer high level government planners and managers spending time and money in analyzing systematically the energy futures of their countries. This is a problem both for

49. Conversations with I. Abdel Rahman.

these countries and for developed nations who are interested in meshing their own energy policies with those of LDCs.

In most LDCs, an institutional capacity needs to be created to perform this role. Policymakers and planners should be trained and institutions developed and supported. It is important that the policy systems developed be integrated with policymaking and operating units that are responsible for the nation's economic and development activities.

Also, each LDC should have the capacity to undertake extensive data collection efforts and to analyze energy use and resources. Unfortunately, most developing countries would find it difficult to finance and staff such programs. Consequently, LDCs require assistance from international organizations and wealthier countries like the United States to support their energy research efforts. Also, it is necessary to finance training of energy policymakers and to create mechanisms for the exchange of policy information and expertise among developing countries. Finally, methodologies should be developed that LDCs could apply to their own energy situations and thus enable them to better understand the relationship between their development strategies and energy.

Development and Demonstration of New Demand and Supply Alternatives.   Many unanswered questions remain regarding the potential for more efficient energy use and new approaches to energy supply. For example, how much can be saved through the redesign of transportation systems, the revamping of manufacturing processes, the introduction of more efficient cookstoves, or the cost-effective retrofit of commercial buildings? Furthermore, what specific actions and technologies are cost-effective in achieving efficiency gains? Far too little investigation into these areas has taken place. For example, in the Caribbean nation of St. Lucia, an international organization gave a significant grant to assess the geothermal energy potential for the country. The study found sufficient resources to provide 1 megawatt or one-tenth of the country's electric needs, a considerable resource. In this tourism-dominated country, however, 60 percent of the electricity is consumed by the hotel industry. Since most of the hotels were constructed prior to the fourfold increase in oil prices, they are excellent candidates for efficiency improvements. A 16 percent increase (experience in the United States indicates retrofit savings often exceed 25 percent) in efficiency in these hotels alone would save an amount equal to the 1 megawatt of power generated by exploiting the geothermal source. This does not in any way argue against developing the geothermal resource. It does suggest that institutions or nations that provide assistance funds for energy studies should look beyond the supply side to the resources produced through efficiency gains.

More research and extensive demonstrations are needed on innovative building designs, the incorporation of passive solar techniques, and the need for building standards in the modern sector. Demonstrations of more energy-efficient techniques should also be sought in the industrial, rural, agricultural, and transportation sectors. In the latter case, experiments in urban planning might be undertaken to reduce the need for travel, especially in group I and II countries that have rapidly growing cities.

New supply technologies, especially renewable resources for rural villages and food production, have much the same need for experimentation and development. What sources of renewable energy or packages of renewable alternatives do villagers determine to be most suitable? What barriers exist to penetrating and utilizing these resources? The answers to questions such as these will require large-scale research and demonstration programs, especially in group II and III countries where a significant part of the population lives in rural areas. These should be carried out by developing countries with the financial and technical assistance of international organizations and countries such as the United States.

Numerous small demonstrations or isolated installations of new energy technologies are currently underway or are being planned, although few important studies or demonstrations are looking at improvements in end use efficiency. Several units within the United Nations, the World Bank, foundations like the al Dir'iyyah Institute and Rockefeller Foundation, AID, OECD nations, and other private organizations are supporting such activities. In addition, private companies are engaged in related projects. Solarex, the world's leading manufacturer of photovoltaic cells, has over one hundred installations in LDCs.[50]

The primary attention of many of these institutions focuses on renewable resources for rural and agricultural use. Unfortunately, there is no mechanism currently in operation for coordinating these efforts. Also, there is no consistent evaluation plan that could provide comparable information about the various research projects. James Howe of the Overseas Development Council and others have called for a method of correcting this problem. In addition, the

---

50. Private discussions with Jay A. Conger, Solarex Corporation, at the Stanley Strategy for Peace Conference held at Airlie House, October 5-7, 1978.

Bonn summit of 1978 resulted in an agreement among the countries involved to coordinate their research support for renewable energy in LDCs. Although there may be an existing institution that can perform the role needed in this area, it is not easily identifiable. What is probably needed is a new international organization on renewable energy and efficiency improvements. The organization would attempt to (1) coordinate research and demonstration activities on renewable resources and efficient use; (2) establish common evaluation procedures for such tests and demonstrations; (3) collect and disseminate information about new activities in these areas and evaluate results of ongoing work; (4) organize and support regional R & D centers on LDC energy to reduce the amount of duplication that is already beginning to appear and will certainly expand in the years ahead; (5) provide technical and financial assistance to all countries on renewable energy supplies and efficient uses; and (6) serve as an advocate for action and an information exchange for these areas.

Such an organization would require broad support. Both policy leadership and its technical staff should include representatives of the academic community, LDCs, OECD countries, international organizations, and private industry. It is especially important to involve industry representatives, since they hold much of the technical information on both the supply and demand issues and also will have a major role in the eventual financing and marketing of innovations.

It is possible that action to launch such an organization could come from the United Nations 1981 Conference on Renewable Energy Resources. It is hoped that steps to organize some of the functions outlined above can take place before that time.

Implementation. In the United States, once a policy direction has been established and the viability of an action proven, mechanisms exist that will allow the innovation to penetrate the market. Financing can usually be obtained through the private sector, and the technical expertise and other necessary infrastructure is already in place. Often this is not the case in developing countries. The capital financing burden for energy facing LDCs, for example, is immense. One study estimated that oil exploration alone in oil-importing countries would require $10-14 billion between 1977 and 1980.[51] The financial needs for efficiency improvements and eventually for renewable energy supplies are also likely to be large.

51. Conversations with Ishrat Usmani, United Nations, New York, New York, 1978.

Much of the financial resources needed to explore for conventional fuels and make efficiency improvements will have to come from multinational corporations and private banks. Those funds are not likely to flow freely enough to meet the needs, unless guarantees exist that reduce the risks associated with political and economic instability in many LDCs. This is especially true for inherently risky investments such as wildcatting for oil. The financing problem will probably be more acute for those countries in the medium and low industrialized groups (II and III), especially those that have few energy resources. Their interaction with multinational corporations and their access to international financial markets have been considerably less than those in the other groups. It is possible that a new international financing and guarantee institution may be necessary to deal with this problem, but a good case can be made that the World Bank can perform these roles effectively. The bank should be urged to continue its move into energy investments not now in its portfolio. Recently, the bank moved tentatively into financing oil and gas development (e.g., $159 million for India's Bombay High). Even more important, however, may be the newly announced financing of oil and gas exploration. A five year, $3 billion program is planned to provide poorer developing countries with low interest loans designed to spur oil and gas exploration and development. Slightly over $2 billion of the program would be used to develop known oil and gas resources and just over $0.5 billion for appraisal drilling and geophysical and geological surveys. This is a difficult area for the bank not only because of the risks, but also because of the problems involved in developing an equitable system that will benefit both countries who use their own national oil companies for exploration work and those who contract with multinational corporations. Despite the difficulties, the bank should advance further in these directions for conventional fuels, for efficiency improvements, and for renewable energy sources. Several fuel wood projects are already underway (e.g., Turkey and Niger) and ten to twelve others are under consideration. Searches are underway for other small-scale renewable projects, but much more should be done.

Because it is presumed that an LDC cannot afford to default and ruin its credit worthiness with the bank, any project in which the bank participates automatically provides a kind of guarantee for private financing sources, thus opening the door to LDCs for private sector funds.

Another financing issue concerns consumer finance. The Ford Motor Company several years ago abandoned a promising program to produce a very simple walk-behind farm tractor for LDC applications. Tests had shown that the tractor was more economical than a horse, could be operated and maintained by unsophisticated owners, could be supplied with service and spare parts in remote locations, but could not be financed. Even though potential buyers had annual cash incomes more than adequate to pay for the machine over its useful life, there were no institutions willing and/or able to lend money for purchase. Some of the energy technologies, especially those on the demand side, may need consumer financing.[52]

Financing, of course, is only one of the implementation barriers to be overcome once the feasibility of an alternative energy action has been demonstrated. Penetrating the LDC with new energy sources or demand innovations is not an easy task. Public and private efforts to accomplish this end need to be researched and tested. Development of extension services, the use of national and international volunteers, and the role of the individual entrepreneur and industry all deserve consideration. In this respect, those countries in the high urbanized industrial group can probably rely more on utilizing entrepreneurs and structured market mechanisms while those in other groups may need to look more to other means.

Raising Awareness

As mentioned above, the level of consciousness about the energy problems and possible solutions is not very high in most LDCs. Even in areas where some individual organizations do exist (usually in the research-academic community) their views do not often reach the political leadership or top government managers and policymakers.

Equally distressing is the lack of understanding in places like the United States about the energy problems of developing countries. The absence of accurate perceptions about the energy situation can lead to inappropriate policy responses, inaction, or indifference.

In both the United States and LDCs, major efforts need to be undertaken to educate and to instill a sense of urgency. This is essential if the problems are to be addressed and overcome. International dialogues on the subject like those recently sponsored by the Rockefeller Foundation in Brazil and the process initiated by the Aspen Institute and the al Dir'iyyah Institute may help. The UN conference on renewables will also highlight the problem, but much more is necessary.

52. Conversations with Richard H. Shackson.

U.S. Response

The U.S. domestic and foreign policies that affect the LDC energy situation are too numerous to discuss individually. They involve everything from AID assistance strategy to domestic education curriculum. In addition, most of the policies involving the United States and LDCs have implications for energy only as a part of a more comprehensive package. However, in response to LDC needs, the United States should consider action in the following eight areas:

1. **Support Energy Research and Demonstrations in LDCs.** General assistance to LDCs has diminished from 0.6 percent of GNP in the 1960s to less than 0.3 percent in 1978. Thus, energy assistance funds are competing for a shrinking pie. Nevertheless, energy is one issue common to LDCs and the United States. Assistance in supporting the needed research and demonstrations described above is important because of the useful information obtained by both parties. Although there are undoubtedly situations in which this financial support can best be provided bilaterally (e.g., to countries in the highest urbanization group who have more difficulty obtaining assistance through international organizations because of their higher income levels), much of this aid should be funneled through international institutions, particularly the United Nations Development Program and the World Bank. These institutions are in a better position than the U.S. government to serve the energy needs of most of the countries in the medium and low urbanized industrialized groups. The United States should increase its support to the bank and urge it to move in the directions recommended earlier. With regard to the wealthier LDCs, the new U.S. Foundation for International Technological Cooperation might prove to be a good vehicle for providing technological assistance and open scientific energy exchanges.

2. **Speed Implementation of a Domestic Energy Strategy that Minimizes Energy Costs by Choosing Those Technologies from Either the Demand or Supply Side That Are Most Cost-Effective in Meeting Energy Requirements.** This will require more emphasis on eliminating the market barriers (such as artificially low prices) that hinder energy-conserving actions. Energy demand and supply options need to be placed on an equal competitive footing. Such a strategy will be likely to result in considerable gains in efficiency. A 10 percent gain in U.S. energy efficiency could theoretically free

supplies sufficient to increase resources available to LDCs by nearly 40 percent.

3. Shift Substantial Energy Research and Demonstration Dollars into Renewables, Efficiency Improvements, and New Ways to Produce and Consume Conventional Fuels that would be Attractive to LDCs. Exports to LDCs have grown at 12 percent per year since 1960. Much of the U.S.'s future economic strength lies in its ability to serve these emerging world markets with technical innovations and services. Its comparative advantage in this area, however, will slip away without a foundation of appropriate research. Almost all government effort at present is focused on systems too large for most of the LDC markets (e.g., large nuclear reactors and/ or breeders). Also, government action does not consider the labor and capital situations in those environments. The United States is thus missing a good opportunity to aid its economic future and at the same time to join with the LDCs in their energy struggle.

4. Incorporate Renewables into the U.S. Energy System. The United States should pursue a special course to allow economically attractive renewable energy resources to penetrate its own markets. Beyond the demonstration stage, it is important that LDCs who watch the United States for leadership see renewables and efficient uses of energy making inroads within the U.S. market.

5. Involve Non-OPEC LDCs in Energy Negotiations. Two relatively closed clubs have existed in the world of energy—one in nuclear and the other in petroleum. Most non-OPEC nations are excluded from both. They are seldom included in either producer or consumer discussions on oil. However, many are producers and are increasing in importance as consumers, especially energy rich countries in the high and medium industrialized groups. In addition, the nuclear circle of nations has become even tighter, with the expressed purpose of limiting weapon proliferation. Leaving LDCs out of discussions about the future of nuclear power, its applicability, technical developments, safeguards, waste disposal, and safety problems probably increases rather than decreases the potential negative implications of expanding nuclear power. The International Nuclear Fuel Cycle Evaluation effort, which includes LDCs, is a start at correcting this situation, but other initiatives might also be considered. In addition, the United States should clarify its policy position on nuclear power. An estimated ten to twenty nations may have interconnected electric power grids of sufficient size to be candidates for a nuclear plant by the year 2000. Each country will have to assess the applicability and economic attractiveness of nuclear energy to its own situation. Attempts to keep an energy source used extensively in the developed world away from a LDC that desires it are both arrogant and hopeless.

6. Avoid Separate DOE-AID Assistance Programs. Energy is important to development, but is only one element in a complex set of issues. We should not impose the U.S. penchant for creating single function organizations on LDCs by creating a separate energy assistance program within the Department of Energy that is operated by individuals outside the overall development assistance framework. This option is not being pursued actively at present but remains a subtle thrust of some government energy specialists. Energy specialists should be involved in information exchanges and technical assistance efforts, but only under the organizational umbrella of the comprehensive U.S. assistance effort.

7. Use Energy-Efficient Principles in Overseas Buildings and Operations. In the past, the United States has built and operated its showcase buildings (embassies, official residences, and some military installations) without regard to energy considerations. New buildings were typically designed by U.S. firms with the same energy-using characteristics found in the United States. There is some indication from U.S. officials that this situation is changing. An important example can be set for LDCs if U.S. buildings exemplify the best in energy efficiency and solar designs.

8. Change Education and Training Policy. Energy education has started to infiltrate the curriculum of the nation's schools, a trend that should continue. However, discussions of LDC problems such as the energy situation and its relationship to the United States seldom receive attention. This could change. In addition, foundations and institutes should become involved in the public education process. For example, more attention should be given to non-OPEC LDCs in the annual Aspen Institute Energy Assessment. The Overseas Development Council, Resources for the Future, and other similar organizations, with the support of government if necessary, must do a better job of improving the American people's understanding of LDC energy issues and their importance to the United States.

Education and training of LDC energy technicians, policymakers, and planners are also important, the most noteworthy of which is the AID-sponsored training workshop for energy planners at the Institute for Energy Research at Stony Brook. However, American institutions need to sponsor more of these kinds of projects both in the United States and in LDCs. Training programs like the Stony Brook operation should be given regionally and even on a country-specific basis. The U.S. government ought to support such efforts through international organizations and American and LDC institutions as well.

CONCLUSION

Developing countries face an energy future with great uncertainties and problems of crisis proportions. The march away from traditional fuels and toward higher levels of petroleum dependency is making many of the countries exceedingly vulnerable. A number of alternatives have the potential to alleviate this situation. However, the applicability of these various options differs according to the supply and demand characteristics of each LDC. To better assess the problems, to develop and test alternatives, and to act on solutions will require LDCs, international organizations, and countries like the United States to work in concert. The United States should seize this excellent opportunity to form an effective partnership with the LDCs. Energy is an issue with which both are struggling. Together, the United States and LDCs can achieve solutions that will prove beneficial to themselves, to other nations, and to the world energy situation as a whole.

Appendix: Comparison of Derived Energy Demands with Fossil Fuel Recoverable Reserves and Ultimate Hydraulic Resources[a]

Country	Total Derived Energy Consumption[b]	Total Energy Recoverable Fossil Fuel (Oil) Reserves[c]	Fossil Fuel Reserve to Demand Ratio[d]	Ultimate Annual Hydraulic Resources[e]	Ultimate Hydraulic Output as Percent of Derived Demand[f]	Net Imports or Exports of Total Energy as Percent of Total Energy Consumption[g] (1978)	
						Imports	Exports
Energy Rich							
Highest Urbanization							
Turkey	537	32,390 (2,257)	60	23,508	44	50	
Yugoslavia	952	189,560 (2,013)	199	228	24	42	
Argentina	1,197	27,970 (15,250)	23	687	57	16	
Brazil	1,426	68,660 (5,368)	48	1,869	131	74	
Colombia	415	10,380 (5,856)	25	1,080	260		22
Guyana	20			259	1,238	100	
Mexico[h]	1,859	45,520 (85,400)	24	357	19	16	
Peru	248	10,310 (2,013)	42	392	158	30	
Trinidad and Tobago	117	20,630 (4,270)	175				74
South Korea	804	19,590	24	35	4	60	
Energy Rich							
Medium Urbanization							
Congo	20	34,430 (2,440)	1,721	162	810		91
Egypt	434	39,170 (15,250)	90	54	12		18
Eq. Guinea	9.5			43	452	98	
Gabon	200	13,870 (-)	69	315	157		91
Liberia	26			108	415	93	
Mozambique	129	3,990 (-)	30	162	125	77	
Rhodesia		40,730 (-)		72		11	
Syria	247			172	69	88	
Tunisia[h]	54	4,130 (16,470)	76	173	3.2		59
Malaysia	163	18,950 (15,250)	116	16	9.8	95	93
Oman	1.89	31,350 (34,770)	16,587				99

India^h	8,432	279,940	(–)	33	1,008	11	21	
Bolivia	62	6,350	(2,440)	102	324	522	88	76
Costa Rica	26				136	523	93	
Nicaragua	29				64	220	61	
Paraguay	41				108	263	97	
Papua New Guinea	20	1,350		67	438	2,190		
Energy Rich								
Low Urbanization								
Angola	91	10,790	(7,320)	118	174	191	100	89
Botswana	100	5,600	(–)		32		87	
Cameroon^h	52	10		0.1	413	413	76	
Central African Republic	128		(366)		158	303	94	
Madagascar	51	11,170		87	1,152	900	107	
Senegal		53,330			63	123	98	70
Swaziland					10		100	
Upper Volta	67				172	256	87	
Zaire	427	87,130	(915)	204	2,376	556	58	
Afghanistan	167	5,820	(512)	34	64	38	38	
Bangladesh		24,930	(–)		23			
Pakistan	1,067	26,860	(1,708)	25	378	35		
Energy Poor								
Highest Urbanization								
Cyprus	26						105	
Lebanon	69						110	
Singapore	95						177	
Taiwan	426	8,310	(73)	20	19		40	
Chile	69	8,580	(2,689)		318	75	84	
Jamaica	33						42	
Panama	26				43	130	88	
Surinam	77						89	
Uruguay			80	1	34	44		
Energy Poor								
Medium Urbanization								
Ivory Coast	62				39	62	106	
Mauritius	9.75		(0.9)	2.3	1.15	11	95	
Morocco	204	470		18	10	4.9	85	
Zambia	72	1,320			55	76	43	

Appendix: continued

Country	Total Derived Energy Consumption [b]	Total Energy Recoverable Fossil Fuel (Oil) Reserves [c]	Fossil Fuel Reserve to Demand Ratio [d]	Ultimate Annual Hydraulic Resources [e]	Ultimate Hydraulic Output as Percent of Derived Demand [f]	Net Imports or Exports of Total Energy as Percent of Total Energy Consumption [g] — Imports Exports (1978)
Jordan	33	300	9			113
Philippines	616	1,090 (610)	1.7	54	8.7	102
Thailand	704	2,310 (1.6)	3.2	81	11	94
Dominican Republic	42					108
El Salvador	54			16	29	89
Guatemala	93	(97.6)		21	22	95
Honduras	45			86	191	110
Fiji	7					100
Energy Poor						
Low Urbanization						
Benin	35			25	71	100
Burundi	54					100
Chad	65			37	56	110
Ethiopia	463			201	43	96
Gambia	7.1					103
Ghana	164			56	34	60
Kenya	209			193	92	88
Lesotho				9.3		
Malawi	72			1.4	1.9	91
Mali	92			38	41	97
Mauritania	28			21	75	100
Niger	54			103	190	100
Rwanda	50					67
Sierra Leone	42			43	102	84
Somalia	45			2.5	5.5	100

Southwest Africa						
Sudan	247			172	69	88
Tanzania	244	5,050	20	299	122	104
Togo	40			6.9	17	99
Uganda	240			259	107	83
Guinea	79			92	116	99
Nepal	179					93
Sri Lanka	233			17	7.2	106
Viet Nam				691		12
Burma	684	9,920 (335)	14.5	810	118	26
Yemen	28					100
Haiti	83					100

a All values in thousands of terjoules.

b *World Energy Conference Survey of Energy Resources, 1974* U.S. National Committee of the World Energy Conference, New York, 1974. The energy consumption figure is calculated by raising the commercial energy consumption statistic to a base where per capita commercial energy consumption is equal to the lowest level in the high urbanized group. For example, the base level (630) is divided by the actual 1975 GNP, then multiplied by its energy consumption level in 1971. This applies only to countries in the medium and low urbanized groups. Energy rich countries are those countries having an energy resource to derived demand ratio of over 23, or substantial hydraulic resources (over 300%). Energy poor countries are defined as having an energy resource to derived demand ratio of 20 or less, with little or no hydraulic resources.

c Ibid. (fossil fuel reserves): Brookhaven National Laboratory, *Energy, Energy Needs, Uses and Resources in Developing Countries* (oil reserves).

d Column 2 divided by derived demand (see note a)

e *World Energy Conference Survey of Energy Resources, 1974.*

f Ibid. (see note a).

g UNCTAD, *Handbook of International Trade and Development Statistics, 1976.*

h Oil reserve figures are based on 1978 estimates and therefore may be somewhat higher than total fossil fuel estimates from 1975.

OPEC and the Political Future of the World Oil Market

Dankwart A. Rustow

FROM COMPANY OLIGOPOLY
TO GOVERNMENT CARTEL

The world price of oil, ever since the emergence of a world oil market, has been set mainly by economic factors. Until the early 1970s it was set by oligopolistic competition among a small group of multinational companies, and since then it has been set by concerted action of the Organization of Petroleum Exporting Countries (OPEC), which established itself as the price leader in the global market.

The position of the seven major companies—British Petroleum, Exxon, Gulf, Mobil, Shell, Socal, and Texaco—went unchallenged until the 1950s. Through an interlocking network of subsidiaries, they owned the major production concessions in the Middle East, where production costs were lower and the potential for future production higher than anywhere else in the world. They responded to the first major challenge to their position, Mossadegh's attempt at nationalization of Iranian oil in 1951-1953, by shutting down their operations in Iran and stepping up production elsewhere in the Middle East so as to more than make up the loss.

Soon the companies faced two additional challenges. One was the intrusion into the Middle East and especially into Libya of aggressive smaller companies willing to cut prices so as to take over some of the seven companies' established markets. One such challenge was Italy's Ente Nazionale Idrocarburi (ENI), whose president, Enrico Mattei, liked to refer to the major companies with mock affection

This paper was updated in August 1979.

393

as the "sette sorelle" or "seven sisters"; others were American so-called "independent" oil companies—that is, refiners without previous access to crude oil of their own. The other major challenge was the demand first by Venezuela and then by Middle Eastern governments for a steeply increasing share in the production profits.

To appease the governments, the companies in the period from 1948 to 1954 negotiated so-called "fifty-fifty" profit-sharing agreements that tripled or quadrupled the governments' income per barrel but—since the added payments were construed as income taxes rather than royalties—enabled the companies to deduct the added payments from their tax bills in the United States or Western Europe.

To meet the competition from ENI and the independents, the major companies in 1958 began to reduce their prices, thereby hastening the conversion of Western Europe and Japan from coal to oil as their major fuel and enabling the companies themselves to market larger and larger amounts of their inexpensive and highly profitable Middle Eastern oil. This expansion of production not only helped the companies to defend their share of the market from the inroads of the smaller competitors; under the fifty-fifty formula it also served to increase the revenues of host governments as well as of major companies.

Economic and political circumstances in the early 1970s interacted to put an end to this exceptional period of falling global energy prices and to prepare the way for the dramatic shift from company oligopoly to government cartel.

Economic developments brought the major companies to the end of their two avenues of retreat. The growing revenues under the fifty-fifty formula whetted the financial appetites of governments in Libya, Venezuela, and the Middle East. Similarly, they strengthened the governments' ability to hold out in any future disputes. No serious contest would be possible between companies with a few weeks' storage of oil and governments with several months' or even years of reserves of foreign exchange. As the oil-producing governments pushed their advantage, by the mid-1960s the companies reached the point where their tax credits under the fifty-fifty formula were beginning to exceed the taxes they owed to home governments on their foreign operations, so that higher payments to oil governments began to cut into profits.

Similarly, Europe and Japan had nearly completed their conversion from coal—and of course customers cannot shift to oil for more than 100 percent of their energy needs any more than companies can write off more than 100 percent of their taxes. As a result of the oil import quota program (1959–1973), moreover, the vast U.S. market remained mostly closed to the companies' foreign oil. Without additional taxes to write off and without new markets to conquer, the companies were quickly approaching the point where they could no longer meet the financial demands of oil-producing governments without raising their prices to global consumers. But this in turn implied that the companies were in danger of surrendering to the governments of oil-producing countries their traditional privilege of setting world prices.

Just such a transfer of pricing power from companies to governments was the major aim of OPEC, founded in 1960 by Venezuela and the four major Middle Eastern oil producers in response to the companies' price cuts of the late 1950s. OPEC's first, and largely unheralded, victory was that the companies henceforth did not attempt to lower the "posted price" on which their payments to the governments depended, but instead started offering discounts, thus in effect absorbing the price cuts of the 1960s out of their own share of the fifty-fifty profit split. Next, the OPEC governments insisted that the 13 to 17 percent royalty be added to, rather than included in, the 50 percent "income tax" paid by the companies. It was these pressures, together with the companies' discounts off the posted price, which by about 1970 had raised the governments' share in oil production profits from 50 to about 80 percent. And by then OPEC governments were beginning to press for increases in the posted price, or the tax rate, or both.

By 1968 OPEC's leaders, foremost among them the Saudi oil minister, Sheikh Ahmad Zaki al-Yamani,[1] had recognized that OPEC's aim of establishing full government control over the export of petroleum need not entail irreconcilable conflict with the companies. In OPEC countries, the companies would continue to act as production managers; abroad their established networks of refineries and sales organizations would help to enforce OPEC's production and pricing decisions. Although the companies fought vigorously against surrendering their control over these decisions, they accepted their defeat gracefully and did, indeed, continue to act as production managers and sales agents for most of OPEC's oil. In turn they have been rewarded through privileged access to large amounts of oil, through a small discount on that oil from the sales price charged by OPEC governments to third parties, and through the opportunity to add their profit margins to a vastly more expensive product.

1. For an account of the rise of OPEC, see Dankwart A. Rustow and John F. Mugno, *OPEC: Success and Prospects* (New York: New York University Press for Council on Foreign Relations, 1976). The policy statement by OPEC issued in 1968 is reprinted in the appendix.

Political factors were crucial in enabling OPEC to win this power contest. In the Mossadegh crisis, the companies had been able to rely on Britain's imperial might to protect their own position in the Middle East. Thus the British Navy had dispatched a battleship to Iranian waters as an implicit warning, and the Royal Air Force had forced a tanker with nationalized Iranian oil into harbor at Aden. But by 1970, Aden was no longer a crown colony; the British had withdrawn their military units from Suez, Jordan, Iraq, Cyprus, and Kuwait, and were about to do so from the Arab Emirates on the Persian Gulf. Similarly, the United States had evacuated its units from the air force base in Wheelus, Libya. These departures left a power vacuum in which the oil-producing governments felt free to assert their economic interests without fear of military intervention.

Soon, moreover, the Arab-Israeli war of 1973 gave OPEC's Arab members, which account for about 60 percent of the cartel's production, a sense of moral justification in reducing their output in the fall and winter of 1973–1974. And it was the panic prices on the spot market created by this curtailment that provided the essential backdrop for the quadrupling of oil prices enforced by Arab and non-Arab oil exporters alike.

The following sections of this chapter will consider the interplay of economic and political factors in OPEC's domination of world energy markets; domestic and regional political factors within and around OPEC countries that might influence the future of the global oil market; the policies of non-OPEC countries, including non-OPEC oil exporters and the major importing countries; and the potential role of the Soviet Union and China.

THE OPEC SYSTEM: ECONOMICS AND POLITICS

OPEC has grown from its original five members of 1960—Iran, Iraq, Kuwait, Saudi Arabia, and Venezuela—to thirteen—Algeria, Ecuador, Gabon, Indonesia, Libya, Nigeria, Qatar, and the United Arab Emirates being the new members. Throughout the two decades of its existence, OPEC has consistently accounted for 80 to 90 percent of the petroleum moving in international trade, and petroleum so traded amounts to about one-half of all petroleum produced and consumed. By wresting control of production amounts and of prices from the multinational companies, OPEC has established itself as the price leader for all petroleum generally and to some extent even for other forms of energy such as coal and uranium.

In the world petroleum market, OPEC's leadership has been direct and unchallenged. For example, non-OPEC exporters such as Oman, Malaysia, Trinidad, Norway, and Mexico have set their prices with a firm eye on OPEC—underbidding OPEC prices slightly while newly carving out their share in the international market, but matching them once they had done so. Domestic U.S. producers have also followed OPEC prices—to the extent that government price controls permit. Even the Soviet Union in selling petroleum to Western countries has matched OPEC levels at once and in selling it to communist countries in Eastern Europe has matched them with some delay.

Although petroleum accounts for only about half of the world's energy consumption, it became the pacesetter in the 1960s, forcing out of business any coal mines that could not, by and large, match the prices of oil. The same price leadership pattern has persisted as oil prices have risen dramatically in the 1970s. Thus the price of coal in the United States rose nearly two and one half-fold from 1972 to 1975, at a time when the domestic price of oil had more than doubled. The estimated price for synthetic oil from coal, in particular, has always been roughly double that of petroleum—rising from $6 per barrel in 1972 to $30 in 1978. As long as this price leadership of oil throughout the energy market is maintained, the only effective limitations on OPEC's ability to push up prices are posed by reductions in demand—whether resulting from elasticity (that is, consumer resistance to higher prices), from government-mandated conservation or import restrictions, or from the effects of economic recession.

The financial benefits to OPEC governments have been striking. When the organization was formed in 1960, the aggregate income of its members from petroleum was about $2 billion; for 1979 it is likely to exceed $200 billion. The sharpest increases came in 1970–1971, when revenues per barrel rose from 95 cents to $1.37; in 1973–1974, when they rose to $9.37; and in 1979, when they rose to over $20. Economic and political factors interacted to make possible each of these dramatic rises.

From 1968 to 1970, the world's demand for oil imports rose by over one-fourth. Libya was in a particularly favorable position in this expanding market. Its oil was low in sulfur and in gravity—that is, of the highest quality. Its transport route to the major West European market was short and direct—whereas tankers from the Persian Gulf after the closing of the Suez canal in 1967 faced the long detour via the Cape of Good Hope. Libya also was in an unusually strong bargaining position with the companies: its population was diminutive, so that most of its oil revenues accumulated as international reserves; and in contrast to the Middle Eastern countries, where a single consortium of companies owned the concession for the entire country, Libya had parceled out its oil production to a dozen different companies or groups.

These longer run economic trends and structural features combined with two distinct political events. In September 1969, an Islamic-fundamentalist junta under Colonel Qaddafi had deposed the aging King Idris of Libya. Unlike the royal regime, which had increased its income by pushing the companies to step up production at prevailing rates of revenue, Qaddafi's junta preferred to increase its income even faster by cutting production and raising prices. A unique opportunity to apply this tactic presented itself in the summer of 1970, when another radical regime, in Syria, refused to allow repairs to the damaged TAP line that had transported much of Saudi Arabia's oil to the Mediterranean and from there on to Europe. The result was an all-time high in oil tanker rates, unprecedented demand for Libyan oil—and a round of negotiations initiated by Qaddafi and soon pursued by the Persian Gulf producers, in which the multinational oil companies for the first time found themselves at a very distinct disadvantage.

In 1973–1974, the political factors were much more obvious: the October war of Egypt and Syria against Israel; the embargo proclaimed by Saudi Arabia and others against the United States as Israel's major arms supplier; the production cuts by most Arab oil producers, amounting to as much as 25 percent by December; and the price increases unilaterally imposed by OPEC governments on multinational companies in the resulting situation of acute shortage. But even here, the longer range economic trends form an essential backdrop. Although the oil companies since 1970 had slowly raised their prices to keep up with higher payments to host governments, demand for OPEC oil had increased by about one-third. The end of the oil import quota program in the spring of 1973, moreover, meant that the United States was rapidly opening up as a vast and fast-growing market for foreign oil.

The events of October 1973 lend themselves to different interpretations. Egypt's aim was to regain its self-esteem by mounting a successful surprise attack, and the "oil weapon" wielded by other Arabs thus was an important auxiliary effort. For Saudi Arabia, on the one hand, the Yom Kippur war may well have been a convenient occasion to implement its long-standing ambition of wresting control from the oil companies, propelling itself among the world's foremost financial powers, and thus adding to its influence in the world's diplomatic councils.

Other details support such a reinterpretation of the events of 1973–1974. Iraq, then priding itself in being the most radical and anti-Zionist Arab regime, joined in the embargo but not in the production limitation that turned out to be the true cutting edge of the "oil weapon." Instead, it actually increased production, in line with its long-standing policy of expanding its market and increasing its revenues to the maximum—and conscious, presumably, that the production cuts by the Saudis and others were quite enough to drive up the price. In December 1973, it was the conservative and pro-Western shah who took the lead in pushing the OPEC price up from $5 to $7. And by mid-1974, when the October war and the embargo were long past, Saudi Arabia quietly took the lead (through a retroactively applied formula for government-company "participation") in raising OPEC government revenues to as much as $9.37 per barrel. The policies of Saudi Arabia in maintaining that new price level for the next four and one-half years will be examined in a later context.

The oil crisis of 1978–79 differs from those of 1970–71 and 1973–74 in that the crucial background factor was not a gradual and steady rise in demand but a sudden curtailment of supply. Once again the political elements were obvious. Production in Iran, as a result of the revolutionary events, dropped sharply in September 1978, virtually ceased by year's end, and early in 1979 resumed at about two-thirds of its former level. The Saudis' spare production capacity, which might have compensated for the shutdown of production in any other exporting country, was insufficient to cover the gap, and the price stability of the 1974–1978 period yielded to a sharp upward spiral.

On the basis of this all too sketchy analysis of the crucial events of the 1970s, one may perhaps venture the following assessment of political and economic factors in the rise of OPEC and its continued ascendancy over the world's energy markets. One economic and one political background factor stand out. In the 1950s and 1960s, major industrial economies shifted to Middle Eastern oil as their principal, or at least marginal, source of energy. And toward 1970 the West's long political hegemony over the Middle East came to an end. The West, that is to say, became economically dependent on the Middle East just when Middle Eastern countries became politically independent of the West.

Free to assert their economic interest without immediate fear of political retaliation, the major oil exporters of the Middle East and other regions wrested from multinational oil companies the power to determine production amounts and to set prices. The basic pattern has thus been one of oligopoly, in which a cartel of thirteen sovereign countries sets the basic price, and other oil exporting countries, as well as the multinational oil companies and the producers of coal and uranium, all stand ready to follow OPEC's price leadership and to enforce the resulting price levels throughout the world.

Within this economic structure, political events act as random shocks, curtailing production or interrupting the distribution of crude oil. This was the effect of Qaddafi's advent and the closing of the Trans-Arabian pipeline (TAP) in 1970, of the production cuts accompanying the embargo of 1973, and of the strikes and disruptions in the Iranian oil fields in 1978–1979. Each such curtailment has served to move the price of oil up sharply, with the integrated and oligopolistic structure of the world oil and energy markets providing the necessary ratchet effect to keep the price at that higher level—until the next random political shock.

Even during the crucial phases of transition from one price level to the next, economic circumstances (such as the sharp upturns in world demand preceding the 1970 and 1973 crises and the erosion of Saudi spare capacity between 1975 and 1979) set the stage for the political drama. Conversely, as we shall see in the following sections, most political upheavals in the absence of such circumstances do not result in major oil crises.

COHESION AND CONFLICT WITHIN OPEC

All thirteen members of OPEC are considered developing countries. Their economies, aside from the petroleum sector, are by and large preindustrial. All thirteen members have a colonial or quasi-colonial past, Venezuela and Ecuador having attained independence in the early nineteenth century and nine other members having proceeded to independence from colonial, mandate, or protectorate status in the period between 1945 and 1970. Saudi Arabia and Iran, although always nominally independent, were in effect under American and British hegemony until the 1950s. This common colonial or quasi-colonial heritage, which also includes resentment at having local oil resources developed by Western companies for their own benefit and that of their Western consumers, has been an important factor in OPEC's formation and in its cohesion as a cartel. OPEC not only pursues the collective economic self-interest of its members, it also sees itself as the vanguard in the movement to redress past injustices inflicted by Western imperialism. Hence no serious thought has been given, on either side, to extending OPEC membership to capitalist-developed or to communist oil-exporting countries.

But let us add at once that, given this solid "Third World" (and hence latently anti-Western or South versus North) ideological bias, the precise composition of OPEC has been of little consequence. As we have seen, all significant non-OPEC exporters, including developing countries such as Oman, Malaysia, and Mexico and industrial countries such as Canada, Norway, and the United Kingdom, have followed OPEC's price lead—as indeed have most of the world's energy producers.

OPEC's lingering anti-Western animus finds expression in the political rhetoric that emanates from such capitals as Tehran (whether under the shah or the ayatollahs), Algiers, Tripoli, and Riyadh. It has aligned OPEC countries behind resolutions in favor of a "New International Economic Order" in the UN General Assembly or at the UN Conference on Trade, Aid, and Development (UNCTAD). And it has prompted efforts, not always successful, to shape a common front of oil-producing and non-oil-producing developing countries in such settings as the Conference on International Economic Cooperation (1975–1977).

Beneath this common ideological surface, there is little political cohesion within OPEC. OPEC's members have been acting from obvious economic interest—their common gain having increased from about $100 billion in 1974 to $200 billion in 1979, and their prospective joint loss in case of basic disunity being commensurate. All significant contacts among OPEC members in different geographic regions relate to oil and oil alone. Even among OPEC members in the same world region, political tensions are rife. For years the shah's Iran and Saudi Arabia were vying for regional predominance in the Persian—or as the Saudis would insist, the "Arab"—Gulf and were engaged in a lively arms race. Iran and Iraq have been at odds in a protracted territorial dispute at the Shatt-al-Arab; Iran for years supported the Kurdish insurgent movement in Iraq, and more recently Iraq has been supporting Arab-speaking insurgents in Iran's oil region of Khuzistan. Through three Arab-Israeli wars, from 1955 to 1973, the shah's Iran continued to supply oil to Israel. Among Arab OPEC countries, there is intense animosity between the radical regimes in Libya, Iraq, and Algeria, on the one hand, and the conservative monarchies in Saudi Arabia and the Arab Emirates, on the other. Even on the common Arab-Israeli issue there has occasionally been a sharp cleavage between the first group, as members of the "rejection front," and the Saudis with their more circumspect position.

Nevertheless, in raising petroleum prices, conservative monarchs, radical colonels, democratic governments in Venezuela, and more recently, Shii ayatollahs in Iran have all cooperated. Economic opportunities, not politics have determined the price strategy of OPEC and other producers. And not surprisingly, the main divisions among

OPEC members that have been of relevance to the price and availability of petroleum have also been economic.

One fundamental division that repeatedly manifested itself in 1974–1978 and that presumably persists is that between "high absorbers" and "low absorbers" of the financial gain from petroleum. The high absorbers are countries with low per capita incomes and with a variety of other economic assets, such as land, labor, and minerals, awaiting economic development. Hence they have no difficulty in spending their current oil incomes on consumption and investment and are eager to increase that income by augmenting production, raising prices, or both. The low absorbers, by contrast, have small populations and few if any economic assets other than petroleum. Unable to spend all their current income, they accumulate large international reserves; and naturally they are more concerned about preserving the value of those financial assets than they are about increasing current revenues. Not surprisingly, the high absorbers, such as Iran, Iraq, Indonesia, Algeria, Venezuela, and Nigeria, are already producing near their respective capacities; in practice their only prospect of increasing revenues is by raising the price. Hence, in the semiannual OPEC meetings on prices from 1974 to 1978, the high absorbers turned out to be the price hawks and the low absorbers the price doves.

Conversely, what spare capacity may exist among OPEC producers will be concentrated among the low absorbers. For example, in 1978 OPEC's total production was 30.2 million barrels per day, but its aggregate production capacity was estimated at 39.2 million barrels. Of the spare capacity of about 9 million barrels a day, about 3.5 million was held by Saudi Arabia alone. This spare capacity, greater than the total production of any one OPEC country except Iran, gave the Saudis the controlling voice in OPEC councils in the 1974–1978 period. If others tried to raise the price beyond the Saudis' preferred level, the Saudis could maintain their lower price and draw customers away from the others by stepping up production. If others tried to start a price war, cutting prices and increasing production, the Saudis could match any cut or increase and continue to make money long after everyone else's initial gains had turned into mounting losses.

The only political variations on the economic division of high absorbers–price hawks versus low absorbers–price doves have been the attitudes of Libya and Kuwait, which have generally sided with those countries in favor of more rapid price increases—Libya out of a generalized "radical," anti-Western attitude, and Kuwait because its large Palestinian population makes compromises in this direction seem opportune.

In the specific situation after the 1973-1974 price jump, there was no concrete danger of price wars: it would be unreasonable to expect the managers of the world's most successful cartel wantonly to tear down the structure they had so spectacularly built up. On the other hand, the contest between price hawks and doves—that is, those wishing to increase the price more steeply or more slowly—was fought behind the scenes at most OPEC meetings and out in the open in the first half of 1977. Invariably the doves, led by Saudi Arabia, won. Thus early in 1977, when the Saudis and the United Arab Emirates raised their prices by 5 percent, they still managed to increase their sales in a shrinking market. By contrast, their Persian Gulf neighbors, Iran, Iraq, Kuwait, and Qatar, which had raised prices by 10 percent, suffered losses in revenue ranging from 12 to 19 percent below the previous six months.[2]

The Saudi's preferred pricing policy, which until 1978 they managed to impose on OPEC as a whole, was to keep nominal prices steady and real prices falling at times of global recession and to have nominal prices rise and real prices continue level at times of recovery. All in all, between 1974 and 1978, when world consumer prices rose by as much as 55 percent, the price of a barrel of Saudi Arabian light petroleum, which then served as OPEC's "marker crude," rose by no more than 27 percent—or just half that amount. Two distinct reasons may be inferred for this cautious price policy. First, the Saudis' spare capacity and accumulated financial reserves make them naturally into OPEC's—and indeed the world's—marginal producer. And this means that it is their sales that will fall most sharply in a recession. Thus, from 1974 to the recession year of 1975, world oil consumption in noncommunist countries dropped by 2.4 percent, OPEC's production by 11.3 percent, and Saudi Arabia's by as much as 16.2 percent. Second, the Saudi government and its monetary agency were fast accumulating the world's largest financial reserves—early in 1977 these amounted to about $50 billion—or more than those of West Germany and the United States combined. This in turn meant that the Saudis had a larger stake in the health of the global economy than anyone else.

The period of comparative price stability and of Saudi predominance within OPEC was interrupted, or perhaps ended, by the Iranian revolution of 1978-1979. The Saudis' spare capacity, it was just noted, exceeded the total production of any one country except Iran; thus when Iran's production was halted late in 1978, the Saudis

---

2. For detailed figures, see Dankwart A. Rustow, "Middle East Oil: International and Regional Developments," in C. Legum and H. Shaked, eds., *Middle East Contemporary Survey* (New York and London: Holmes and Meier, 1979), p. 311.

could not single-handedly compensate for the loss—and this meant that they were no longer in control of OPEC's price levels. For a time, additional production in Libya, Nigeria, Kuwait, and Iraq as well as in Saudi Arabia made up for part of the Iranian shortfall. But the others, all of them price hawks, were glad to see OPEC prices rise sharply; hence they reimposed production limits as Iranian oil resumed its flow at about two-thirds of its former level. With the situation in Iran still highly uncertain, the Saudis evidently felt it unwise to engage their entire spare capacity or to provoke a public showdown with the other OPEC members. The result by mid-1979 was a Saudi production level about 12 percent higher than in 1978; an average OPEC price of about $20.50 per barrel, or about 60 percent above 1978; and an unusually wide spread of OPEC prices, with the Saudi price at the lower end rather than in the middle of that range. Whether the Saudis once again will establish themselves as OPEC's unquestioned price setters would seem to depend on their ability and willingness to increase their capacity sufficiently so as to counteract any deliberate or accidental curtailments of supply from other OPEC members.

POLITICAL INSTABILITY IN AND AROUND OPEC COUNTRIES

Six of OPEC's members are located in the Middle East, four in Africa, two in Latin America, and one in Southeast Asia. All of these are areas of long-standing and deepseated domestic and regional political instability—characterized by coups, successful or attempted revolutions, civil wars, and interstate conflict. An earlier section has sought to assess the contributing or decisive role that certain of these political events played in bringing about the dramatic structural changes and price increases of 1971, 1973, and 1979. The present section will attempt a more systematic examination of the impact of political instability on the availability and price of oil.

Among the more notable political upheavals in oil-producing countries in the past three decades have been the overthrow of the shah of Iran and his restoration by the Zahedi coup (1953), the Nigerian civil war of the mid-1960s, the extremely bloody upheaval in Indonesia that replaced Sukarno with the military regime under Suharto (1965), a series of military coups in Iraq since 1958, the intermittent insurgency of Kurdish tribesmen in northern Iraq, the military coup in Libya (1969) that replaced Idris with Qaddafi, the assassination of King Faisal of Saudi Arabia (1975), the Iranian revolution (1978–1979) and subsequent secessionist movements, recurrent coups d'etat in Ecuador, and sporadic instances of urban terrorism in Venezuela.

The most prominent regional conflicts affecting oil, of course, have been the four Arab-Israeli wars of 1948, 1956, 1967, and 1973. Yet there is much additional potential for interstate conflict in the vicinity of OPEC countries and especially in the Middle East. The recurrent dispute between Iraq and Iran and the rivalry between Iran and Saudi Arabia have already been referred to. Iran in the mid-1970s also provided military support for the sultan of Oman against communist-supported insurgents in the province of Dhofar—an operation viewed with some alarm in Riyadh. There have been recurrent tensions between Saudi Arabia and communist-controlled Southern Yemen; recurrent bitter disputes between Iraq and Syria; Libyan-inspired attempts at subversion in Egypt, Sudan, Tunisia, and other Arab countries; one major border war between Egypt and Libya; a prolonged conflict between Algeria and Morocco in the formerly Spanish Sahara; and various territorial claims of Iran against Iraq and Bahrain, of Iraq against Kuwait, and so on.

By and large it is remarkable how little effect this domestic and regional instability has had on the global oil situation in the past. In the Iranian crisis of 1951–1953, as we saw, the multinational companies were able to compensate for the loss of Iranian production by increasing the flow from other Persian Gulf countries. The civil war in Nigeria significantly delayed and curtailed production in 1967 and 1968; yet the Indonesian upheaval of 1965 and the Kurdish insurgency in Iraq have had no noticeable effect on oil production. More recently, oil development in Angola continued at full pace in the midst of a civil war—with Cuban soldiers assigned to guard the operations of the Gulf Oil Company.

Even where the political instability does interfere with oil production, the seriousness of the effect depends, of course, on the size of the country's oil operation. Nigerian production in 1967–1968 was cut in half—that is, from about 2 percent to about 1 percent of the world's oil trade; the impact, in other words, was negligible. Libya's tough bargaining stance in 1970 posed serious problems because Libya at the time accounted for 14 percent of OPEC's output, as against 16 percent each for Iran, Saudi Arabia, and Venezuela. In the 1970s, only Saudi Arabia and Iran have controlled large portions of OPEC's output, their 1978 shares being 28 and 17 percent respectively; whereas eight other members (Iraq, Venezuela, Kuwait, Libya, Nigeria, the United Arab Emirates, Indonesia, and Algeria, in that descending order) supplied from 9 to 4 percent each, and the three others (Qatar, Ecuador, Gabon) 1 percent or less apiece.

The Libyan coup of 1969 illustrates a phenomenon also known from election campaigns in Venezuela—that rival political forces in oil countries will tend to differentiate their oil policies. After Qaddafi's accession, the shift from the policy of increasing revenues via production to increasing them via price turned out to be of crucial significance not only for Libya but for all of OPEC and the entire world market. Yet it can be argued that the Qaddafi coup acted mainly as a catalyst to make Libya and other OPEC countries take fuller advantage of their latent bargaining power and that by now that determination is widely shared throughout OPEC. Hence the crucial variables become other factors, such as the increases in world oil demand preceding the 1970 and 1973 crises, or random shocks unforeseen or even unintended by oil governments, such as the disrepair of the TAP in 1970 or the strikes in the Iranian oil fields in 1978.

The most notable effect of regional conflicts has been on the pattern of oil transportation. The 1948 Arab-Israeli war led to the permanent closing of the Iraq Petroleum Company's pipeline to Haifa. The 1956 conflict interrupted passage through the Suez Canal, which then constituted part of the major oil route from the Middle East to Europe. From 1967 to 1975 the canal once again remained closed. And the 1973 war, of course, resulted in the largest disruption of all—the Arab oil embargo. The possibility of its recurrence will be examined in the following section.

Although manmade transport facilities such as canals and pipelines remain highly vulnerable to manmade wars, it is also notable that these disruptions of transport were only temporary and that alternative routes were quickly developed. After 1948, the Iraqi pipelines to Lebanon and Syria were beginning to handle the full flow of oil from northern Iraq. When these lines were closed down in a dispute between Iraq and Syria in 1975, Iraq developed two alternative pipeline routes, one to its own Persian Gulf coast and the other via Turkey to the Mediterranean.

Similarly, the massive flow of oil that used to go by the older, smaller tankers through the Suez Canal before 1967 was soon handled by supertankers plying the route around the Cape of Good Hope. The world's tanker fleet was vastly expanded between 1967 and 1973, on the expectation that seaborne oil trade would continue its spectacular expansion of around 10 percent a year. But the price jump of 1973-1974 caused the oil trade to stagnate (or rather to decline first and then to return, in 1976-1977, to about the level of 1973), so that the world's supply of oil tanker space has been about 50 percent larger than the typical demand. It is highly unlikely that the volume of that trade will grow quickly (or indeed will ever grow) so as to absorb that surplus fully. It follows that oil transport routes in the future are likely to be less vulnerable to the kinds of disruption that they have suffered in the past.

Oil production—except during the Iranian revolution of 1978–1979—has proved even less vulnerable to regional political or military conflicts than have routes of transport. In 1956, 1967, and 1973, military operations on the Sinai and along the Suez Canal temporarily suspended production of fields on either side of the Gulf of Suez. But for most of the period since 1967, a tacit understanding between Israelis and Egyptians allowed continued operations of fields or refineries on both sides of the gulf, even though—or precisely because —each operation was within easy artillery range from hostile forces across the gulf. As long as political or military conflict is carried on by organized governments, the revenues from oil production would be likely to be considered a major prize that neither side, in struggling for its possession, would wish to destroy.

There has been some concern in the international relations literature about a transport crisis involving the Strait of Hormuz. The mining of that strait would be a relatively simple military operation, and it would suspend the flow of more than half of the oil in the international market. But such a measure would interrupt equally the flow from each of the six Persian Gulf producers, so that none of them would be interested in bringing about such a blockage. On the other hand, such a mining operation is too complex to be carried out by saboteurs against the wishes of the coastal states; and the navigable channel at Hormuz is too deep and too wide to be blocked by a few sunken vessels.

The scenario changes if one imagines one or the other superpower becoming directly drawn into a military conflict in the Persian Gulf region. In such a situation, destruction of oil fields or terminal facilities or mining of the Strait of Hormuz might readily occur as a result of the military action itself or of deliberate sabotage by the defending forces. But it is hard to conceive of involvement by one superpower that would not provoke similar involvement by the other. A confrontation in the Persian Gulf may not be the likeliest opening scenario for such a superpower confrontation; yet if the United States and the Soviet Union did proceed to such a conflict, the oil fields of the Persian Gulf and oil transport routes on all of the world's high seas would, in any event, be among the most vulnerable targets.

Regional conflicts of a nature similar to those in the Middle East are readily conceivable in other regions where oil is produced or past which oil is transported. Most Southeast Asian countries have in the last generation been embroiled in conflicts with one or more of their neighbors. The Horn of Africa and the southern part of the continent are likely to remain centers of regional or internal racial conflict, as well as targets for Soviet penetration; and of course, most of the oil in global trade passes by tanker close to the coasts of Somalia, Mozambique, South Africa, Namibia, and Angola. The Caribbean has long been a region of political instability, and various scenarios of domestic or regional conflict involving oil-producing nations such as Mexico or Venezuela could plausibly be developed.

Yet in assessing such scenarios, past experience as reviewed in these pages should be borne in mind. Oil production might continue even while parts of a country are embroiled in civil war, as it did in Iraq and Angola. Oil production might continue despite a continuing regional military conflict, as it did along the Gulf of Suez. New regimes installed by military coup might wish to distinguish their oil policy from that of their predecessors and to increase government revenues; yet it is an open question whether they would do so by curtailing production, as Qaddafi did in 1970, or by increasing it, as did successive regimes in Iraq. Above all, the production of most OPEC countries is relatively small; hence even a complete shutdown could be compensated for by increased production elsewhere—unless it happened to occur during an unusually tight market. Finally, the long-term glut of tanker space has made oil transport less vulnerable than ever; and a complete disruption of tanker routes is plausible only as a prelude or accompaniment of a third world war—a contingency excluded from the scope of this study.

In sum, a review of events of the past quarter century indicates that the world's major oil-exporting regions offer a high potential for domestic and regional political conflict, but that most of this conflict has had a negligible impact, or no impact at all, on the flow and the price of oil. Not every political crisis in these tension-laden regions, that is to say, has developed the explosive potential of the Yom Kippur war or of the Khomeini revolution in Iran. Still, the impact of these two events on the global oil market was so decisive that we must inquire, in the following section, into the likelihood of their repetition.

ANOTHER EMBARGO? ANOTHER IRAN?

Each of the four Arab-Israeli wars, as previously noted, involved some disruption of the flow of Arab oil. From 1956 and 1967 to 1973, moreover, Arab solidarity increased considerably—leading up to the spectacular application of the "oil weapon." The Egyptian-Israeli peace treaty of 1979 may have diminished the chances of a fifth Arab-Israeli war, but has certainly not excluded it. And if there should be another such outbreak, it is widely assumed that oil would be directly involved in such a confrontation. For the policymakers of leading consumer countries, and particularly of the United States, this is probably a good assumption to make.

Yet on closer examination, the connection between a future Arab-Israeli conflict and a new embargo may not be quite as automatic as that. Much would depend on specific circumstances and on Washington's attitude toward the conflict. If the war resulted from an Israeli preemptive strike, for example, the United States might well adopt a critical attitude, and Israel would be unlikely to receive American military equipment during the conflict. In such a situation, any application of the Arab "oil weapon" would be counterproductive and likely to change an evenhanded American attitude into a hostile one.

If, as in 1973, the war started with an Arab invasion of Israeli-held territory, and if the United States once again extended tangible and intangible support to Israel, this could easily trigger another embargo against the United States. The consequences of a conflict somewhere in the gray area between these extremes would be harder to predict; much would depend on Arab perceptions of American evenhandedness.

The impact of the Arab oil weapon, if and when it were applied, would depend mainly on the size and duration of the production cuts. Two circumstances could make the outcome far more serious than last time. First, the leading Arab oil-producing countries—Saudi Arabia, Libya, Iraq, Kuwait, and the United Arab Emirates—have accumulated far larger foreign exchange reserves and therefore could sustain without major hardship production cuts far deeper and longer than those of 1973. Second, American dependence on imported oil generally and on Arab oil specifically has increased in the past few years; between 1973 and 1977 our oil imports rose by as much as 40 percent, and the share of Arab oil in the imported total doubled (from 22 to 41 percent).

Although in 1973 it was the production cuts rather than the embargo itself that caused the disruption of the global (including the American) oil market, in the future, even a destination embargo could cause considerable harm quite apart from any cutbacks in volume. In 1973 our imports were equivalent to only about one-fourth of the total oil exports of non-Arab countries; hence the rerouting of tankers required by the embargo was relatively smoothly accomplished. Today, our imports are equivalent to more than half of the non-Arab oil in world trade (and nearly three-fourths of the non-Arab and non-Iranian oil); and since not all qualities of oil can be readily substituted at most refineries, even a destination embargo without production cuts might have a palpable impact.

In recognition of the potential threat of a new embargo, most major importing countries have joined together in an emergency oil-sharing program under the auspices of the International Energy Agency (IEA) and are also increasing their strategic oil reserves. There are problems with both these precautions. For example, it became evident during the Iranian crisis of 1978–1979 that even a total shutdown of production in the second largest exporting country was insufficient to trigger the IEA sharing mechanism. It should not necessarily be assumed, moreover, that the European countries and Japan will be willing to renew the ten-year sharing plan beyond 1984—since it commits them to supporting what many of them view as a combination of American profligacy in energy consumption and idiosyncrasy in Middle Eastern policy. Moreover, the United States strategic petroleum reserve is building up slowly and present pumping equipment is suitable only for putting the oil into the storage caverns, not yet for getting it back out. (See Chapter 6 for extensive discussion)

Still, if a future embargo with accompanying production cutbacks occurred while the IEA arrangement was in force and if it lasted no longer than the actual armed conflict, its impact could be readily absorbed by the importing countries under the emergency program—judging by the duration of previous Mideast conflicts. On the other hand, if the full force of the Arab oil weapon were brought to bear for an extended period and if (as at the moment seems likely) Iran would join in the embargo, the impact on the industrial countries of the world would be very serious indeed. However, in such an eventuality, other considerations would also come into play, such as retaliatory actions on the part of the importing countries—as broadly hinted by former Secretary of State Henry Kissinger in his veiled threat in December 1974 about the use of force in case of "actual strangulation" of the West.

In summary, the threat of an effective future embargo is real but limited. It is quite unlikely in the absence of an armed Arab-Israeli conflict; it is likely but by no means certain in case of such a conflict; and it would probably have to be maintained well beyond the duration of the conflict itself to cause major damage. If and when an embargo came, the United States would be far more vulnerable than in 1973—although the effect would be attenuated through application of the IEA emergency sharing rules.

The Iranian events of 1978–1979 were unique in their impact on world oil and even in a historical perspective find their close analogy probably only in France in 1789 and in England in 1640. No close repetition of the Iranian scenario is thus likely to occur in other oil-exporting countries such as Iraq or Saudi Arabia.

Saudi Arabia specifically is a Sunni rather than a Shii country, and its government is an oligarchy rather than an autocracy. The split between Sunni and Shii Muslims is far older and deeper than that between Roman Catholics and Protestants or Orthodox Greeks; hence the events of Iran will not spread to the south by power of example. The present Saudi government, moreover, already includes distinct theocratic elements; even for its Sunni clergy, a change of regime could only be a change for the worse. And in contrast to the shah's centralized and repressive autocracy, the Saudi pattern of collective decisionmaking by the family council of hundreds of princes proved its resilience on many occasions, including the replacement of the incompetent King Saud by King Faisal and, on the latter's assassination, the establishment of the duumvirate of King Khalid and Prince Fahd. It is perhaps significant that through all these changes of monarch, Sheikh Yamani retained his post as petroleum minister.

Valid as are these distinctions between Saudi Arabia and Iran, they are rather beside the point. What mattered about the Iranian revolution was not the specific circumstances of the upheaval or the particular coloration of the new regime. What mattered was that, in the world's second largest oil-exporting country, power passed into the hands of several groups, such as the Shii clergy in Qom and the workers' committees in the Khuzistan oil region, which made it impossible for foreign technicians to continue their work and put a low priority on the income from oil exports. In the swirling interaction of these and other groups, Iranian exports first ceased altogether and then resumed at about two-thirds of their previous level; the effect was that of the severest oil shortage and the steepest price rises since 1973.

The Saudi government seems to be one of the more stable regimes in the Middle East. Yet possibilities such as a palace coup led by a violently anti-Western faction, a military overthrow by puritanical officers of the Qaddafi type, or even mounting unrest among the hundreds of thousands of foreign workers from Egypt, Yemen, and elsewhere cannot be totally excluded. We saw in a previous section that one of the major restraining forces on past Saudi oil policy has been the country's vast accumulation of foreign funds. Any new regime that was willing to sacrifice large portions of those funds would certainly acquire an unprecedented flexibility in its oil policy. Saudi Arabia, which in mid-1979 produced 9.5 million barrels of crude oil per day, could cover its current foreign exchange requirements at perhaps half that level and its bare necessities at an even smaller fraction. In short, the likelihood of a drastic change in Saudi politics leading to a complete reversal of oil policies may be very small; yet the effects of such a reversal for the United States and other oil-importing countries might be little short of catastrophic.

POLICIES OF NON-OPEC EXPORTERS

When OPEC was founded in 1960, its five original members (Venezuela, Kuwait, Saudi Arabia, Iran, and Iraq—according to the size of their production that year) produced an aggregate of under 8 million barrels of oil a day. OPEC as a whole supplied 83 percent of the international oil trade, and more than one-third of that amount came from Venezuela. Several major shifts in the world petroleum market have occurred since then. Venezuelan production has declined since the early 1970s. Production around the Persian Gulf has increased sharply, with Saudi Arabia and Iran becoming OPEC's and the world's leading exporters. In response to the disruption of the Middle East oil trade in 1956, 1967, and 1973, additional discoveries were made, and production was expanded in such locations as Libya, Nigeria, the North Sea, Alaska, Angola, and Mexico. Yet none of these developments have threatened OPEC's position, which, on the contrary, was consolidated during this very period of geographic diversification. OPEC's membership has grown from five to thirteen, its exports have quadrupled, and its share of the world oil market has remained virtually unchanged (82 percent in 1970, 83 percent in 1978).

Countries in the Third World that joined the ranks of major exporters typically offered some discounts below prevailing world prices while completing their oil development and carving out for themselves a commensurate share of the market. Having done so, they subsequently joined OPEC—Libya in 1962, Abu Dhabi in 1967, Algeria in 1969, Nigeria in 1971—conforming thereafter to its price-setting patterns. Indeed, we saw that one of those newcomers, Libya, was instrumental in hastening OPEC's meteoric advance in the early 1970s. Much the same pattern of initial discounts and later observance of OPEC-set prices seems to be followed by other new exporters—Norway, Mexico, Angola—that have not, or not yet, joined OPEC. The largest of these new producers, Mexico, supplies only 1 million barrels per day or the equivalent of 3 percent of OPEC's total exports.

In the post-1974 world oil market, each additional source of supply, such as Norway or Mexico, does have something of a

moderating effect on prices. The advent of new producers strengthens the hand of OPEC's price doves, makes nominal prices rise more slowly than they otherwise might, and thus even helps bring about periodic slight drops in the real price. But note that OPEC's total annual exports have declined substantially only once, during the recession year of 1975, and that the additional supplies from Norway, Mexico, and elsewhere have been absorbed in an expanding market without cutting into any existing market shares. In 1979, these new supplies were insufficient to prevent the tight market and panic in the wake of events in Iran. While this pattern lasts, newly discovered or developed supplies are likely at most to slow down the rising trend of prices, rather than to bring about any stagnation or decline.

The picture might change somewhat if some recent or future new discovery should add a source of petroleum exports of truly major dimensions—that is, if a new Iran or Saudi Arabia were to appear on the horizon. The chances of this happening seem slight, for the simple reason that the more promising a given oil area on geologic grounds, the more likely it is already to have been explored. But assume for a moment that the highly controversial estimates that would place ultimate Mexican reserves in the neighborhood of Saudi Arabia's proved accurate. It seems likely that Mexico, because of its proximity to the United States and its dependence on the United States for the export of labor and the import of tourists and technology, might refrain from joining OPEC. Also, until it had established itself as a major supplier to the United States, Mexico might offer a slight discount below other OPEC prices—for example, by forgoing part of its comparative advantage in transport costs. Yet Mexico would be extremely unlikely to let such temporary discounting deteriorate into a full-fledged price war. Indeed, its large population and need for development capital naturally would align it with OPEC's "high-absorbers" or price hawks, such as Iran and Algeria. Within OPEC, the result might be a shift from a pattern of unilateral control, such as the Saudis exercised in 1974–1978, to one of dual control negotiated, say, between Riyadh and Mexico City. Once again, the net effect of the development of a major new source of oil exports would thus be a slowing down of OPEC-imposed price rises rather than a collapse of the OPEC-dominated price structure.

POLICIES OF CONSUMER COUNTRIES

The policies of major oil-importing countries obviously have a considerable effect on price and availability of oil on the world market. To mention just three examples, the protectionist oil import quota program in the United States between 1959 and 1973 increased the pressure on international oil companies to sell Middle Eastern oil in Western Europe and Japan; traditionally high gasoline taxes in Europe have had a profound effect on the volume and type of refined products consumed in Europe; and according to recent OECD estimates, "accelerated policies" for conserving energy consumption and stimulating production of energy alternatives in its member countries might reduce their oil import needs by as much as 30 percent below levels that would otherwise obtain in 1985.[3]

Efforts to expand oil supplies in the high energy-consuming countries have resulted in substantial new supplies from Alaska and the British part of the North Sea (and from Norway, as discussed in the preceding section). Yet these discoveries have not substantially lessened the import dependence of the United States or the OECD area as a whole. In the United States specifically, the new Alaskan supplies, even if rapidly developed, would be inadequate to offset the combined effect of declining production of oil and natural gas in the contiguous forty-eight states, of declining Canadian imports, and of growing energy consumption (which after a slight dip in 1974–75 resumed its secular rise, albeit at a slower rate than before 1973). To the problems of an energy-hungry and import-dependent West, Alaska and the North Sea have offered a reprieve, not a solution.

Development of coal in the United States and of nuclear, solar, and other forms of energy throughout the OECD area is likely to contribute new energy supplies; yet in view of the necessary technological lead times and capital expenditures (and of the unresolved problems of nuclear waste disposal and coal transport), their contribution is likely to be slight until the end of this century. Hence the OECD's "accelerated policies" scenario of 1977 puts as much emphasis on energy conservation as it does on new supplies.

Other policies have been proposed for both the United States and other industrial countries in the OECD that would be aimed not at preventing a future shortage that would enhance the power of the OPEC cartel but at breaking the cartel's existing power. Among these are proposals to secretly auction import tickets for the United States and the proposal to break up the vertical integration of the international oil companies through enforced divestiture. Such measures, it would seem, would be at best ineffectual and at worst counterproductive. It is difficult to conceive of OPEC countries, which have

3. See OECD, *World Energy Outlook* (Paris: OECD, January 1977); and Dankwart A. Rustow "U.S.–Saudi Relations and the Oil Crises of the 1980s," *Foreign Affairs* 55 no. 3 (April 1977): 494–516.

maintained their economic cohesion despite bitter political differ- ences, turning over their marketing to anonymous agents just so as to enable their largest customer to break up their cartel.

The vertical divestiture proposal overlooks the fact that OPEC's control of the market rests on control not of downstream operations but of prices at the upstream end. And such control would, of course, be unaffected by any rearrangement downstream.

It should be emphasized that "accelerated policies," such as en- visaged by OECD, are designed to prevent a supply and price crisis in the mid-or late 1980s, not to break up the present structure of OPEC. Even with its exports reduced to about 10 percent below current levels, OPEC as a whole would still run a foreign payments surplus, and those members that ran a payments deficit could readily balance their budgets by using up accumulated reserves, or by bor- rowing from other OPEC members or elsewhere in the financial mar- kets, or by scaling down some of their development projects—or indeed by raising the price of oil.

The greatest single variable on the consumer country side is con- sumer attitudes and government policies in the United States. Presi- dent Carter's 1977 energy program proposed a tax to bring the domestic American oil price up to international levels and thereby hoped to reduce imports from the 1977 high of 8.2 million barrels a day (mbd) to 6 mbd in 1985. His 1979 program kept the limit at 8.2 mbd, but by development of synthetic oil from shale and coal and other measures hoped to bring that amount down by half by 1990. Meanwhile energy conservation remains a quicker and surer option available to Americans. We use two and one-half times as much energy per capita as do the Japanese or West Europeans. Even per unit of gross domestic product, our energy use exceeds that in Japan, West Germany, and France by 18, 25, and 53 percent respec- tively.[4] Thus, if we could adjust our automobile efficiency from our present average of fourteen miles per gallon to the European stan- dard of twenty-one miles we could save 2.5 mbd in imports—which is the very amount President Carter hopes to save by his uncertain and costly venture into synthetics. It is also an amount slightly in excess of the total petroleum consumption of the country of France —which illustrates sharply the major effect that even modest Amer- ican measures of conservation would have on the world market.

4. Calculated from data in Joy Dunkerley, ed., *International Comparisons of Energy Consumption* (Washington, D.C.: Resources for the Future, 1978), pp. 179-97. See also the earlier pathbreaking study by Joel Darmstadter et al., *How Industrial Societies Use Energy* (Baltimore: Johns Hopkins University Press for Resources for the Future, 1977).

THE ROLES OF THE SOVIET UNION
AND CHINA

Among Communist countries, Russia has for some time been an oil exporter, and China is becoming one. But oil consumption in the Soviet Union is increasing steadily, and some estimates are that the Soviet surplus will barely be enough to supply the needs of other Soviet Bloc (COMECON) countries by the early 1980s and that the COMECON area as a whole will be in balance by the mid-1980s. China's domestic needs for oil also are rising with growing industrialization, but need for foreign exchange provides a potent motive for oil export. Again, according to informed estimates, China is likely to remain a modest net exporter. Here too, the quantities are not likely to be large enough to substantially affect the global picture of price or availability. (See Chapter 10 for extended discussion)

The Soviet Union's quiet but very active policy in various Third World regions may, however, become a political factor to be reckoned with. The Soviet Union's drive for an active or even a dominant role in the Middle East since the mid-1950s has gone through many advances and setbacks. Its most notable net contribution probably has been to speed the drive of the region toward full independence in the late 1950s and 1960s, and the aggressive price policy of OPEC may thus be seen as a partial consequence. In the 1960s and 1970s, relations were closest with Iraq, although there has been some recent cooling (and conversely a rapprochement between Iraq and major Western oil companies). Soviet relations continue to be close with Syria; there is strong Soviet influence in Afghanistan, South Yemen, and the Horn of Africa; and closer relations have recently been initiated with Libya. The most active recent drives have been in southern and eastern Africa, and Cuba has played a major role in this effort. The close political cooperation between Havana and Moscow again raises at least the possibility of a new Soviet bid for influence, at some opportune point in the future, in the Caribbean and parts of Latin America.

The question relevant in the present context is how such growing Soviet influence would affect the international oil picture—and the most plausible answer, for the time being, would seem to be very little. Iraq's experience since the 1960s shows that the Soviets do not possess the advanced technology to help substantially in the development of oil resources in the developing world; nor have Iraq's close political ties with the Soviets in any way reduced the volume of its exports to the West. Pro-Soviet takeovers are thus unlikely to change the direction of petroleum trade that would otherwise prevail. Pro-communist governments must manage the same oil reserves as the preceding conservative regimes and sell the product on the same global market. This of course in no way denies the strategic and financial gain that the Soviets would derive from such a takeover (especially of a country like Iran); but to reap the financial gain, the country in question would have to continue exporting to capitalist hard currency countries.

As far as price is concerned, on the other hand, strongly conservative or even fiercely anti-Soviet regimes such as the shah's or Khomeini's Iran or democratic Venezuela have been just as militant in driving up the price of petroleum as have the more radical or pro-Soviet regimes in Iraq or Libya.

The most serious danger would be a communist takeover in Iran—and in view of the political disarray and the disintegrative tendencies that have come to the fore since the Iranian revolution, this possibility would seem to have moved considerably closer. The danger, presumably, would not be the wholesale diversion to the Soviet Union of oil supplies previously destined to the West, but rather the entrenchment of Soviet power near the world's major sources of petroleum on the Persian Gulf. In such a situation, disruption of Middle Eastern oil exports through closure of the Strait of Hormuz would become a readily available alternative. Any flagrant resort to this possibility would—as suggested before—become the likely prelude to a great power confrontation or even to World War Three. Yet one can easily think of scenarios where the provocation would be less clear-cut and the damage to the West's economic and military position equally disastrous.

SUMMARY

The major determinants of the price and availability of petroleum in the past have been economic factors—until the early 1970s the oligopolistic competition among multinational oil companies and since then the concerted price setting of the OPEC countries. The intrusion of new competitors in the 1950s and 1960s brought a period of declining oil prices from about 1958 to 1970, whereas the escalating financial demands of host governments began to drive up the price of oil after 1970. In the years of OPEC's ascendancy, restrained demand and surplus capacity resulted in a slight decline in the real price of oil between 1974 and 1978. But a sharp increase in demand in 1973 and a sharp decline in supply as a result of the Iranian turmoil in 1978–1979 resulted in steep price increases in 1973–1974 and in 1979.

The same economic variables may be expected to retain their

significance for the remainder of the century. Sharp upswings in demand or sudden drops in supply will strengthen the hand of the price hawks among the exporting countries, those eager to sell their oil at the highest possible price. Substantial additions to supply or reductions in demand, whether due to recession or deliberate conservation, will strengthen the position of the price doves, those eager to keep price increases moderate so as to preserve the health of the global economy and the value of their investments in it. If the trend of increasing energy consumption and oil imports, particularly in the United States, continues, one may expect the periods of shortage or at least of tight markets—and hence of rising prices—to become more rather than less frequent.

Major new oil discoveries are unlikely to change the picture fundamentally. With world oil consumption increasing at annual rates of 2 or 3 percent a year and American oil imports since 1973 at a compound annual rate of more than 5 percent, the world has needed a new North Sea, a new Alaska, or a new Mexico every other year or so just to keep its dependence on OPEC oil at the level reached in 1973. It seems unlikely that fields of even larger size still remain to be discovered, but even if they do, technological lead times are such that more than a decade would pass between discovery and development to full productive capacity. Even longer lead times are likely to apply to the development of other energy sources (synthetics from coal or shale, tarsands; fusion; solar) on scales sufficient to change the basic balance of forces in the world oil market. In short, for the world's oil problems there is no *deus ex machina* —and no *deus ex mexico*. This means that the role of petroleum as the source of about half the world's energy supply appears assured for the remainder of this century. And barring some major political upheaval, so does OPEC's role as the price setter for petroleum and perhaps even for other forms of energy.

To the effects of these essentially economic factors must be added the workings of certain political variables. All OPEC countries are located in some of the politically most unstable regions of the world. Many of them have been politically highly unstable in the past; many of them have a potential for such instability in the future. Indeed, considering how often OPEC countries or their neighbors have been involved in military coups, civil wars, or regional conflict, it seems remarkable, not how often, but how rarely political events have had a distinct impact on the flow or price of oil. Governments of diverse political structure and ideological orientation have responded to the same economic incentives and opportunities. Petroleum has continued to flow before and after coups, in the midst of civil wars, and in the immediate vicinity of armistice lines. Transport routes for oil, which in the past have proven highly vulnerable, appear to have acquired a new degree of immunity as a result of the long-term glut in the world tanker market.

Nonetheless, it would be rash to discount the effect of future political upheavals. Two considerations in particular should be kept in mind. First, the effect of most political events on the oil market may be slight, but the effect almost invariably is in the direction of shorter supplies and higher prices. That is, economic forces make for the exploration, discovery, and production of oil and for its delivery to consumers. By and large, political factors can only reduce or interrupt that flow.

Second, while it may be an exceptional political event that has an impact on oil, the magnitude of that impact, if and when it comes, tends to be truly exceptional. The Qaddafi coup of 1969 prepared for the change of market control from multinationals to OPEC beginning in 1971. The Yom Kippur war of 1973 and the Arab embargo led to a quadrupling of oil prices. The Iranian revolution of 1978–1979 started another upward price spiral, the end of which is not yet in sight.

For the future, the most distinctive political dangers would seem to be a Soviet takeover in Iran or a violent change of regime in Saudi Arabia. Nothing in the foregoing analysis, of course, leads us to predict either of these events or even enables us to assess the precise degree of their probability or improbability. But the analysis does establish that if either of these events did occur, the impact on the global oil market and on the major industrial economies, foremost among them that of the United States, could be very serious indeed.

It follows that a gradual but steady reduction of the level of U.S. dependence on oil imports—through deliberate measures of conservation for the next decade and through systematic development of alternative energy sources for future decades—should remain a matter of the very highest national priority.

Contents for Energy: The Next Twenty Years

A report by a study group sponsored by
the Ford Foundation and administered
by Resources for the Future

Index

Advanced gas-cooled reactor (AGR), 297, 301, 305, 309
Africa, 358, 362, 366, 372-73, 376, 416
Agency for International Development (AID), 355, 380, 386-87
Air pollution, 2. *See also* Environment
  and cogeneration, 171, 181-82
  in USSR, 328
Alaska, 213, 222, 412, 414, 418
al Dir'iyyah Institute, 355, 380, 383
Alternative energy sources. *See* Coal; Natural gas; Nuclear energy
Animal draft power, 350
Annual Report to Congress, 31-32, 68, 91
Arab-Israeli Wars, 396, 401, 406, 408
Argentina, 372, 375
Arrow, K., 159
Aspen Institute, 383, 386
Australia
  coal in, 213
  as exporter, 231, 235
  uranium in, 315-16
Austria, 232, 248, 305, 311-13
Automatic adjustment clause, 131-32, 156
Auto efficiency, 35. *See also* Gas consumption; Mean auto fuel efficiency
  and consumption of gasoline, 100-13
  under EPCA efficiency standards, 104-13, 115, 118-20

and federal programs, 94-98, 117-18
and gasoline price, 99-100, 102-03, 115-17, 120-21
and mean fuel efficiency, 100-104, 112-14, 123-25
Auto efficiency standards, 94-98, 104, 245
  and consumption of gasoline, 94, 104
  effect on demand for energy, 10, 18, 35
Auto emission standards, 94-95, 104, 114, 118

Balance of payments, 149-50
Bangladesh, 350, 355, 365
Basic Petroleum Data Book, 91
Belgium, 232
  coal production in, 269, 272, 275, 287
  nuclear energy in, 299, 301, 306
Biogas, 375
Bonneville Power Administration, 155n, 166
Bottoming cycles, 169, 184
Brazil
  consumption of energy in, 350, 353, 357
  nuclear energy in, 229, 375
  oil in, 371
  wood in, 376
Breeder reactors, 249-53, 299, 316-17

List of Contributors

Dennis W. Bakke, Deputy Director, Energy Productivity Center, Mellon Institute, Arlington, Virginia

Norman L. Dean, Jr., Attorney, Washington, D.C.

Marshall I. Goldman, Professor of Economics, Wellesley College and Associate Director, Russian Research Center, Harvard University

William W. Hogan, Professor of Political Economy, John F. Kennedy School of Government, Harvard University

Edward N. Krapels, Oil Consultant, Washington, D.C.

Gerald Manners, Reader in Geography, University College, London, England

Philip J. Mause, Attorney, Washington, D.C.

Horst Mendershausen, Consultant, Santa Monica, California

Dankwart A. Rustow, Professor of Political Science, Graduate School, City University of New York

Irwin M. Stelzer, President, National Economic Research Associates, Inc., New York

James L. Sweeney, Associate Professor Engineering-Economic Systems, and Director, Energy Modeling Forum, Stanford University